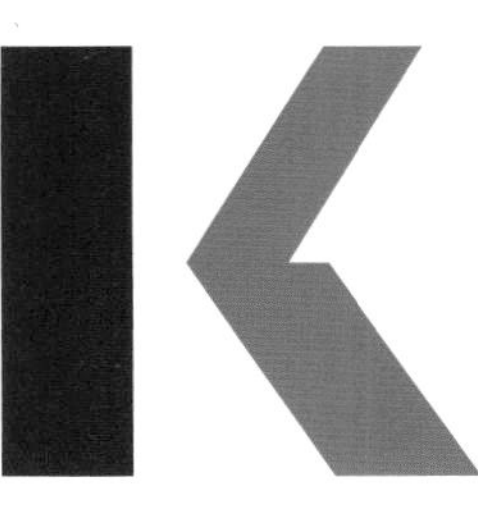

Kaplan Publishing are constantly finding new ways to make a difference to your studies and our exciting online resources really do offer something different to students looking for exam success.

This book comes with free MyKaplan online resources so that you can study anytime, anywhere

Having purchased this book, you have access to the following online study materials:

CONTENT	ACCA (including FFA,FAB,FMA)		AAT		FIA (excluding FFA,FAB,FMA)	
	Text	Kit	Text	Kit	Text	Kit
iPaper version of the book	✓	✓	✓	✓	✓	✓
Interactive electronic version of the book	✓					
Progress tests with instant answers	✓		✓			
Mock assessments online			✓	✓		
Material updates	✓	✓	✓	✓	✓	✓
Latest official ACCA exam questions		✓				
Extra question assistance using the signpost icon*		✓				
Timed questions with an online tutor debrief using the clock icon*		✓				
Interim assessment including questions and answers	✓				✓	
Technical articles	✓	✓			✓	✓

* Excludes F1, F2, F3, FFA, FAB, FMA

How to access your online resources

Kaplan Financial students will already have a MyKaplan account and these extra resources will be available to you online. You do not need to register again, as this process was completed when you enrolled. If you are having problems accessing online materials, please ask your course administrator.

If you are already a registered MyKaplan user go to www.MyKaplan.co.uk and log in. Select the 'add a book' feature and enter the ISBN number of this book and the unique pass key at the bottom of this card. Then click 'finished' or 'add another book'. You may add as many books as you have purchased from this screen.

If you purchased through Kaplan Flexible Learning or via the Kaplan Publishing website you will automatically receive an e-mail invitation to MyKaplan. Please register your details using this email to gain access to your content. If you do not receive the e-mail or book content, please contact Kaplan Flexible Learning.

If you are a new MyKaplan user register at www.MyKaplan.co.uk and click on the link contained in the email we sent you to activate your account. Then select the 'add a book' feature, enter the ISBN number of this book and the unique pass key at the bottom of this card. Then click 'finished' or 'add another book'.

Your Code and Information

This code can only be used once for the registration of one book online. This re online content will expire when the final sittings for the examinations covered t taken place. Please allow one hour from the time you submit your book details your request.

Please scratch the film to access your MyKaplan code.

Please be aware that this code is case-sensitive and you will need to include the dashes within the passcode, but not when entering the ISBN. For further technical support, please visit www.MyKaplan.co.uk

Professional Examinations

Paper F6

Taxation
(Finance Act 2013)

EXAM KIT

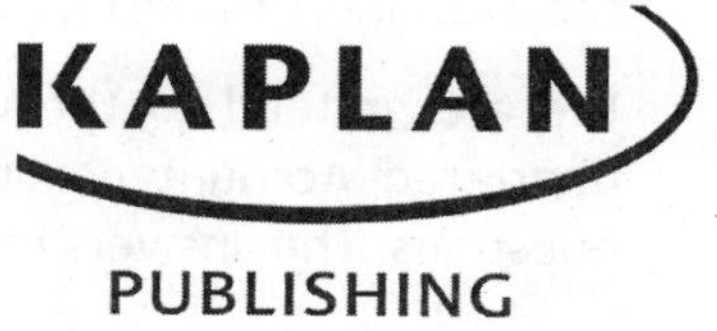

British Library Cataloguing-in-Publication Data

A catalogue record for this book is available from the British Library.

Published by:

Kaplan Publishing UK

Unit 2 The Business Centre

Molly Millar's Lane

Wokingham

Berkshire

RG41 2QZ

ISBN: 978 0 85732 825 0

Printed and bound in Great Britain.

Acknowledgements

The past ACCA examination questions are the copyright of the Association of Chartered Certified Accountants. The original answers to the questions from June 1994 onwards were produced by the examiners themselves and have been adapted by Kaplan Publishing.

We are grateful to the Chartered Institute of Management Accountants and the Institute of Chartered Accountants in England and Wales for permission to reproduce past examination questions. The answers have been prepared by Kaplan Publishing.

CONTENTS

Section

Key features in this edition

In addition to providing a wide ranging bank of real past exam questions, we have also included in this edition:

- An analysis of all of the recent examination papers.
- Paper specific information and advice on exam technique.
- Our recommended approach to make your revision for this particular subject as effective as possible.

  This includes step by step guidance on how best to use our Kaplan material (Complete text, pocket notes and exam kit) at this stage in your studies.
- An increased number of enhanced tutorial answers packed with specific key answer tips, technical tutorial notes and exam technique tips from our experienced tutors.
- Complementary online resources including full tutor debriefs and question assistance to point you in the right direction when you get stuck.

June and December 2012, June and December 2013 – Real examination questions

The real June 2012, December 2012, June 2013 and December 2013 exam papers are available on **My**Kaplan at:

www.mykaplan.co.uk

You will find a wealth of other resources to help you with your studies on the following sites:

www.mykaplan.co.uk

www.accaglobal.com/en/student.html

INDEX TO QUESTIONS AND ANSWERS

INTRODUCTION

The current syllabus was first introduced in June 2011 and brought in a new tax, Inheritance tax, and a few small additional topics to other taxes. The format of the exam changed slightly, but not significantly, and the style of some questions changed.

Accordingly, we have included some new questions on Inheritance tax in line with recent exams, and adapted many of the old ACCA questions within this kit. The adaptations have been made to reflect the new style of paper, the new legislative changes in recent Finance Acts, Tax law rewrites and IAS terminology. We have included the new topics brought into the syllabus in some questions.

The questions within the kit are past ACCA exam questions, the more recent questions (from 2005) are labelled as such in the index. Note that if a question within this kit has been changed in any way from the original version, this is indicated in the end column of the index below with the mark *(A)*.

KEY TO THE INDEX

PAPER ENHANCEMENTS

We have added the following enhancements to the answers in this exam kit:

Key answer tips

All answers include key answer tips to help your understanding of each question.

Tutorial note

All answers include more tutorial notes to explain some of the technical points in more detail.

Top tutor tips

For selected questions, we "walk through the answer" giving guidance on how to approach the questions with helpful 'tips from a top tutor', together with technical tutor notes.

These answers are indicated with the "footsteps" icon in the index.

ONLINE ENHANCEMENTS

Timed question with Online tutor debrief

For selected questions, we recommend that they are to be completed in full exam conditions (i.e. properly timed in a closed book environment).

In addition to the examiner's technical answer, enhanced with key answer tips and tutorial notes in this exam kit, online you can find an answer debrief by a top tutor that:

- works through the question in full
- points out how to approach the question
- how to ensure that the easy marks are obtained as quickly as possible, and
- emphasises how to tackle exam questions and exam technique.

These questions are indicated with the "clock" icon in the index.

Online question assistance

Have you ever looked at a question and not know where to start, or got stuck part way through?

For selected questions, we have produced "Online question assistance" offering different levels of guidance, such as:

- ensuring that you understand the question requirements fully, highlighting key terms and the meaning of the verbs used
- how to read the question proactively, with knowledge of the requirements, to identify the topic areas covered
- assessing the detailed content of the question body, pointing out key information and explaining why it is important
- help in devising a plan of attack

With this assistance, you should then be able to attempt your answer confident that you know what is expected of you.

These questions are indicated with the "signpost" icon in the index.

Online question enhancements and answer debriefs will be available from Spring 2014 on **My**Kaplan at:

www.mykaplan.co.uk

INCOME TAX AND NATIONAL INSURANCE

CHARGEABLE GAINS

INHERITANCE TAX

CORPORATION TAX

VALUE ADDED TAX

ANALYSIS OF PAST PAPERS

The table below summarises the key topics that have been tested in the new syllabus examinations to date.

Note that the references are to the number of the question in this edition of the exam kit.

	Dec 2008	Jun 2009	Dec 2009	Jun 2010	Dec 2010	Jun 2011	Dec 2011
Ethics							
Tax avoidance vs tax evasion				Q32			
Ethics of non-disclosure				Q32			
Money laundering				Q32			
Income tax							
Exempt income	Q4	Q15	Q17			Q19	
Basic income tax computation	Q4	Q15	Q17	Q71	Q5	Q19	Q7
		Q16	Q18				
Gift Aid donation	Q4	Q15					Q7
Reduction of personal allowance					Q5	Q19	Q7
Personal age allowance		Q15					Q7
Property income	Q4						Q8
Furnished holiday lettings							Q8
Rent-a-room relief							Q8
ISAs			Q17				
Residence				Q27			
Employed individual							
Factors indicating employment		Q16					
Salary and bonus	Q4					Q19	
Exempt benefits					Q5		
Car and fuel benefit	Q4				Q6		Q7
Living accommodation	Q4				Q5		
Beneficial loan					Q5		
Use of assets	Q4				Q5		
Mileage allowance		Q15					
Self-employed individual							
Adjustment to profits			Q17	Q27		Q19	
			Q18				
Capital allowances	Q26	Q15		Q27			
Basis of assessment rules	Q26		Q17	Q27		Q19	Q7
Partnerships - allocation	Q26			Q27		Q19	
Pensions							
Pension income		Q15					Q7
Occupational pension		Q15			Q5		Q7
Personal pension contributions	Q30	Q15			Q5	Q40	Q7
Annual allowance	Q30						
No relevant earnings	Q30						

	Dec 2008	Jun 2009	Dec 2009	Jun 2010	Dec 2010	Jun 2011	Dec 2011
Income tax losses							
Choice of loss relief					Q24		
Ongoing losses					Q24		
Relief against gains					Q24		
National insurance contributions							
Class 1	Q4	Q16		Q71	Q6	Q19	Q7
Class 1A	Q4				Q6		
Class 2		Q16	Q17			Q19	Q7
Class 4		Q16	Q17	Q27		Q19	Q7
Capital gains							
Basic CGT computation	Q43	Q37	Q18	Q44	Q39		
Enhancement		Q37			Q39		
Exempt assets		Q37					Q41
Chattels		Q37					Q41
Part disposal	Q43			Q44	Q39		Q41
Shares	Q43	Q37	Q38	Q44	Q39	Q40	
Takeover	Q43				Q39	Q40	
Wasting asset		Q37					Q41
Insurance for damaged assets				Q44			
Husband and wife							Q41
Capital losses		Q37					
Reliefs							
Entrepreneurs' relief		Q37			Q39	Q40	
Principal private residence relief		Q37	Q38				Q41
Gift relief			Q38				Q41
Rollover relief				Q44			
Self-assessment – individual							
Pay dates			Q17		Q39		
Payments on account			Q17			Q19	
Filing dates		Q15					
HMRC enquiry				Q32			
Retention of records		Q15					
Discovery assessment				Q32			
Interest and penalties				Q32		Q19	
PAYE administration					Q5		
Inheritance tax							
PETs						Q49	
CLTs						Q49	Q50
Estate computation						Q49	
Due dates						Q49	

	Dec 2008	Jun 2009	Dec 2009	Jun 2010	Dec 2010	Jun 2011	Dec 2011
Corporation tax							
Residence			Q55				
Definition of accounting periods							Q61
Adjustment to profits		Q70	Q55		Q6 Q72	Q57	Q61
Capital allowances		Q70	Q55	Q71	Q72	Q57	Q61
Lease premiums		Q70		Q71	Q72	Q57	
Basic TTP computation	Q43		Q55	Q71 Q56	Q39 Q72	Q57	
Property income		Q70		Q71		Q57	
Interest income		Q70		Q71	Q72	Q57	Q61
Chargeable gains	Q43			Q44	Q39	Q57	
Straddling 31 March liability comp			Q55	Q56			
Corporation tax losses							
Choice of loss relief – factors			Q65				
Trading losses			Q65	Q71			
Capital losses	Q43						
Groups							
Associated companies		Q70	Q55	Q71 Q56	Q72		
Group relief				Q71			Q50
Capital gains group		Q70					
Self-assessment – companies							
Due dates and interest		Q70		Q56			
Quarterly instalments						Q57	
Value added tax							
Registration			Q55			Q80	
Pre-registration input VAT			Q55				
Deregistration		Q79					
VAT return computation		Q79		Q27	Q72		Q61
Tax point				Q27			
Due dates						Q80	
VAT invoices					Q72	Q80	
Default surcharge					Q72		
Errors in a VAT return			Q55			Q80	
Transfer of going concern		Q79					Q61
Overseas supplies						Q80	
Annual accounting scheme						Q80	
Cash accounting scheme		Q79					
Flat rate scheme				Q27			
Net after tax cost comparison					Q6		

ANALYSIS OF MOST RECENT EXAMS

The table below summarises the key topics that have been tested in the most recent exams.

Note that the references are to the number of the question in the original exam. These exams can be found, with enhanced "walk through answers", updated in line with legislation relevant to your exam sitting, on **My**Kaplan at:

www.mykaplan.co.uk

	Jun 12	Dec 12	Jun 13
Income tax			
Exempt income	Q4	Q1	
Basic income tax computation	Q1	Q1, Q4	Q1, Q5
Gift Aid donation		Q1	
Reduction of personal allowance		Q1	
Property income	Q1	Q1	Q1, Q5
Furnished holiday lettings		Q1	Q1
ISAs		Q5	
Employed individual			
Salary and bonus	Q1		
Car and fuel benefit			Q1
Living accommodation	Q1		
Beneficial loan			Q1
Use of assets	Q1		
Mileage allowance			Q1
Self-employed individual			
Capital allowances	Q1	Q1	Q4
Basis of assessment rules		Q1	Q4
Partnerships – allocation	Q1		
Choice of accounting date	Q1		
Pensions			
Pension income			Q1
Occupational pension			Q1
Personal pension contributions		Q5	Q1
Annual allowance		Q5	Q1
Income tax losses			
Relief against income	Q4		
Opening year loss relief	Q4		
Terminal loss relief	Q4		
Tax savings	Q4		
National insurance contributions			
Class 1	Q1	Q4	Q1
Class 1A	Q1		Q1
Class 2	Q1		
Class 4	Q1		

	Jun 12	Dec 12	Jun 13
Capital gains			
Chargeable person	Q3		
Basic CGT computation	Q3		Q3, Q5
Enhancement		Q3	
Part disposal		Q3	
Shares		Q3	Q3
Insurance for damaged assets		Q3	
Capital losses		Q4	
Reliefs			
Entrepreneurs' relief	Q3, Q4		Q3
Gift relief			Q3
Rollover relief	Q3		Q3
Self-assessment – individual			
Payments on account		Q1	
Corporation tax			
Residence	Q3		
Adjustment to profits	Q2	Q2	Q2
Capital allowances	Q2	Q2	Q2, Q4
Lease premiums	Q2		
Basic TTP computation	Q2	Q2, Q4	Q2
Interest income		Q2	
Chargeable gains	Q2, Q3	Q3	
Long period of account	Q2		Q4
Straddling 31 March liability comp	Q2		
Corporation tax losses			
Capital losses		Q3	
Groups			
Associated companies	Q2	Q2	Q2
Group relief			Q2
Capital gains group	Q2		
Self-assessment – companies			
Due dates and interest		Q2	
iXBRL		Q2	

	Jun 12	Dec 12	Jun 13
Value added tax			
Registration	Q1		
VAT return computation			Q2
Tax point	Q1		Q2
Default surcharge			Q2
Overseas supplies		Q2	
VAT groups			Q2
Annual accounting scheme		Q2	
Cash accounting scheme		Q2	
Flat rate scheme	Q1		
Inheritance tax			
PETs	Q5	Q5	Q5
CLTs		Q5	
Exemptions	Q5		Q5
Estate computation	Q5		Q5
Due dates			Q5
Transfer of nil rate band	Q5		
Net after tax cost comparison		Q4	

EXAM TECHNIQUE

- Use the allocated **15 minutes reading and planning time** at the beginning of the exam:
  - read the questions and examination requirements carefully, and
  - begin planning your answers.

  See the Paper Specific Information for advice on how to use this time for this paper.
- **Divide the time** you spend on questions in proportion to the marks on offer:
  - there are 1.8 minutes available per mark in the examination
  - within that, try to allow time at the end of each question to review your answer and address any obvious issues

  Whatever happens, always keep your eye on the clock and **do not over run on any part of any question!**
- Spend the last **five minutes** of the examination:
  - reading through your answers, and
  - **making any additions or corrections**.
- If you **get completely stuck** with a question:
  - leave space in your answer book, and
  - **return to it later.**
- Stick to the question and **tailor your answer** to what you are asked.
  - pay particular attention to the verbs in the question.
- If you do not understand what a question is asking, **state your assumptions**.

  Even if you do not answer in precisely the way the examiner hoped, you should be given some credit, if your assumptions are reasonable.
- You should do everything you can to make things easy for the marker.

  The marker will find it easier to identify the points you have made if your **answers are legible**.
- **Written questions**:

  Your answer should have:
  - a clear structure
  - a brief introduction, a main section and a conclusion.

  Be concise.

  It is better to write a little about a lot of different points than a great deal about one or two points.
- **Computations**:

  It is essential to include all your workings in your answers.

  Many computational questions require the use of a standard format:

  e.g. income tax computations, corporation tax computations and capital gains.

  Be sure you know these formats thoroughly before the exam and use the layouts that you see in the answers given in this book and in model answers.
- **Reports, memos and other documents**:

  Some questions ask you to present your answer in the form of a report, a memo, a letter or other document.

  Make sure that you use the correct format – there could be easy marks to gain here.

PAPER SPECIFIC INFORMATION

THE EXAM

FORMAT OF THE EXAM

		Number of marks
5 compulsory questions which will be **predominantly computational**:		
Question 1:	Income tax	25 or 30
Question 2:	Corporation tax	25 or 30
Question 3:	Chargeable gains (personal or corporate)	15
Question 4:	Any area of the syllabus	15
Question 5:	Any area of the syllabus	15
		100

Total time allowed: 3 hours plus 15 minutes reading and planning time.

Note that:

- Question 1 will focus on income tax and question 2 will focus on corporation tax. The two questions will be for a total of 55 marks, with one of the questions being for 30 marks and the other being for 25 marks.
- There will always be a minimum of 10 marks on VAT. These marks will normally be included within question 1 or 2, although there could be a separate question on value added tax.
- National Insurance Contributions will not be examined as a separate question, but may be examined in any question involving income tax or corporation tax.
- Inheritance tax will be tested for between 5 and 15 marks and can be included within questions 3, 4 or 5.
- Groups and overseas aspects of corporation tax may be examined within question 2 or 5.
- Questions 1 and 2 may include a small element of chargeable gains.
- Any of the five questions might include the consideration of issues relating to the minimisation or deferral of tax liabilities.

PASS MARK

The pass mark for all ACCA Qualification examination papers is 50%.

READING AND PLANNING TIME

Remember that all three hour paper based examinations have an additional 15 minutes reading and planning time.

ACCA GUIDANCE

ACCA guidance on the use of this time is as follows:

This additional time is allowed at the beginning of the examination to allow candidates to read the questions and to begin planning their answers before they start to write in their answer books.

This time should be used to ensure that all the information and, in particular, the exam requirements are properly read and understood.

During this time, candidates may only annotate their question paper. They may not write anything in their answer booklets until told to do so by the invigilator.

KAPLAN GUIDANCE

As all questions are compulsory, there are no decisions to be made about choice of questions, other than in which order you would like to tackle them.

Therefore, in relation to F6, we recommend that you take the following approach with your reading and planning time:

- **Skim through the whole paper**, assessing the level of difficulty of each question.
- **Write down** on the question paper next to the mark allocation **the amount of time you should spend on each part.** Do this for each part of every question.
- **Decide the order** in which you think you will attempt each question:

  This is a personal choice and you have time on the revision phase to try out different approaches, for example, if you sit mock exams.

  A common approach is to tackle the question you think is the easiest and you are most comfortable with first.

  Others may prefer to tackle the longest questions first, or conversely leave them to the last.

  Psychologists believe that you usually perform at your best on the second and third question you attempt, once you have settled into the exam, so not tackling the bigger Section A questions first may be advisable.

  It is usual however that student tackle their least favourite topic and/or the most difficult question in their opinion last.

  Whatever you approach, you must make sure that you leave enough time to attempt all questions fully and be very strict with yourself in timing each question.

- **For each question** in turn, read the requirements and then the detail of the question carefully.

  Always read the requirement first as this enables you to **focus on the detail of the question with the specific task in mind**.

  For computational questions:

  Highlight key numbers/information and key words in the question, scribble notes to yourself on the question paper to remember key points in your answer.

  Jot down pro formas required if applicable.

  For written questions:

  Take notice of the format required (e.g. letter, memo, notes) and identify the recipient of the answer. You need to do this to judge the level of financial sophistication required in your answer and whether the use of a formal reply or informal bullet points would be satisfactory.

  Plan your beginning, middle and end and the key areas to be addressed and your use of titles and sub-titles to enhance your answer.

  For all questions:

  Spot the easy marks to be gained in a question and parts which can be performed independently of the rest of the question. For example, writing down due dates of payment of tax, due dates for making elections, laying out basic pro formas correctly.

  Make sure that you do these parts first when you tackle the question.

  Don't go overboard in terms of planning time on any one question – you need a good measure of the whole paper and a plan for all of the questions at the end of the 15 minutes.

  By covering all questions you can often help yourself as you may find that facts in one question may remind you of things you should put into your answer relating to a different question.

- With your plan of attack in mind, **start answering your chosen question** with your plan to hand, as soon as you are allowed to start.

Always keep your eye on the clock and do not over run on any part of any question!

DETAILED SYLLABUS

The detailed syllabus and study guide written by the ACCA can be found at:

www.accaglobal.com/en/student.html

KAPLAN'S RECOMMENDED REVISION APPROACH

QUESTION PRACTICE IS THE KEY TO SUCCESS

Success in professional examinations relies upon you acquiring a firm grasp of the required knowledge at the tuition phase. In order to be able to do the questions, knowledge is essential.

However, the difference between success and failure often hinges on your exam technique on the day and making the most of the revision phase of your studies.

The **Kaplan complete text** is the starting point, designed to provide the underpinning knowledge to tackle all questions. However, in the revision phase, pouring over text books is not the answer.

Kaplan Online fixed tests help you consolidate your knowledge and understanding and are a useful tool to check whether you can remember key topic areas.

Kaplan pocket notes are designed to help you quickly revise a topic area, however you then need to practice questions. There is a need to progress to full exam standard questions as soon as possible, and to tie your exam technique and technical knowledge together.

The importance of question practice cannot be over-emphasised.

The recommended approach below is designed by expert tutors in the field, in conjunction with their knowledge of the examiner and their recent real exams.

The approach taken for the fundamental papers is to revise by topic area. However, with the professional stage papers, a multi topic approach is required to answer the scenario based questions.

You need to practice as many questions as possible in the time you have left.

OUR AIM

Our aim is to get you to the stage where you can attempt exam standard questions confidently, to time, in a closed book environment, with no supplementary help (i.e. to simulate the real examination experience).

Practising your exam technique on real past examination questions, in timed conditions, is also vitally important for you to assess your progress and identify areas of weakness that may need more attention in the final run up to the examination.

In order to achieve this we recognise that initially you may feel the need to practice some questions with open book help and exceed the required time.

The approach below shows you which questions you should use to build up to coping with exam standard question practice, and references to the sources of information available should you need to revisit a topic area in more detail.

Remember that in the real examination, all you have to do is:

- attempt all questions required by the exam
- only spend the allotted time on each question, and
- get them at least 50% right!

Try and practice this approach on every question you attempt from now to the real exam.

EXAMINER COMMENTS

We have included the examiner's comments to the specific new syllabus examination questions in this kit for you to see the main pitfalls that students fall into with regard to technical content.

However, too many times in the general section of the report, the examiner comments that students had failed due to:

- "misallocation of time"
- "running out of time" and
- showing signs of "spending too much time on an earlier questions and clearly rushing the answer to a subsequent question".

Good exam technique is vital.

THE KAPLAN PAPER F6 REVISION PLAN

Stage 1: Assess areas of strengths and weaknesses

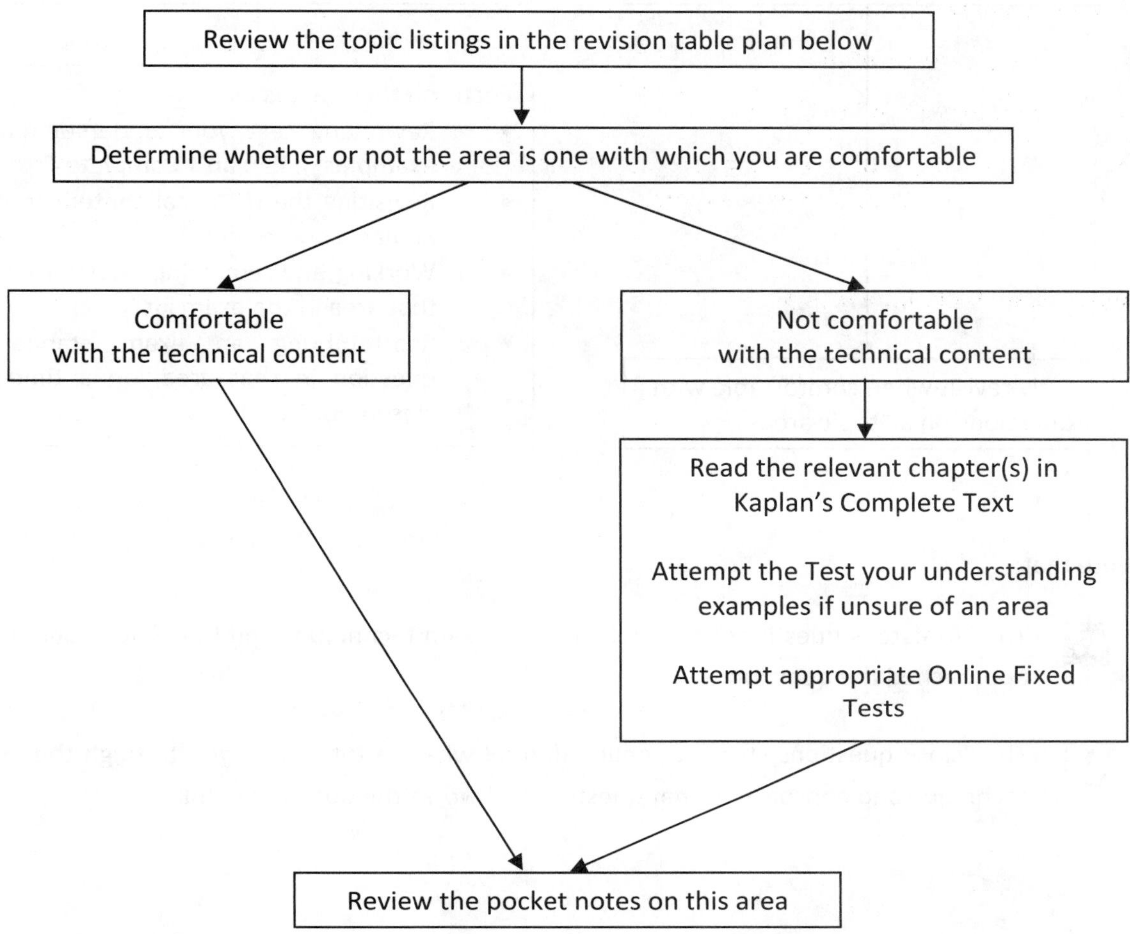

Stage 2: Practice questions

Follow the order of revision of topics as recommended in the revision table plan below and attempt the questions in the order suggested. Note that although the plan is organised into different subject areas, the real exam questions will cover more than one topic, and therefore some parts of the exam questions set below will be on topics covered later in the revision plan.

Try to avoid referring to text books and notes and the model answer until you have completed your attempt.

Try to answer the question in the allotted time.

Review your attempt with the model answer and assess how much of the answer you achieved in the allocated exam time.

Fill in the self-assessment box below and decide on your best course of action.

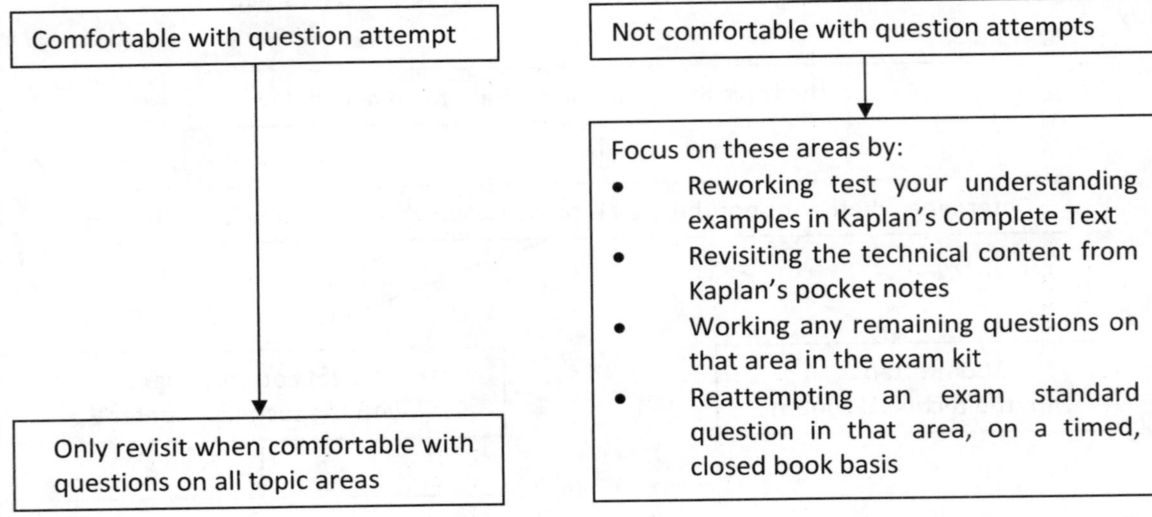

Note that:

The "footsteps questions" give guidance on exam techniques and how you should have approached the question.

The "clock questions" have an online debrief where a tutor talks you through the exam technique and approach to that question and works the question in full.

Stage 3: Final pre-exam revision

We recommend that you **attempt at least one three hour mock examination** containing a set of previously unseen exam standard questions.

It is important that you get a feel for the breadth of coverage of a real exam without advanced knowledge of the topic areas covered – just as you will expect to see on the real exam day.

Ideally this mock should be sat in timed, closed book, real exam conditions and could be:

- a mock examination offered by your tuition provider, and/or
- the last real examination paper (available shortly afterwards on **My**Kaplan with "enhanced walk through answers" and a full "tutor debrief").

THE DETAILED REVISION PLAN

Topic	*Complete Text Chapter*	*Pocket note Chapter*	*Questions to attempt*	*Tutor guidance*	*Date attempted*	*Self assessment*
Personal income tax computation	2	1	–	Review the layout of an income tax computation and rates of tax. Question 1 in the exam will include at least one income tax computation, and it is crucial that you are comfortable with the pro forma.		
– Residence	2	1	Q27(a) Q36(a)	The rules to determine whether an individual is resident in the UK became much more complex in FA13. Revise the rules from the pocket notes and practice these two questions.		
– Employment income and assessable benefits	4	2	2 4 5 16	A popular exam topic, almost guaranteed to form part of the exam. There are many questions on this area. Start with Q2 which is a basic warm up question covering a number of employment benefits. Build up to Q4 and Q5 which are more demanding past exam questions on this area. Q4 includes the new child benefit income tax charge. Q16 tests the rules for determining whether an individual is employed or self-employed and the consequences of this decision.		
– Property income	3	1	8	This is a detailed question solely on property income which is an excellent test of your retention of these rules. However, be aware that this topic often appears as part of a big income tax computation, where property is just one of a few sources of income for an individual.		

Topic	*Complete Text Chapter*	*Pocket note Chapter*	*Questions to attempt*	*Tutor guidance*	*Date attempted*	*Self assessment*
– Badges of trade	5	3	18	Revise the badges of trade rules from the pocket notes, before attempting this question. Note that although you are not required to apply the rules to a particular scenario in this question, you may be asked to do so in the exam. The consequences of the decision are however covered and this question demonstrates the importance of the badges of trade and how an individual is taxed as a consequence.		
– Adjusted trading profit, including capital allowances and cash basis	5 & 6	3 & 4	12 14 10	An adjustment of profits calculation is almost certain to be tested in the exam, although it may form part of question 1 for a sole trader/partnership or question 2 for a company. Q12 tests many of the typical adjustments you may see, and having practiced this question you can then attempt Q14 to time. Q10 tests the new rules on the cash basis of assessment.		
– Basis of assessment	7	5	11 13	You may benefit from practicing the test your understandings from the complete text before attempting these questions. The opening year rules are commonly tested and Q13 provides good practice.		
– National insurance	11	8	29(a)	National insurance regularly forms part of a longer question, and can provide easy marks to a well-prepared student. This question covers NICs for both an employee and a self-employed individual.		

Topic	***Complete Text Chapter***	***Pocket note Chapter***	***Questions to attempt***	***Tutor guidance***	***Date attempted***	***Self assessment***
– Trading losses for individuals	9	7	23 22 20	These questions cover the range of ways losses can be tested – in an ongoing business, losses in the opening years and losses on cessation. Q23 also now tests the cap on income tax reliefs introduced in FA13. In the current climate, losses are topical and it is important to be familiar with each of the reliefs.		
– Partnerships	8	6	27(b)	The allocation of profits between partners is a relatively straightforward computation, but does require practice.		
– Pensions	10	8	28 30	Like National Insurance, pensions is a topic which is likely to form a small part of a longer question, however the two questions listed here provide excellent practice of the various ways this topic could be tested.		
– Tax admin for individuals	12	9	31 32	Administration rarely appears as a standalone question (although this was the case in June 2010); however, it is regularly tested at the end of a longer income tax question. It is vital to learn the dates for submission and payment as well as the potential penalties and interest.		
Consolidation of personal tax			17 26	Having revised all of the above topics, attempt Q17 and Q26 which are recent questions incorporating many aspects of the taxation of individuals.		
Inheritance tax (IHT)	17	13	45 49 50	IHT is examined for 5-15 marks in each exam and therefore it is important to study this area. Use your pocket notes to revise the key facts and techniques. Warm up with Q45 then practice questions 49 and 50, which were the first two questions on IHT after it was introduced to the F6 syllabus.		

Topic	*Complete Text Chapter*	*Pocket note Chapter*	*Questions to attempt*	*Tutor guidance*	*Date attempted*	*Self assessment*
Corporation tax computation	18	14	–	Review the layout of a corporation tax computation and the rates of tax. Question 2 will include a corporation tax computation, and it is crucial that you are comfortable with the pro forma. You should also ensure you know how to calculate the tax liability for an accounting period which straddles 31 March 2013 as this is highly examinable.		
– Adjustment of profits and capital allowances	19	14	52 59(a)	It is important to be comfortable with the differences between sole traders and companies for adjustments to profits and capital allowances. Use Q52 to check that you are clear about these differences, then attempt Q59, which is classic example of this type of question.		
– Property income	19	14	71(a)	There are minor but important differences between taxing property income for individuals and companies. This question covers property income for a company, and also covers group relief, which you could leave until you revise that area, or have a go and see what you remember!		
– Long periods of account	19	14	54 58	In order to deal with a long period of account, you need to learn the rules regarding apportioning different types of income between the two periods. Having revised these rules from the pocket notes, practice them using these questions.		

Topic	***Complete Text Chapter***	***Pocket note Chapter***	***Questions to attempt***	***Tutor guidance***	***Date attempted***	***Self assessment***
– Corporation tax losses	21	16	65	Many students are daunted by loss questions, however a systematic approach is all that is required and practice is key. Remind yourself of the layout required using the pocket notes, and practice the test your understandings from the complete text if you are not confident, before attempting Q65.		
– Groups	22	17	64 68 69	Groups are often tested as part of question 2. Q64 tests group relief, Q68 covers both group relief and the capital gains aspects of groups and Q69 tests the rules for determining a capital gains group and the number of associates.		
– Tax admin for a company	23	18	56	It is rare to see a standalone question on administration in the exam (although this was the case in June 2010), however there are often easy marks available as part of other questions. It is therefore very important to learn the submission and payment dates as well as the penalty and interest rules.		
Chargeable gains for individuals	13	10	–	Chargeable gains will be tested in question 3 in the exam, and these questions will usually test a wide variety of the topics below. Revise the basic computation using the pocket notes before looking at the detailed areas.		
– Chattels, shares, PPR, Entrepreneurs relief	14 & 16	11 & 12	35 33 39 41	These questions demonstrate how various aspects of capital gains will be tested in one question. Few of these areas are technically challenging, however, it is important that you can tackle them all.		

Topic	***Complete Text Chapter***	***Pocket note Chapter***	***Questions to attempt***	***Tutor guidance***	***Date attempted***	***Self assessment***
– Deferral reliefs	16	12	36 38	Recognising which deferral reliefs apply and whether they are available in full is important These questions cover all these reliefs and provide excellent practice.		
Chargeable gains for companies	20	15	43	Remind yourself of the different gains rules for companies, and test your understanding using Q43.		
– Quoted shares	15 & 20	11 & 15	44	A brief revision of the share pool and matching rules from the pocket notes may be useful. The attempt Q44 which tests the capital gains rules for companies, including share pooling and also asks for calculations of the indexed base costs of assets retained, which had not previously been required.		
Value added tax	24 & 25	19	79 80 27(d) 29(b) 55(b) 60(b) 72(b)	Start by reviewing the examiner's VAT article. VAT usually appears as part of question 1 or question 2 (for a minimum of 10 marks); however Q79 and Q80 are standalone VAT questions. The remainder of the questions listed here contain VAT but are not included in the VAT section of the kit; however any of Qs 73-78 also provide further practice.		
Scenario style exam questions	N/A	20	6 7 19 71(b)-(d)	These questions test a range of subjects and the tax rules covered are not complex, however, the style of questions differs from the others in the kit. Look at the different styles of question using the chapter in the pocket notes, and then ensure you are comfortable with the different question styles by practicing each of these questions.		

Note that not all of the questions are referred to in the programme above.

We have recommended an approach to build up from the basic to exam standard questions.

The remaining questions are available in the kit for extra practice for those who require more questions on some areas.

TAX RATES AND ALLOWANCES

Throughout this exam kit:

1 **Calculations and workings need only to be made to the nearest £.**

2 **All apportionments should be made to the nearest month.**

3 **All workings should be shown.**

The tax rates and allowances below will be reproduced in the examination paper for Paper F6 in the 2014 examination sittings. In addition, other specific information necessary for candidates to answer individual questions will be given as part of the question.

INCOME TAX

		Normal rates	Dividend rates
		%	%
Basic rate	£1 – £32,010	20	10
Higher rate	£32,010 – £150,000	40	32.5
Additional rate	£150,001 and above	45	37.5

A starting rate of 10% applies to savings income where it falls within the first £2,790 of taxable income.

Personal allowances

Personal allowance

Born on or after 6 April 1948	£9,440
Born between 6 April 1938 and 5 April 1948	£10,500
Born before 6 April 1938	£10,660

Income limit

Personal allowance	£100,000
Personal allowance (born before 6 April 1948)	£26,100

Residence status

Days in UK	Previously resident	Not previously resident
Less than 16	Automatically not resident	Automatically not resident
16 to 45	Resident if 4 UK ties (or more)	Automatically not resident
46 to 90	Resident if 3 UK ties (or more)	Resident if 4 UK ties
91 to 120	Resident if 2 UK ties (or more)	Resident if 3 UK ties (or more)
121 to 182	Resident if 1 UK tie (or more)	Resident if 2 UK ties (or more)
183 or more	Automatically resident	Automatically resident

Child benefit income tax charge

Where income is between £50,000 and £60,000, the charge is 1% of the amount of child benefit received for every £100 of income over £50,000.

Car benefit percentage

The relevant base level of CO_2 emissions is 95 grams per kilometre.

The percentage rates applying to petrol cars with CO_2 emissions up to:

75 grams per kilometre or less	5%
76 to 94 grams per kilometre	10%
95 grams per kilometre	11%

Car fuel benefit

The base level figure for calculating the car fuel benefit is £21,100.

Individual Savings Accounts (ISAs)

The overall investment limit is £11,520, of which £5,760 can be invested in a cash ISA.

Pension scheme limits

Annual allowance	£50,000

The maximum contribution that can qualify for tax relief without evidence of earnings is £3,600.

Authorised mileage allowance: cars

Up to 10,000 miles	45p
Over 10,000 miles	25p

Capital allowances: rates of allowance

	%
Plant and machinery	
Main pool	18
Special rate pool	8
Motor cars	
New cars with CO_2 emissions up to 95 grams per kilometre	100
CO_2 emissions between 96 and 130 grams per kilometre	18
CO_2 emissions above 130 grams per kilometre	8
Annual investment allowance	
First £250,000 of expenditure (since 1 January 2013)	100

Cap on income tax reliefs

Unless otherwise restricted, reliefs are capped at the higher of £50,000 or 25% of income.

CORPORATION TAX

Financial year	*2011*	*2012*	*2013*
Small profits rate	20%	20%	20%
Main rate	26%	24%	23%
Lower limit	£300,000	£300,000	£300,000
Upper limit	£1,500,000	£1,500,000	£1,500,000
Standard fraction	3/200	1/100	3/400

Marginal relief

Standard fraction × (U – A) × N/A

VALUE ADDED TAX

Standard rate of VAT	20.0%
Registration limit	£79,000
Deregistration limit	£77,000

INHERITANCE TAX: Tax rates

£1 – £325,000	Nil
Excess – Death rate	40%
– Lifetime rate	20%

Inheritance tax: Taper relief

Years before death:	Percentage reduction %
Over 3 but less than 4 years	20
Over 4 but less than 5 years	40
Over 5 but less than 6 years	60
Over 6 but less than 7 years	80

CAPITAL GAINS TAX

Rates of tax	– Lower rate	18%
	– Higher rate	28%
Annual exempt amount		£10,900
Entrepreneurs' relief	– Lifetime limit	£10,000,000
	– Rate of tax	10%

NATIONAL INSURANCE CONTRIBUTIONS
(not contracted out rates)

			%
Class 1	Employee	£1 – £7,755 per year	Nil
		£7,756 – £41,450 per year	12.0
		£41,451 and above per year	2.0
Class 1	Employer	£1 – £7,696 per year	Nil
		£7,697 and above per year	13.8
Class 1A			13.8
Class 2		£2.70 per week	
		Small earnings exception limit	£5,725
Class 4		£1 – £7,755 per year	Nil
		£7,756 – £41,450 per year	9.0
		£41,451 and above per year	2.0

RATES OF INTEREST (assumed)

Official rate of interest:	4.0%
Rate of interest on underpaid tax:	3.0%
Rate of interest on overpaid tax:	0.5%

TIME LIMITS AND ELECTION DATES

Income tax

Election/claim	Time limit	For 2013/14
Agree the amount of trading losses to carry forward	4 years from the end of the tax year in which the loss arose	5 April 2018
Current and prior year set-off of trading losses against total income (and chargeable gains)	12 months from 31 January following the end of the tax year in which the loss arose	31 January 2016
Three year carry back of trading losses in the opening years	12 months from 31 January following the end of the tax year in which the loss arose	31 January 2016
Three year carry back of terminal trading losses in the closing years	4 years from the end of the last tax year of trading	5 April 2018

National Insurance Contributions

Class 1 primary and secondary – pay days	14 days after the end of each tax month under PAYE system (17 days if paid electronically)	19th of each month 22nd (electronic)
Class 1 A NIC – pay day	19 July following end of tax year 22 July if paid electronically	19 July 2014 22 July 2014
Class 2 NICs – pay days	Monthly direct debit or six monthly invoicing	31 January 2014 & 31 July 2014
Class 4 NICs – pay days	Paid under self-assessment with income tax	

Capital gains tax

Replacement of business asset relief for individuals (Rollover relief)	4 years from the end of the tax year: – in which the disposal occurred or – the replacement asset was acquired whichever is later	5 April 2018 for 2012/13 sale and 2013/14 acquisition
Holdover relief of gain on the gift of a business asset (Gift relief)	4 years from the end of the tax year in which the disposal occurred	5 April 2018
Entrepreneurs' relief	12 months from 31 January following the end of the tax year in which the disposal occurred	31 January 2016
Determination of principal private residence	2 years from the acquisition of the second property	

Self-assessment – individuals

Election/claim	Time limit	For 2013/14
Pay days for income tax and Class 4 NIC	1st instalment: 31 January in the tax year 2nd instalment: 31 July following the end of tax year Balancing payment: 31 January following the end of tax year	 31 January 2014 31 July 2014 31 January 2015
Pay day for CGT	31 January following the end of tax year	31 January 2015
Filing dates If return issued by 31 October in the tax year If return issued after 31 October in the tax year	 Paper return: 31 October following end of tax year Electronic return: 31 January following end of tax year 3 months from the date of issue of the return	 31 October 2014 31 January 2015
Retention of records Business records Personal records	 5 years from 31 January following end of the tax year 12 months from 31 January following end of the tax year	 31 January 2020 31 January 2016
HMRC right of repair	9 months from date the return was filed	
Taxpayers right to amend a return	12 months from 31 January following end of the tax year	31 January 2016
Taxpayers claim for overpayment relief	4 years from the end of the tax year	5 April 2018
HMRC can open an enquiry	12 months from submission of the return	
HMRC can raise a discovery assessment – No careless or deliberate behaviour – Tax lost due to careless behaviour – Tax lost due to deliberate behaviour	 4 years from the end of the tax year 6 years from the end of the tax year 20 years from the end of the tax year	 5 April 2018 5 April 2020 5 April 2034
Taxpayers right of appeal against an assessment	30 days from the assessment – appeal in writing	

Corporation tax

Election/claim	**Time limit**
Replacement of business asset relief for companies (Rollover relief)	4 years from the end of the chargeable accounting period: – in which the disposal occurred or – the replacement asset was acquired whichever is later
Agree the amount of trading losses to carry forward	4 years from the end of the chargeable accounting period in which the loss arose
Current year set-off of trading losses against total profits (income and gains), and 12 month carry back of trading losses against total profits (income and gains)	2 years from the end of the chargeable accounting period in which the loss arose
Surrender of current period trading losses to other group companies (Group relief)	2 years after the claimant company's chargeable accounting period
Election for transfer of capital gain or loss to another company within the gains group	2 years from the end of the chargeable accounting period in which the disposal occurred by the company actually making the disposal

Self-assessment – companies

Election/claim	**Time limit**
Pay day for small and medium companies	9 months and one day after the end of the chargeable accounting period
Pay day for large companies	Instalments due on 14th day of: – Seventh, Tenth, Thirteenth, and Sixteenth month **after the start** of the chargeable accounting period
Filing dates	Later of: – 12 months from the end of the chargeable accounting period – 3 months from the issue of a notice to deliver a corporation tax return
Companies claim for overpayment relief	4 years from the end of the chargeable accounting period
HMRC can open an enquiry	12 months from the actual submission of the return
Retention of records	6 years from the end of the chargeable accounting period

Value added tax

Election/claim	**Time limit**
Compulsory registration Historic test: – Notify HMRC – Charge VAT Future test: – Notify HMRC – Charge VAT	 30 days from end of the month in which the threshold was exceeded Beginning of the month, one month after the end of the month in which the threshold was exceeded 30 days from the date it is anticipated that the threshold will be exceeded the date it is anticipated that the threshold will be exceeded (i.e. the beginning of the 30 day period)
Compulsory deregistration	30 days from cessation
Filing of VAT return and payment of VAT	One month and seven days after the end of the return period

Section 1

PRACTICE QUESTIONS

INCOME TAX AND NATIONAL INSURANCE

INCOME TAX BASICS AND EMPLOYMENT INCOME

1 SALLY AND SANDRA BURTON (ADAPTED) 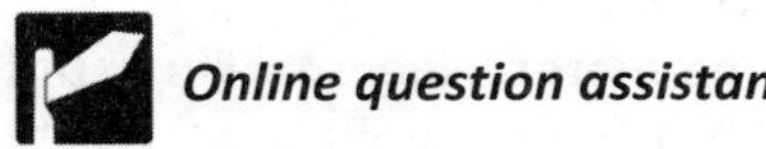

Sally and Sandra Burton, born on 6 February 1948 and 4 November 1937 respectively, are sisters.

The following information is available for 2013/14:

Sally Burton

(1) Sally is employed by Burton plc as a part time manager working 3 days a week in one of the company's nationwide chain of retail clothing shops. She is paid a gross annual salary of £19,000 from which PAYE of £2,400 was deducted by her employer.

(2) On 6 June 2013 Sally was provided with a petrol powered motor car which has a list price of £17,118. Sally made a capital contribution of £2,000 towards the cost of the motor car when it was first provided. The official CO_2 emission rate for the motor car is 177 grams per kilometre. Burton plc paid for all of the motor car's maintenance costs of £2,400 during 2013/14 as well as car parking costing £1,200. Her employer did not provide any fuel for private journeys.

(3) Burton plc has provided Sally with living accommodation since 2012. The property was purchased in 2005 for £105,000, and was valued at £120,000 when first provided to Sally. It has an annual value of £1,632. Sally was not required by her job to live in the accommodation provided by her employer. Sally was required to reimburse her employer £75 each month for the use of the accommodation.

(4) In addition to her employment income, Sally received interest of £1,000 on the maturity of a savings certificate from the National Savings & Investments bank during the tax year 2013/14. This was the actual cash amount received.

(5) During 2013/14 Sally received building society interest of £1,800. This was the actual cash amount received.

Sandra Burton

(1) Sandra is self-employed running a retail grocery shop. Her statement of profit or loss for the year ended 5 April 2014 is as follows:

	£	£
Gross profit		60,105
Depreciation	2,425	
Motor expenses (Note 2)	5,400	
Property expenses (Note 3)	9,600	
Other expenses (all allowable)	24,680	
		(42,105)
Net profit		18,000

(2) The motor expenses all relate to Sandra's motor car. During the year ended 5 April 2014 Sandra drove a total of 12,000 miles, of which 4,000 were for private journeys. The car was acquired in March 2011, and has an official CO_2 emission rate of 125 grams per kilometre. At 6 April 2013 the car had a tax written down value of £9,600. She does not own any other assets that qualify for capital allowances.

(3) Sandra purchased her grocery shop in 2005 for £105,000. She lives in a flat that is situated above the shop, and one-third of the total property expenses of £9,600 relate to this flat.

(4) In addition to her self-employed income, Sandra received £895 from an investment account at the National Savings & Investment bank during 2013/14. This was the actual cash amount received.

(5) During 2013/14 Sandra received dividends of £1,080. This was the actual cash amount received.

Required:

(a) Calculate Sally's income tax payable for 2013/14. **(13 marks)**

(b) Calculate Sandra's income tax payable for 2013/14. **(12 marks)**

(Total 25 marks)

Online question assistance

2 VIGOROUS PLC (ADAPTED)

Vigorous plc runs a health club. The company has three employees who received benefits during 2013/14, and it therefore needs to prepare forms P11D for them. Each of the three employees is paid an annual salary of £60,000.

The following information is relevant:

Andrea Lean

(1) Andrea was employed by Vigorous plc throughout 2013/14.

(2) Throughout 2013/14 Vigorous plc provided Andrea with a petrol powered company motor car with a list price of £19,400. The official CO_2 emission rate for the motor car is 260 grams per kilometre. Vigorous plc paid for all of the motor car's running costs of £6,200 during 2013/14, including petrol used for private journeys. Andrea pays £150 per month to Vigorous plc for the use of the motor car.

(3) Vigorous plc has provided Andrea with living accommodation since 1 November 2011. The property was purchased on 1 January 2009 for £130,000. The company spent £14,000 improving the property during March 2010, and a further £8,000 was spent on improvements during May 2013.

The value of the property on 1 November 2011 was £170,000, and it has an annual value of £7,000. The furniture in the property cost £6,000 during November 2011. Andrea personally pays for the annual running costs of the property amounting to £4,000.

(4) Throughout 2013/14 Vigorous plc provided Andrea with a mobile telephone costing £500. The company paid for all business and private telephone calls.

Ben Slim

(1) Ben commenced employment with Vigorous plc on 1 July 2013.

(2) On 1 July 2013 Vigorous plc provided Ben with an interest free loan of £120,000 so that he could purchase a new main residence. He repaid £20,000 of the loan on 1 December 2013.

(3) During 2013/14 Vigorous plc paid £9,300 towards the cost of Ben's relocation. His previous main residence was 125 miles from his place of employment with the company. The £9,300 covered the cost of disposing of Ben's old property and of acquiring his new property.

(4) From 1 July 2013 Vigorous plc provided Ben with a petrol powered second hand motor car which has a list price of £9,200. The official CO_2 emission rate for the motor car is 90 g/km. No fuel was provided by the company; Ben just claimed fuel for his business mileage. Ben had the use of the car until 30 September 2013 when his new company car arrived.

(5) During the period from 1 October 2013 until 5 April 2014 Vigorous plc provided Ben with a new diesel powered company motor car which has a list price of £11,200. The official CO_2 emission rate for the motor car is 119 g/km. Ben reimburses Vigorous plc for the fuel used for private journeys.

(6) On 1 July 2013 Ben joined the company's childcare scheme which provides employees with childcare vouchers of £60 per week to buy care from an approved child carer. Ben received vouchers to provide care for 36 weeks in 2013/14.

Chai Trim

(1) Chai was employed by Vigorous plc throughout 2013/14.

(2) During 2013/14 Vigorous plc provided Chai with a two-year old company van, which was available for private use. The van was unavailable during the period 1 August to 30 September 2013. Chai was also provided with private fuel for the van.

(3) Vigorous plc has provided Chai with a television for her personal use since 6 April 2011. The television cost Vigorous plc £800 in April 2011. On 6 April 2013 the company sold the television to Chai for £150, although its market value on that date was £250.

(4) Throughout 2013/14 Vigorous plc provided Chai with free membership of its health club. The normal annual cost of membership is £800. This figure is made up of direct costs of £150, fixed overhead costs of £400 and profit of £250. The budgeted membership for the year has been exceeded, but the health club has surplus capacity.

(5) On 1 January 2014 Vigorous plc provided Chai with a new computer costing £1,900. She uses the computer at home for personal study purposes.

Required:

(a) **Explain what is meant by the term 'P11D employee'.** **(3 marks)**

(b) **Calculate the benefit figures that Vigorous plc will have to include on the forms P11D for Andrea, Ben, and Chai for 2013/14.** **(19 marks)**

(c) **Explain how the income tax liability in respect of benefits is collected by HM Revenue & Customs.** **(3 marks)**

(Total: 25 marks)

3 ALI PATEL (ADAPTED)  *Walk in the footsteps of a top tutor*

You should assume that today's date is 15 March 2013.

Ali Patel has been employed by Box plc since 1 January 2010, and is currently paid an annual salary of £29,000. On 6 April 2013 Ali is to be temporarily relocated for a period of 12 months from Box plc's head office to one of its branch offices. He has been offered two alternative remuneration packages:

First remuneration package

(1) Ali will continue to live near Box plc's head office, and will commute on a daily basis to the branch office using his private motor car.

(2) He will be paid additional salary of £500 per month.

(3) Box plc will pay Ali an allowance of 38 pence per mile for the 1,600 miles that Ali will drive each month commuting to the branch office.

Ali's additional cost of commuting for 2013/14 will be £1,800.

Second remuneration package

(1) Box plc will provide Ali with rent-free living accommodation near the branch office.

(2) The property will be rented by Box plc at a cost of £800 per month. The annual value of the property is £4,600.

(3) Ali will rent out his main residence near Box plc's head office, and this will result in property business income of £6,000 for 2013/14.

Required:

(a) **Calculate Ali's income tax liability and Class 1 national insurance contributions for 2013/14, if he:**

(i) **accepts the first remuneration package offered by Box plc;** **(6 marks)**

(ii) **accepts the second remuneration package offered by Box plc.** **(5 marks)**

(b) **Advise Ali as to which remuneration package is the most beneficial from a financial perspective.**

Your answer should be supported by a calculation of the amount of income, net of all costs including income tax and Class 1 national insurance contributions, which he would receive for 2013/14 under each alternative. **(4 marks)**

(Total: 15 marks)

4 PETER CHIC (ADAPTED)  *Walk in the footsteps of a top tutor*

Peter Chic is employed by Haute-Couture Ltd as a fashion designer. The following information is available for the tax year 2013/14:

Employment

(1) During the tax year 2013/14 Peter was paid a gross annual salary of £75,600 by Haute-Couture Ltd. Income tax of £42,000 was deducted from this figure under PAYE.

(2) In addition to his salary, Peter received two bonus payments from Haute-Couture Ltd during the tax year 2013/14. The first bonus of £14,300 was paid on 30 April 2013 and was in respect of the year ended 31 December 2012. Peter became entitled to this first bonus on 10 April 2013. The second bonus of £13,700 was paid on 31 March 2014 and was in respect of the year ended 31 December 2013. Peter became entitled to this second bonus on 25 March 2014.

(3) Throughout the tax year 2013/14 Haute-Couture Ltd provided Peter with a diesel powered motor car which has a list price of £22,500. The motor car cost Haute-Couture Ltd £21,200, and it has an official CO_2 emission rate of 212 g/km.

Peter made a capital contribution of £2,000 towards the cost of the motor car when it was first provided to him. Haute-Couture Ltd also provided Peter with fuel for private journeys.

(4) Haute-Couture Ltd has provided Peter with living accommodation since 1 January 2011. The company had purchased the property in 2010 for £160,000, and it was valued at £185,000 on 1 January 2011. Improvements costing £13,000 were made to the property during June 2012. The annual value of the property is £9,645.

(5) Throughout the tax year 2013/14 Haute-Couture Ltd provided Peter with two mobile telephones. The telephones had each cost £250 when purchased by the company in January 2013 and are both used for both private and business calls.

(7) During February 2014 Peter spent five nights overseas on company business. Haute-Couture Ltd paid Peter a daily allowance of £10 to cover the cost of personal expenses such as telephone calls to his family.

Property income

(1) Peter owns two properties, which are let out. Both properties are freehold houses, with the first property being let out furnished and the second property being let out unfurnished.

(2) The first property was let from 6 April 2013 to 31 August 2013 at a monthly rent of £500, payable in advance. On 31 August 2013 the tenant left owing two months' rent which Peter was unable to recover. The property was not re-let before 5 April 2014. During March 2014 Peter spent £600 repairing the roof of this property.

(3) The second property was purchased on 1 July 2013, and was then let from 1 August 2013 to 5 April 2014 at a monthly rent of £2,820, payable in advance. During July 2013 Peter spent £875 on advertising for tenants. For the period 1 July 2013 to 5 April 2014 he paid loan interest of £7,800 in respect of a loan that was taken out to purchase this property.

(4) Peter insured both of his rental properties at a total cost of £660 for the year ended 30 June 2013, and £1,080 for the year ended 30 June 2014. The insurance is payable annually in advance.

(5) Where possible, Peter claims the wear and tear allowance.

Other information

(1) During the tax year 2013/14 Peter received building society interest of £4,760 and dividends of £2,700. These were the actual cash amounts received.

(2) On 4 August 2013 Peter received a premium bond prize of £100.

(3) During the tax year 2013/14 Peter made Gift Aid donations totalling £2,340 (net) to national charities.

(4) Peter received child benefit of £1,056 during 2013/14.

Required:

(a) Calculate the income tax payable by Peter Chic for the tax year 2013/14. (21 marks)

(b) Calculate the total amount of national insurance contributions that will have been paid by Peter Chic and Haute-Couture Ltd in respect of Peter's earnings and benefits for the tax year 2013/14. (4 marks)

(Total: 25 marks)

5 JOE JONES (ADAPTED) 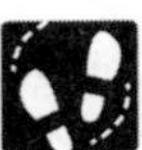 *Walk in the footsteps of a top tutor*

On 31 December 2013 Joe Jones resigned as an employee of Firstly plc, and on 1 January 2014 commenced employment with Secondly plc. Joe was employed by both companies as a financial analyst. Joe Jones's employment income has always exceeded £150,000 until 2012/13. The following information is available for the tax year 2013/14:

Employment with Firstly plc

(1) From 6 April 2013 to 31 December 2013 Joe was paid a salary of £11,400 per month. In addition to his salary, Joe was paid a bonus of £12,000 on 12 May 2013. He had become entitled to this bonus on 22 March 2013.

(2) Joe contributed 6% of his monthly gross salary of £11,400 into Firstly plc's HM Revenue and Customs' registered occupational pension scheme.

(3) On 1 May 2013 Firstly plc provided Joe with an interest free loan of £120,000 so that he could purchase a holiday cottage. Joe repaid £50,000 of the loan on 31 July 2013, and repaid the balance of the loan of £70,000 when he ceased employment with Firstly plc on 31 December 2013.

(4) During the period from 6 April 2013 to 31 December 2013 Joe's three-year-old daughter was provided with a place at Firstly plc's workplace nursery. The total cost to the company of providing this nursery place was £11,400 (190 days at £60 per day).

(5) During the period 6 April 2013 to 31 December 2013 Firstly plc paid gym membership fees of £1,050 for Joe.

(6) Firstly plc provided Joe with a home entertainment system for his personal use costing £4,400 on 6 April 2013. The company gave the home entertainment system to Joe for free, when he left the company on 31 December 2013, although its market value at that time was £3,860.

Employment with Secondly plc

(1) From 1 January 2014 to 5 April 2014 Joe was paid a salary of £15,200 per month.

(2) During the period 1 January 2014 to 5 April 2014 Joe contributed a total of £3,000 (gross) into a personal pension scheme.

(3) From 1 January 2014 to 5 April 2014 Secondly plc provided Joe with living accommodation. The property has an annual value of £10,400 and is rented by Secondly plc at a cost of £2,250 per month.

(4) During the period 1 January 2014 to 5 April 2014 Secondly plc provided Joe with 13 weeks of childcare vouchers costing £70 per week. Joe used the vouchers to provide childcare for his three-year-old daughter at a registered nursery near to his workplace.

(5) During the period 1 January 2014 to 5 April 2014 Joe used Secondly plc's company gym which is only open to employees of the company. The cost to Secondly plc of providing this benefit to Joe was £340.

(6) During the period 1 January 2014 to 5 April 2014 Secondly plc provided Joe with a mobile telephone costing £560. The company paid for all of Joe's business and private telephone calls.

Required:

(a) Calculate Joe Jones' taxable income for the tax year 2013/14. (17 marks)

(b) (i) For each of the PAYE forms P45, P60 and P11D, briefly describe the circumstances in which the form will be completed, state who will provide it, the information to be included, and the dates by which they should have been provided to Joe Jones for the tax year 2013/14. (6 marks)

Your answer should be confined to the details that are relevant to Joe Jones.

(ii) State how and when Secondly plc will submit information to HMRC regarding Joe's income tax and NIC on his employment income and the deadline for the final submission for the year. (2 marks)

(Total: 25 marks)

6 SAMMI SMITH (ADAPTED)  *Walk in the footsteps of a top tutor*

You should assume that today's date is 20 March 2013.

Sammi Smith is a director of Smark Ltd. The company has given her the choice of being provided with a leased company motor car or alternatively being paid additional director's remuneration and then privately leasing the same motor car herself.

Company motor car

The motor car will be provided throughout the tax year 2013/14, and will be leased by Smark Ltd at an annual cost of £26,540. The motor car will be petrol powered, will have a list price of £81,858, and will have an official CO_2 emission rate of 310 grams per kilometre.

The lease payments will cover all the costs of running the motor car except for fuel. Smark Ltd will not provide Sammi with any fuel for private journeys.

Additional director's remuneration

As an alternative to having a company motor car, Sammi will be paid additional gross director's remuneration of £26,000 during the tax year 2013/14. She will then privately lease the motor car at an annual cost of £26,540.

Other information

The amount of business journeys that will be driven by Sammi will be immaterial and can therefore be ignored.

Sammi's current annual director's remuneration is in excess of £45,000. Smark Ltd prepares its accounts to 5 April, and pays corporation tax at the main rate of 23%. The lease of the motor car will commence on 6 April 2013.

Required:

(a) Advise Sammi Smith of the income tax and national insurance contribution implications for the tax year 2013/14 if she

(1) is provided with the company motor car, and

(2) receives additional director's remuneration of £26,000. (5 marks)

(b) Advise Smark Ltd of the corporation tax and national insurance contribution implications for the year ended 5 April 2014 if the company

(1) provides Sammi Smith with the company motor car, and

(2) pays Sammi Smith additional director's remuneration of £26,000.

You should ignore value added tax (VAT). (5 marks)

(c) Determine which of the two alternatives is the most beneficial from each of the respective points of view of Sammi Smith and Smark Ltd. (5 marks)

(Total: 15 marks)

7 PHILIP, CHARLES & WILLIAM (ADAPTED)  *Walk in the footsteps of a top tutor*

 ***Timed question with Online tutor debrief***

Philip, Charles and William Wind are grandfather, father and son. The following information is available for the tax year 2013/14:

Philip Wind

Philip was born on 1 October 1935. During the tax year 2013/14 he received pensions of £11,600.

In addition to his pension income, Philip received building society interest of £14,880 during the tax year 2013/14. This was the actual cash amount received.

Charles Wind

Charles was born on 30 March 1965. He is self-employed as an architect, and his tax adjusted trading profit for the year ended 31 December 2013 was £109,400.

During the tax year 2013/14 Charles made a gift aid donation of £800 (gross) to a national charity.

William Wind

William was born on 23 April 1990. He is employed as a security consultant by Crown plc, a company that supplies security services. During the tax year 2013/14 William was paid a gross annual salary of £182,700.

During the tax year 2013/14 William contributed £7,300 into Crown plc's HM Revenue and Customs' registered occupational pension scheme. The company contributed a further £10,950 on his behalf.

Throughout the tax year 2013/14 Crown plc provided William with a petrol-powered motor car which has a list price of £83,100. The motor car cost Crown plc £78,800, and it has an official CO_2 emission rate of 222 grams per kilometre. Crown plc also provided William with fuel for private journeys.

During the tax year 2013/14 William made contributions of £8,000 to Crown plc in respect of the motor car. This consisted of £4,800 for the use of the motor car, and £3,200 towards the cost of fuel for private journeys. The total cost of the fuel for private journeys was £4,400.

Required:

(a) Calculate the respective income tax liabilities for the tax year 2013/14 of:

- **(i) Philip Wind** **(4 marks)**
- **(ii) Charles Wind** **(4 marks)**
- **(iii) William Wind.** **(7 marks)**

(b) Calculate the respective national insurance contributions, if any, suffered by Philip, Charles and William Wind for the tax year 2013/14. **(4 marks)**

(c) Explain to Charles and William Wind, with supporting calculations, how their respective income tax liabilities for the tax year 2013/14 would have been reduced if:

(i) Charles Wind had contributed £8,600 (gross) into a personal pension scheme during the tax year 2013/14; (3 marks)

(ii) William Wind's contributions of £8,000 to Crown plc in respect of the company motor car for the tax year 2013/14 had been allocated on a more beneficial basis. (3 marks)

(Total: 25 marks)

 ***Calculate your allowed time, allocate the time to the separate parts...................***

8 LETICIA STONE  *Walk in the footsteps of a top tutor*

 ***Timed question with Online tutor debrief***

Leticia Stone owns three properties which are let out. The following information relates to the tax year 2013/14:

Property one

This is a freehold house that qualifies as a trade under the furnished holiday letting rules. Leticia purchased this property on 1 July 2013 for £282,000. The purchase price included £4,600 for furniture and kitchen equipment.

Leticia borrowed £220,000 to purchase this property. During the period 1 July 2013 to 5 April 2014 she made loan repayments totalling £14,300, of which £12,700 was in respect of loan interest.

The property was let for 22 weeks at £425 per week during the period 1 July 2013 to 5 April 2014.

Due to a fire, £12,200 was spent on replacing the roof of the house during March 2014. Only £10,900 of this was paid for by Leticia's property insurance.

During the tax year 2013/14 Leticia drove 1,170 miles in her motor car in respect of the furnished holiday letting business. She uses HM Revenue and Customs' authorised mileage rates to calculate her expense deduction. The mileage was for the following purposes:

	Miles
Purchase of property	160
Running the business on a weekly basis	880
Property repairs	130

The other expenditure on this property for the period 1 July 2013 to 5 April 2014 amounted to £3,770, and this is all allowable.

Property two

This is a leasehold shop that is let out unfurnished. The property was acquired on 1 May 2013 and was immediately let to a tenant, with Leticia receiving a premium of £45,000 for the grant of a five-year lease. During the period 1 May 2013 to 5 April 2014 Leticia received four quarterly rental payments of £2,160 per quarter, payable in advance.

Leticia pays a monthly rent of £1,360 for this property, but did not pay a premium when she acquired it.

Property three

This is a freehold house that is let out unfurnished. The property was let from 6 April 2013 to 31 January 2014 at a monthly rent of £580. On 31 January 2014 the tenant left, owing three months' rent. Leticia recovered two months of the outstanding rent by retaining the tenant's security deposit, but was unable to recover the balance.

On 1 March 2014 a new tenant paid Leticia a security deposit of £1,200, being two months' rent, although the new tenancy did not commence until 15 April 2014.

During the tax year 2013/14 Leticia paid loan interest of £9,100 in respect of a loan that was taken out to purchase this property.

Other expenditure

The other expenditure on properties two and three for the tax year 2013/14 amounted to £36,240, and this is all allowable.

Furnished room

During the tax year 2013/14 Leticia rented out one furnished room of her main residence. During the year she received rent of £3,170, and incurred allowable expenditure of £4,840 in respect of the room. Leticia always uses the most favourable basis as regards the tax treatment of the furnished room.

Required:

(a) Calculate Leticia Stone's property business loss for the tax year 2013/14.
Your answer should separately identify the furnished holiday letting loss.

(13 marks)

(b) Advise Leticia Stone as to the possible ways in which her property business loss for the tax year 2013/14 can be relieved. **(2 marks)**

(Total: 15 marks)

 ***Calculate your allowed time, allocate the time to the separate parts..................***

INCOME TAX BASICS AND INCOME FROM SELF-EMPLOYMENT

9 CAROL COURIER

For the purposes of this question you should assume that today's date is 15 March 2013.

Carol Courier is employed by Quick-Speed plc as a delivery driver, and is paid a salary of £37,500 p.a. She contributes 5% of her gross salary into Quick-Speed plc's HM Revenue & Customs registered occupational pension scheme.

As an alternative to being employed, Quick-Speed plc have offered Carol the opportunity to work for the company on a self-employed basis.

The details of the proposed arrangement for the year ended 5 April 2014 are as follows:

(1) Carol will commence being self-employed on 6 April 2013.

(2) Her income from Quick-Speed plc is expected to be £43,500.

(3) When not working for Quick-Speed plc, Carol will be allowed to work for other clients. Her income from this work is expected to be £8,000.

(4) Carol will lease a delivery van from Quick-Speed plc, and 100% of the mileage will be for business purposes. The cost of leasing and running the van will be £4,400.

(5) When she is unavailable Carol will have to provide a replacement driver to deliver for Quick-Speed plc. This will cost her £2,800.

(6) Carol will contribute £3,000 (gross) into a personal pension scheme during 2013/14. This will provide her with the same benefits as the occupational pension scheme provided by Quick-Speed plc.

Required:

(a) Assuming that Carol does not accept the offer from Quick-Speed plc and continues to be employed by the company, calculate her income tax and Class 1 NIC liability for 2013/14. (5 marks)

(b) Assuming that Carol accepts the offer to work for Quick-Speed plc on a self-employed basis from 6 April 2013 onwards, calculate her income tax, Class 2 NIC and Class 4 NIC liability for 2013/14. (6 marks)

(c) Advise Carol as to whether it will be beneficial to accept the offer to work for Quick-Speed plc on a self-employed basis.

Your answer should be supported by a calculation of the amount by which Carol's income for 2013/14 (net of outgoings, income tax and NIC) will increase or decrease if she accepts the offer. (4 marks)

(Total: 15 marks)

10 IDRIS WILLIAMS  *Walk in the footsteps of a top tutor*

(a) Idris Williams is planning to start a private tutoring business and is considering whether to prepare his accounts to 5 April or 30 June.

Required:

Advise Idris of the advantages for tax purposes of choosing an accounting date of either 5 April or 30 June. (4 marks)

(b) Idris commences trade on 6 April 2013 and decides to prepare his first set of accounts to 5 April 2014.

The following information is available regarding his statement of profit and loss for the first year of trading:

	Notes	£	£
Revenue	(1)		57,510
Less: Cost of sales	(2)		(17,660)
Gross profit			39,850
Expenses:			
Depreciation	(3)	1,250	
Property expenses	(4)	7,600	
Motor expenses	(5)	9,340	
Other expenses	(6)	1,485	
			(19,675)
Net profit			20,175

(1) Revenue includes £8,275 which is still receivable at 5 April 2014.

(2) Idris paid for 95% of his purchases by 5 April 2014 and the remainder in May 2014. There is no closing inventory at 5 April 2014.

(3) The depreciation charge relates to the office equipment bought in the period for £3,500 and a motor car purchased on 6 April 2013. Idris purchased the motor car with CO_2 emissions of 105 g/km for £9,000.

(4) Idris plans to live in a room behind his tuition office for the first year of the business to save costs. 50% of the expenses relate to his private room.

(5) The motor expenses of £9,340 relate to Idris' car and in the period he drove 13,000 business miles and 20,000 miles in total.

(6) The other expenses are all allowable for tax purposes. £400 of these expenses were unpaid at 6. April 2014.

The cash basis private use adjustment for one occupant in a business premises for a 12 month period is £4,200.

Required:

(i) Calculate Idris' tax adjusted trading profit for the year ended 5 April 2014, assuming he uses the normal accruals basis. **(4 marks)**

(ii) State why Idris is entitled to use the cash basis and calculate Idris' tax adjusted trading profit for the year ended 5 April 2014, assuming he uses the cash basis. **(6 marks)**

(iii) State which basis would be more beneficial for Idris for 2013/14. **(1 mark)**

(Total: 15 marks)

11 CHATRU (ADAPTED)  *Walk in the footsteps of a top tutor*

(1) Chatru started trading on 1 November 2009. His first accounts were prepared to 30 April 2011 and thereafter to 30 April annually. He ceased trading on 31 March 2014.

His trading results, adjusted for income tax purposes were:

	£
1.11.09 – 30.4.11	40,500
Year ended 30.4.12	12,000
Year ended 30.4.13	24,000
Period to 31.3.14	50,000

Required:

(a) Calculate the assessable income for all years in question. **(8 marks)**

(b) Calculate whether there would have been any income tax benefit in Chatru continuing to trade one extra month and preparing final accounts to his normal accounting date, on the assumption that his tax-adjusted profit for April 2014 was £4,200. **(3 marks)**

(2) Chatru, who was born on 24 October 1950, had the following additional income and expenditure in 2013/14:

Investment income

(i) He received dividends of £33,500, bank interest of £2,500 and interest from an Individual Savings Account of £1,500.

Property income

(i) He rented out a room in his house to a student and charged rent of £150 per month.

(ii) From 6 April 2013 he rented out a furnished property on which he received rent of £11,100. During the year he made payments on a loan which he had taken out to acquire the property of which £500 related to interest charges. He incurred allowable expenses of £1,600 which included £800 council tax and £300 water rates. He also spent £400 on a cooker for the property.

(iii) Chatru and his wife, Sandra, jointly owned a piece of land in the ratio 25:75. They received rent of £4,000 per annum from renting the land to a local farmer.

Other information

(i) On 1 March 2014 Chatru made a payment of £5,000 to a national charity under the Gift Aid scheme.

(ii) Sandra works part-time earning £8,000 per annum and has no other income other than mentioned above.

(iii) Chatru and Sandra have not made any elections in respect of their income.

For the purposes of this part assume that Chatru ceased to trade on 31 March 2014.

Required:

(a) Compute the income tax payable by Chatru for the tax year 2013/14. **(15 marks)**

(b) Advise Chatru and Sandra of two ways in which they may have reduced their joint income tax liability in 2013/14. **(4 marks)**

(Total: 30 marks)

12 OLIVE GREEN (ADAPTED)  *Walk in the footsteps of a top tutor*

Olive Green is self-employed running a health food shop. Her statement of profit or loss for the year ended 31 March 2014 is as follows:

	£	£
Gross profit		130,750
Expenses:		
Depreciation	2,350	
Light and heat (Note 1)	1,980	
Motor expenses (Note 2)	9,700	
Rent and rates (Note 1)	5,920	
Sundry expenses (Note 3)	2,230	
Wages and salaries (Note 4)	78,520	
		(100,700)
Net profit		30,050

Note 1 – Private accommodation

Olive lives in a flat that is situated above the health food shop. 30% of the expenditure included in the statement of profit or loss for light, heat, rent and rates relates to the flat.

Note 2 – Motor expenses

Motor expenses include £4,700 for the running of Olive's car. During the year ended 31 March 2014 Olive drove a total of 20,000 miles, of which 8,000 were for business purposes.

The motor expenses also include £3,000 leasing costs. This relates to the lease of a car with CO_2 emissions of 145 grams per kilometre which is used by the shop manager.

Note 3 – Sundry expenses

The figure of £2,230 for sundry expenses includes £220 for a fine in respect of health and safety regulations, £180 for the theft of cash by an employee, £100 for a donation to a political party, and £140 for a trade subscription to the Health and Organic Association.

Note 4 – Wages and salaries

The figure of £78,520 for wages and salaries includes an annual salary of £14,000 paid to Olive's daughter. She works in the health food shop as a sales assistant. The other sales assistants doing the same job are paid an annual salary of £10,500.

Note 5 – Goods for own use

Each week Olive takes health food from the shop for her personal use without paying for it. The weekly cost of this food is £30, and it has a selling price of £45.

Note 6 – Plant and machinery

The only item of plant and machinery is Olive's motor car which was purchased in October 2010 and has CO_2 emissions of 125 grams per kilometre. The tax written down value of this vehicle at 1 April 2013 was £15,800.

Note 7 – Patent royalties

Olive pays a patent royalty of £150 (gross) every quarter for the use of equipment that allows her to make her own organic breakfast cereal. This has not been accounted for in arriving at the net profit of £30,050.

Other income

(1) Olive has a part-time employment for which she was paid a gross salary of £6,000 during 2013/14. Income tax of £1,195 has been deducted from this figure under PAYE.

(2) During 2013/14 Olive received building society interest of £1,440 and dividends of £1,080. These were the actual cash amounts received.

(3) On 30 November 2013 Olive sold some investments, and this resulted in a chargeable gain of £12,800.

Other information

(1) During 2013/14 Olive paid interest of £220 (gross) on a loan taken out on 1 January 2012 to purchase equipment for use in her part-time employment.

(2) Olive contributed £2,600 (gross) into a personal pension scheme during 2013/14.

(3) Olive's payments on account of income tax in respect of 2013/14 totalled £4,900.

Required:

(a) Calculate Olive's tax adjusted trading profit for the year ended 31 March 2014.

Your computation should commence with the net profit figure of £30,050, and should list all of the items referred to in Notes (1) to (7), indicating by the use of zero (0) any items that do not require adjustment. **(8 marks)**

(b) (i) Calculate the income tax and capital gains tax payable by Olive for 2013/14 **(11 marks)**

(ii) Calculate Olive's balancing payment for 2013/14 and her payments on account for 2014/15, stating the relevant due dates.

You should ignore National Insurance contributions. **(3 marks)**

(c) Advise Olive of the consequences of not making the balancing payment for 2013/14 until 30 April 2015. **(3 marks)**

(Total: 25 marks)

13 FOO DEE (ADAPTED)

On 31 December 2013 Foo Dee resigned as an employee of Gastronomic-Food plc. The company had employed her as a chef since 2001. On 1 January 2014 Foo commenced self-employment running her own restaurant, preparing accounts to 30 September.

The following information is available for 2013/14:

Employment

(1) During the period 6 April 2013 to 31 December 2013 Foo's total gross salary from her employment with Gastronomic-Food plc was £38,000. Income tax of £5,600 was deducted from this figure under PAYE.

(2) Foo used her private motor car for both business and private purposes during the period from 6 April 2013 to 31 December 2013. She received no reimbursement from Gastronomic-Food plc for any of the expenditure incurred.

Foo's total mileage during this period was 15,000 miles, made up as follows:

	miles
Normal daily travel between home and permanent workplace	4,650
Travel between home and permanent workplace in order to turn off a fire alarm	120
Travel between permanent workplace and Gastronomic-Food plc's suppliers	750
Travel between home and a temporary workplace for two months	3,800
Private travel	5,680
	15,000

(3) On 1 October 2013 Gastronomic-Food plc paid £12,900 towards Foo's removal expenses when she was permanently relocated to a different restaurant owned by the company. The £12,900 covered the cost of disposing of Foo's old property and of acquiring her new property.

(4) Foo contributed 6% of her gross salary of £38,000 into Gastronomic-Food plc's HM Revenue & Customs' registered occupational pension scheme.

Self-employment

(1) Foo's statement of profit or loss for her restaurant business for the nine-month period ended 30 September 2014 is as follows:

	£	£
Gross profit		202,054
Depreciation	3,500	
Motor expenses (Note 2)	4,200	
Property expenses (Note 3)	12,800	
Other expenses (all allowable)	50,700	
		(71,200)
Net profit		130,854

(2) During the period 1 January 2014 to 30 September 2014 Foo drove a total of 6,000 miles, of which 2,000 were for private journeys.

(3) Foo purchased her restaurant on 1 January 2014. She lives in a flat that is situated above the restaurant, and one-quarter of the total property expenses of £12,800 relate to this flat.

(4) On 1 January 2014 Foo purchased a motor car with CO_2 emissions of 115 grams per kilometre for £14,600 (see note 2 above) and equipment for £81,200.

Other income

(1) During the tax year 2013/14 Foo received building society interest of £640 and dividends of £360. These were the actual cash amounts received.

(2) On 10 July 2013 Foo sold some investments, and this resulted in a capital gain of £17,600.

Other information

(1) Foo contributed £1,600 (net) into a personal pension scheme during the period 1 January 2014 to 5 April 2014.

(2) Foo received child benefit of £1,752 during 2013/14.

(2) She did not make any payments on account of income tax in respect of the tax year 2013/14.

Required:

(a) Calculate Foo's tax adjusted trading profit for the nine-month period ended 30 September 2014.

Assume that the current tax rates and allowances apply throughout. (5 marks)

(b) (i) Calculate the income tax and capital gains tax payable by Foo for the tax year 2013/14. (16 marks)

(ii) Calculate Foo's balancing payment for the tax year 2013/14 stating the due date. Ignore National Insurance contributions. (1 marks)

(c) Advise Foo of the consequences of not making the balancing payment for the tax year 2013/14 until 31 May 2015. (3 marks)

(Total: 25 marks)

14 SAM AND KIM WHITE (ADAPTED) 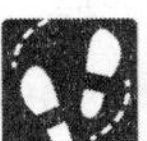 *Walk in the footsteps of a top tutor*

 ***Timed question with Online tutor debrief***

Sam and Kim White are a married couple. Sam was born on 22 August 1967 and Kim was born on 15 March 1962. The following information is available for the tax year 2013/14:

Sam White

(1) Sam is self-employed running a retail clothing shop. His statement of profit or loss for the year ended 5 April 2014 is as follows:

	Note	£	£
Gross profit			190,300
Depreciation		7,600	
Motor expenses	2	8,800	
Patent royalties	3	700	
Professional fees	4	1,860	
Other expenses	5	71,340	
			(90,300)
Net profit			100,000

(2) During the year ended 5 April 2014 Sam drove a total of 25,000 miles, of which 5,000 miles were driven when he visited his suppliers in Europe. The balance of the mileage is 25% for private journeys and 75% for business journeys in the United Kingdom.

(3) During the year ended 5 April 2014 Sam paid patent royalties of £700 (gross) in respect of specialised technology that he uses when altering clothes for customers.

(4) The figure for professional fees consists of £1,050 for legal fees in connection with an action brought against a supplier for breach of contract and £810 for accountancy. Included in the figure for accountancy is £320 in respect of personal capital gains tax advice for the tax year 2012/13.

(5) The figure for other expenses of £71,340 includes £560 for gifts to customers of food hampers costing £35 each and £420 for gifts to customers of pens carrying an advertisement for the clothing shop costing £60 each.

(6) Sam uses one of the eight rooms in the couple's house as an office for when he works at home. The total running costs of the house for the year ended 5 April 2014 were £5,120. This cost is not included in the expenses in the statement of profit or loss of £90,300.

(7) Sam uses his private telephone to make business telephone calls. The total cost of the private telephone for the year ended 5 April 2014 was £1,600, and 25% of this related to business telephone calls. The cost of the private telephone is not included in the expenses in the statement of profit or loss of £90,300.

(8) During the year ended 5 April 2014 Sam took goods out of the clothing shop for his personal use without paying for them and no entry has been made in the accounts to record this. The goods cost £820, and had a selling price of £1,480.

(9) The tax written down values for capital allowance purposes at 6 April 2013 were:

General pool	£14,800
Motor car bought January 2011	£20,200

The motor car is used by Sam (see note 2) and has an official CO_2 emission rate of 190 g/km.

Kim White

(1) Kim is employed as a sales person by Sharp-Suit plc, a clothing manufacturing company. During the tax year 2013/14 she was paid a gross annual salary of £21,600.

(2) On 1 June 2013 Sharp-Suit plc provided Kim with an interest free loan of £14,250 so that she could purchase a new motor car.

(3) During the period from 1 June 2013 to 5 April 2014 Kim used her private motor car for business and private purposes. She received no reimbursement from Sharp-Suit plc for any of the expenditure incurred.

Kim's mileage during this period included the following:

	Miles
Normal daily travel between home and permanent workplace	3,400
Travel between permanent workplace and Sharp-Suit plc's customers	11,200
Travel between home and a temporary workplace for one month	1,300

(4) During the tax year 2013/14 Kim paid interest of £140 (gross) on a personal loan taken out on 1 January 2012 to purchase a laptop computer for use in her employment with Sharp-Suit plc. She also made a charitable contribution of £800 under the Gift Aid scheme, which she does every year.

Joint income – Building society deposit account

The couple have savings of £25,000 in a building society deposit account which is in their joint names.

During the tax year 2013/14 Sam and Kim received building society interest totalling £1,200 from this joint account. This was the actual cash amount received.

Required:

(a) Calculate Sam's tax adjusted trading profit for the year ended 5 April 2014.

Your computation should start with the net profit of £100,000 and should list all the items referred to in Notes (1) to (8), indicating with a zero (0) any items that do not require adjustment. (11 marks)

(b) Calculate Sam and Kim's respective income tax liabilities for the tax year 2013/14.

You should ignore any capital allowances that Kim might be entitled to. (10 marks)

(c) Explain to Sam and Kim how their overall income tax liability could be reduced if they were to either:

(i) transfer their joint building society deposit account into individual savings accounts (ISAs); or **(2 marks)**

(ii) transfer their joint building society deposit account into Kim's sole name. **(2 marks)**

Assume that 2013/14 rates and allowances continue to apply.

(Total: 25 marks)

 ***Calculate your allowed time, allocate the time to the separate parts...................***

15 GOMEZ BROTHERS (ADAPTED)  *Walk in the footsteps of a top tutor*

Domingo, Erigo and Fargo Gomez are three brothers. The following information is available for the tax year 2013/14:

Domingo Gomez

(1) Domingo was born on 1 November 1946.

(2) During the tax year 2013/14 he received the state pension of £4,500 and a private pension of £3,300.

(3) In addition to his pension income Domingo received building society interest of £15,200 and interest of £600 on the maturity of a savings certificate from the National Savings and Investments Bank during the tax year 2013/14. These were the actual cash amounts received.

(4) During the tax year 2013/14 Domingo made donations of £300 (gross) to local charities. These were not made under the Gift Aid scheme.

Erigo Gomez

(1) Erigo was born on 28 August 1957.

(2) He is employed as a business journalist by Economical plc, a magazine publishing company. During the tax year 2013/14 Erigo was paid a gross annual salary of £36,000.

(3) During the tax year 2013/14 Erigo used his private motor car for business purposes. He drove 18,000 miles in the performance of his duties for Economical plc, for which the company paid an allowance of 20 pence per mile.

(4) During June 2013 Economical plc paid £11,400 towards the cost of Erigo's relocation when he was required to move his place of employment. Erigo's previous main residence was 140 miles from his new place of employment with the company. The £11,400 covered the cost of disposing of Erigo's old property and of acquiring a new property.

(5) Erigo contributed 6% of his gross salary of £36,000 into Economical plc's HM Revenue and Customs' registered occupational pension scheme.

(6) During the tax year 2013/14 Erigo donated £100 (gross) per month to charity under the payroll deduction scheme.

Fargo Gomez

(1) Fargo was born on 5 June 1960.

(2) He commenced self-employment as a business consultant on 6 July 2013. Fargo's tax adjusted trading profit based on his draft accounts for the nine-month period ended 5 April 2014 is £112,800. This figure is before making any adjustments required for:

  (i) Advertising expenditure of £2,600 incurred during May 2013. This expenditure has not been deducted in calculating the profit of £112,800.

  (ii) Capital allowances.

(3) The only item of plant and machinery owned by Fargo is his motor car. This cost £11,000 on 6 July 2013 and has CO_2 emissions of 122 g/km. During the nine-month period ended 5 April 2014 Fargo drove a total of 24,000 miles, of which 8,000 were for private journeys.

(4) During the tax year 2013/14 Fargo contributed £5,200 (gross) into a personal pension scheme, and made Gift Aid donations totalling £2,400 (net) to national charities.

Tax returns

For the tax year 2013/14 Domingo wants to file a paper self-assessment tax return and have HM Revenue and Customs prepare a self-assessment on his behalf. Erigo also wants to file a paper tax return but will prepare his own self-assessment. Fargo wants to file his tax return online.

Required:

(a) Calculate the respective income tax liabilities for the tax year 2013/14 of:

  (i) Domingo Gomez **(6 marks)**

  (ii) Erigo Gomez **(6 marks)**

  (iii) Fargo Gomez. **(7 marks)**

(b) Advise Domingo, Erigo and Fargo Gomez of the latest dates by which their respective self-assessment tax returns for the tax year 2013/14 will have to be submitted given their stated filing preferences. **(3 marks)**

(c) Advise Domingo, Erigo and Fargo Gomez as to how long they must retain the records used in preparing their respective tax returns for the tax year 2013/14, and the potential consequences of not retaining the records for the required period. **(3 marks)**

(Total: 25 marks)

16 ANDREW ZOOM  *Walk in the footsteps of a top tutor*

Andrew Zoom is a cameraman who started working for Slick-Productions Ltd on 6 April 2013. The following information is available in respect of the year ended 5 April 2014:

(1) Andrew received gross income of £50,000 from Slick-Productions Ltd.

He works a set number of hours each week and is paid an hourly rate for the work that he does.

When Andrew works more than the set number of hours he is paid overtime.

(2) Andrew is under an obligation to accept the work offered to him by Slick-Productions Ltd, and the work is carried out under the control of the company's production manager.

He is obliged to do the work personally, and this is all performed at Slick-Productions Ltd's premises.

(3) All of the equipment that Andrew uses is provided by Slick-Productions Ltd.

Andrew has several friends who are cameramen, and they are all treated as self-employed. He therefore considers that he should be treated as self-employed as well in relation to his work for Slick-Productions Ltd.

Required:

(a) List those factors that indicate that Andrew Zoom should be treated as an employee in relation to his work for Slick-Productions Ltd rather than as self-employed.

You should confine your answer to the information given in the question. (4 marks)

(b) Calculate Andrew Zoom's income tax liability and national insurance contributions for the tax year 2013/14 if he is treated:

(i) As an employee in respect of his work for Slick-Productions Ltd;

You are not required to calculate the employers' National Insurance contributions. (3 marks)

(ii) As self-employed in respect of his work for Slick-Productions Ltd. (3 marks)

(Total: 10 marks)

17 NA STYLE  *Walk in the footsteps of a top tutor*

Na Style commenced self-employment as a hairdresser on 1 January 2011. She had tax adjusted trading profits of £25,200 for the six-month period ended 30 June 2011, and £21,600 for the year ended 30 June 2012.

The following information is available for the tax year 2013/14:

Trading profit for the year ended 30 June 2013

(1) Na's statement of profit or loss for the year ended 30 June 2013 is as follows:

	Note	£	£
Income			61,300
Expenses			
Depreciation		1,300	
Motor expenses	2	2,200	
Professional fees	3	1,650	
Property expenses	4	12,900	
Purchases	5	4,700	
Other expenses	6	16,550	
			(39,300)
Net profit			22,000

(2) Na charges all the running expenses for her motor car to the business. During the year ended 30 June 2013 Na drove a total of 8,000 miles, of which 7,000 were for private journeys.

(3) The figure for professional fees consists of £390 for accountancy and £1,260 for legal fees in connection with the grant of a new five-year lease of parking spaces for customers' motor cars.

(4) Na lives in a flat that is situated above her hairdressing studio, and one-third of the total property expenses of £12,900 relate to this flat.

(5) During the year ended 30 June 2013 Na took goods out of the hairdressing business for her personal use without paying for them, and no entry has been made in the accounts to record this. The goods cost £250, and had a selling price of £450.

(6) The figure for other expenses of £16,550 includes £400 for a fine in respect of health and safety regulations, £80 for a donation to a political party, and £160 for a trade subscription to the Guild of Small Hairdressers.

(7) Na uses her private telephone to make business telephone calls. The total cost of the private telephone for the year ended 30 June 2013 was £1,200, and 20% of this related to business telephone calls. The cost of the private telephone is not included in the expenses in the statement of profit or loss of £39,300.

(8) Capital allowances for the year ended 30 June 2013 are £810.

Other information

(1) During the tax year 2013/14 Na received dividends of £1,080, building society interest of £560, interest of £310 from an individual savings account (ISA), interest of £1,100 on the maturity of a savings certificate from the National Savings & Investments Bank, and interest of £370 from government stocks (gilts). These were the actual cash amounts received in each case.

(2) Na's payments on account of income tax in respect of the tax year 2013/14 totalled £3,200.

Required:

(a) Calculate the amount of trading profits that will have been assessed on Na Style for the tax years 2010/11, 2011/12 and 2012/13 respectively, clearly identifying the amount of any overlap profits. (5 marks)

(b) Calculate Na Style's tax adjusted trading profit for the year ended 30 June 2013.

Your computation should commence with the net profit figure of £22,000, and should list all of the items referred to in Notes (1) to (8) indicating by the use of zero (0) any items that do not require adjustment. (8 marks)

(c) (i) Calculate the income tax payable by Na Style for the tax year 2013/14. (6 marks)

(ii) Calculate Na Style's balancing payment for the tax year 2013/14 and her payments on account for the tax year 2014/15, stating the relevant due dates.

You should ignore national insurance contributions. (3 marks)

(d) Advise Na Style of the consequences of not making the balancing payment for the tax year 2013/14 until 31 May 2015.

Your answer should include calculations as appropriate. (3 marks)

(Total: 25 marks)

18 SIMON HOUSE (ADAPTED)  *Walk in the footsteps of a top tutor*

On 1 May 2013 Simon House purchased a derelict freehold house for £127,000. Legal fees of £1,800 were paid in respect of the purchase.

Simon then renovated the house at a cost of £50,600, with the renovation being completed on 10 August 2013. He immediately put the house up for sale, and it was sold on 31 August 2013 for £260,000. Legal fees of £2,600 were paid in respect of the sale.

Simon financed the transaction by a bank loan of £150,000 that was taken out on 1 May 2013 at an annual interest rate of 6%. The bank loan was repaid on 31 August 2013.

Simon had no other income or capital gains for the tax year 2013/14 except as indicated above.

Simon has been advised that whether or not he is treated as carrying on a trade will be determined according to the 'badges of trade', which include:

(1) Subject matter of the transaction.

(2) Length of ownership.

(3) Frequency of similar transactions.

(4) Work done on the property.

(5) Circumstances responsible for the realisation.

(6) Motive.

Required:

(a) Briefly explain the meaning of each of the six 'badges of trade' listed in the question.

You are not expected to quote from decided cases. (3 marks)

(b) Calculate Simon House's income tax liability and his Class 2 and Class 4 national insurance contributions for the tax year 2013/14, if he is treated as carrying on a trade in respect of the disposal of the freehold house. (8 marks)

(c) Calculate Simon House's capital gains tax liability for the tax year 2013/14, if he is not treated as carrying on a trade in respect of the disposal of the freehold house. (4 marks)

(Total 15 marks)

19 BAYLE DEFENDER (ADAPTED)  *Walk in the footsteps of a top tutor*

(a) You should assume that today's date is 20 November 2013.

Bayle Defender is self-employed as a lawyer. She is also a director of Acquit & Appeal Ltd. The following information is available for the tax year 2013/14:

Self-employment

(1) Bayle's statement of profit or loss for the year ended 30 September 2013 is as follows:

	Note	£	£
Revenue	2		324,100
Expenses			
Gifts and donations	3	8,680	
Lease of motor car	4	10,360	
Professional fees	5	3,240	
Property expenses	6	46,240	
Travel expenses	7	16,770	
Other expenses	8	66,410	
			(151,700)
Net profit			172,400

(2) Revenue includes £2,800 received during May 2013 in respect of an impairment loss that Bayle had written off when calculating her trading profit for the year ended 30 September 2011.

(3) Gifts and donations are as follows:

	£
Gifts to customers	
(clocks costing £110 each and displaying Bayle's name)	3,300
Gifts to customers	
(bottles of champagne costing £40 each, displaying Bayle's name)	2,480
Donations to political parties	2,900
	8,680

(4) The lease commenced on 1 May 2013, and is in respect of a motor car with CO_2 emissions of 144 grams per kilometre. There is no private use of the motor car.

(5) The figure of £3,240 for professional fees is in respect of accountancy services, of which £600 is for inheritance tax planning advice.

(6) Bayle lives in an apartment that is situated above her office, and two-fifths of the total property expenses of £46,240 relate to this apartment.

(7) The figure of £16,770 for travel expenses includes £520 for parking fines incurred by Bayle.

(8) The figure for other expenses of £66,410 includes £670 for Bayle's professional subscription to the Law Society, and £960 for her golf club membership fee.

Director's remuneration

(9) Bayle will be paid gross director's remuneration of £42,000 by Acquit & Appeal Ltd during the tax year 2013/14.

(10) In addition to her director's remuneration, Bayle received two bonus payments of £6,000 from Acquit & Appeal Ltd during June 2013, both of which were in respect of the year ended 31 December 2012. Bayle became entitled to the first bonus payment of £6,000 on 10 March 2013, and to the second bonus payment of £6,000 on 20 April 2013.

(11) Acquit & Appeal Ltd deducts PAYE at a flat rate of 45% from all of Bayle's earnings.

Other information

(12) During the tax year 2013/14 Bayle will receive dividends of £9,900, interest of £5,240 on the maturity of a savings certificate issued by National Savings & Investments (NS&I), and interest of £3,600 from government stocks (gilts). These are the actual cash amounts that will be received.

(13) Bayle's payments on account of income tax in respect of the tax year 2013/14 will total £53,400.

Required:

(i) Calculate Bayle Defender's tax adjusted trading profit for the year ended 30 September 2013.

Your computation should commence with the net profit figure of £172,400, and you should also list all of the items referred to in Notes (2) to (8) indicating by the use of zero (0) any items that do not require adjustment.

(6 marks)

(ii) Calculate the income tax payable by Bayle Defender for the tax year 2013/14. **(8 marks)**

(iii) Calculate the amount of income tax that will be due for payment by Bayle Defender on 31 January 2015, and advise her of the consequences if this amount is not paid until 31 August 2015.

You should ignore national insurance contributions. **(5 marks)**

(b) On 1 December 2013 Bayle Defender is planning to bring a newly qualified lawyer, Fyle Guardian, into her business. Fyle will either be taken on as an employee, being paid a gross monthly salary of £3,300, or join Bayle as a partner, receiving a 20% share of the new partnership's profits.

Bayle has forecast that her tax adjusted trading profit will be £216,000 for the year ended 30 September 2014, and £240,000 for the year ended 30 September 2015.

Fyle does not have any other income for the tax year 2013/14.

Required:

(i) Assuming that Fyle Guardian is employed from 1 December 2013, calculate the total amount of National Insurance contributions that will be paid by Bayle Defender and Fyle Guardian, if any, in respect of his earnings for the tax year 2013/14.

You are not expected to calculate the National Insurance contributions that will be paid in respect of Bayle Defender's earnings. **(4 marks)**

(ii) Assuming that Fyle Guardian becomes a partner from 1 December 2013:

(1) Calculate his trading income assessments for the tax years 2013/14 and 2014/15.

You are not expected to calculate any overlap profits. **(4 marks)**

(2) Calculate the total amount of National Insurance contributions that will be paid by Bayle Defender and Fyle Guardian, if any, in respect of his trading income assessment for the tax year 2013/14.

You are not expected to calculate the National Insurance contributions that will be paid in respect of Bayle Defender's trading income assessment. **(3 marks)**

(Total: 30 marks)

TRADING LOSSES

20 NORMA (ADAPTED)

Norma, who had been in business as a confectioner since 1 May 2009, disposed of the business and retired on 31 May 2013. She does not intend to start any other business, but will be employed part-time from 1 June 2013 on an annual salary of £11,400.

Her trading profits/(losses), as adjusted for taxation were:

	£	
Period ended 31.12.09	21,000	Profit
Year ended 31.12.10	17,000	Profit
Year ended 31.12.11	15,500	Profit
Year ended 31.12.12	7,835	Profit
Period ended 31.5.13	(11,000)	Loss

Norma has received bank interest of £2,000 (gross) each year since April 2009. In addition she realised a taxable gain (i.e. after the annual exempt amount), of £35,000 in June 2012.

Required:

(a) **Calculate Norma's taxable income and gains for each tax year that she was in business before any relief for the loss arising in the period ended 31 May 2013.**

(b) **Explain the options available to Norma to utilise the loss and explain the effect on her tax liability of the loss relief claims identified.**

Assume that rates and allowances for 2013/14 apply throughout. **(15 marks)**

21 LEONARDO

Leonardo, an art dealer commenced to trade on 1 September 2010. His trading results, adjusted for income tax, are:

	£	
1.9.10 to 31.5.11	40,500	Profit
1.6.11 to 31.5.12	(54,000)	Loss
1.6.12 to 31.5.13	(27,000)	Loss
1.6.13 to 31.5.14	11,000	Profit

Leonardo does not foresee making any significant profits in the next 2 or 3 years.

Leonardo has not had any other income in any of the years in question, or earlier.

Required:

(a) **Show how his trading loss can be utilised most effectively, giving your reasons.** **(8 marks)**

(b) **State by what date(s) the claims you are proposing in part (a) should be submitted to HM Revenue & Customs.** **(2 marks)**

(Total: 10 marks)

22 DEE ZYNE  *Walk in the footsteps of a top tutor*

On 5 July 2013 Dee Zyne resigned as an employee of Trendy-Wear plc. The company had employed her as a fashion designer since 2003. On 6 July 2013 Dee commenced self-employment running her own clothing business, preparing accounts to 5 April.

The following information is available for 2013/14.

Employment

(1) During the period 6 April 2013 to 5 July 2013 Dee's total gross salary from her employment with Trendy-Wear plc was £26,000. Income tax of £5,400 was deducted from this figure under PAYE.

(2) During the period 6 April 2013 to 5 July 2013 Trendy-Wear plc provided Dee with a petrol-powered company motor car with a list price of £17,500. The official CO_2 emission rate for the motor car was 198 grams per kilometre. Trendy-Wear plc also provided Dee with fuel for private journeys. Dee paid £100 per month to Trendy-Wear plc for the use of the motor car, and she also made a capital contribution of £1,500 towards the cost of the motor car when it was first provided to her. The motor car was not available to Dee after 5 July 2013.

(3) On 1 January 2012 Trendy-Wear plc had provided Dee with an interest-free loan of £60,000 so that she could purchase a yacht. Dee repaid £45,000 of the loan on 5 May 2013, and repaid the balance of the loan of £15,000 on 6 July 2013.

(4) During the period from 6 April 2013 to 5 July 2013 Dee was provided with free meals in Trendy-Wear plc's staff canteen. The total cost of these meals to the company was £350.

Self-employment

(1) Dee's tax adjusted trading loss for the period 6 July 2013 to 5 April 2014 was £11,440. This figure is before taking account of the information in Note (2) and capital allowances.

(2) During the period 6 July 2013 to 5 April 2014 Dee paid patent royalties of £500 (gross) in respect of specialised technology that she uses in her clothing business.

(3) Dee purchased the following assets during the period ended 5 April 2014:

		£
10 July 2013	Computer	1,257
16 August 2013	Office furniture	2,175
13 November 2013	Motor car (1)	10,400
21 January 2014	Motor car (2)	17,800

Motor car (1) purchased on 13 November 2013 has CO_2 emissions of 105 grams per kilometre, is used by an employee, and 15% of the mileage is for private purposes.

Motor car (2) purchased on 21 January 2014 has CO_2 emissions of 135 grams per kilometre, is used by Dee, and 20% of the mileage is for private purposes.

Other information

(1) During the period 6 April 2013 to 5 July 2013 Dee paid interest of £110 (gross) on a personal loan taken out on 1 August 2012 to purchase a computer for use in her employment with Trendy-Wear plc.

(2) Dee's total income for each of the years 2007/08 to 2012/13 was £80,000.

Required:

(a) **Calculate Dee's tax adjusted trading loss for 2013/14.** **(6 marks)**

(b) **Assuming that Dee claims loss relief against her total income for 2013/14, calculate the income tax repayable to her for 2013/14.** **(15 marks)**

(c) **Describe the alternative ways in which Dee could have relieved her trading loss for 2013/14 against total income, and explain why these claims would have been more beneficial than the actual claim made in (b) above.**

You should assume that the tax rates for 2013/14 apply throughout. **(4 marks)**

(Total: 25 marks)

23 SAMANTHA FABRIQUE (ADAPTED)

Samantha Fabrique has been a self-employed manufacturer of clothing since 2002. She has the following gross income and chargeable gains for the tax years 2012/13 to 2014/15:

	2012/13	*2013/14*	*2014/15*
	£	£	£
Trading profit/(loss)	21,600	(81,900)	10,500
Building society interest	52,100	3,800	1,500
Chargeable gains/(loss)	53,300	(3,400)	11,300

The chargeable gains do not qualify for Entrepreneurs' relief.

Required:

(a) **State the factors that will influence an individual's choice of loss relief claims.** **(3 marks)**

(b) **Calculate Samantha's taxable income and taxable gains for each of the tax years 2012/13, 2013/14 and 2014/15 on the assumption that she relieves the trading loss of £81,900 for the tax year 2013/14 on the most favourable basis.**

Explain your reasoning behind relieving the loss on the most favourable basis.

You should assume that the tax allowances for the tax year 2013/14 apply throughout. **(12 marks)**

(Total: 15 marks)

24 GOFF GREEN (ADAPTED)  *Walk in the footsteps of a top tutor*

Goff Green has been a self-employed manufacturer of golf equipment since 6 April 2004. For the year ended 5 April 2014 he made a trading loss of £55,000. Goff's recent trading profits are as follows:

	£
Year ended 5 April 2012	14,800
Year ended 5 April 2013	23,600

For each of the tax years from 2011/12 to 2013/14 Goff received gross building society interest of £3,800.

On 16 July 2013 Goff disposed of an investment and this resulted in a chargeable gain of £19,700. He disposed of another investment on 19 January 2014 and this resulted in a capital loss of £4,800.

Required:

(a) Calculate Goff Green's taxable income and taxable gains for each of the tax years from 2011/12 to 2013/14 on the assumption that he relieves the maximum possible amount of the trading loss of £55,000 for the year ended 5 April 2014 as early as possible.

Your answer should clearly show the amount of the trading loss that is unrelieved.

You should assume that the tax allowances for the tax year 2013/14 apply throughout. **(5 marks)**

(b) Assuming that for the year ended 5 April 2015 Goff Green will make a trading profit of £37,600, explain why it would probably not be beneficial for him to make a loss relief claim against the chargeable gain of £19,700 arising on the disposal of the investment on 16 July 2013.

You should assume that the tax rates and allowances for the tax year 2013/14 will continue to apply. **(5 marks)**

(Total: 10 marks)

PARTNERSHIPS

25 PETER, QUINTON AND ROGER (ADAPTED)

(1) Peter and Quinton commenced in partnership on 1 January 2011. Roger joined as a partner on 1 January 2012, and Peter resigned as a partner on 31 December 2013. Profits and losses have always been shared equally.

The partnership's tax adjusted profits and losses are as follows:

	£	
Year ended 31 December 2011	40,000	Profit
Year ended 31 December 2012	90,000	Profit
Year ended 31 December 2013	(30,000)	Loss

All of the partners were in employment prior to becoming partners, and each of them has investment income. None of the partners has any capital gains.

Required:

(a) Briefly explain the basis by which trading profits are assessed on partners when they join a partnership. (2 marks)

(b) Calculate the trading income assessments of Peter, Quinton and Roger for 2010/11, 2011/12 and 2012/13. (6 marks)

(c) State the possible ways in which Peter, Quinton and Roger can relieve their share of the trading loss for 2013/14.

Your answer should include a calculation of the amount of loss available for relief to each partner. (7 marks)

(2) Following Peter's retirement from the partnership Quinton has recently taken over responsibility for the partnership's Value Added Tax (VAT) affairs. He has contacted you with some queries regarding VAT interest charges and penalties.

Required:

(a) State when a VAT 'default surcharge' arises and for how long a 'default surcharge period' lasts (3 marks)

(b) State under what circumstances HM Revenue & Customs may raise assessments for VAT 'default interest' and the period for which interest is charged. (3 marks)

(c) Explain the consequences of Quentin finding an error on an earlier VAT return submitted by the partnership. (4 marks)

(Total: 25 marks)

26 AE, BEE, CAE, DEE AND EUE (ADAPTED)  *Walk in the footsteps of a top tutor*

(a) Ae and Bee commenced in partnership on 1 July 2011 preparing accounts to 30 June. Cae joined as a partner on 1 July 2013. Profits have always been shared equally.

The partnership's trading profits since the commencement of trading have been:

	£
Year ended 30 June 2012	54,000
Year ended 30 June 2013	66,000
Year ended 30 June 2014	87,000

Required:

Calculate the trading income assessments of Ae, Bee and Cae for each of the tax years 2011/12, 2012/13 and 2013/14. (5 marks)

(b) Dee has been self-employed for many years. The business has been loss making for the last two years. In the year ended 5 April 2015 she is planning to bring her sister, Di, into the business as a partner, in an attempt to turn the business around. She anticipates that the business will make a small loss in the year ended 5 April 2015, but will make growing profits going forward.

Dee's losses have been as follows:

	£
Year ended 5 April 2013	5,000
Year ended 5 April 2014	165,000

Dee has savings income of £85,000 each year.

Required:

(i) Explain how the loss in the year ended 5 April 2014 can be relieved, assuming Dee always claims relief for her losses as soon as possible. (3 marks)

(ii) Explain the claims available to Di to obtain relief for her share of any trading losses in the year ended 5 April 2015. (2 marks)

(c) Eue ceased trading on 30 September 2014, having been self-employed since 1 July 2005.

(1) Eue's trading profits for the final two periods of trading were as follows:

	£
Year ended 30 June 2013	61,200
Fifteen-month period ended 30 September 2014	72,000

Both these figures are before taking account of capital allowances.

(2) The capital allowances for the year ended 30 June 2013 were £2,100.

The tax written-down value of the capital allowances general pool at 1 July 2013 was £6,300. On 15 November 2013 Eue purchased a motor car with CO_2 emissions of 112 grams per kilometre for £2,400. All of the items included in the general pool were sold for £4,300 on 30 September 2014.

(3) Until the final period of trading Eue had always prepared accounts to 30 June. Her overlap profits for the period 1 July 2005 to 5 April 2006 were £19,800.

Required:

Calculate the amount of trading profits that will be assessed on Eue for each of the tax years 2013/14 and 2014/15. (5 marks)

(Total: 15 marks)

27 AUY MAN AND BIM MEN (ADAPTED)  *Walk in the footsteps of a top tutor*

Auy Man and Bim Men have been in partnership since 6 April 2003 as management consultants. The following information is available for the tax year 2013/14:

Personal information

Auy was born on 3 July 1981. During the tax year 2013/14 she spent 190 days in the United Kingdom (UK). Auy was resident in the UK during 2012/13.

Bim was born on 4 January 1958. During the tax year 2013/14 she spent 100 days in the UK. Bim has spent the same amount of time in the UK for each of the previous five tax years, and was treated as resident in the UK during each of the previous three years. Bim's time in the UK is spent living in her holiday home in the Lake District.

Statement of profit or loss for the year ended 5 April 2014

The partnership's summarised statement of profit or loss for the year ended 5 April 2014 is:

	Notes	£	£
Sales	1		142,200
Expenses:	2		
Depreciation		3,400	
Motor expenses	3	4,100	
Other expenses	4	1,800	
Wages and salaries	5	50,900	
			(60,200)
Net profit			82,000

Notes

(1) The sales figure of £142,200 is exclusive of output value added tax (VAT) of £28,440.

(2) The expenses figures are exclusive of recoverable input VAT of:

Motor expenses	£180
Other expenses	£140

(3) The figure of £4,100 for motor expenses includes £2,600 in respect of the partners' motor cars, with 30% of this amount being in respect of private journeys.

(4) The figure of £1,800 for other expenses includes £720 for entertaining employees. The remaining expenses are all allowable.

(5) The figure of £50,900 for wages and salaries includes the annual salary of £4,000 paid to Bim (see the profit sharing note below), and the annual salary of £15,000 paid to Auy's husband, who works part-time for the partnership. Another part-time employee doing the same job is paid a salary of £10,000 per annum.

Plant and machinery

On 6 April 2013 the tax written down values of the partnership's plant and machinery were:

	£
Main pool	3,100
Motor car (1)	18,000
Motor car (2)	14,000

The following transactions took place during the year ended 5 April 2014:

		Cost/(Proceeds)
		£
8 May 2013	Sold motor car (2)	(13,100)
8 May 2013	Purchased motor car (3)	11,600
21 November 2013	Purchased motor car (4)	14,200
14 January 2014	Purchased motor car (5)	8,700

Motor car (1) was purchased in March 2011 and has a CO_2 emission rate of 155 grams per kilometre. It is used by Auy, and 70% of the mileage is for business journeys.

Motor car (2) was purchased in December 2010 and had a CO_2 emission rate of 115 grams per kilometre. It was used by Bim, and 70% of the mileage was for business journeys.

Motor car (3) is a new car purchased on 8 May 2013 has a CO_2 emission rate of 85 grams per kilometre. It is used by Bim, and 70% of the mileage is for business journeys.

Motor car (4) purchased on 21 November 2013 has a CO_2 emission rate of 105 grams per kilometre. Motor car (5) purchased on 14 January 2014 has a CO_2 emission rate of 170 grams per kilometre. These two motor cars are used by employees of the business.

Profit sharing

Profits are shared 80% to Auy and 20% to Bim. This is after paying an annual salary of £4,000 to Bim, and interest at the rate of 5% on the partners' capital account balances.

The capital account balances are:

	£
Auy Man	56,000
Bim Men	34,000

VAT

The partnership has been registered for VAT since 6 April 2003. However, the partnership has recently started invoicing for its services on new payment terms, and the partners are concerned about output VAT being accounted for at the appropriate time.

Required:

(a) **Explain why both Auy Man and Bim Men will each be treated for tax purposes as resident in the United Kingdom for the tax year 2013/14.** **(2 marks)**

(b) **Calculate the partnership's tax adjusted trading profit for the year ended 5 April 2014, and the trading income assessments of Auy Man and Bim Men for the tax year 2013/14.**

Your computation should commence with the net profit figure of £82,000, and should also list all of the items referred to in Notes (2) to (5) indicating by the use of zero (0) any items that do not require adjustment. **(15 marks)**

(c) **Calculate the Class 4 National Insurance contributions payable by Auy Man and Bim Men for the tax year 2013/14.** **(3 marks)**

(d) **(i)** **Advise the partnership of the VAT rules that determine the tax point in respect of a supply of services;** **(3 marks)**

(ii) **Calculate the amount of VAT paid by the partnership to HM Revenue & Customs throughout the year ended 5 April 2014;**

You should ignore the output VAT scale charges due in respect of fuel for private journeys. **(2 marks)**

(iii) **Advise the partnership of the conditions that it must satisfy in order to join and continue to use the VAT flat rate scheme, and calculate the tax saving if the partnership had used the flat rate scheme to calculate the amount of VAT payable throughout the year ended 5 April 2014.**

You should assume that the relevant flat rate scheme percentage for the partnership's trade was 14% throughout the whole of the year ended 5 April 2014. **(5 marks)**

(Total: 30 marks)

PENSIONS AND NIC

28 DUKE AND EARL UPPER-CRUST (ADAPTED)

Duke and Earl Upper-Crust, born on 29 August 1969, are twin brothers.

Duke is employed by the High-Brow Bank plc as a financial adviser. During the tax year 2013/14 Duke was paid a gross salary of £115,000. He also received a bonus of £40,000 on 15 March 2014. On 31 March 2014 Duke made a contribution of £45,000 (gross) into a personal pension scheme. He is not a member of High-Brow Bank plc's occupational pension scheme.

Earl is self-employed as a financial consultant. His trading profit for the year ended 5 April 2014 was £34,000. On 31 March 2014 Earl made a contribution of £40,000 (gross) into a personal pension scheme.

Neither Duke nor Earl has any other income.

In previous years Duke and Earl Upper-Crust had the same level of income. Duke paid £45,000 (gross) into his pension scheme and Earl paid £10,000 (gross).

Required:

(a) **Calculate Duke and Earl's income tax liabilities for the tax year 2013/14, together with the actual net of tax amounts that Duke and Earl will have paid to their personal pension companies. (9 marks)**

(b) **Explain the effect of the pension scheme annual allowance limit, and the tax implications if contributions are made in excess of this limit. (2 marks)**

(c) **Advise Duke and Earl of the maximum additional amounts that they could have contributed into personal pension schemes for the tax year 2013/14 without incurring an annual allowance charge, and the date by which any qualifying contributions would have had to have been paid. (4 marks)**

(Total: 15 marks)

29 VANESSA AND SERENE (ADAPTED)  *Walk in the footsteps of a top tutor*

(a) Vanessa Serve and Serene Volley, born on 28 June 1981 and 11 July 1978 respectively, are sisters. The following information is available for the tax year 2013/14:

Vanessa Serve

(1) Vanessa is self-employed as a tennis coach. Her tax adjusted trading profit for the year ended 31 March 2014 is £52,400. However, this figure is before taking account of capital allowances.

(2) The only item of plant and machinery owned by Vanessa is her motor car. This was bought in January 2011 and has an official CO_2 emission rate of 100 grams per kilometre. At 1 April 2013 it had a tax written down value of £10,400.

During the year ended 31 March 2014 Vanessa drove a total of 20,000 miles, of which 6,000 were for private journeys.

(3) Vanessa contributed £6,400 (gross) into a personal pension scheme during the tax year 2013/14.

(4) In addition to her self-employed income, Vanessa received interest of £1,100 from an investment account at the National Savings & Investments Bank during the tax year 2013/14. This was the actual cash amount received.

(5) Vanessa's payments on account in respect of the tax year 2013/14 totalled £8,705.

Serene Volley

(1) Serene is employed as a sports journalist by Backhand plc, a newspaper publishing company.

During the tax year 2013/14 she was paid a gross annual salary of £26,400. Income tax of £3,710 was deducted from this figure under PAYE.

(2) Throughout the tax year 2013/14 Backhand plc provided Serene with a diesel powered motor car which has a list price of £26,600. The official CO_2 emission rate for the motor car is 87 grams per kilometre.

The company did not provide Serene with any fuel for private journeys.

(3) Serene contributed 5% of her gross salary of £26,400 into Backhand plc's HM Revenue and Customs' registered occupational pension scheme.

(4) In addition to her employment income, Serene received interest of £1,200 on the maturity of a savings certificate from the National Savings & Investments Bank during the tax year 2013/14. This was the actual cash amount received.

(5) Serene did not make any payments on account in respect of the tax year 2013/14.

Required:

(i) Calculate the income tax payable by Vanessa and Serene respectively for the tax year 2013/14. (11 marks)

(ii) Calculate the national insurance contributions payable by Vanessa and Serene respectively for the tax year 2013/14. (4 marks)

(iii) Calculate Vanessa and Serene's respective balancing payments for the tax year 2013/14 and their payments on account, if any, for the tax year 2014/15.

You should state the relevant due dates. (5 marks)

(b) Note that in answering this part of the question you are not expected to take account of any of the information provided in part (a) above.

Unless stated otherwise all of the figures below are exclusive of VAT.

Vanessa Serve is registered for value added tax (VAT), and is in the process of completing her VAT return for the quarter ended 30 June 2014.

The following information is available:

(1) Sales invoices totalling £18,000 were issued in respect of standard rated sales. All of Vanessa's customers are members of the general public.

(2) During the quarter ended 30 June 2014 Vanessa spent £600 on mobile telephone calls, of which 40% related to private calls.

(3) On 3 April 2014 Vanessa purchased a motor car for £12,000. On 18 June 2014 £882 was spent on repairs to the motor car.

The motor car is used by Vanessa in her business, although approximately 10% of the mileage is for private journeys. Both figures are inclusive of VAT at the standard rate.

(4) On 29 June 2014 coaching equipment was purchased for £1,760. Vanessa paid for the equipment on this date, but did not take delivery of the equipment or receive an invoice until 3 July 2014. This purchase was standard rated.

(5) In addition to the above, Vanessa also had other standard rated expenses amounting to £2,200 in the quarter ended 30 June 2014.

This figure includes £400 for entertaining UK suppliers and £200 for entertaining overseas customers.

Required:

(i) Calculate the amount of VAT payable by Vanessa for the quarter ended 30 June 2014. (5 marks)

(ii) Advise Vanessa of the conditions that she must satisfy before being permitted to use the VAT flat rate scheme, and the advantages of joining the scheme.

The relevant flat rate scheme percentage for Vanessa's trade as notified by HM Revenue and Customs for the period is 8.5%.

Your answer should be supported by appropriate calculations of the amount of tax saving if Vanessa had used the flat rate scheme to calculate the amount of VAT payable for the quarter ended 30 June 2014. (5 marks)

(Total: 30 marks)

30 ANN, BASIL AND CHLOE (ADAPTED)  *Walk in the footsteps of a top tutor*

You are a trainee accountant and your manager has asked for your help regarding three taxpayers who have all made personal pension contributions during the tax year 2013/14.

Ann Peach

Ann, born on 31 May 1983, is self-employed as an estate agent. Her trading profit for the year ended 5 April 2014 was £48,000. Ann made contributions of £52,000 (gross) into a personal pension scheme during the tax year 2013/14.

Basil Plum

Basil, born on 15 September 1971, is employed by the Banana Bank plc as a fund manager. During the tax year 2013/14 Basil was paid a gross salary of £120,000. Basil has made monthly contributions into a personal pension plan totalling £40,000 (gross) each year for the last four years. In 2013/14 he makes total gross contributions of £50,000.

He is not a member of Banana Bank plc's occupational pension scheme but the bank contributed to Basil's personal pension in 2013/14.

Chloe Pear

Chloe, born on 24 December 1959, lets out unfurnished property. For the tax year 2012/13 her property business profit was £23,900. Chloe made contributions of £8,200 (gross) into a personal pension scheme during the tax year 2013/14.

Neither Ann nor Basil nor Chloe has any other income.

Required:

(a) **For each of the three taxpayers Ann Peach, Basil Plum and Chloe Pear, state, giving reasons, the amount of personal pension contributions that will have qualified for tax relief for the tax year 2013/14, and calculate their income tax liabilities for that year.**

Marks are allocated as follows:

Ann Peach 3 marks; Basil Plum 5 marks; and Chloe Pear 2 marks. **(10 marks)**

(b) **Explain the tax consequences of Banana Bank plc contributing £100,000 into Basil's personal pension in 2013/14 and the purpose of the annual allowance.** **(5 marks)**

(Total: 15 marks)

SELF-ASSESSMENT

31 PI CASSO

Pi Casso has been a self-employed artist since 2002, preparing her accounts to 30 June.

Pi's tax liabilities for the tax years 2011/12, 2012/13 and 2013/14 are as follows:

	2011/12	*2012/13*	*2013/14*
	£	£	£
Income tax liability	3,240	4,100	2,730
Class 2 National Insurance contributions	130	138	140
Class 4 National Insurance contributions	1,240	1,480	990
Capital gains tax liability	–	4,880	–

No income tax has been deducted at source.

Required:

(a) **Prepare a schedule showing the payments on account and balancing payments that Pi will have made or will have to make during the period from 1 July 2013 to 31 March 2015, assuming that Pi makes any appropriate claims to reduce her payments on account.**

Your answer should clearly identify the relevant due date of each payment.

(7 marks)

(b) **State the implications if Pi had made a claim to reduce her payments on account for the tax year 2013/14 to £Nil.** **(2 marks)**

(c) **Advise Pi of the latest date by which her self-assessment tax return for the tax year 2013/14 should be submitted if she wants HM Revenue and Customs (HMRC) to prepare the self-assessment tax computation on her behalf. (3 marks)**

(d) **State the date by which HMRC will have to notify Pi if they intend to enquire into her self-assessment tax return for the tax year 2013/14 and the possible reasons why such an enquiry would be made. (3 marks)**

(Total: 15 marks)

32 ERNEST VADER (ADAPTED)  *Walk in the footsteps of a top tutor*

You should assume that today's date is 30 June 2015.

You are a trainee Chartered Certified Accountant and are dealing with the tax affairs of Ernest Vader.

Ernest's self-assessment tax return for the tax year 2013/14 was submitted to HM Revenue & Customs (HMRC) on 15 May 2014, and Ernest paid the resulting income tax liability by the due date of 31 January 2015. However, you have just discovered that during the tax year 2013/14 Ernest disposed of a freehold property, the details of which were omitted from his self-assessment tax return. The capital gains tax liability in respect of this disposal is £18,000, and this amount has not been paid.

Ernest has suggested that since HMRC's right to raise an enquiry into his self-assessment tax return for the tax year 2013/14 expired on 15 May 2015, no disclosure should be made to HMRC of the capital gain.

Required:

(a) **Briefly explain the difference between tax evasion and tax avoidance, as well as the general anti-abuse rule and how HMRC would view the situation if Ernest Vader does not disclose his capital gain. (4 marks)**

(b) **Briefly explain from an ethical viewpoint how you, as a trainee Chartered Certified Accountant, should deal with the suggestion from Ernest Vader that no disclosure is made to HMRC of his capital gain. (3 marks)**

(c) **Explain why, even though the right to raise an enquiry has expired, HMRC will still be entitled to raise an assessment should they discover that Ernest Vader has not disclosed his capital gain. (2 marks)**

(d) **Explain the penalties which your firm, as tax agents, could be liable to, if they fail to supply the information requested by HMRC. (2 marks)**

(e) **Assuming that HMRC discover the capital gain and raise an assessment in respect of Ernest Vader's capital gains tax liability of £18,000 for the tax year 2013/14, and that this amount is then paid on 31 July 2015:**

   (i) **Calculate the amount of interest that will be payable;**

   You should assume that the rates for the tax year 2013/14 continue to apply. (2 marks)

   (ii) **Advise Ernest Vader as to the amount of penalty that is likely to be charged as a result of the failure to notify HMRC, and how this could have been reduced if the capital gain had been disclosed. (4 marks)**

(Total: 17 marks)

CHARGEABLE GAINS

Tutorial note:

In the new syllabus, Question 3 will be the question on capital gains and will be allocated 15 marks. Past exam questions in the old syllabus however were 20 marks.

Some of the old questions have become easier than when they were originally set with the simplification of the capital gains tax rules. These questions would now be worth 15 marks but they are still comparable to the sort of question you will see in the new syllabus.

However, more recent questions cannot be easily reduced and so they are reproduced here as they were originally set (but updated to FA2013 and are worth 20 marks).

In the new syllabus, the questions on capital gains will be very similar to these questions but they will not be as long, with possibly less disposals to deal with.

INDIVIDUALS – CAPITAL GAINS TAX

33 CHANDRA KHAN (ADAPTED)

Chandra Khan disposed of the following assets during 2013/14:

(a) On 15 June 2013 Chandra sold 10,000 £1 ordinary shares (a 30% shareholding) in Universal Ltd, an unquoted trading company, to her daughter for £75,000. The market value of the shares on this date was £110,000.

The shareholding was purchased on 10 July 2000 for £38,000. Chandra and her daughter have elected to hold over the gain as a gift of a business asset. Chandra is not employed by Universal Ltd.

(b) On 8 November 2013 Chandra sold a freehold factory for £146,000. The factory was purchased on 3 January 2000 for £72,000.

75% of the factory has been used in a manufacturing business run by Chandra as a sole trader. However, the remaining 25% of the factory has never been used for business purposes.

Chandra has claimed to rollover the gain on the factory against the replacement cost of a new freehold factory that was purchased on 10 November 2013 for £156,000. The new factory is used 100% for business purposes by Chandra.

(c) On 1 April 2014 Chandra sold a house for £350,000. She had purchased the house, as her main residence, for £75,000 on 1 April 2006.

Chandra occupied the house until 1 April 2010 when she went to live with a friend. She rented out the house until it was sold on 1 April 2014.

Required:

Calculate the chargeable gains, if any, arising from Chandra's disposals during 2013/14.

Each of the three sections of this question carries equal marks (5 marks each).

(Total: 15 marks)

34 MICHAEL CHIN (ADAPTED)  *Online question assistance*

Michael Chin made the following gifts of assets to his daughter, Mika, during 2013/14:

(1) On 30 June 2013 Michael gave Mika a business that he had run as a sole trader since 1 January 2009. The market value of the business on 30 June 2013 was £250,000, made up as follows:

	£
Goodwill	60,000
Freehold property	150,000
Net current assets	40,000
	250,000

The goodwill has been built up since 1 January 2009, and had a nil cost. The freehold property had cost £86,000 on 20 May 2011. Michael used 75% of this property for business purposes, but the other 25% has never been used for business purposes.

(2) On 8 December 2013 Michael gave Mika his entire holding of 50,000 50p ordinary shares (a 60% holding) in Minnow Ltd, an unquoted trading company. The market value of the shares on that date was £180,000.

Michael had originally purchased the shares on 5 January 2013 for £87,500. On 8 December 2013 the market value of Minnow Ltd's chargeable assets was £250,000, of which £200,000 was in respect of chargeable business assets. Michael has never been employed by Minnow Ltd.

(3) On 15 February 2014 Michael gave Mika 18,000 £1 ordinary shares in Whale plc, a quoted trading company. On that date the shares were quoted at £6.36 – £6.52.

Michael had originally purchased 15,000 shares in Whale plc on 7 December 2012 for £63,000, and he purchased a further 12,000 shares on 21 August 2013 for £26,400. The total shareholding was less than 1% of Whale plc's issued share capital.

(4) On 28 February 2014 Michael gave Mika a painting. On that date the painting was valued at £7,500. He had originally acquired the painting on 1 June 2012 for £4,000.

(5) On 2 March 2014 Michael gave Mika five acres of land attached to an investment property. He had acquired the property, together with the land for £500,000 in May 2013. The value of the land given to Mika on 2 March 2014 was £50,000 and the value of the investment property which Michael retained was £600,000.

(6) On 15 March 2014 Michael gave Mika an antique necklace. On that date the necklace was valued at £4,000. Michael had acquired the necklace for £2,000 on 1 April 2012.

Where possible, Michael and Mika have elected to hold over any gains arising.

Michael incurred a capital loss of £16,800 during 2011/12, and made a capital gain of £12,100 during 2012/13. Michael's taxable income is £41,250.

Required:

Calculate Michael's capital gains tax liability for 2013/14, clearly showing the amount of any gains that can be held over. Ignore Entrepreneurs' relief.

You should assume that the annual exempt amount for 2013/14 applies throughout.

(15 marks)

Online question assistance

35 DAVID AND ANGELA BROOK (ADAPTED)  *Walk in the footsteps of a top tutor*

David and Angela Brook are a married couple. They disposed of the following assets during the tax year 2013/14:

Jointly owned property

(1) On 29 July 2013 David and Angela sold a classic Ferrari motor car for £34,400. The motor car had been purchased on 17 January 2002 for £27,200.

(2) On 30 September 2013 David and Angela sold a house for £381,900. The house had been purchased on 1 October 1993 for £86,000.

David and Angela occupied the house as their main residence from the date of purchase until 31 March 1997. The house was then unoccupied between 1 April 1997 and 31 December 2000 due to Angela being required by her employer to work elsewhere in the United Kingdom.

From 1 January 2001 until 31 December 2007 David and Angela again occupied the house as their main residence. The house was then unoccupied until it was sold on 30 September 2013.

Throughout the period 1 October 1993 to 30 September 2013 David and Angela did not have any other main residence.

David Brook

(1) On 18 April 2013 David sold an antique table for £5,600. The antique table had been purchased on 27 May 2010 for £3,200.

(2) On 5 May 2013 David transferred his entire shareholding of 20,000 £1 ordinary shares in Bend Ltd, an unquoted trading company, to Angela. On that date the shares were valued at £64,000. David's shareholding had been purchased on 21 June 2011 for £48,000.

(3) On 14 February 2014 David made a gift of 15,000 £1 ordinary shares in Galatico plc to his son. On that date the shares were quoted on the Stock Exchange at £2.90 – £3.10. David had originally purchased 8,000 shares in Galatico plc on 15 June 2012 for £17,600, and he purchased a further 12,000 shares on 24 August 2012 for £21,600. David's total shareholding was less than 1% of Galatico plc's issued share capital.

Angela Brook

(1) On 5 May 2013 Angela sold an antique clock for £7,200. The antique clock had been purchased on 14 June 2011 for £3,700.

(2) On 7 July 2013 Angela sold 15,000 of the 20,000 £1 ordinary shares in Bend Ltd that had been transferred to her from David. The sale proceeds were £62,400.

Angela has taxable income of £31,310 for the tax year 2013/14. David does not have any taxable income.

Required:

Compute David and Angela's respective capital gains tax liabilities for the tax year 2013/14. **(20 marks)**

36 WILSON BIAZMA (ADAPTED)

Wilson Biazma is resident in the United Kingdom for tax purposes. He is a higher rate taxpayer.

He disposed of the following assets during the tax year 2013/14:

(1) On 21 July 2013 Wilson sold a freehold office building for £246,000. The office building had been purchased on 3 January 1994 for £104,000. Wilson has made a claim to rollover the gain on the office building against the replacement cost of a new freehold office building that was purchased on 14 January 2013 for £136,000. Both office buildings have always been used entirely for business purposes in a wholesale business run by Wilson as a sole trader.

(2) On 26 July 2012 Wilson sold a retail business that he had run as a sole trader since 1 June 2008. The disposal proceeds for the business on were £200,000.

The only chargeable asset of the business was goodwill and this was valued at £120,000 on 26 July 2012. The goodwill has a nil cost.

(3) On 17 August 2013 Wilson made a gift of his entire holding of 10,000 £1 ordinary shares (a 100% holding) in Gandua Ltd, an unquoted trading company, to his daughter. The market value of the shares on that date was £160,000. The shares had been purchased on 8 January 2013 for £112,000. On 17 August 2013 the market value of Gandua Ltd's chargeable assets was £180,000, of which £150,000 was in respect of chargeable business assets. Wilson and his daughter have elected to hold over the gain on this gift of a business asset. Wilson has never worked for Gandua Ltd.

(4) On 3 October 2013 an antique vase owned by Wilson was destroyed in a fire. The antique vase had been purchased on 7 November 2010 for £49,000. Wilson received insurance proceeds of £68,000 on 20 December 2013 and on 22 December 2013 he paid £69,500 for a replacement antique vase. Wilson has made a claim to defer the gain arising from the receipt of the insurance proceeds.

(5) On 9 March 2014 Wilson sold ten acres of land for £85,000. He had originally purchased twenty acres of land on 29 June 2004 for £120,000. The market value of the unsold ten acres of land as at 9 March 2014 was £65,000. The land has never been used for business purposes.

Required:

(a) **Briefly explain the automatic UK residence tests and state how a person's residence status establishes whether or not they are liable to capital gains tax.** **(4 marks)**

(b) **Calculate Wilson's capital gains tax liability for 2013/14, clearly identifying the effects of the reliefs claimed in respect of disposals (1) to (4).** **(16 marks)**

(Total: 20 marks)

37 NIM AND MAE LOM (ADAPTED)  *Walk in the footsteps of a top tutor*

Nim and Mae Lom are a married couple. They disposed of the following assets during the tax year 2013/14:

Nim Lom

(1) On 20 July 2013 Nim made a gift of 10,000 £1 ordinary shares in Kapook plc to his daughter. On that date the shares were quoted on the Stock Exchange at £3·70 – £3·90, with recorded bargains of £3·60, £3·75 and £3·80. Nim has made the following purchases of shares in Kapook plc:

19 February 2005	8,000 shares for £16,200
6 June 2010	6,000 shares for £14,600
24 July 2013	2,000 shares for £5,800

Nim's total shareholding was less than 5% of Kapook plc, and so holdover relief is not available.

(2) On 13 August 2013 Nim transferred his entire shareholding of 5,000 £1 ordinary shares in Jooba Ltd, an unquoted company, to his wife, Mae. On that date the shares were valued at £28,200. Nim's shareholding had been purchased on 11 January 2011 for £16,000.

(3) On 26 November 2013 Nim sold an antique table for £8,700. The antique table had been purchased on 16 May 2009 for £5,200.

(4) On 2 April 2014 Nim sold UK Government securities (Gilts) for £12,400. The securities had been purchased on 18 August 2011 for £10,100.

Mae Lom

(1) On 28 August 2013 Mae sold 2,000 of the 5,000 £1 ordinary shares in Jooba Ltd that had been transferred to her from Nim (see (2) above). The sale proceeds were £30,400. Entrepreneurs' relief is not available in respect of this disposal.

(2) On 30 September 2013 Mae sold a house for £186,000. The house had been purchased on 1 October 2003 for £122,000.

Throughout the period of ownership the house was occupied by Nim and Mae as their main residence, but one of the house's eight rooms was always used exclusively for business purposes by Mae.

Entrepreneurs' relief is not available in respect of this disposal.

(3) On 30 November 2013 Mae sold a business that she had run as a sole trader since 1 December 2004. The sale resulted in the following capital gains:

	£
Goodwill	80,000
Freehold office building	136,000
Investment property	34,000

The assets were all owned for more than one year prior to the date of disposal. The investment property has always been rented out.

Mae claimed Entrepreneurs' relief in respect of this disposal.

(4) On 31 March 2014 Mae sold a copyright for £9,600. The copyright had been purchased on 1 April 2009 for £10,000 when it had an unexpired life of 20 years.

Other information

Nim does not have any taxable income for the tax year 2013/14. He has unused capital losses of £16,700 brought forward from the tax year 2012/13.

Mae has taxable income of £30,000 for the tax year 2013/14. She has unused capital losses of £8,500 brought forward from the tax year 2012/13.

Required:

Compute Nim and Mae Lom's respective capital gains tax liabilities, if any, for the tax year 2013/14.

In each case, the amount of unused capital losses carried forward to future tax years, if any, should be clearly identified. **(20 marks)**

38 ALICE, BO AND CHARLES (ADAPTED)  *Walk in the footsteps of a top tutor*

You are a trainee accountant and your manager has asked for your help regarding three taxpayers who have all disposed of assets during the tax year 2013/14.

(a) **Alice Lim**

On 24 June 2013 Alice sold a freehold office building for £152,000. The office building had been purchased on 2 March 2012 for £134,000.

Prior to this on 15 April 2012 Alice had sold a freehold warehouse for £149,000 making a gain of £56,000. Alice made a claim to roll over the gain arising on the disposal of the warehouse against the cost of the office building.

Both the office building and the warehouse were used entirely for business purposes in a manufacturing business run by Alice as a sole trader.

Required:

Calculate Alice's chargeable gain, if any, for the tax year 2013/14. **(2 marks)**

You should ignore Entrepreneurs' relief.

(b) **Bo Neptune**

On 31 July 2013 Bo made a gift of his entire holding of 50,000 £1 ordinary shares (a 100% holding) in Botune Ltd, an unquoted trading company, to his son. The market value of the shares on that date was £210,000. The shares had been purchased by Bo on 22 January 2007 for £94,000. Bo and his son have elected to hold over the gain as a gift of a business asset.

Required:

(i) **Calculate Bo Neptune's chargeable gain, if any, for the tax year 2013/14, and the base cost of his son's 50,000 £1 ordinary shares in Botune Ltd. (3 marks)**

(ii) **Explain how your answer to (i) above would have differed if the shares in Botune Ltd had instead been sold to Bo Neptune's son for £160,000. (2 marks)**

You should ignore Entrepreneurs' relief.

(c) **Charles Orion**

On 30 September 2013 Charles sold a house for £282,000. The house had been purchased on 1 October 2001 for £110,000.

He occupied the house as his main residence from the date of purchase until 31 March 2003. The house was unoccupied between 1 April 2003 and 31 December 2011 when Charles went to live with his parents due to his father's illness. From 1 January 2012 until 30 September 2013 Charles again occupied the house as his main residence.

Throughout the period 1 October 2001 to 30 September 2013 Charles did not have any other main residence.

Required:

(i) **Calculate Charles Orion's chargeable gain, if any, for the tax year 2013/14. (5 marks)**

(ii) **Explain how your answer to (i) above would have differed if Charles Orion had rented out his house during the period 1 April 2003 to 31 December 2011. (3 marks)**

(Total: 15 marks)

39 LIM LAM  *Walk in the footsteps of a top tutor*

Lim Lam is the controlling shareholder and managing director of Mal-Mil Ltd, an unquoted trading company that provides support services to the oil industry.

Lim Lam

Lim disposed of the following assets during the tax year 2013/14:

(1) On 8 July 2013 Lim sold five acres of land to Mal-Mil Ltd for £260,000, which was the market value of the land on that date. The land had been inherited by Lim upon the death of her mother on 17 January 2006, when the land was valued at £182,000. Lim's mother had originally purchased the land for £137,000.

(2) On 13 August 2013 Lim made a gift of 5,000 £1 ordinary shares in Oily plc, a quoted trading company, to her sister. On that date the shares were quoted on the Stock Exchange at £7.40 – £7.56, with recorded bargains of £7.36, £7.38 and £7.60.

Lim had originally purchased 1,000 shares in Greasy plc on 8 July 2007 for £18,200. On 23 November 2007 Greasy plc was taken over by Oily plc. Lim received five £1 ordinary shares and two £1 preference shares in Oily plc for each £1 ordinary share held in Greasy plc.

Immediately after the takeover each £1 ordinary share in Oily plc was quoted at £3·50 and each £1 preference share was quoted at £1.25.

Entrepreneurs' relief and holdover relief are not available in respect of this disposal.

(3) On 22 March 2014 Lim sold 40,000 £1 ordinary shares in Mal-Mil Ltd for £280,000.

She had originally purchased 125,000 shares in the company on 8 June 2005 for £142,000, and had purchased a further 60,000 shares on 23 May 2007 for £117,000.

Mal-Mil Ltd has a total share capital of 250,000 £1 ordinary shares. Lim has made no previous disposals eligible for Entrepreneurs' relief.

Lim had taxable income of £30,000 in 2013/14.

Mal-Mil Ltd

On 20 December 2013 Mal-Mil Ltd sold two of the five acres of land that had been purchased from Lim on 8 July 2013. The sale proceeds were £162,000 and legal fees of £3,800 were incurred in connection with the disposal.

The market value of the unsold three acres of land as at 20 December 2013 was £254,000. During July 2013 Mal-Mil Ltd had spent £31,200 levelling the five acres of land.

The relevant retail price indexes (RPIs) are as follows:

July 2013	249.9
December 2013	254.6

Mal-Mil Ltd's only other income for the year ended 31 March 2014 was a trading profit of £163,000.

Required:

(a) Explain why Lim Lam's disposal of 40,000 £1 ordinary shares in Mal-Mil Ltd on 22 March 2014 qualifies for Entrepreneurs' relief. (2 marks)

(b) Calculate Lim Lam's capital gains tax liability for the tax year 2013/14, and state by when this should be paid. (11 marks)

(c) Calculate Mal-Mil Ltd's corporation tax liability for the year ended 31 March 2014, and state by when this should be paid. (7 marks)

(Total: 20 marks)

40 ALPHABET LTD  *Walk in the footsteps of a top tutor*

On 15 October 2013 Alphabet Ltd, an unquoted trading company, was taken over by XYZ plc. Prior to the takeover Alphabet Ltd's share capital consisted of 100,000 £1 ordinary shares and under the terms of the takeover the shareholders received either cash of £6 per share or one £1 ordinary share in XYZ plc for each £1 ordinary share in Alphabet Ltd.

The following information is available regarding the four shareholders of Alphabet Ltd:

Aloi

Aloi has been the managing director of Alphabet Ltd since the company's incorporation on 1 January 2003, and she accepted XYZ plc's cash alternative of £6 per share in respect of her shareholding of 60,000 £1 ordinary shares in Alphabet Ltd. Aloi had originally subscribed for 50,000 shares in Alphabet Ltd on 1 January 2003 at their par value, and purchased a further 10,000 shares on 20 May 2005 for £18,600.

On 6 February 2014 Aloi sold an investment property, and this disposal resulted in a chargeable gain of £22,600.

For the tax year 2013/14 Aloi has taxable income of £60,000.

Bon

Bon has been the sales director of Alphabet Ltd since 1 February 2013, having not previously been an employee of the company. She accepted XYZ plc's share alternative of one £1 ordinary share for each of her 25,000 £1 ordinary shares in Alphabet Ltd. Bon had purchased her shareholding on 1 February 2013 for £92,200.

On 4 March 2014 Bon made a gift of 10,000 of her £1 ordinary shares in XYZ plc to her brother. On that date the shares were quoted on the Stock Exchange at £7.10 – £7.18. There were no recorded bargains. Holdover relief is not available in respect of this disposal.

For the tax year 2013/14 Bon has taxable income of £55,000.

Cherry

Cherry has never been an employee or a director of Alphabet Ltd. She accepted XYZ plc's cash alternative of £6 per share in respect of her shareholding of 12,000 £1 ordinary shares in Alphabet Ltd. Cherry had purchased her shareholding on 27 July 2006 for £23,900.

For the tax year 2013/14 Cherry has taxable income of £31,000, and during the year she contributed £3,400 (gross) into a personal pension scheme.

Dinah

Dinah has been an employee of Alphabet Ltd since 1 May 2004. She accepted XYZ plc's share alternative of one £1 ordinary share for each of her 3,000 £1 ordinary shares in Alphabet Ltd. Dinah had purchased her shareholding on 20 June 2005 for £4,800.

On 13 November 2013 Dinah sold 1,000 of her £1 ordinary shares in XYZ plc for £6,600.

Dinah died on 5 April 2014, and her remaining 2,000 £1 ordinary shares in XYZ plc were inherited by her daughter. On that date these shares were valued at £15,600.

For the tax year 2013/14 Dinah had taxable income of £12,000.

Required:

(a) **State why Bon, Cherry and Dinah did not meet the qualifying conditions for Entrepreneurs' relief as regards their shareholdings in Alphabet Ltd.** **(3 marks)**

(b) **Calculate the capital gains tax liabilities of Aloi, Bon, Cherry and Dinah for the tax year 2013/14.**

In each case, the taxable income is stated after the deduction of the personal allowance. **(12 marks)**

(Total: 15 marks)

41 JORGE JUNG  *Walk in the footsteps of a top tutor*

 ***Timed question with Online tutor debrief***

Jorge Jung disposed of the following assets during the tax year 2013/14:

(1) On 30 June 2013 Jorge sold a house for £308,000. The house had been purchased on 1 January 1996 for £98,000, and throughout the 210 months of ownership had been occupied by Jorge as follows:

Months	
16	Occupied
18	Unoccupied – Travelling overseas
24	Unoccupied – Required to work overseas by his employer
11	Occupied
30	Unoccupied – Required to work elsewhere in the United Kingdom by his employer
22	Unoccupied – Travelling overseas
26	Unoccupied – Required to work elsewhere in the United Kingdom by his employer
17	Occupied
12	Unoccupied – Required to work overseas by his employer
13	Unoccupied – Travelling overseas
21	Unoccupied – Lived with sister
210	

Jorge let the house out during all of the periods when he did not occupy it personally. Throughout the period 1 January 1996 to 30 June 2013 Jorge did not have any other main residence.

(2) On 30 September 2013 Jorge sold a copyright for £8,200. The copyright had been purchased on 1 October 2011 for £7,000 when it had an unexpired life of 10 years.

(3) On 6 October 2013 Jorge sold a painting for £5,400. The painting had been purchased on 18 May 2009 for £2,200.

(4) On 29 October 2013 Jorge sold a motor car for £10,700. The motor car had been purchased on 21 December 2011 for £14,600.

(5) On 3 December 2013 Jorge sold two acres of land for £92,000. Jorge's father-in-law had originally purchased three acres of land on 4 August 2001 for £19,500. The father-in-law died on 17 June 2008, and the land was inherited by Jorge's wife. On that date the three acres of land were valued at £28,600. Jorge's wife transferred the land to him on 14 November 2011. On that date the three acres of land were valued at £39,000. The market value of the unsold acre of land as at 3 December 2013 was £38,000.

(6) On 14 January 2014 Jorge sold 5,000 £1 ordinary shares in Futuristic Ltd, an unquoted trading company, to his sister for £40,000. The market value of the shares on that date was £64,800. The shares had been purchased on 21 March 2009 for £26,300. Jorge and his sister have elected to hold over the gain as a gift of a business asset.

Required:

Calculate Jorge Jung's taxable gains for the tax year 2013/14. (15 marks)

 ***Calculate your allowed time, allocate the time to the separate parts..................***

COMPANIES – CHARGEABLE GAINS

42 FORWARD LTD (ADAPTED)

(i) Forward Ltd sold the following assets during the year ended 31 March 2014:

(1) On 31 May 2013 Forward Ltd sold a freehold office building for £290,000. The office building had been purchased on 15 July 1994 for £148,000. The retail price index (RPI) for July 1994 was 144.0, and for May 2013 it was 250.2.

Forward Ltd purchased a replacement freehold office building on 1 June 2013 for £260,000.

(2) On 30 November 2013 Forward Ltd sold 5,000 £1 ordinary shares in Backward plc for £62,500. Forward Ltd had originally purchased 9,000 shares in Backward plc on 20 April 1988 for £18,000, and purchased a further 500 shares on 1 November 2013 for £6,500. Assume the retail price index for April 1988 was 105.8, and for November 2013 it was 253.4.

Forward Ltd purchased 10,000 £1 ordinary shares in Sideways plc on 1 December 2013 for £65,000.

(ii) On 1 May 1999 Forward Ltd had purchased a painting for the conference room for £15,000. On 1 December 2013, when it was worth £45,000, the painting was damaged. After the damage the painting was worth £20,000. Insurance proceeds of £22,000 were received on 1 February 2014. The proceeds were not used to repair the painting. Assume the retail price index for May 1999 was 165.6, for December 2013 was 254.6 and for February 2014 was 255.5.

Where possible, Forward Ltd has claimed to roll over any gains arising.

Forward Ltd's only other income for the year ended 31 March 2014 is its tax adjusted trading profit of £78,000. There are no associated companies.

Required:

(a) **Calculate Forward Ltd's corporation tax liability for the year ended 31 March 2014, and state by when this should be paid.**

Your answer should clearly identify the amount of any gains that have been rolled over. Capital allowances should be ignored. **(12 marks)**

(b) **Explain how Forward Ltd's rollover relief claim would have altered if on 1 June 2013 it had acquired a leasehold office building on a 15-year lease for £300,000, rather than purchasing the freehold office building for £260,000.** **(3 marks)**

(Total: 15 marks)

43 HAWK LTD  *Walk in the footsteps of a top tutor*

Hawk Ltd sold the following assets during the year ended 31 March 2014:

(1) On 30 April 2013 a freehold office building was sold for £260,000. The office building had been purchased on 2 July 1993 for £81,000, and had been extended at a cost of £43,000 during May 2005.

Hawk Ltd incurred legal fees of £3,200 in connection with the purchase of the office building, and legal fees of £3,840 in connection with the disposal. The office building has always been used by Hawk Ltd for business purposes.

The relevant retail prices indexes (RPIs) are as follows:

July 1993	140.7
May 2005	192.0
April 2013	250.3

(2) On 29 August 2013 5,000 £1 ordinary shares in Albatross plc were sold for £42,500. Hawk Ltd had purchased 6,000 shares in Albatross plc on 1 August 2013 for £18,600, and purchased a further 2,000 shares on 17 August 2013 for £9,400.

(3) On 27 October 2013 10,000 £1 preference shares in Cuckoo plc were sold for £32,000. Hawk Ltd had originally purchased 5,000 £1 ordinary shares in Cuckoo plc on 2 October 2013 for £60,000. On 18 October 2013 Cuckoo plc had a reorganisation whereby each £1 ordinary share was exchanged for three new £1 ordinary shares and two £1 preference shares. Immediately after the reorganisation each new £1 ordinary share was quoted at £4.50 and each £1 preference share was quoted at £2.25.

(4) On 28 March 2014 two acres of land were sold for £120,000. Hawk Ltd had originally purchased three acres of land on 1 March 2014 for £203,500. The market value of the unsold acre of land as at 28 March 2014 was £65,000.

Hawk Ltd's only other income for the year ended 31 March 2014 was a trading profit of £125,000.

Hawk Ltd does not have any associated companies.

Required:

(a) Calculate Hawk Ltd's corporation tax liability for the year ended 31 March 2014. **(16 marks)**

(b) Advise Hawk Ltd of:

(i) The minimum amount that will have to be reinvested in qualifying replacement business assets in order for the company to claim the maximum possible amount of rollover relief in respect of its chargeable gains for the year ended 31 March 2014. **(2 marks)**

(ii) The period during which the reinvestment must take place. **(1 mark)**

(iii) The amount of corporation tax that will be deferred if the maximum possible amount of rollover relief is claimed for the year ended 31 March 2014. **(1 mark)**

(Total: 20 marks)

44 PROBLEMATIC LTD  *Walk in the footsteps of a top tutor*

Problematic Ltd sold the following assets during the year ended 31 March 2014:

(1) On 14 June 2013 16,000 £1 ordinary shares in Easy plc were sold for £54,400. Problematic Ltd had originally purchased 15,000 shares in Easy plc on 26 June 1996 for £12,600. On 28 September 2008 Easy plc made a 1 for 3 rights issue.

Problematic Ltd took up its allocation under the rights issue in full, paying £2.20 for each new share issued.

The relevant retail prices indexes (RPIs) are as follows:

June 1996	153.0
September 2008	218.4
June 2013	249.6

(2) On 1 October 2013 an office building owned by Problematic Ltd was damaged by a fire. The indexed cost of the office building on that date was £169,000. The company received insurance proceeds of £36,000 on 10 October 2013, and spent a total of £41,000 during October 2013 on restoring the office building. Problematic Ltd has made a claim to defer the gain arising from the receipt of the insurance proceeds. The office building has never been used for business purposes.

(3) On 28 January 2014 a freehold factory was sold for £171,000. The indexed cost of the factory on that date was £127,000. Problematic Ltd has made a claim to holdover the gain on the factory against the cost of a replacement leasehold factory under the rollover relief (replacement of business assets) rules. The leasehold factory has a lease period of 20 years, and was purchased on 10 December 2013 for £154,800. The two factory buildings have always been used entirely for business purposes.

(4) On 20 February 2014 an acre of land was sold for £130,000. Problematic Ltd had originally purchased four acres of land, and the indexed cost of the four acres on 20 February 2014 was £300,000. The market value of the unsold three acres of land as at 20 February 2014 was £350,000. Problematic Ltd incurred legal fees of £3,200 in connection with the disposal. The land has never been used for business purposes.

Problematic Ltd's only other income for the year ended 31 March 2014 is a tax adjusted trading profit of £108,056.

Required:

(a) Calculate Problematic Ltd's taxable total profits for the year ended 31 March 2014. **(16 marks)**

(b) Advise Problematic Ltd of the carried forward indexed base costs for capital gains purposes of any assets included in (1) to (4) above that are still retained at 31 March 2014. **(4 marks)**

(Total: 20 marks)

INHERITANCE TAX

45 BRUCE VINCENT

Bruce Vincent died in August 2013 owning the following assets and owing the following liabilities:

	£
Assets:	
House	450,000
Holiday cottage	280,000
Quoted shares	145,000
Bank and cash	10,000
Personal chattels	50,000
Liabilities:	
Mortgage (interest only)	100,000
Credit card debt	12,000
Outstanding income tax	8,000

The executors paid £7,500 in funeral expenses and £4,500 in executor's fees.

Bruce left £10,000 to his wife, who is independently wealthy, and the remainder of the estate to his son.

During his lifetime he made the following gifts:

1 January 2009: Gift to a trust for £350,000

2 May 2010: Gift to nephew for £100,000.

Bruce paid any IHT arising on the gift to the trust.

Required:

Calculate the inheritance tax payable during Bruce's lifetime and as a result of his death. State the due dates of payment and who will pay the tax in each case.

The nil rate bands for earlier years are as follows:

2008/09	**£312,000**	
2010/11	**£325,000**	**(15 marks)**

46 PAUL MASTERS

Paul Masters, due to ill health, is expected to die in the near future. You should assume that today's date is 31 December 2013.
The current value of his estate is as follows:

	£
20,000 shares (1% holding) in Banjo plc, a quoted company	50,000
8,000 shares (2% holding) in Guitar plc, a quoted company	70,000
Main residence	330,000
Holiday cottage	130,000
	580,000

Under the terms of the will, Paul left all of his assets to his son. His son has two children.

Paul's wife is also ill, and is not expected to live for more than three months. She does not have any assets of her own, but Paul is confident that his son will look after her upon his death.

Paul has made the following transfers of value during his lifetime:

(1) On 1 November 2005, he made a gift of £203,000 into a trust. The trust paid any IHT arising on the gift.

(2) On 1 October 2010, he gave his son £150,000 as a wedding gift.

(3) On 1 July 2011, he gave £200 to a niece.

Required:

(a) Calculate the IHT liabilities that would arise if Paul were to die on 31 December 2013 and state the relevant due dates of payment.

The nil rate bands for earlier years are as follows:

2005/06	**£275,000**	
2010/11	**£325,000**	
2011/12	**£325,000**	**(10 marks)**

(b) Explain:

(i) The main advantages in lifetime giving for IHT purposes.

(ii) The main factors that need to be considered in deciding which assets to gift.

(5 marks)

(Total: 15 marks)

47 HENRY HIGGINS  *Walk in the footsteps of a top tutor*

 ***Timed question with Online tutor debrief***

Henry Higgins, born on 28 February 1944, died on 5 October 2013. He was survived by his wife, Sally, born on 5 November 1943, and two children, Cecil and Ida.

Sally is herself in a frail condition and not expected to live for much longer. Both Cecil and Ida have children of their own and are relatively wealthy in their own right.

Henry owned the following assets:

(1) 100,000 £1 ordinary shares in Petal plc, a quoted company, with an issued share capital of 10,000,000 £1 ordinary shares.

On 5 October 2013, the value of these shares was 202p per share.

(2) £20,000 20% Government Stock valued at £20,100.

(3) The following capital deposits both of which have been held for several years:

- £25,000 deposited with a building society
- £18,000 invested in an ISA account.

(4) A house valued on 5 October 2013 at £450,000. This property was his and Sally's family home but was owned outright by Henry.

Under the terms of his will, Henry has left £20,000 to Cecil, £675,000 to his wife and the remainder of his estate to Ida. Sally's will currently leaves her estate equally to their two children.

The only gifts made by Henry during his lifetime were cash gifts of £193,000 on 1 January 2006 and £164,000 on 1 January 2009 respectively. Both gifts were made to a trust. Henry had agreed to pay any inheritance tax arising on these lifetime gifts.

Henry was due an income tax repayment for 2013/14 of £1,650.

Required:

(a) Calculate the inheritance tax liabilities arising:

(i) From the lifetime gifts of cash into the trust; and (5 marks)

(ii) Arising as a consequence of Henry's death on 5 October 2013. (7 marks)

(b) Explain the tax implications of the executors of Sally's estate claiming to transfer Henry's unused nil rate band to Sally on her death.

State the date by which such an election must be made. (3 marks)

The nil rate bands for earlier years are as follows:

2005/06 £275,000

2008/09 £312,000

(15 marks)

 ***Calculate your allowed time, allocate the time to the separate parts...................***

48 HELGA EVANS  *Walk in the footsteps of a top tutor*

Assume today's date is 30 June 2013.

Helga was born on 25 September 1935. She is married to Gordon, who is independently wealthy in his own right. They have one child, Louise.

Helga has unfortunately recently become terminally ill and is expected to live for only another four years.

She owns the following assets:

(1) 10,000 ordinary £1 shares in Starling plc, a quoted UK resident trading company with an issued share capital of 1 million ordinary shares. The shares are currently valued at £14.62 p per share.

(2) A 25% interest in £100,000 10% loan stock in Wren plc, currently valued at £25,750.

(3) Main residence valued at £500,000.

(4) Cash deposits amount to £151,333.

(5) Sundry personal chattels collectively worth £20,000.

Under the terms of Helga's will, all of her assets are to be left to Louise with the exception of the house and her sundry personal chattels which are bequeathed to Gordon.

Due to her failing health, Helga and her family are considering whether she should either:

(i) Gift all of her assets, with the exception of the house and her sundry personal chattels, to Louise upon her death in four years' time, or

(ii) Make these gifts to Louise now.

In four years' time her assets are expected to be valued at the following amounts for inheritance tax purposes:

	£
Starling plc shares	200,000
25% of the Wren loan stock	25,000
Residence	600,000
Cash deposits	180,000
Sundry personal chattels	20,000
	1,025,000

The only previous gift made by Helga was a cash gift, net of annual exemptions, of £360,000 made to Louise in September 2011.

Required:

Advise Helga whether she should:

(i) Make the transfers of the selected assets to Louise upon her death in four years' time, or

(ii) Make the transfers on 6 July 2013.

Your answer should consider the likely IHT implications and should include a calculation of any tax likely to arise under each option.

You should assume that the rates and allowances for 2013/14 continue to apply.

The nil rate band for 2011/12 was £325,000. (15 marks)

49 JIMMY  *Walk in the footsteps of a top tutor*

Jimmy died on 14 February 2014. He had made the following gifts during his lifetime:

(1) On 2 August 2012 Jimmy made a cash gift of £50,000 to his grandson as a wedding gift when he got married.

(2) On 14 November 2012 Jimmy made a cash gift of £800,000 to a trust. Jimmy paid the inheritance tax arising from this gift.

At the date of his death Jimmy owned the following assets:

(1) His main residence valued at £260,000.

(2) Building society deposits of £515,600.

(3) A life assurance policy on his own life. On 14 February 2014 the policy had an open market value of £182,000, and proceeds of £210,000 were received following Jimmy's death. The cost of Jimmy's funeral amounted to £5,600.

Under the terms of his will Jimmy left £300,000 to his wife, with the residue of his estate to his daughter.

The nil rate band for the tax year 2012/13 is £325,000.

Required:

(a) Explain why it is important to differentiate between potentially exempt transfers and chargeable lifetime transfers for inheritance tax purposes. (2 marks)

(b) Calculate the inheritance tax that will be payable as a result of Jimmy's death. (12 marks)

(c) State by when the personal representatives must pay the inheritance tax due on Jimmy's estate. (1 mark)

(Total: 15 marks)

50 BLACK LTD (ADAPTED)  *Walk in the footsteps of a top tutor*

 ***Timed question with Online tutor debrief***

(a) Black Ltd owns 100% of the ordinary share capital of White Ltd. The results of Black Ltd and White Ltd for the year ended 31 March 2014 are as follows:

	Black Ltd	*White Ltd*
	£	£
Trading profit/(loss)	396,800	(351,300)
Property business profit	21,100	26,700
Capital loss	–	(17,200)
Qualifying charitable donations	(4,400)	(5,600)

As at 1 April 2013 Black Ltd had unused trading losses of £57,900, and unused capital losses of £12,600, whilst White Ltd had unused trading losses of £21,800.

Required:

Advise Black Ltd as to the maximum amount of group relief that can be claimed from White Ltd in respect of its losses for the year ended 31 March 2014.

Clearly identify any losses that cannot be surrendered by White Ltd as part of the group relief claim.

You are not expected to calculate either company's corporation tax liability.
(5 marks)

(b) Ethel Brown started to run a small bed and breakfast business as a sole trader on 6 April 2013. She prepared her first accounts for the year to 5 April 2014.

She has read in the newspapers about a new cash basis of accounting and new HMRC flat rate expense adjustments which are intended to simplify tax accounting for small businesses.

In the year to 5 April 2014 she has the following transactions:

(1) Payments of £25,000 in respect of premises costs. She lives in part of the bed and breakfast premises with her husband and two children and 35% of the premises costs relate to their private use. The HMRC flat rate private use adjustment for four occupants of business premises is £7,800.

(2) On 1 June 2013 Ethel paid a car dealer £14,000 by cheque for a car with CO_2 emissions of 125g/km. She also made payments totalling £3,000 related to the running costs of the car for the year. She has used the car 40% of the time for private purposes and she drove 11,000 business miles during the year.

(3) On 1 March 2014 she acquired an item of kitchen equipment for £350 on credit terms. She paid the supplier's invoice on 15 April 2014.

Ignore VAT.

Required:

Prepare brief notes which you can use to advise Ethel on how the transactions in notes (1) to (3) should be treated for tax purposes in the accounts for the year to 5 April 2014 assuming that she opts to prepare her accounts using the cash basis and the HMRC flat rate expense adjustments. (4 marks)

(c) On 15 January 2014 Blu Reddy made a gift of 200,000 £1 ordinary shares in Purple Ltd, an unquoted investment company, to a trust. Blu paid the inheritance tax arising from this gift.

Before the transfer Blu owned 300,000 shares out of Purple Ltd's issued share capital of 500,000 £1 ordinary shares. On 15 January 2014 Purple Ltd's shares were worth £2 each for a holding of 20%, £3 each for a holding of 40%, and £4 each for a holding of 60%.

Blu has not made any previous gifts.

Required:

Calculate the inheritance tax that will be payable as a result of Blu Reddy's gift to the trust, and the additional inheritance tax that would be payable if Blu were to die on 31 May 2018.

You should ignore annual exemptions, and should assume that the nil rate band for the tax year 2013/14 remains unchanged. (6 marks)

(Total: 15 marks)

Calculate your allowed time, allocate the time to the separate parts....................

CORPORATION TAX

CORPORATION TAX BASICS AND ADMINISTRATION

51 ARABLE LTD (ADAPTED)

Timed question with Online tutor debrief

Arable Ltd commenced trading on 1 February 2013 as a manufacturer of farm equipment, preparing its first accounts for the nine-month period ended 31 October 2013. The following information is available:

Trading profit

The tax adjusted trading profit is £414,111. This figure is before taking account of capital allowances and any deduction arising from the premiums paid in respect of leasehold property.

Plant and machinery

Arable Ltd purchased the following assets in respect of the nine-month period ended 31 October 2013.

		£
5 January 2013	Machinery	199,750
18 January 2013	Building alterations necessary for the installation of the machinery	3,700
20 February 2013	Lorry	22,000
12 March 2013	Motor car (1)	11,200
14 March 2013	Motor car (2)	14,600
17 March 2013	Motor car (3)	13,000
29 July 2013	Computer	5,400

Motor car (1) purchased on 12 March 2013 for £11,200 has a CO_2 emission rate of 106 grams per kilometre. Motor car (2) purchased on 14 March 2013 for £14,600 has a CO_2 emission rate of 138 grams per kilometre. Motor car (3), purchased on 17 March 2013 for £13,000, has CO_2 emissions of 79 grams per kilometre.

The company will not make any short life asset elections.

Leasehold property

On 1 February 2013 Arable Ltd acquired a leasehold office building. A premium of £75,000 was paid for the grant of a 15-year lease. The office building was used for business purposes by Arable Ltd throughout the period ended 31 October 2013.

On 1 June 2013 Arable Ltd acquired the freehold of a second office building. This office building was empty until 31 July 2013, and was then let to a tenant. On that date Arable Ltd received a premium of £50,000 for the grant of a five-year lease, and annual rent of £14,800 which was payable in advance.

Loan interest received

Loan interest of £6,000 was received on 31 July 2013, and £3,000 was accrued at 31 October 2013. The loan was made for non-trading purposes.

Dividends received

During the period ended 31 October 2013 Arable Ltd received dividends of £18,000 from Ranch plc, an unconnected UK company. This figure was the actual cash amount received.

Profit on disposal of shares

On 5 September 2013 Arable Ltd sold 10,000 £1 ordinary shares in Ranch plc for £37,576. Arable Ltd had originally purchased 15,000 shares in Ranch plc on 10 February 2013 for £12,000.

A further 5,000 shares were purchased on 20 May 2013 for £11,250. Arable Ltd's shareholding never represented more than a 1% interest in Ranch plc.

Assume that the relevant indexation factors are as follows:

February 2013	247.6
May 2013	250.2
September 2013	252.0

Other information

Arable Ltd has two associated companies.

Required:

(a) **Calculate Arable Ltd's corporation tax liability for the nine-month period ended 31 October 2013.** **(27 marks)**

(b) **State the date by which Arable Ltd's self-assessment corporation tax return for the period ended 31 October 2013 should be submitted, and explain how the company can correct the return if it is subsequently found to contain an error or mistake.** **(3 marks)**

(Total: 30 marks)

Calculate your allowed time, allocate the time to the separate parts...................

52 ZOOM PLC (ADAPTED)  *Online question assistance*

Zoom plc is a manufacturer of photographic equipment. The company had taxable total profits of £863,652 for the year ended 31 March 2014.

The statement of profit or loss of Zoom plc for the year ended 31 March 2014 shows:

	£	£
Operating profit (Note 1)		812,500
Other operating income (Note 3)		16,400
Income from investments		
Bank interest (Note 4)	10,420	
Loan interest (Note 5)	22,500	
Income from property (Note 6)	44,680	
Dividends (Note 7)	49,500	
		127,100
		956,000
Interest payable (Note 8)		(46,000)
Profit before taxation		910,000

Note 1 – Operating profit

Depreciation of £59,227 has been deducted in arriving at the operating profit of £812,500.

Note 2 – Plant and machinery

On 1 April 2013 the tax written down values of plant and machinery were as follows:

	£
General pool	19,600
Short life asset	20,200

The following transactions took place during the year ended 31 March 2014:

		Cost/Proceeds
		£
15 April 2013	Purchased equipment	8,600
19 July 2013	Purchased computer	12,300
29 July 2013	Sold short life asset	(19,200)
30 July 2013	Purchased motor car (1)	16,600
3 August 2013	Sold a lorry	(9,800)
22 December 2013	Purchased motor car (2)	11,850
1 February 2014	Purchased motor car (3)	14,200
28 February 2014	Sold equipment (original cost £1,900)	(1,000)

Motor car (1) purchased on 30 July 2013 for £16,600 has a CO_2 emission rate of 140 grams per kilometre. Motor car (2) purchased on 22 December 2013 for £11,850 has a CO_2 emission rate of 126 grams per kilometre. Motor car (3), purchased on 1 February 2014 for £14,200, has CO_2 emissions of 76 grams per kilometre.

The short life asset sold on 29 July 2013 for £19,200 originally cost £31,500 in May 2011. The lorry sold on 3 August 2013 for £9,800 originally cost £17,200.

Note 3 – Other operating income

The other operating income consists of trade-related patent royalties that were received during the year ended 31 March 2014.

Note 4 – Bank interest received

The bank interest was received on 31 March 2014. The bank deposits are held for non-trading purposes.

Note 5 – Loan interest receivable

The loan was made for non-trading purposes on 1 July 2013. Loan interest of £15,000 was received on 30 December 2013, and interest of £7,500 was accrued at 31 March 2014.

Note 6 – Income from property

Zoom plc lets out two unfurnished office buildings that are surplus to requirements.

The first office building was let from 1 April 2013 until 31 January 2014 at a rent of £3,200 per month. On 31 January 2014 the tenant left owing two months' rent which Zoom plc was unable to recover. This office building was not re-let until May 2014.

The second office building was not let from 1 April 2013 to 31 July 2013. During this period Zoom plc spent £4,800 on advertising for new tenants, and £5,200 on decorating the office building. On 1 August 2013 the office building was let at an annual rent of £26,400, payable in advance.

Zoom plc insured its two office buildings at a total cost of £3,360 for the year ended 31 December 2013, and £3,720 for the year ended 31 December 2014. The insurance is payable annually in advance.

Note 7 – Dividends received

The dividends were all received from unconnected UK companies. The figure of £49,500 is the actual cash amount received.

Note 8 – Interest payable

The interest is in respect of a loan note that has been used for trading purposes. Interest of £23,000 was paid on 30 September 2013 and again on 31 March 2014.

Note 9 – Other information

Zoom plc made quarterly instalment payments in respect of its corporation tax liability for the year ended 31 March 2013.

Zoom plc has three associated companies.

For the year ended 31 March 2013 Zoom plc had taxable total profits of £780,000.

Required:

(a) (i) Calculate the amount of capital allowances that Zoom plc can claim for the year ended 31 March 2014. (12 marks)

(ii) Prepare a computation for the year ended 31 March 2014 reconciling Zoom plc's profit before taxation with its taxable total profits.

Your reconciliation should commence with the profit before taxation figure of £910,000, clearly identify the tax adjusted trading profit and the amount of property business profit, and end with the figure of £863,652 for taxable total profits.

You should list all of the items referred to in Notes (1) and (3) to (8) that are relevant, indicating by use of zero (0) any items that do not require adjustment. (8 marks)

(b) Explain why Zoom plc was required to make quarterly instalment payments in respect of its corporation tax liability for the year ended 31 March 2014. (3 marks)

(c) Calculate Zoom plc's corporation tax liability for the year ended 31 March 2014 and explain how and when this will have been paid.

You should assume that the company's taxable total profits of £863,652 accrued evenly throughout the year. (3 marks)

(d) Explain how your answer to part (c) above would differ if Zoom plc had no associated companies.

Your answer should include a calculation of the revised corporation tax liability for the year ended 31 March 2014. (4 marks)

(Total: 30 marks)

Online question assistance

53 BALLPOINT LTD (ADAPTED)  *Walk in the footsteps of a top tutor*

Ballpoint Ltd is a manufacturer of pens and other writing implements in the UK. The company is incorporated overseas, although its directors are based in the UK and hold their board meetings in the UK.

Ballpoint Ltd's summarised statement of profit or loss for the year ended 31 March 2014 is:

	£	£
Gross profit		968,388
Operating expenses:		
Depreciation	71,488	
Gifts and donations (Note 1)	4,100	
Repairs and renewals (Note 2)	40,800	
Professional fees (Note 3)	8,800	
Car lease costs (Note 4)	4,000	
Other expenses (Note 5)	330,000	
		(459,188)
Operating profit		509,200
Income from investments: Dividends (Note 6)		45,000
Profit from sale of fixed assets: Disposal of factory (Note 7)		60,000
		614,200
Interest payable (Note 8)		(94,200)
Profit before taxation		520,000

Note 1 – Gifts and donations

	£
Gifts to customers (pens costing £20 each displaying Ballpoint Ltd's name)	2,040
Gifts to customers (food hampers costing £35 each)	770
Gifts to employees	270
Donation to national charity	600
Donation to a local charity (Ballpoint Ltd received free advertising in the charity's magazine)	120
Donation to a political party	300
	4,100

Note 2 – Repairs and renewals

The figure of £40,800 for repairs and renewals includes £14,800 for replacing the roof of a warehouse, which was in a bad state of repair, and £13,900 for initial repairs to an office building that was acquired on 20 March 2013.

The office building was not usable until the repairs were carried out, and this fact was reflected by a reduced purchase price.

Note 3 – Professional fees

	£
Accountancy and audit fee	2,300
Legal fees in connection with the issue of share capital	3,100
Legal fees in connection with the issue of a loan note to purchase machinery that was subsequently cancelled	1,800
Legal fees in connection with the defence of the company's internet domain name	1,600
	8,800

Note 4 – Car lease costs

Ballpoint Ltd leases a car for its production manager at a cost of £4,000 p.a. The car has a CO_2 emission rate of 129 grams per kilometre.

Note 5 – Other expenses

The figure of £330,000 for other expenses includes £3,700 for entertaining overseas customers, £1,700 for entertaining employees, £400 for counselling services provided to an employee who was made redundant, and a fine of £2,600 for publishing a misleading advertisement. The remaining expenses are all allowable.

Note 6 – Dividends received

During the year ended 31 March 2014 Ballpoint Ltd received dividends of £27,000 from Paper Ltd, an unconnected UK company, and dividends of £18,000 from Pencil Ltd, its 100% UK subsidiary company. Both figures are the actual cash amounts received.

Note 7 – Disposal of factory

The profit of £60,000 is in respect of a factory that was sold on 30 June 2013 for £300,000. The factory had been purchased on 1 April 2009 for £240,000. The indexation allowance from April 2009 to June 2013 is £43,200.

Note 8 – Interest payable

The interest payable is in respect of the company's loan note that was issued in the year 2008. The proceeds of the issue were used to finance the company's trading activities. Interest of £47,100 was paid on 30 September 2013 and again on 31 March 2014.

Note 9 – Plant and machinery

On 1 April 2013 the tax written down values of plant and machinery were as follows:

	£
Main pool	8,200
Special rate pool	9,800

The following transactions took place during the year ended 31 March 2014:

		Cost/(Proceeds)
		£
2 May 2013	Purchased equipment	61,260
4 June 2013	Purchased motor car (1)	18,200
4 June 2013	Purchased motor car (2)	11,400
4 June 2013	Purchased motor car (3)	9,200
18 August 2013	Purchased equipment	4,300
12 November 2013	Sold equipment	(2,700)
20 December 2013	Sold motor car (2)	(10,110)

Motor car (1) purchased for £18,200 has a CO_2 emission rate of 134 grams per kilometre. Motor car (2) purchased for £11,400 has a CO_2 emission rate of 119 grams per kilometre. Motor car (3) purchased for £9,200 has CO_2 emissions of 72 grams per kilometre.

The equipment sold on 12 November 2013 for £2,700 was originally purchased for £13,800 on 10 July 2009.

Note 10 – Group relief

For the year ended 31 March 2014 Ballpoint Ltd has claimed group relief of £42,000 from its 100% subsidiary company, Pencil Ltd.

Note 11 – Other information

Ballpoint Ltd has only one associated company, Pencil Ltd.

Required:

(a) **Explain why Ballpoint Ltd is treated as being resident in the United Kingdom, and state what difference it would make if the directors were based overseas and were to hold their board meetings overseas. (3 marks)**

(b) **Calculate Ballpoint Ltd's tax adjusted trading profit for the year ended 31 March 2014.**

Your computation should commence with the profit before taxation figure of £520,000, and should list all of the items referred to in Notes (1) to (8) indicating by the use of zero (0) any items that do not require adjustment. (20 marks)

(c) **Calculate Ballpoint Ltd's corporation tax liability for the year ended 31 March 2014. (7 marks)**

(Total: 30 marks)

54 DO-NOT-PANIC LTD (ADAPTED)

Do-Not-Panic Ltd is a United Kingdom resident company that installs burglar alarms.

The company commenced trading on 1 January 2013 and its results for the fifteen-month period ended 31 March 2014 are summarised as follows:

(1) The trading profit as adjusted for tax purposes is £437,500. This figure is before taking account of capital allowances.

(2) Do-Not-Panic Ltd purchased equipment for £24,000 on 20 February 2014.

(3) On 21 December 2013 Do-Not-Panic Ltd disposed of some investments and this resulted in a capital loss of £4,250. On 28 March 2014 the company made a further disposal and this resulted in a chargeable gain of £42,000.

(4) Franked investment income of £25,000 was received on 22 February 2014.

Do-Not-Panic Ltd has no associated companies.

Required:

(a) Calculate Do-Not-Panic Ltd's corporation tax liabilities in respect of the fifteen-month period ended 31 March 2014 and advise the company by when these should be paid. (10 marks)

(b) Calculate Do-Not-Panic Ltd's corporation tax liabilities and advise the company by when these should be paid, assuming that instead of producing a fifteen-month period of account, they decided to produce:

- **a three month set of accounts to 31 March 2013, and then**
- **a twelve month set of accounts to 31 March 2014.**

Assume that trading profits accrue evenly over the fifteen month period. (9 marks)

(c) State which approach will give the lower total tax bill. (1 mark)

(Total: 20 marks)

55 CRASH BASH LTD (ADAPTED)  *Walk in the footsteps of a top tutor*

(a) Crash-Bash Ltd commenced trading on 1 February 2013 as a manufacturer of motor cycle crash helmets in the United Kingdom. The company is incorporated overseas, although its directors are based in the United Kingdom and hold their board meetings in the United Kingdom.

Crash-Bash Ltd prepared its first accounts for the nine-month period ended 31 October 2013. The following information is available:

Trading profit

The tax adjusted trading profit based on the draft accounts for the nine-month period ended 31 October 2013 is £553,434.

This figure is before making any adjustments required for:

(1) Capital allowances.

(2) Advertising expenditure of £12,840 incurred during January 2013. This expenditure has not been deducted in arriving at the tax adjusted trading profit for the period ended 31 October 2013 of £553,434.

Plant and machinery

The accounts for the nine-month period ended 31 October 2013 showed the following additions and disposals of plant and machinery:

		Cost
		£
2 May 2013	Purchased machinery	193,750
28 June 2013	Purchased a motor car (1)	13,200
1 September 2013	Sold machinery	11,000
12 September 2013	Purchased motor car (2)	14,000

Motor car (1) purchased on 28 June 2013 for £13,200 has a CO_2 emission rate of 79 grams per kilometre. Motor car (2) purchased on 12 September 2013 has a CO_2 emission rate of 110 grams per kilometre. The machinery sold on 1 September 2013 was acquired on 2 May 2013 for £10,000.

Dividends received

During the period ended 31 October 2013 Crash-Bash Ltd received a dividend of £14,250 from a 100% owned subsidiary company, Safety Ltd and received dividends of £36,000 from Flat-Out plc, an unconnected company. This figure was the actual cash amount received.

Other information

With the exception of Safety Ltd, Crash-Bash Ltd does not have any associated companies.

Required:

(i) Explain why Crash-Bash Ltd is treated as being resident in the United Kingdom. (2 marks)

(ii) Calculate Crash-Bash Ltd's corporation tax liability for the nine-month period ended 31 October 2013. (14 marks)

(iii) State the date by Crash-Bash Ltd's self-assessment corporation tax return for the year ended 31 October 2013 should be submitted, and advise the company of the penalties that will be due if the return is submitted eight months late.

You should assume that the company pays its corporation tax liability at the same time that the self-assessment tax return is submitted. (4 marks)

(b) *Note that in answering this part of the question you are not expected to take account of any of the information provided in part (a) above.*

Crash-Bash Ltd's outputs and inputs for the first two months of trading from 1 February 2013 to 31 March 2013 were as follows:

	February	*March*
	£	£
Outputs		
Sales	13,200	18,800
Inputs		
Goods purchased	94,600	193,100
Services incurred	22,300	32,700

The above figures are stated exclusive of value added tax (VAT).

On 1 April 2013 Crash-Bash Ltd realised that its sales for April 2013 were going to exceed £100,000, and therefore immediately registered for VAT. On that date the company had a stock of goods that had cost £108,600 (exclusive of VAT).

During September 2013 Crash-Bash Ltd discovered that a number of errors had been made when completing its VAT return for the quarter ended 30 June 2013. As a result of these errors the company will have to make an additional payment of VAT to HM Revenue and Customs (HMRC).

Required:

(i) **Explain why Crash-Bash Ltd was required to compulsorily register for VAT from 1 April 2013, and state what action the company then had to take as regards notifying HM Revenue and Customs of the registration. (3 marks)**

(ii) **Calculate the amount of input VAT that Crash-Bash Ltd was able to recover in respect of inputs incurred prior to registering for VAT on 1 April 2013.**

Your answer should include an explanation as to why the input VAT is recoverable. (4 marks)

(iii) **Explain how Crash-Bash Ltd could have voluntarily disclosed the errors relating to the VAT return for the quarter ended 30 June 2013, and state the circumstances in which default interest would have been due.**

(3 marks)

(Total: 30 marks)

56 QUAGMIRE LTD  *Walk in the footsteps of a top tutor*

For the year ended 31 January 2014 Quagmire plc had taxable total profits of £1,200,000 and franked investment income of £200,000.

For the year ended 31 January 2013 the company had taxable total profits of £1,600,000 and franked investment income of £120,000.

Quagmire plc's profits accrue evenly throughout the year. Quagmire plc has one associated company.

Required:

(a) **Explain why Quagmire plc will have been required to make quarterly instalment payments in respect of its corporation tax liability for the year ended 31 January 2014. (3 marks)**

(b) **Calculate Quagmire plc's corporation tax liability for the year ended 31 January 2014, and explain how and when this will have been paid.** **(3 marks)**

(c) **Explain how your answer to part (b) above would differ if Quagmire plc did not have an associated company.**

Your answer should include a calculation of the revised corporation tax liability for the year ended 31 January 2014. **(4 marks)**

(Total: 10 marks)

57 MOLTEN METAL PLC (ADAPTED)  *Walk in the footsteps of a top tutor*

Molten-Metal plc is a manufacturer of machine tools. The following information is available for the year ended 31 March 2014:

Trading profit

The tax adjusted trading profit for the year ended 31 March 2014 is £2,090,086. This figure is **before** making any deductions required for:

(1) Interest payable.

(2) Capital allowances.

(3) Any revenue expenditure that may have been debited to the company's capital expenditure account in error.

Interest payable

During the year ended 31 March 2014 Molten-Metal plc paid loan stock interest of £22,500. Loan stock interest of £3,700 was accrued at 31 March 2014, with the corresponding accrual at 1 April 2013 being £4,200. The loan is used for trading purposes.

The company also incurred a loan interest expense of £6,800 in respect of a loan that is used for non-trading purposes.

Capital expenditure account

The following items of expenditure have been debited to the capital expenditure account during the year ended 31 March 2014:

1 May 2013	Purchase of a second-hand freehold office building for £378,000. This figure included £83,000 for a ventilation system and £10,000 for a lift. Both the ventilation system and the lift are integral to the office building.
	During May 2013 Molten-Metal plc spent a further £97,400 on repairs. The office building was not usable until these repairs were carried out, and this fact was represented by a reduced purchase price.
26 June 2013	Purchase of machinery for £140,000. During June 2013 a further £7,000 was spent on building alterations that were necessary for the installation of the machinery.
8 August 2013	A payment of £41,200 for the construction of a new decorative wall around the company's premises.

27 August 2013	Purchase of movable partition walls for £22,900. Molten-Metal plc uses these to divide up its open plan offices, and the partition walls are moved around on a regular basis.
11 March 2014	Purchase of two motor cars each costing £17,300. Each motor car has a CO_2 emission rate of 120 grams per kilometre. One motor car is used by the factory manager, and 60% of the mileage is for private journeys. The other motor car is used as a pool car.

Written down value

On 1 April 2013 the tax written down value of plant and machinery in Molten-Metal plc's main pool was £87,800.

Property income

Since 1 February 2014 Molten-Metal plc has let out an unfurnished freehold office building that is surplus to requirements. On that date the tenant paid the company £78,800, consisting of a premium of £68,000 for the grant of a six-year lease, and the advance payment of three months' rent.

Interest receivable

Molten-Metal plc made a loan for non-trading purposes on 1 August 2013. Loan interest of £9,800 was received on 31 January 2014, and £3,100 was accrued at 31 March 2014.

The company also received bank interest of £2,600 during the year ended 31 March 2014. The bank deposits are held for non-trading purposes.

Disposal of office building

On 20 May 2013 Molten-Metal plc sold a freehold office building for £872,000. The office building had been purchased on 13 June 2005 for £396,200 (including legal fees).

During June 2009 the office building was extended at a cost of £146,000, and during the same month the company spent £48,000 replacing part of the office building roof following a fire.

Molten-Metal plc incurred legal fees of £28,400 in connection with the disposal. Indexation factors are as follows:

June 2005 to May 2013	0.302
June 2009 to May 2013	0.172

Quarterly instalment payments

Molten-Metal plc makes quarterly instalment payments in respect of its corporation tax liability. The first three instalment payments for the year ended 31 March 2014 totalled £398,200.

Required:

(a) **Calculate Molten-Metal plc's corporation tax liability for the year ended 31 March 2014.**

You should ignore any chargeable gain arising from the grant of the lease and also ignore rollover relief. **(23 marks)**

(b) **Calculate the final quarterly instalment payment that will have to be made by Molten-Metal plc for the year ended 31 March 2014, and state when this will be due.** **(2 marks)**

(Total: 25 marks)

WITH VAT ASPECTS

58 STRETCHED LTD (ADAPTED)

(1) Stretched Ltd has always prepared its accounts to 31 December, but has decided to change its accounting date to 31 March. The company's results for the 15-month period ended 31 March 2014 are as follows:

(i) The tax adjusted trading profit is £330,000. This figure is before taking account of capital allowances.

(ii) Until January 2014 the company has never been entitled to capital allowances as all assets were leased. However, on 15 January 2014 the company bought a machine for £70,000.

(iii) There is a property business profit of £45,000 for the 15-month period ended 31 March 2014.

(iv) On 15 April 2013 the company disposed of some investments, and this resulted in a chargeable gain of £44,000. On 8 February 2014 the company made a further disposal, and this resulted in a capital loss of £6,700.

(v) Franked investment income of £30,000 was received on 10 September 2013.

(vi) A qualifying charitable donation of £5,000 was made on 31 March 2014.

As at 1 January 2013 Stretched Ltd had unused trading losses of £23,000, and unused capital losses of £3,000.

Stretched Ltd has no associated companies.

Required:

(a) Calculate Stretched Ltd's corporation tax liabilities in respect of the 15-month period ended 31 March 2014, and advise the company by when these should be paid. (13 marks)

(b) State the advantages for tax purposes of a company having an accounting date of 31 March instead of 31 December. (2 marks)

(2) Stretched Ltd is registered for VAT. The following information is available in respect of its VAT return for the quarter ended 30 June 2014.

(i) On 10 June 2014 Stretched Ltd received an order for goods, together with a deposit of £5,000. It despatched the goods to the customer on 20 June 2014 and raised an invoice for the balance due of £25,000 on 1 July 2014. The invoice was paid on 30 July 2014.

(ii) On 1 June 2014 Stretched Ltd received an invoice for £12,500 in respect of a new car for the sales director. On 1 June 2014 the director's old car was taken to auction and the company received a cheque for £7,000 in respect of the sale of the car. The private use of both cars by the sales director was 20%. In the quarter to 30 June 2014 the company paid fuel bills of £600 in respect of the sales director's cars. No charge was made to the sales director by the company for the cost of the private fuel.

(iii) During the quarter ended 30 June 2014 the company incurred standard-rated costs of £1,000, in respect of the company's annual dinner dance for staff, and £500 on entertaining potential UK customers.

All figures are inclusive of VAT.

In the quarter to 30 September 2013 the company had submitted and paid its VAT liability late. The returns and payment for the quarters to 31 December 2013 and 31 March 2014 were submitted on time.

Required:

(a) **Advise Stretched Ltd how the transactions in (i) to (iii) above should be dealt with in the VAT return for the quarter to 30 June 2014.** **(7 marks)**

(b) **Explain the implications if Stretched Ltd is two months late in submitting its VAT return and in paying the related VAT liability for the quarter ended 30 June 2014.** **(3 marks)**

(Total: 25 marks)

59 SCUBA LTD (ADAPTED)  *Walk in the footsteps of a top tutor*

(a) Scuba Ltd is a manufacturer of diving equipment. The following information is relevant for the year ended 31 March 2014:

Operating profit

The operating profit is £198,400.

The expenses that have been deducted in calculating this figure include:

	£
Depreciation and amortisation of lease	45,200
Entertaining customers	7,050
Entertaining employees	2,470
Gifts to customers (diaries costing £25 each displaying Scuba Ltd's name)	1,350
Gifts to customers (food hampers costing £80 each)	1,600

Leasehold property

On 1 July 2013 Scuba Ltd acquired a leasehold office building that is used for business purposes. The company paid a premium of £80,000 for the grant of a twenty-year lease.

Plant and machinery

On 1 April 2013 the tax written down values of plant and machinery were as follows:

	£
General pool	47,200
Special rate pool	22,400

The following transactions took place during the year ended 31 March 2014:

		Cost/(Proceeds)
		£
3 April 2013	Purchased machinery	22,800
29 May 2013	Purchased a computer	1,100
4 August 2013	Purchased a motor car (1)	10,400
1 September 2013	Purchased a motor car (2)	15,400
18 November 2013	Purchased machinery	7,300
1 February 2014	Purchased a motor car (3)	20,000
15 February 2014	Sold a lorry	(12,400)

Motor car (1) purchased on 4 August 2013 for £10,400 has CO_2 emissions of 110 grams per kilometre and is used by the factory manager, and 40% of the mileage is for private journeys.

Motor car (2) purchased on 1 September 2013 for £15,400 has CO_2 emissions of 140 grams per kilometre and has no private use.

Motor car (3) purchased on 1 February 2014 for £20,000 has CO_2 emissions of 75 grams per kilometre and has no private use.

The lorry sold on 15 February 2014 for £12,400 originally cost £19,800.

Property income

Scuba Ltd lets a retail shop that is surplus to requirements. The shop was let until 31 March 2013 but was then empty from 1 April 2013 to 31 July 2013. During this period Scuba Ltd spent £6,200 on decorating the shop, and £1,430 on advertising for new tenants. The shop was let from 1 August 2013 to 31 March 2014 at a quarterly rent of £7,200, payable in advance.

Interest received

Interest of £430 was received from HM Revenue & Customs on 31 October 2013 in respect of the overpayment of corporation tax for the year ended 31 March 2012.

Other information

Scuba Ltd has no associated companies, and the company has always had an accounting date of 31 March.

Required:

(i) **Compute Scuba Ltd's tax adjusted trading profit for the year ended 31 March 2014.**

Your computation should commence with the operating profit of £198,400, and should list all of the items referred to that are relevant to the adjustment of profits, indicating by the use of zero (0) any items that do not require adjustment.

You should ignore value added tax (VAT). **(15 marks)**

(ii) **Compute Scuba Ltd's corporation tax liability for the year ended 31 March 2014.** **(4 marks)**

(b) Scuba Ltd registered for value added tax (VAT) on 1 April 2011.

The company's VAT returns have been submitted as follows:

Quarter ended	*VAT paid/ (refunded)* £	*Submitted*
30 June 2011	18,600	One month late
30 September 2011	32,200	One month late
31 December 2011	8,800	On time
31 March 2012	3,400	Two months late
30 June 2012	(6,500)	One month late
30 September 2012	42,100	On time
31 December 2012	(2,900)	On time
31 March 2013	3,900	On time
30 June 2013	18,800	On time
30 September 2013	57,300	Two months late
31 December 2013	9,600	On time

Scuba Ltd always pays any VAT that is due at the same time that the related return is submitted.

During February 2014 Scuba Ltd discovered that a number of errors had been made when completing its VAT return for the quarter ended 31 December 2013.

As a result of these errors the company will have to make an additional payment of VAT to HM Revenue & Customs.

Required:

(i) State, giving appropriate reasons, the default surcharge consequences arising from Scuba Ltd's submission of its VAT returns for the quarter ended 30 June 2011 to the quarter ended 30 September 2013 inclusive. (8 marks)

(ii) Explain how Scuba Ltd can voluntarily disclose the errors relating to the VAT return for the quarter ended 31 December 2013, and state whether default interest will be due. (3 marks)

(Total: 30 marks)

60 WIRELESS LTD (ADAPTED)  *Walk in the footsteps of a top tutor*

(a) Wireless Ltd, a United Kingdom resident company, commenced trading on 1 October 2013 as a manufacturer of computer routers. The company prepared its first accounts for the six-month period ended 31 March 2014.

The following information is available:

Trading profit

The tax adjusted trading profit based on the draft accounts for the six-month period ended 31 March 2014 is £195,626.

This figure is before making any adjustments required for:

(1) Capital allowances.

(2) Director's remuneration of £23,000 paid to the managing director of Wireless Ltd, together with the related employer's Class 1 national insurance contributions.

The remuneration is in respect of the period ended 31 March 2014 but was not paid until 5 April 2014. No accrual has been made for this remuneration in the draft accounts.

The managing director received no other remuneration from Wireless Ltd during the tax year 2013/14.

Plant and machinery

Wireless Ltd purchased the following assets in respect of the six-month period ended 31 March 2014:

		£
20 September 2013	Office equipment	10,400
5 October 2013	Machinery	60,200
6 October 2013	Van	15,000
10 October 2013	Computer (including software of £8,000)	40,000
11 October 2013	Building alterations necessary for the installation of the machinery	4,700
18 February 2014	Motor car	10,600

The van purchased on 6 October 2013 has a CO_2 emission rate of 135 grams per kilometre. The motor car purchased on 18 February 2014 for £10,600 has a CO_2 emission rate of 106 grams per kilometre. It is used by the sales manager, and 15% of the mileage is for private journeys.

Loan interest received

Loan interest of £1,110 was received on 31 March 2014. The loan was made for non-trading purposes.

Dividend

On 31 March 2014 Wireless Ltd received a dividend of £14,680 (net) from a 100% owned subsidiary company.

Income from property

Wireless Ltd lets out an unfurnished freehold office building that is surplus to requirements. The office building was let throughout the year ended 31 March 2014. On 1 April 2013 Wireless Ltd received a premium of £10,000 for the grant of a ten-year lease, and the annual rent of £4,400 which is payable in advance.

Donation

A qualifying charitable donation of £1,800 was paid on 20 March 2014.

Required:

(i) Explain when an accounting period starts for corporation tax purposes. (2 marks)

(ii) Calculate Wireless Ltd's taxable total profits for the six-month period ended 31 March 2014.

In your adjustment of profits computation you should commence with £195,626, and you should adjust for capital allowances and costs relating to the employment of the director. (14 marks)

(b) *Note that in answering this part of the question you are not expected to take account of any of the information provided in part (a) above.*

Wireless Ltd's sales since the commencement of trading on 1 October 2013 have been:

		£
2013	October	9,700
	November	18,200
	December	21,100
2014	January	14,800
	February	23,300
	March	24,600

The above figures are stated exclusive of value added tax (VAT).

The company's sales are all standard rated and are made to VAT registered businesses.

Wireless Ltd only sells goods and since registering for VAT has been issuing sales invoices to customers that show:

(1) the invoice date and the tax point

(2) Wireless Ltd's name and address

(3) the VAT-exclusive amount for each supply

(4) the total VAT-exclusive amount, and

(5) the amount of VAT payable.

The company does not offer any discount for prompt payment.

Required:

(i) Explain from what date Wireless Ltd was required to compulsorily register for VAT and state what action the company then had to take as regards notifying HM Revenue and Customs (HMRC) of the registration. (4 marks)

(ii) Explain the circumstances in which Wireless Ltd would have been allowed to recover input VAT incurred on goods purchased and services incurred prior to the date of VAT registration. (4 marks)

(iii) Explain why it would have been beneficial for Wireless Ltd to have voluntarily registered for VAT from 1 October 2013. (3 marks)

(iv) State the additional information that Wireless Ltd must show on its sales invoices in order for them to be valid for VAT purposes. (3 marks)

(Total: 30 marks)

61 STARFISH LTD (ADAPTED)  *Walk in the footsteps of a top tutor*

 ***Timed question with Online tutor debrief***

Starfish Ltd, a retailer of scuba diving equipment, was incorporated on 15 October 2009, and commenced trading on 1 December 2009. The company initially prepared accounts to 31 March, but changed its accounting date to 31 December by preparing accounts for the nine-month period ended 31 December 2013. Starfish Ltd ceased trading on 31 March 2014, and a resolution was subsequently passed to commence winding up procedures.

Starfish Ltd's results for each of its periods of account up to 31 December 2013 are:

	Tax adjusted trading profit/(loss)	*Bank interest*	*Gift aid donations*
	£	£	£
Four-month period ended 31 March 2010	(12,600)	600	(800)
Year ended 31 March 2011	64,200	1,400	(1,000)
Year ended 31 March 2012	53,900	1,700	(900)
Year ended 31 March 2013	14,700	0	(700)
Nine-month period ended 31 December 2013	49,900	0	(600)

The company's summarised statement of profit or loss for its final three-month period of trading ended 31 March 2014 is as follows:

	Notes	£	£
Gross profit			16,100
Expenses			
Depreciation		25,030	
Donations	1	1,650	
Impairment loss	2	2,000	
Legal fees	3	9,370	
Other expenses	4	168,050	
			(206,100)
Loss before taxation			(190,000)

Note 1 – Donations

Donations were made to the following:	£
A political party	300
Gift to national charity	1,350
	1,650

Note 2 – Impairment loss

On 31 March 2014 Starfish Ltd wrote off an impairment loss of £2,000 in respect of a trade debt.

Note 3 – Legal fees

Legal fees were in connection with the following:

	£
Defence of the company's internet domain name	3,490
Court action for publishing a misleading advertisement	2,020
Issue of 6% loan notes to purchase machinery - the loan note issue was subsequently cancelled	3,860
	9,370

Note 4 – Other expenses

Other expenses are as follows:

	£
Entertaining customers	3,600
Entertaining employees	1,840
Counselling services provided to employees who were made redundant	8,400
Balance of expenditure (all allowable)	154,210
	168,050

Note 5 – Plant and machinery

On 1 January 2014 the tax written down values of the company's plant and machinery were:

	£
Main pool	23,600
Special rate pool	13,200

On 10 January 2014 Starfish Ltd purchased a laptop computer for £3,120. This figure is inclusive of value added tax (VAT).

On 31 March 2014 the company sold all of the items included in the main pool for £31,200, and the laptop computer for £1,800.

The only item in the special rate pool was a car which had been acquired for £16,000 and which was sold on 31 March 2014 for £9,600. The car was used by the managing director, and 20% of the mileage was for private journeys.

All of the above figures are inclusive of VAT where applicable. None of the items included in the main pool was sold for more than its original cost, and all of the items in the main pool were standard rated.

Note 6 – Final VAT return

Starfish Ltd deregistered from VAT on 31 March 2014. The following information relates to the company's final VAT return for the quarter ended 31 March 2014:

(i) Cash sales revenue amounted to £41,160, of which £38,520 was in respect of standard rated sales and £2,640 was in respect of zero-rated sales.

(ii) Sales invoices totalling £2,200 were issued in respect of credit sales revenue. This figure is exclusive of VAT, and the sales were all standard rated. Starfish Ltd offered all of its credit sale customers a 4% discount for payment within 14 days of the date of the sales invoice, and 60% of the customers paid within this period.

(iii) In addition to the above sales revenue, Starfish Ltd sold its remaining inventory of scuba diving equipment on 31 March 2014 for £28,800. The inventory had originally cost £32,400.

(iv) There were no purchases of inventory during the period.

(v) Standard rated expenses amounted to £69,960, of which £4,320 was in respect of entertaining customers.

(vi) The impairment loss which Starfish Ltd wrote off on 31 March 2014 (as per note (2) above) was in respect of a sales invoice (exclusive of VAT) that was due for payment on 8 August 2013. Output VAT of £384 was originally paid in respect of this sale.

(vii) Purchases and sales of non-current assets during the period are as per note (5) above.

Unless otherwise stated, all of the above figures are inclusive of VAT where applicable.

Starfish Ltd did not use the VAT cash accounting scheme.

Required:

(a) State when an accounting period starts and when an accounting period finishes for corporation tax purposes. (4 marks)

(b) Calculate Starfish Ltd's tax adjusted trading loss for the three-month period ended 31 March 2014.

Notes:

(1) Your computation should commence with the loss before taxation figure of £190,000, and should also list all of the items referred to in notes (1) to (4) indicating by the use of zero (0) any items that do not require adjustment.

(2) In answering this part of the question you are not expected to take account of any of the information provided in note (6) above regarding the final VAT return. (12 marks)

(c) Assuming that Starfish Ltd claims relief for its trading losses on the most beneficial basis, calculate the company's taxable total profits for the four-month period ended 31 March 2010, the years ended 31 March 2011, 2012 and 2013 and the nine-month period ended 31 December 2013. (5 marks)

(d) (i) Calculate the amount of VAT payable by Starfish Ltd in respect of its final VAT return for the quarter ended 31 March 2014;

Notes:

(1) In answering this part of the question you are not expected to take account of any of the information provided in notes (1), (3) or (4) above.

(2) You should ignore the output VAT scale charge due in respect of fuel for private journeys. (7 marks)

(ii) Explain, with supporting calculations, how your answer to part (d)(i) above would differ if Starfish Ltd had instead sold its entire business as a going concern to a single VAT registered purchaser. (2 marks)

(Total: 30 marks)

Calculate your allowed time, allocate the time to the separate parts...................

RELIEF FOR TRADING LOSSES

62 HALF-LIFE LTD (ADAPTED)

Half-Life Ltd commenced trading on 1 April 2010 and ceased trading on 30 June 2014.

The company's results for all its periods of trading are as follows:

	y/e 31.3.11	*y/e 31.3.12*	*y/e 31.3.13*	*p/e 30.6.13*	*y/e 30.6.14*
	£	£	£	£	£
Tax adjusted profit/(loss)	224,000	67,400	38,200	(61,700)	(308,800)
Property business profit	8,200	12,200	6,500	4,400	–
Chargeable gains	–	–	5,600	–	23,700
Charitable donations	(1,200)	(1,000)	–	–	(700)

Half-Life Ltd does not have any associated companies.

Required:

(a) Assuming that Half-Life Ltd claims the maximum possible relief for its trading losses, calculate the company's taxable total profits for the years ended 31 March 2011, 2012 and 2013, the period ended 30 June 2013, and the year ended 30 June 2014.

Your answer should clearly identify the amounts of any losses and qualifying charitable donations that are unrelieved. (9 marks)

(b) State the dates by which Half-Life Ltd must make the loss relief claims in part (a). (2 marks)

(c) Calculate the amount of corporation tax that will be repaid to Half-Life Ltd as a result of making the loss relief claims in part (a).

The corporation tax rates for FY 2010 were 21% and 28%, with a marginal relief fraction of 7/400. The upper and lower limits were the same as in FY 2011. (4 marks)

(Total: 15 marks)

63 LOSER LTD (ADAPTED)

Loser Ltd 's results for the year ended 30 June 2011, the nine month period ended 31 March 2012, the year ended 31 March 2013 and the year ended 31 March 2014 are:

	y/e 30.6.11	*p/e 31.3.12*	*y/e 31.3.13*	*y/e 31.3.14*
	£	£	£	£
Trading profit/(loss)	86,600	(25,700)	27,300	(78,300)
Property business profit	–	4,500	8,100	5,600
Charitable donations	(1,400)	(800)	(1,200)	(1,100)

Loser Ltd does not have any associated companies.

Required:

(a) State the factors that will influence a company's choice of loss relief claims. (3 marks)

(b) Assuming that Loser Ltd claims relief for its losses as early as possible, compute the company's taxable total profits for the year ended 30 June 2011, the period ended 31 March 2012, the year ended 31 March 2013 and the year ended 31 March 2014.

Your answer should clearly identify the amount of any losses that are unrelieved. **(5 marks)**

(c) Explain how your answer to (b) above would have differed if Loser Ltd had ceased trading on 31 March 2014. **(2 marks)**

(Total: 10 marks)

64 SOFA LTD (ADAPTED)  *Online question assistance*

(a) Sofa Ltd is a manufacturer of furniture.

The company's summarised statement of profit or loss for the year ended 31 March 2014 is as follows:

	Note	£	£
Gross profit			427,200
Operating expenses			
Depreciation		150,820	
Professional fees	1	19,900	
Repairs and renewals	2	22,800	
Other expenses	3	304,000	
			(497,520)
Operating loss			(70,320)
Profit from sale of fixed assets			
Disposal of shares	4		4,300
Income from investments			
Bank interest	5		8,400
			(57,620)
Interest payable	6		(31,200)
Loss before taxation			(88,820)

Note 1 – Professional fees

Professional fees are as follows:

	£
Accountancy and audit fee	3,400
Legal fees in connection with the issue of share capital	7,800
Legal fees in connection with the renewal of a ten year property lease	2,900
Legal fees in connection with the issue of a loan note (see Note 6)	5,800
	19,900

Note 2 – Repairs and renewals

The figure of £22,800 for repairs and renewals includes £9,700 for constructing a new wall around the company's premises and £3,900 for repairing the wall of an office building after it was damaged by a lorry. The remaining expenses are all fully allowable.

Note 3 – Other expenses

The figure of £304,000 for other expenses includes £1,360 for entertaining suppliers; £700 for entertaining employees; £370 for counselling services provided to an employee who was made redundant; and a fine of £420 for infringing health and safety regulations. The remaining expenses are all fully allowable.

Note 4 – Profit on disposal of shares

The profit on the disposal of shares of £4,300 is in respect of a shareholding that was sold on 29 October 2013.

Note 5 – Bank interest received

The bank interest was received on 31 March 2014. The bank deposits are held for non-trading purposes.

Note 6 – Interest payable

Sofa Ltd issued a loan note on 1 July 2013, and this was used for trading purposes. Interest of £20,800 was paid on 31 December 2013, and £10,400 was accrued at 31 March 2014.

Note 7 – Plant and machinery

On 1 April 2013 the tax written down values of plant and machinery were as follows:

	£
Main pool	16,700
Short life asset	16,400

The following transactions took place during the year ended 31 March 2014:

		Cost/(Proceeds)
		£
12 May 2013	Purchased equipment	211,400
8 June 2013	Sold the short life asset	(15,800)
8 June 2013	Purchased motor car (1)	22,200
2 August 2013	Purchased motor car (2)	10,900
19 October 2013	Purchased motor car (3)	13,800
8 January 2014	Sold a lorry	(7,600)
18 January 2014	Sold motor car (2)	(8,800)
10 February 2014	Purchased a second-hand office building	280,000

Motor car (1) purchased on 8 June 2013 for £22,200 has a CO_2 emission rate of 132 grams per kilometre. Motor car (2) purchased on 2 August 2013 for £10,900, has CO_2 emissions of 127 grams per kilometre. Motor car (3) purchased on 19 October 2013 for £13,800 has CO_2 emissions of 78 grams per kilometre.

The short life asset sold on 8 June 2013 for £15,800 originally cost £25,625 in May 2011. The lorry sold on 8 January 2014 for £7,600 originally cost £24,400.

The cost of the second-hand office building purchased on 10 February 2014 for £280,000 includes fixtures qualifying as plant and machinery integral features. £44,800 of the purchase price of the office relates to these fixtures.

Required:

Calculate Sofa Ltd's tax adjusted trading loss for the year ended 31 March 2014.

Your answer should commence with the loss before taxation figure of £88,820, and should list all of the items referred to in Notes (1) to (6) indicating by the use of zero (0) any items that do not require adjustment.

You should assume that the company claims the maximum available capital allowances. **(20 marks)**

(b) Sofa Ltd has three subsidiary companies:

Settee Ltd

Sofa Ltd owns 100% of the ordinary share capital of Settee Ltd. For the year ended 30 June 2013 Settee Ltd had taxable total profits of £240,000, and for the year ended 30 June 2014 will have taxable total profits of £90,000.

Couch Ltd

Sofa Ltd owns 60% of the ordinary share capital of Couch Ltd. For the year ended 31 March 2014 Couch Ltd had taxable total profits of £64,000.

Futon Ltd

Sofa Ltd owns 80% of the ordinary share capital of Futon Ltd. Futon Ltd commenced trading on 1 January 2014, and for the three-month period ended 31 March 2014 had taxable total profits of £60,000.

Required:

Advise Sofa Ltd as to the maximum amount of group relief that can potentially be claimed by each of its three subsidiary companies in respect of its trading loss for the year ended 31 March 2014.

For the purposes of answering this part of the question, you should assume that Sofa Ltd's tax adjusted trading loss for the year ended 31 March 2014 is £200,000.

(5 marks)

(Total: 25 marks)

Online question assistance

65 VOLATILE LTD (ADAPTED)  *Walk in the footsteps of a top tutor*

Volatile Ltd commenced trading on 1 January 2009. The company's recent results are:

	y/e *31 Dec 2011*	*p/e* *30 Sept 2012*	*y/e* *30 Sept 2013*
	£	£	£
Trading profit/(loss)	15,200	78,700	(101,800)
Property business profit	6,500	–	–
Chargeable gains	–	–	9,700
Qualifying charitable donations	(1,200)	(1,000)	(800)

Required:

(a) **State the factors that will influence a company's choice of loss relief claims. You are not expected to consider group relief.** **(3 marks)**

(b) **Assuming that Volatile Ltd claims relief for its trading losses as early as possible, calculate the company's taxable total profits for the year ended 31 December 2011, nine month period ended 30 September 2012, and year ended 30 September 2013.**

Your answer should also clearly identify the amount of any unrelieved trading losses as at 30 September 2013. **(7 marks)**

(Total: 10 marks)

WITH GROUP ASPECTS

66 STRAIGHT PLC (ADAPTED)

Straight plc is the holding company for a group of companies as follows.

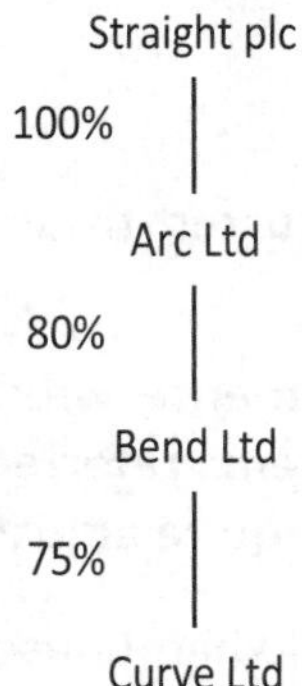

All of the companies in the group have an accounting date of 31 March.

(a) **Straight plc**

For the year ended 31 March 2014 the following information is relevant:

Operating profit

The operating profit is £173,915.

The expenses that have been deducted in calculating this figure include:

	£
Depreciation	21,200
Car lease cost (Note 1)	8,500
Entertaining (Note 2)	12,000
Fine for breach of Health and Safety regulations	1,250

Notes

(1) On 1 April 2013 Straight plc entered into an agreement for the lease of a car for one of the company's salesmen. The car has CO_2 emissions of 132 grams per kilometre.

(2) Entertaining costs consist of £10,000 for entertaining potential overseas customers and £2,000 for a Christmas party for the company's ten staff.

(3) **Plant and machinery**

On 1 April 2013 the tax written down values of plant and machinery were:

	£
Main pool	35,200
Special rate pool	18,400

The following transactions took place during the year ended 31 March 2014:

		Cost/(Proceeds)
		£
3 April 2013	Purchased machinery	12,400
1 May 2013	Sold a motor car	(15,200)

The motor car sold on 1 May 2013 was used by a salesman, and 40% of his mileage was for private journeys. The car had originally cost £23,000 in June 2012 and had a CO_2 emission rate of 162 grams per kilometre. It was the only asset in the special rate pool.

Required:

Calculate Straight plc's tax adjusted trading profit for the year ended 31 March 2014.

Your computation should commence with the operating profit of £173,915, and should list all of the relevant items referred to in part (a), indicating by the use of zero (0) any items that do not require adjustment. **(10 marks)**

(b) As at 31 March 2013 Straight plc had unused trading losses of £15,000 and unused capital losses of £10,000.

Straight plc sold a freehold office building on 20 June 2013 for £350,000, and this resulted in a capital gain of £140,000. The company has made a rollover relief claim in respect of a replacement building purchased for £270,000.

During the year ended 31 March 2014 Straight plc received dividends of £18,000 from Arc Ltd, and dividends of £9,000 from Triangle plc, an unconnected company. These figures are the actual amounts received.

Arc Ltd sold a freehold warehouse on 10 March 2014, and this resulted in a capital loss of £40,000.

Required:

(i) Explain why Straight plc, Arc Ltd, Bend Ltd and Curve Ltd form a group for capital gains purposes, and why Curve Ltd would be excluded from the group if Straight plc's holding in Arc Ltd were only 80% instead of 100%. (4 marks)

(ii) Before taking into account any transfer of capital gains or losses, calculate the corporation tax payable by Straight plc for the year ended 31 March 2014. (8 marks)

(iii) State the time limit for Straight plc and Arc Ltd to make a joint election to transfer the capital gain arising on the disposal of Arc Ltd's freehold warehouse, and explain why such an election will be beneficial.

You are not expected to consider any alternative joint elections. (3 marks)

(Total: 25 marks)

67 ANIMAL LTD (ADAPTED)

Animal Ltd is the holding company for a group of companies.

The results of each group company for the year ended 31 March 2014 are as follows:

	Tax adjusted trading profit/(loss)	*Property business income*	*Franked Investment Income*
	£	£	£
Animal Ltd	450,000	5,000	20,000
Bat Ltd	65,000	15,000	–
Cat Ltd	85,000	–	–
Dog Ltd	100,000	–	–
Elk Ltd	–	–	–
Fox Ltd	60,000	–	5,000
Gnu Ltd	(200,000)	–	–

Animal Ltd owned 100% of each subsidiary company's ordinary share capital throughout the year ended 31 March 2014 with the following exceptions:

(1) Animal Ltd only owned 90% of Bat Ltd's ordinary share capital.

(2) Animal Ltd's shareholding in Cat Ltd was disposed of on 31 December 2013. The tax adjusted trading profit of £85,000 is for the year ended 31 March 2014.

(3) Animal Ltd's shareholding in Dog Ltd was acquired on 1 January 2014. The tax adjusted trading profit of £100,000 is for the year ended 31 March 2014.

Elk Ltd was a dormant company throughout the year ended 31 March 2014.

Required:

(a) Explain the group relationship that must exist in order that group relief can be claimed. (3 marks)

(b) Explain why there are six associated companies in the Animal Ltd group of companies. Your answer should identify the six associated companies. (3 marks)

(c) Assuming that relief is claimed for Gnu Ltd's trading loss of £200,000 in the most beneficial manner; calculate the taxable total profits of Animal Ltd, Bat Ltd, Cat Ltd, Dog Ltd and Fox Ltd for the year ended 31 March 2014.

Explain your strategy for claiming group relief in the most beneficial manner.
(9 marks)

(Total: 15 marks)

68 TOCK-TICK LTD (ADAPTED)

Tock-Tick Ltd is a clock manufacturer. The company's summarised statement of profit or loss for the year ended 31 March 2014 is as follows:

	£	£
Gross profit		825,020
Operating expenses		
Impaired debts (Note 1)	9,390	
Depreciation	99,890	
Gifts and donations (Note 2)	9,290	
Professional fees (Note 3)	12,400	
Repairs and renewals (Note 4)	128,200	
Other expenses (Note 5)	420,720	
		(679,890)
Operating profit		145,130
Profit from sale of fixed assets		
Disposal of office building (Note 6)		78,100
Income from investments		
Loan interest (Note 7)		12,330
		235,560
Interest payable (Note 8)		(48,600)
Profit before taxation		186,960

Note 1 – Impaired debts

Impaired debts are as follows:

	£
Trade debts recovered from previous years	(1,680)
Trade debts written off	7,970
Increase in allowance for trade receivables	3,100
	9,390

Note 2 – Gifts and donations

Gifts and donations are as follows:

	£
Gifts to customers (pens costing £45 each displaying Tock-Tick Ltd's name)	1,080
Gifts to customers (food hampers costing £30 each)	720
Donation to a recognised political party	6,450
Long service award to an employee	360
Donation to a national charity	600
Donation to a local charity (Tick-Tock Ltd received free advertising in the charity's magazine)	80
	9,290

Note 3 – Professional fees

Professional fees are as follows:

	£
Accountancy and audit fee	5,400
Legal fees in connection with the issue of share capital	2,900
The cost of registering the company's trademark	800
Legal fees in connection with the renewal of a 35-year property lease	1,300
Debt collection	1,100
Legal fees in connection with a court action for not complying with health and safety legislation	900
	12,400

Note 4 – Repairs and renewals

The figure of £128,200 for repairs and renewals includes £41,800 for replacing the roof of an office building, which was in a bad state of repair, and £53,300 for extending the office building.

Note 5 – Other expenses

Other expenses include £2,160 for entertaining suppliers; £880 for counselling services provided to two employees who were made redundant; and the cost of seconding an employee to a charity of £6,400. The remaining expenses are all fully allowable.

Note 6 – Disposal of office building

The profit of £78,100 is in respect of a freehold office building that was sold on 20 February 2014 for £300,000. The office building was purchased on 18 November 2000 for £197,900. Assume the indexation allowance from November 2002 to February 2014 is £85,889.

The building has always been used by Tock-Tick Ltd for trading purposes.

Note 7 – Loan interest received

The loan interest is in respect of a loan that was made on 1 July 2013. Interest of £8,280 was received on 31 December 2013, and interest of £4,050 was accrued at 31 March 2014. The loan was made for non-trading purposes.

Note 8 – Interest payable

The interest payable is in respect of a loan note that is used for trading purposes. Interest of £24,300 was paid on 30 September 2013 and again on 31 March 2014.

Note 9 – Plant and machinery

On 1 April 2013 the tax written down values of plant and machinery were:

	£
General pool	12,200
Special rate pool	21,600
Short-life asset	2,300

The following transactions took place during the year ended 31 March 2014:

		Cost/(Proceeds)
		£
28 May 2013	Sold a motor car	(34,800)
7 June 2013	Purchased a motor car	14,400
1 August 2013	Sold the short-life asset	(460)
15 August 2013	Purchased equipment	6,700

The motor car purchased on 7 June 2013 has a CO_2 emission rate of 79 g/km.

The motor car sold on 28 May 2013 for £34,800 originally cost £33,600 in June 2011 and had a CO_2 emission rate of 169 g/km.

Required:

(a) **Calculate Tock-Tick Ltd's tax adjusted trading profit for the year ended 31 March 2014.**

Your computation should commence with the profit before taxation figure of £186,960, and should list all of the items referred to in Notes (1) to (8), indicating by the use of zero (0) any items that do not require adjustment. **(19 marks)**

(b) **Calculate Tock-Tick Ltd's taxable total profits for the year ended 31 March 2014.** **(5 marks)**

(c) **It has now been discovered that Tock-Tick Ltd had acquired a 100% shareholding in Clock Ltd on 31 March 2013.**

Clock Ltd made a tax adjusted trading loss of £62,400 for the year ended 31 December 2013 but was profitable in the following year.

On 15 March 2014 Clock Ltd purchased a new freehold office building for £294,000 that is to be used 100% for trading purposes.

(i) State the effect on Tock-Tick Ltd's taxable total profits for the year ended 31 March 2014 of the acquisition of Clock Ltd, assuming all beneficial elections and claims are made in respect of Clock Ltd's trading loss and its acquisition of the office building. (4 marks)

(ii) Compute the corporation tax liability of Tock-Tick Ltd for the year ended 31 March 2014 assuming the beneficial claims and elections identified in (c)(i) above are made. (2 marks)

(Total: 30 marks)

69 MUSIC PLC (ADAPTED)

Music plc is the holding company for a group of companies. The group structure is as follows:

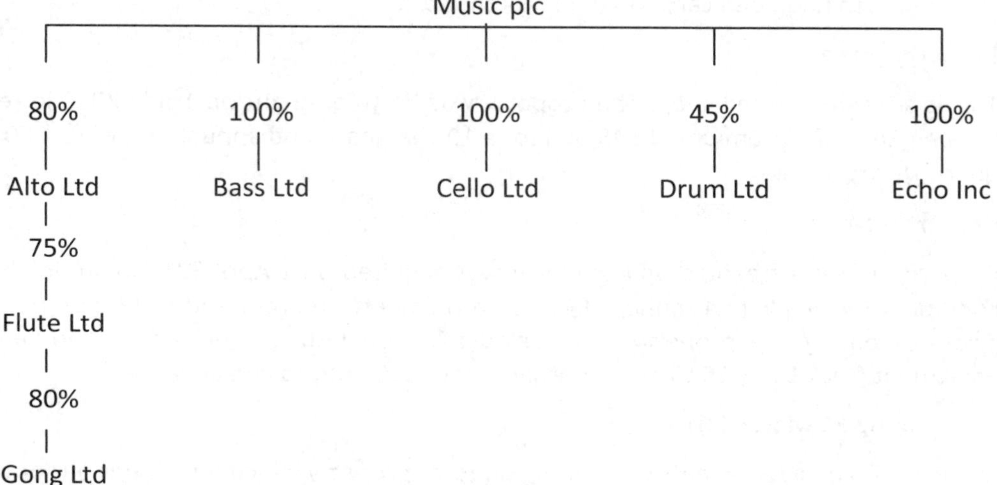

Music plc's shareholding in Bass Ltd was disposed of on 31 December 2013, and the shareholding in Cello Ltd was acquired on 1 January 2014. The other shareholdings were all held throughout the year ended 31 March 2014.

Echo Inc is resident overseas. The other companies are all resident in the United Kingdom.

For the year ended 31 March 2014 Music plc had a tax adjusted trading profit of £92,000. During the year Music plc received franked investment income of £15,000 from an unconnected company, bank interest of £12,000 and a dividend of £5,400 from Bass Ltd.

As at 31 March 2013 Music plc had unused capital losses of £32,000. On 5 January 2014 the company sold a freehold office building, and this resulted in a further capital loss of £65,000.

Alto Ltd sold a freehold warehouse on 10 March 2014, and this resulted in a capital gain of £120,000. An election has been made so that the gain is treated as Music plc's gain.

Music plc also owns a number of properties which it lets out. The following information relates to the properties let out during the year ended 31 March 2014. Music plc claims the wear and tear allowance on its properties, where appropriate.

Property one

Property one is a freehold house which is let out furnished. It was let out from 1 September 2013 at a quarterly rent of £2,500, payable in advance. In April 2013 Music plc incurred £2,500 on redecorating the house and £400 on a new dishwasher. During the year the company also incurred £1,500 on advertising for new tenants and agents fees, council tax of £1,200 and water rates of £600.

Property two

This is a freehold house which is let out unfurnished. It was let until 1 January 2014 at a monthly rent of £650, payable in advance. The tenants left owing the last month's rent, which the company never recovered.

New tenants occupied the house from 1 March 2014 at a rent of £700 per month. The tenants were unable to supply appropriate references and Music plc therefore required the tenants to pay the first six months' rent up front.

On 10 April 2014 Music plc paid £500 in connection with repairs to the central heating system which had been carried out in March 2014.

Property three

This is a freehold retail shop. The property was let to a tenant on 1 July 2013 in return for the payment of a premium of £45,000 for a 10 year lease and annual rent of £2,000 payable quarterly in advance.

Property four

Property four is a freehold apartment. It was acquired on 1 April 2013 in an uninhabitable condition. Music plc had to incur £4,000 on repairs to the roof and £2,000 on new fittings prior to renting the property. It incurred £250 on letting agency fees and rented the apartment from 1 July 2013 at a monthly rent of £500 payable in advance.

Year ending 31 March 2015

Music plc is considering either acquiring another property which it will rent out or investing in new plant and machinery in the year ending 31 March 2015. In either case it will take out a new bank loan of £100,000 at a 10% interest rate to partly fund the acquisition. Bank arrangement fees will be £300.

Required:

(a) **State, giving appropriate reasons, which companies in the Music plc group of companies form a group for capital gains purposes. (5 marks)**

(b) **Explain why Music plc has six associated companies.**

Your answer should identify the six associated companies. (4 marks)

(c) **Calculate Music plc's property business profit for the year ended 31 March 2014. (8 marks)**

(d) **Calculate Music plc's corporation tax liability for the year ended 31 March 2014. (6 marks)**

(e) **Explain how the bank fees and interest costs will be treated for tax purposes if the company acquires another property or it acquires new plant and machinery in the year ended 31 March 2015. (2 marks)**

(Total: 25 marks)

70 GASTRON LTD (ADAPTED)  *Walk in the footsteps of a top tutor*

Gastron Ltd, a United Kingdom resident company, is a luxury food manufacturer.

Its summarised statement of profit or loss for the year ended 31 March 2014 is as follows:

	Note	£	£
Gross profit			876,500
Operating expenses			
Depreciation		85,660	
Amortisation of leasehold property	1	6,000	
Gift and donations	2	2,700	
Professional fees	3	18,800	
Other expenses	4	230,240	
			(343,400)
Operating profit			533,100
Income from investments			
Income from property	5	20,600	
Bank interest	6	12,400	
Dividends	7	54,000	
			87,000
Profit from sale of fixed assets			
Disposal of shares	8		80,700
			700,800
Interest payable	9		(60,800)
Profit before taxation			640,000

Note 1 – Leasehold property

On 1 April 2013 Gastron Ltd acquired a leasehold office building, paying a premium of £60,000 for the grant of a new ten-year lease. The office building was used for business purposes by Gastron Ltd throughout the year ended 31 March 2014. No legal costs were incurred by Gastron Ltd in respect of this lease.

Note 2 – Gifts and donations

Gifts and donations are as follows:

	£
Gifts to customers (pens costing £60 each and displaying Gastron Ltd's name)	1,200
Gifts to customers (hampers of food costing £25 each)	1,100
Donation to local charity	
(Gastron Ltd received free advertising in the charity's magazine)	400
	2,700

Note 3 – Professional fees

Professional fees are as follows:

	£
Legal fees in connection with the renewal of a 45-year property lease in respect of a warehouse	3,600
Legal fees in connection with the issue of a loan note (see Note 9)	15,200
	18,800

Note 4 – Other expenses

The figure of £230,240 for other expenses includes £1,300 for entertaining suppliers and £900 for entertaining employees.

Note 5 – Income from property

Gastron Ltd lets out the whole of an unfurnished freehold office building that is surplus to requirements. The office building was let from 1 April 2013 to 31 December 2013 at a monthly rent of £1,800, payable in advance. On 31 December 2013 the tenant left owing two months' rent which Gastron Ltd was unable to recover. During January 2014 the company spent £3,700 decorating the property. The office building was then re-let from 1 February 2014 at a monthly rent of £1,950, on which date the new tenant paid six months' rent in advance.

Note 6 – Bank interest received

The bank interest was received on 31 March 2014. The bank deposits are held for non-trading purposes.

Note 7 – Dividends received

During the year ended 31 March 2014 Gastron Ltd received dividends of £36,000 from Tasteless plc, an unconnected UK company, and dividends of £18,000 from Culinary Ltd, a 100% UK subsidiary company (see Note 11). Both figures are the actual cash amounts received.

Note 8 – Profit on disposal of shares

The profit on disposal of shares is in respect of a 1% shareholding that was sold on 14 October 2013. The disposal resulted in a chargeable gain of £74,800. This figure is after taking account of indexation.

Note 9 – Interest payable

The interest payable is in respect of the company's loan note that was issued on 1 April 2013. The proceeds of the issue were used to finance the company's trading activities. Interest of £30,400 was paid on 30 September 2013 and again on 31 March 2014.

Note 10 – Plant and machinery

On 1 April 2013 the tax written down values of plant and machinery were as follows:

	£
Main pool	16,700
Special rate pool	18,400

The following transactions took place during the year ended 31 March 2014:

		Cost/ (Proceeds)
		£
19 May 2013	Purchased equipment	6,800
12 July 2013	Purchased motor car (1)	9,800
11 August 2013	Purchased motor car (2)	16,200
5 October 2013	Purchased a lorry	17,200
5 March 2014	Sold equipment	(3,300)

Motor car (1) purchased on 12 July 2013 for £9,800 has a CO_2 emission rate of 117 grams per kilometre. Motor car (2), purchased on 11 August 2013 for £16,200, has a CO_2 emission rate of 79 grams per kilometre. The equipment sold on 5 March 2014 for £3,300 was originally purchased in 2007 for £8,900.

Note 11 – Subsidiary company

Gastron Ltd owns 100% of the ordinary share capital of Culinary Ltd. On 13 February 2014 Culinary Ltd sold a freehold factory and this resulted in a capital loss of £66,000. For the year ended 31 March 2014 Culinary Ltd made no other disposals and paid corporation tax at the small profits rate of 20%.

Required:

(a) **Calculate Gastron Ltd's tax adjusted trading profit for the year ended 31 March 2014, after deducting capital allowances.**

Your computation should commence with the profit before taxation figure of £640,000, and should list all of the items referred to in Notes (1) to (9) indicating by the use of zero (0) any items that do not require adjustment. (15 marks)

(b) **Calculate Gastron Ltd's corporation tax liability for the year ended 31 March 2014, on the basis that no election is made between Gastron Ltd and Culinary Ltd in respect of capital gains. (7 marks)**

(c) **State the date by which Gastron Ltd's corporation tax liability for the year ended 31 March 2014 should be paid, and advise the company of the interest that will be due if the liability is not paid until 31 August 2015. (3 marks)**

(d) **Explain the group relationship that must exist in order for two or more companies to form a group for capital gains purposes. (2 marks)**

(e) **State the time limit for Gastron Ltd and Culinary Ltd to make a joint election such that Culinary Ltd is treated as making the chargeable gain on the disposal of shares (see Note 8), and explain why such an election will be beneficial. (3 marks)**

(Total: 30 marks)

71 MICE LTD (ADAPTED)  *Walk in the footsteps of a top tutor*

(a) You should assume that today's date is 28 March 2014.

Mice Ltd commenced trading on 1 July 2010 as a manufacturer of computer peripherals.

The company prepares accounts to 31 March, and its results for the first three periods of trading were as follows:

	Period ended 31 March 2011	*Year ended 31 March 2012*	*Year ended 31 March 2013*
	£	£	£
Trading profit	83,200	24,700	51,200
Property business profit	2,800	7,100	12,200
Qualifying charitable donations	(1,000)	(1,500)	–

The following information is available in respect of the year ended 31 March 2014:

Trading loss

Mice Ltd expects to make a trading loss of £180,000.

Business property income

Mice Ltd lets out three office buildings that are surplus to requirements.

The first office building is owned freehold. The property was let throughout the year ended 31 March 2014 at a quarterly rent of £3,200, payable in advance. Mice Ltd paid business rates of £2,200 and insurance of £460 in respect of this property for the year ended 31 March 2014. During June 2013 Mice Ltd repaired the existing car park for this property at a cost of £1,060, and then subsequently enlarged the car park at a cost of £2,640.

The second office building is owned leasehold. Mice Ltd pays an annual rent of £7,800 for this property, but did not pay a premium when the lease was acquired. On 1 April 2013 the property was sub-let to a tenant, with Mice Ltd receiving a premium of £18,000 for the grant of an eight-year lease. The company also received the annual rent of £6,000 which was payable in advance. Mice Ltd paid insurance of £310 in respect of this property for the year ended 31 March 2014.

The third office building is also owned freehold. Mice Ltd purchased the freehold of this building on 1 January 2014, and it will be empty until 31 March 2014. The building is to be let from 1 April 2014 at a monthly rent of £640, and on 15 March 2014 Mice Ltd received three months' rent in advance.

On 1 January 2014 Mice Ltd paid insurance of £480 in respect of this property for the year ended 31 December 2014, and during February 2014 spent £680 on advertising for tenants. Mice Ltd paid loan interest of £1,800 in respect of the period 1 January 2014 to 31 March 2014 on a loan that was taken out to purchase this property.

Loan interest received

On 1 July 2013 Mice Ltd made a loan for non-trading purposes. Loan interest of £6,400 was received on 31 December 2013, and £3,200 will be accrued at 31 March 2014.

Dividend received

On 15 October 2013 Mice Ltd received a dividend of £7,400 (net) from a 3% shareholding in USB Ltd.

Chargeable gain

On 20 December 2013 Mice Ltd sold its 3% shareholding in USB Ltd. The disposal resulted in a chargeable gain of £10,550, after taking account of indexation.

Required:

(i) **Calculate Mice Ltd's property business profit for the year ended 31 March 2014** **(8 marks)**

(ii) **Assuming that Mice Ltd claims relief for its trading loss as early as possible, calculate the company's taxable total profits for the nine-month period ended 31 March 2011, and each of the years ended 31 March 2012, 2013 and 2014.** **(7 marks)**

(b) Mice Ltd has owned 100% of the ordinary share capital of Web-Cam Ltd since it began trading on 1 April 2013. For the three-month period ended 30 June 2013 Web-Cam Ltd made a trading profit of £28,000, and is expected to make a trading profit of £224,000 for the year ended 30 June 2014. Web-Cam Ltd has no other taxable profits or allowable losses.

Required:

Assuming that Mice Ltd does not make any loss relief claim against its own profits, advise Web-Cam Ltd as to the maximum amount of group relief that can be claimed from Mice Ltd in respect of the trading loss of £180,000 for the year ended 31 March 2014. **(3 marks)**

(c) Mice Ltd has surplus funds of £350,000 which it is planning to spend before 31 March 2014. The company will either purchase new equipment for £350,000, or alternatively it will purchase a new ventilation system for £350,000, which will be installed as part of its factory.

Mice Ltd has not made any other purchases of assets during the year ended 31 March 2014, and neither has its subsidiary company Web-Cam Ltd.

Required:

Explain the maximum amount of capital allowances that Mice Ltd will be able to claim for the year ended 31 March 2014 in respect of each of the two alternative purchases of assets.

You are not expected to recalculate Mice Ltd's trading loss for the year ended 31 March 2014, or redo any of the calculations made in parts (a) and (b) above.

(4 marks)

(d) Mice Ltd is planning to pay its managing director a bonus of £40,000 on 31 March 2014. The managing director has already been paid gross director's remuneration of £55,000 during the tax year 2013/14, and the bonus of £40,000 will be paid as additional director's remuneration. The director has no other income.

Required:

Advise the managing director as to the additional amount of income tax and National Insurance contributions (both employee's and employer's) that will be payable as a result of the payment of the additional director's remuneration of £40,000.

You are not expected to recalculate Mice Ltd's trading loss for the year ended 31 March 2014, or redo any of the calculations made in parts (a) and (b) above.

(3 marks)

(Total: 25 marks)

72 NEUNG LTD (ADAPTED)  *Walk in the footsteps of a top tutor*

(a) Neung Ltd is a UK resident company that runs a business providing financial services. The company's summarised statement of profit or loss for the year ended 31 March 2014 is as follows:

	Note	£
Operating profit	1	627,300
Income from investments		
Loan interest	2	37,800
Dividends	3	54,000
Profit before taxation		719,100

Note 1 – Operating profit

Depreciation of £11,830 and amortisation of leasehold property of £7,000 have been deducted in arriving at the operating profit of £627,300.

Note 2 – Loan interest receivable

The loan was made for non-trading purposes on 1 July 2013. Loan interest of £25,200 was received on 31 December 2013, and interest of £12,600 was accrued at 31 March 2014.

Note 4 – Dividends received

Neung Ltd holds shares in four UK resident companies as follows:

	Percentage shareholding	*Status*
Second Ltd	25%	Trading
Third Ltd	60%	Trading
Fourth Ltd	100%	Dormant
Fifth Ltd	100%	Trading

During the year ended 31 March 2014 Neung Ltd received a dividend of £37,800 from Second Ltd, and a dividend of £16,200 from Third Ltd. These figures were the actual cash amounts received.

Fifth Ltd made a trading loss of £15,700 for the year ended 31 March 2014.

Additional information

Leasehold property

On 1 April 2013 Neung Ltd acquired a leasehold office building, paying a premium of £140,000 for the grant of a 20-year lease. The office building was used for business purposes by Neung Ltd throughout the year ended 31 March 2014.

Plant and machinery

On 1 April 2013 the tax written down values of Neung Ltd's plant and machinery were as follows:

	£
Main pool	4,800
Short life asset	22,800
Special rate pool	12,700

The company purchased the following assets during the year ended 31 March 2014:

		£
19 July 2013	Motor car [1]	15,400
12 December 2013	Motor car [2]	28,600
20 December 2013	Ventilation system	312,000

The short life asset is a specialised piece of machinery which was purchased on 1 January 2013. Motor car [1] purchased on 19 July 2013 has a CO_2 emission rate of 212 grams per kilometre. Motor car [2] purchased on 12 December 2013 has a CO_2 emission rate of 118 grams per kilometre.

The ventilation system purchased on 20 December 2013 for £312,000 is integral to the freehold office building in which it was installed.

Required:

(i) **State, giving reasons, which companies will be treated as being associated with Neung Ltd for corporation tax purposes; (2 marks)**

(ii) **Calculate Neung Ltd's corporation tax liability for the year ended 31 March 2014;**

You should assume that the whole of the annual investment allowance is available to Neung Ltd, that the company wishes to maximise its capital allowances claim, and that any favourable claims are made in respect of group losses. (15 marks)

(iii) **Advise Neung Ltd of the taxation consequences if it were to dispose of 40% of the shares in Fifth Ltd on 1 April 2014. You are not expected to consider any chargeable gains that may arise due to this disposal. (3 marks)**

(b) *Note that in answering this part of the question you are not expected to take account of any of the information provided in part (a) above.*

The following information is available in respect of Neung Ltd's value added tax (VAT) for the quarter ended 31 March 2014:

(1) Invoices were issued for sales of £44,600 to VAT registered customers. Of this figure, £35,200 was in respect of exempt sales and the balance in respect of standard rated sales. The standard rated sales figure is exclusive of VAT.

(2) In addition to the above, on 1 March 2014 Neung Ltd issued a VAT invoice for £8,000 plus VAT of £1,600 to a VAT registered customer. This was in respect of a contract for standard rated financial services that will be completed on 15 April 2014. The customer paid for the contracted services in two instalments of £4,700 on 31 March 2014 and 30 April 2014 respectively.

(3) Invoices were issued for sales of £289,300 to non-VAT registered customers. Of this figure, £241,300 was in respect of exempt sales and the balance in respect of standard rated sales. The standard rated sales figure is inclusive of VAT.

(4) The managing director of Neung Ltd is provided with free fuel for private mileage driven in her company motor car. During the quarter ended 31 March 2014 this fuel cost Neung Ltd £260. The relevant quarterly scale charge is £404. Both these figures are inclusive of VAT.

For the quarters ended 30 September 2012 and 30 June 2013 Neung Ltd was one month late in submitting its VAT returns and in paying the related VAT liabilities. All of the company's other VAT returns have been submitted on time.

Required:

(i) Calculate the amount of output VAT payable by Neung Ltd for the quarter ended 31 March 2014; (4 marks)

(ii) Advise Neung Ltd of the default surcharge implications if it is one month late in submitting its VAT return for the quarter ended 31 March 2014 and in paying the related VAT liability; (3 marks)

(iii) State the circumstances in which Neung Ltd is and is not required to issue a VAT invoice, and the period during which such an invoice should be issued. (3 marks)

(Total: 30 marks)

VALUE ADDED TAX

The examiner has stated that there will be a minimum of 10 marks on VAT in the exam.

These marks will often be in question one or two, and past exam questions where this has been the case are included in the kit under the heading of the primary tax being examined.

However, the examiner sometimes sets a separate question on VAT, which could be worth up to 15 marks.

73 CONFUSED LTD

(a) Confused Ltd will commence trading in the near future. The company operates a small aeroplane, and is considering three alternative types of business. These are

(1) training, in which case all sales will be standard rated for VAT,

(2) transport, in which case all sales will be zero-rated for VAT, and

(3) an air ambulance service, in which case all sales will be exempt from VAT.

For each alternative Confused Ltd's sales will be £80,000 per month (exclusive of VAT), and standard rated expenses will be £10,000 per month (inclusive of VAT).

Required:

For each of the three alternative types of business

(i) State whether Confused Ltd will be required or permitted to register for VAT when trading commences, and

(ii) Calculate the monthly amount of output VAT due and input VAT recoverable. **(6 marks)**

(b) Puzzled Ltd has discovered that a number of errors have been made when preparing its VAT returns for the previous four quarters. As a result of the errors the company will have to make an additional payment of VAT to HM Revenue & Customs.

Required:

Explain how Puzzled Ltd can voluntarily disclose the errors that have been discovered, and when default interest will be due. **(3 marks)**

(c) Perplexed Ltd has been registered for VAT since 1995, but intends to cease trading on 31 December 2014. On the cessation of trading Perplexed Ltd can either sell its fixed assets on a piecemeal basis to individual purchasers, or it can sell its entire business as a going concern to a single purchaser.

Required:

Advise Perplexed Ltd as to what will happen to its VAT registration, and whether output VAT will be due, if the company ceases trading on 31 December 2014 and:

(i) sells its fixed assets on a piecemeal basis, or

(ii) sells its entire business as a going concern. **(6 marks)**

(Total: 15 marks)

74 ASTUTE LTD (ADAPTED)

(a) Astute Ltd registered for VAT on 1 July 2013. The company has annual standard rated sales of £350,000. This figure is inclusive of VAT. As a result of bookkeeping problems Astute Ltd has been late in submitting its VAT returns to date.

Required:

Advise Astute Ltd of the conditions that it must satisfy before being permitted to use the VAT annual accounting scheme, and the advantages of joining the scheme. **(4 marks)**

(b) Bright Ltd registered for VAT on 1 January 2014. The company has annual standard rated sales of £82,000, and these are all made to the general public. The company has annual standard rated expenses of £17,000. Both figures are inclusive of VAT. The relevant flat rate scheme percentage for the company's trade for the first twelve months is 11%.

Required:

Advise Bright Ltd of the conditions that it must satisfy before being permitted to use the VAT flat rate scheme, and the advantages of joining the scheme.

Your answer should be supported by appropriate calculations of the potential annual tax saving. **(4 marks)**

(c) Clever Ltd registered for VAT on 1 June 2013. The company has annual standard rated sales of £250,000. This figure is inclusive of VAT. The company pays its expenses on a cash basis, but allows customers three months' credit when paying for sales. Several of Clever Ltd's customers have recently defaulted on the payment of their debts.

Required:

Advise Clever Ltd of the conditions that it must satisfy before being permitted to use the VAT cash accounting scheme, and the advantages of joining the scheme. **(4 marks)**

(d) Robert has owned all of the issued share capital of two UK resident companies, Talent Limited and Gifted Limited, for a number of years.

Talent Limited and Gifted Limited trade with each other.

Required:

Advise Robert whether Talented Limited and Gifted Limited can be group registered for VAT purposes and the effect of a VAT group registration. **(3 marks)**

(Total: 15 marks)

75 VICTOR STYLE  *Online question assistance*

Victor Style has been a self-employed hairdresser since 1 January 2011. His sales from the date of commencement of the business to 30 September 2013 were £5,800 per month.

On 1 October 2013 Victor increased the prices that he charged customers, and from that date his sales have been £10,900 per month. Victor's sales are all standard rated.

As a result of the price increase, Victor was required to register for value added tax (VAT) and charge VAT on sales from 1 January 2014.

As all of his customers are members of the general public, it was not possible to increase prices any further as a result of registering for VAT.

Victor's standard rated expenses are £400 per month.

Where applicable, the above figures are inclusive of VAT.

Assume that the VAT registration threshold for 2013/14 applied throughout.

Required:

(a) **Explain why Victor was required to compulsorily register for VAT from 1 January 2014, and state what action he then had to take as regards notifying HM Revenue & Customs of the registration. (5 marks)**

(b) **Calculate the total amount of VAT payable by Victor during the year ended 31 December 2014.**

You should ignore pre-registration input VAT. (3 marks)

(c) **Advise Victor why it would have been beneficial to have used the VAT flat rate scheme from 1 January 2014.**

Your answer should include a calculation of the amount of VAT that Victor would have saved for the year ended 31 December 2014 by joining the scheme.

The flat rate scheme percentage for hairdressing for Victor in the year ended 31 December 2014 is 13%. (3 marks)

(d) **Calculate the effect on Victor's net profit for the year ended 31 December 2014 as a consequence of the price increase and subsequent VAT registration. (4 marks)**

(Total: 15 marks)

 *Online question assistance*

76 VECTOR LTD (ADAPTED)

Vector Ltd is registered for VAT, and is in the process of completing its VAT return for the quarter ended 31 March 2014. The following information is available.

(1) Sales invoices totalling £128,000 were issued in respect of standard rated sales in the UK. Vector Ltd offers its UK customers a 2.5% discount for prompt payment.

(2) On 15 March 2014 Vector Ltd received an advance deposit of £4,500 in respect of a contract with a UK company that is due to be completed during April 2014. The total value of the contract is £10,000. Both figures are inclusive of VAT.

(3) Vector Ltd also made sales to companies in Ruritania (not in the EU) totalling £35,000, to VAT registered EU companies totalling £48,000 and non-VAT registered EU customers totalling £14,250.

(4) Standard rated expenses amounted to £74,800. This includes £4,200 for entertaining UK customers.

(5) On 31 March 2014 Vector Ltd wrote off £12,000 due from a customer as an impaired debt. The debt was in respect of three invoices, each of £4,000, that were due for payment on 15 August, 15 September and 15 October 2013 respectively. No discounts were offered on the sales.

(6) On 1 January 2014 the company purchased a motor car costing £9,800 for the use of its sales manager. The sales manager is provided with free petrol for private mileage. The car has CO_2 emissions of 205 g/km and the relevant quarterly scale charge is £523. Both figures are inclusive of VAT.

Unless stated otherwise all of the above figures are exclusive of VAT.

Required:

(a) Calculate the amount of VAT payable by Vector Ltd for the quarter ended 31 March 2014. (8 marks)

(b) State the conditions that Vector Ltd must satisfy before it will be permitted to use the cash accounting scheme, and advise the company of the implications of using the scheme. (4 marks)

(c) If Vector Ltd were a subsidiary in a UK group of companies, explain the advantages and disadvantages of Vector Ltd joining a group VAT registration rather than being registered separately. (3 marks)

(Total: 15 marks)

77 LITHOGRAPH LTD (ADAPTED)

Lithograph Ltd runs a printing business, and is registered for VAT. Because its annual taxable turnover is only £250,000, the company uses the annual accounting scheme so that it only has to prepare one VAT return each year. The annual VAT period is the year ended 31 December.

Year ended 31 December 2013

The total amount of VAT payable by Lithograph Ltd for the year ended 31 December 2013 was £10,200.

Year ended 31 December 2014

The following information is available:

(1) Sales invoices totalling £250,000 were issued to VAT registered customers, of which £160,000 were for standard rated sales and £90,000 were for zero-rated sales.

(2) Purchase invoices totalling £45,000 were received from VAT registered suppliers, of which £38,000 were for standard rated purchases and £7,000 were for zero-rated purchases.

(3) Standard rated expenses amounted to £28,000. This includes £3,600 for entertaining overseas customers.

(4) On 1 January 2014 Lithograph Ltd purchased a motor car costing £18,400 for the use of its managing director. The manager director is provided with free petrol for private mileage, and the cost of this is included in the standard rated expenses in Note (3). The car has CO_2 emissions of 210 g/km and the relevant annual scale charge is £2,160. Both figures are inclusive of VAT.

(5) During the year ended 31 December 2014 Lithograph Ltd purchased machinery for £24,000, and sold office equipment for £8,000. Input VAT had been claimed when the office equipment was originally purchased.

(6) On 31 December 2014 Lithograph Ltd wrote off £4,800 due from a customer as an impaired debt. The debt was in respect of an invoice that was due for payment on 31 May 2014.

Unless stated otherwise all of the above figures are exclusive of VAT.

Required:

(a) Calculate the monthly payments on account of VAT that Lithograph Ltd will have made in respect of the year ended 31 December 2014, and state in which months these will have been paid. (2 marks)

(b) (i) Calculate the total amount of VAT payable by Lithograph Ltd for the year ended 31 December 2014. (6 marks)

(ii) Based on your answer to part (i) above, calculate the balancing payment that would have been paid with the annual VAT return, and state the date by which this return was due for submission. (2 marks)

(Total: 10 marks)

78 DENZIL DYER (ADAPTED)

Denzil Dyer has been a self-employed printer since 2007. He has recently registered for value added tax (VAT).

Denzil's sales consist of printed leaflets, some of which are standard rated and some of which are zero-rated. He sells to both VAT registered customers and to non-VAT registered customers.

For a typical printing contract, Denzil receives a 10% deposit at the time that the customer makes the order. The order normally takes fourteen days to complete, and Denzil issues the sales invoice three to five days after completion. Some customers pay immediately upon receiving the sales invoice, but many do not pay for up to two months.

Customers making an order of more than £500 are given a discount of 5% from the normal selling price. Denzil also offers a discount of 2.5% of the amount payable to those customers that pay within one month of the date of the sales invoice.

All of Denzil's printing supplies are purchased from a VAT registered supplier. He pays by credit card and receives a VAT invoice. However, Denzil also purchases various office supplies by cash without receiving any invoices.

Denzil does not use the annual accounting scheme, the cash accounting scheme or the flat rate scheme.

Required:

(a) **Explain why it is important for Denzil to correctly identify whether a sale is standard rated or whether it is zero-rated.** **(2 marks)**

(b) **Advise Denzil as to when he should account for the output VAT relating to a typical standard rated printing supply.** **(4 marks)**

(c) **Explain the VAT implications of the two types of discount that Denzil gives or offers to his customers.** **(3 marks)**

(d) **Advise Denzil of the conditions that will have to be met in order for him to recover input VAT.**

You are not expected to list those goods and services for which input VAT is non-recoverable. **(3 marks)**

(e) **State the circumstances in which Denzil is and is not required to issue a VAT invoice, and the period during which such an invoice should be issued.** **(3 marks)**

(Total: 15 marks)

79 ANNE ATTIRE  *Walk in the footsteps of a top tutor*

 ***Timed question with Online tutor debrief***

Anne Attire runs a retail clothing shop. She is registered for value added tax (VAT), and is in the process of completing her VAT return for the quarter ended 31 May 2014.

The following information is available (all figures are exclusive of VAT):

(1) Cash sales amounted to £42,000, of which £28,000 was in respect of standard rated sales and £14,000 was in respect of zero-rated sales.

(2) Sales invoices totalling £12,000 were issued in respect of credit sales. These sales were all standard rated. Anne offers all of her credit sale customers a 5% discount for payment within one month of the date of the sales invoice, and 90% of the customers pay within this period. The sales figure of £12,000 is stated before any deduction for the 5% discount.

(3) Purchase and expense invoices totalling £19,200 were received from VAT registered suppliers. This figure is made up as follows:

	£
Standard rated purchases and expenses	11,200
Zero rated purchases	6,000
Exempt expenses	2,000
	19,200

Anne pays all of her purchase and expense invoices two months after receiving the invoice.

(4) On 31 May 2014 Anne wrote off two impairment losses (bad debts) that were in respect of standard rated credit sales. The first impairment loss was for £300, and was in respect of a sales invoice due for payment on 15 April 2014. The second impairment loss was for £800, and was in respect of a sales invoice due for payment on 10 November 2013.

Anne does not use the cash accounting scheme.

Anne will soon be 60 years old and is therefore considering retirement. On the cessation of trading Anne can either sell the fixed assets of her business on a piecemeal basis to individual VAT registered purchasers, or she can sell the entire business as a going concern to a single VAT registered purchaser.

Required:

(a) Calculate the amount of VAT payable by Anne Attire for the quarter ended 31 May 2014, and state the date by which the VAT return for this period was due for submission. (6 marks)

(b) State the conditions that Anne Attire must satisfy before she will be permitted to use the cash accounting scheme, and advise her of the implications of using the scheme. (5 marks)

(c) Advise Anne Attire as to what will happen to her VAT registration, and whether output VAT will be due in respect of the fixed assets, if she ceases trading and then:

(i) Sells her fixed assets on a piecemeal basis to individual VAT registered purchasers; (2 marks)

(ii) Sells her entire business as a going concern to a single VAT registered purchaser. (2 marks)

(Total: 15 marks)

Calculate your allowed time, allocate the time to the separate parts..................

80 ASTON MARTYN (ADAPTED)

Walk in the footsteps of a top tutor

Aston Martyn commenced self-employment on 1 September 2013 providing consultancy services to the motor industry. His sales revenue has been as follows:

		Standard rated	*Zero-rated*
		£	£
2013	September	2,300	–
	October	6,400	–
	November	20,900	4,800
	December	10,700	–
2014	January	16,100	–
	February	15,800	2,200
	March	4,200	–
	April	31,500	3,300
	May	44,600	6,600

Where applicable, the above figures are stated exclusive of value added tax (VAT).

Aston only supplies services and all of his supplies are to VAT registered businesses. He does not offer any discount for prompt payment.

The following is a sample of the new sales invoice that Aston is going to issue to his customers:

SALES INVOICE

Aston Martyn		**Customer:**	Faster Motors plc
111 Long Road		**Address:**	22 Short lane
London W1 9MG			Manchester M1 8MB
Telephone 0207 123 3456			
Invoice Date	6 June 2014		
Tax Point	6 June 2014		

Description of services
Business advice

	£
Total price (excluding VAT)	12,000.00
Total price (including VAT)	14,400.00

Aston sometimes receives supplies of standard rated services from VAT registered businesses situated elsewhere within the European Union. As business to business services these are treated as being supplied in the United Kingdom. Aston wants to know how he should account for these services for VAT purposes.

Because of the complexity of the VAT legislation, Aston is concerned that despite his best efforts he will incorrectly treat a standard rated supply as zero-rated, thus understating the amount of VAT payable. He wants to know if such an error will result in a penalty, and if so how much the penalty will be.

Aston understands that he is entitled to use the annual accounting scheme so that he would only have to submit one VAT return each year, but wants to know how using the scheme will otherwise affect him as regards the submission of VAT returns and the payment of VAT.

Required:

(a) **Explain from what date Aston Martyn's business was required to be registered for VAT.** **(3 marks)**

(b) **State the FOUR additional pieces of information that Aston Martyn will have to show on his new sales invoices in order for them to be valid for VAT purposes.** **(2 marks)**

(c) **Explain when and how Aston Martyn should account for VAT in respect of the supplies of services he receives from VAT registered businesses situated elsewhere within the European Union.** **(2 marks)**

(d) **Assuming that Aston Martyn incorrectly treats a standard rated supply as zero-rated with the result that the amount of VAT payable is understated, advise him as to the maximum amount of penalty that is likely to be charged by HM Revenue and Customs, and by how much this penalty would be reduced as a result of a subsequent unprompted disclosure.** **(3 marks)**

(e) **(i)** **If Aston Martyn does not use the annual accounting scheme, advise him as to how and when he will have to submit his quarterly VAT returns and pay the related VAT;** **(2 marks)**

(ii) **If Aston Martyn uses the annual accounting scheme, advise him as to when he will have to pay VAT and submit his annual VAT return.** **(3 marks)**

(Total: 15 marks)

Section 2

ANSWERS TO PRACTICE QUESTIONS

INCOME TAX AND NATIONAL INSURANCE

INCOME TAX BASICS AND EMPLOYMENT INCOME

1 SALLY AND SANDRA BURTON (ADAPTED)  *Online question assistance*

Key answer tips

This question requires two income tax computations for taxpayers entitled to a personal age allowance. However, due to the level of income, abatement of the allowance is necessary.

One sister is employed, the other self-employed, allowing the examiner to test a wide range of the personal tax syllabus.

Always watch out for exempt income and consider whether income is received gross or net.

(a) **Sally Burton**

Income tax computation – 2013/14

	Total	*Other income*	*Savings income*
	£	£	£
Salary	19,000		
Car benefit (W1)	3,402		
Living accommodation (W2)	2,532		
	———		
Employment income	24,934	24,934	
NS&I Savings Certificate interest	Exempt		
Building society interest (£1,800 × 100/80)	2,250		2,250
	———	———	———
Total income	27,184	24,934	2,250
Less: PAA (W3)	(9,958)	(9,958)	
	———	———	———
Taxable income	17,226	14,976	2,250
	———	———	———

Income tax

£			£
14,976	× 20%	(Other income)	2,995
2,250	× 20%	(Savings income)	450
17,226			

	£
Income tax liability	3,445
Less: Tax suffered at source	
PAYE	(2,400)
Building society interest (£2,250 × 20%)	(450)
Income tax payable	595

(b) **Sandra Burton**

Income tax computation – 2013/14

	Total	*Other income*	*Savings income*	*Dividend income*
	£	£	£	£
Trading income (W4)	24,273	24,273		
NS&I Investment account interest (received gross)	895		895	
Dividends (£1,080 × 100/90)	1,200			1,200
Total income	26,368	24,273	895	1,200
Less: PAA (W3)	(10,526)	(10,526)		
Taxable income	15,842	13,747	895	1,200

Income tax

£			£
13,747	× 20%	(Other income)	2,749
895	× 20%	(Savings income)	179
1,200	× 10%	(Dividend income)	120
15,842			

	£
Income tax liability	3,048
Less: Tax credit	
Dividends (£1,200 × 10%)	(120)
Income tax payable	2,928

Tutorial note

NS&I Savings Certificate income is exempt from income tax.

NS&I Investment account interest is taxable and received gross

Workings

(W1) **Car benefit**

CO_2 emissions = 177 g/km (rounded down to 175), available for 10 months

	%
Petrol	11
Plus: (175 – 95) × 1/5	16
Appropriate percentage	27

	£
List price of car	17,118
Less: Capital contributions	(2,000)
	15,118
Car benefit (£15,118 × 27% × 10/12)	3,402

Tutorial note

The maintenance costs are ignored as they are covered in the car benefit percentage. The car parking cost is an exempt benefit

(W2) **Living accommodation**

	£
Annual value	1,632
Additional benefit for expensive accommodation (£120,000 (Note) – £75,000) × 4%	1,800
	3,432
Less: Contributions to employer (£75 × 12 months)	(900)
	2,532

Tutorial note

The property was bought in 2005, which is more than 6 years before it was made available to Sally. Therefore in the calculation of the additional benefit, the cost must be replaced with the market value of the accommodation when the property was first made available.

(W3) **Personal age allowance**

	£		£
Sally			
PAA (born between 6.4.1938 and 5.4.1948)			10,500
Less: Abatement			
Total income	27,184		
Income limit	(26,100)		
Excess	1,084	× 50%	(542)
Reduced PAA			9,958
Sandra			
PAA (born before 6.4.1938)			10,660
Less: Abatement			
Total income	26,368		
Income limit	(26,100)		
Excess	268	× 50%	(134)
Reduced PAA			10,526

(W4) **Computation of tax adjusted trading profit**

	£
Net profit as per accounts	18,000
Add: Depreciation	2,425
Motor expenses (£5,400 × 4,000/12,000)	1,800
Private accommodation (£9,600 × 1/3)	3,200
Adjusted trading profit	25,425
Less: Capital allowances (W5)	(1,152)
Tax adjusted trading profit	24,273

(W5) **Capital allowances**

	Private use car	*Business use*	*Allowances*
	£		£
TWDV b/f	9,600		
Less: WDA (18%)	(1,728)	× (8,000/12,000)	1,152
TWDV c/f	7,872		

Key answer tips

A full blown capital allowances computation is given in the workings to this answer to show how the allowances are calculated. However, where there are not many transactions it is perfectly acceptable to do one or two lines and just calculate the allowances available on each asset acquired rather than a full computation. If you do this however, be careful and make sure you explain your calculations clearly.

2 VIGOROUS PLC (ADAPTED)

Key answer tips

This question required the calculation of three benefit packages for three P11D (i.e. higher paid) employees. All of the key benefits that you need to be able to deal with in the F6 examination appear in this question!

Easy marks were available in parts (a) and (c) for explaining the term P11D and how benefits are assessed.

However, careful calculation is required for the benefits as there are many places where calculations can go wrong. Remember to time apportion the calculation where the benefit is not available all year, and don't forget to deduct any employee contributions paid.

(a) **P11D employees**

- Employees earning at a rate of £8,500 p.a. a year or more, and most directors (irrespective of earnings), are P11D employees.
- Benefits must be included when calculating the figure of £8,500, and these are calculated as if they were received by a P11D employee.
- Full-time working directors are excluded if they earn less than £8,500 p.a. and do not own more than 5% of their company's ordinary share capital.

(b) **Assessable benefits – 2013/14**

Andrea Lean

	£
Car benefit (W1)	4,990
Fuel benefit (W1)	7,385
Living accommodation	
– Annual value	7,000
– Additional benefit (W2)	2,760
– Furniture (£6,000 at 20%)	1,200
Mobile telephone	Nil

Tutorial note

1. *The living accommodation cost in excess of £75,000 so there will be an additional benefit.*

   Since the property was purchased within six years of first being provided, the benefit is based on the cost of the property plus improvements prior to 6 April 2013 (see W2).

2. *The annual running costs are personally borne by Andrea and therefore are not included as a benefit. Had her employer paid the costs, a £4,000 benefit would arise which she would have reduced to £Nil if she reimbursed the company directly.*

3. *The provision of one mobile telephone does not give rise to a taxable benefit, even if there is private use.*

Workings

(W1) **Car and fuel benefits**

CO_2 emissions = 260 g/km, available all year

	%	
Petrol	11	
Plus: (255 – 95) × $^1/_5$	32	
Appropriate percentage	43	Restricted to 35%

	£
Car benefit (£19,400 × 35%)	6,790
Less: Contributions (£150 × 12)	(1,800)
	4,990
Fuel benefit (£21,100 × 35%)	7,385

(W2) **Additional benefit for expensive accommodation**

	£	
Cost of property (January 2009)	130,000	
Improvements before 6 April 2013	14,000	
	144,000	
Less: Limit	(75,000)	
	69,000	
Additional benefit	× 4%	£2,760

Tutorial note

Improvements in May 2013 are not taken into account in calculating the benefit for 2013/14, as only improvements up to the start of the tax year are included.

However, they will be taken into account next year in calculating the benefit for 2014/15.

Ben Slim

	£
Beneficial loan (W1)	3,300
Relocation costs (£9,300 – £8,000) (Note 1)	1,300
Car benefit (W2) – Car 1 (Note 2)	230
Car benefit (W3) – Car 2	1,008
Childcare vouchers ((£60 – £28) × 36) (Note 4)	1,152

Tutorial note

1 *Only £8,000 of relocation costs is exempt.*

2 *A reduced percentage of 10% applies to petrol cars with CO_2 emissions between 76 – 94 g/km. If it had been a diesel car, the percentage would be 13%.*

If the car had CO_2 emissions of less than 76 g/km, the percentage would have been 5% (8% if diesel).

3 *There is no fuel benefit as Ben reimburses the company for the full cost of private diesel.*

4 *For a higher rate taxpayer the payment of up to £28 per week for approved childcare is an exempt benefit.*

Workings

(W1) **Beneficial loan**

Average method	£	
Loan at start of year	120,000	
Loan at end of year	100,000	
	220,000	
Average loan (£220,000 ÷ 2)	110,000	
Assessable benefit (£110,000 × 4% × 9/12)		£3,300
Precise method		
(£120,000 × 4% × 5/12)	2,000	
(£100,000 × 4% × 4/12)	1,333	
		£3,333

Ben will not elect for the precise method and in view of the small difference it is unlikely that HMRC will make the election so the benefit will therefore be £3,300.

(W2) **Car benefit – Car 1**

CO_2 emissions = 90 g/km, available 3 months

Appropriate rate = 10% (petrol car with CO_2 emissions between 76 – 94 g/km)

Car benefit = (£9,200 × 10% × 3/12) = £230

(W3) **Car benefit – Car 2**

CO_2 emissions = 119 g/km (rounded down to 115 g/km), available 6 months

	%
Diesel	14
Plus: (115 – 95) × 1/5	4
Appropriate percentage	18
Car benefit (£11,200 × 18% × 6/12)	£1,008

Chai Trim

	£
Van benefit (£3,000 × 10/12) (Note 1)	2,500
Fuel benefit (£564 × 10/12) (Note 2)	470
Television (W)	330
Health club membership (Note 3)	150
Computer (£1,900 × 20% × 3/12) (Note 4)	95

Tutorial note

1 *The van was only available for ten months of 2013/14 so the fixed annual £3,000 benefit is time apportioned.*

2 *Private fuel for the van was provided for ten months of 2013/14 so the benefit is time apportioned.*

3 *In-house benefits are valued according to the marginal cost. The taxable benefit in relation to the health club membership is therefore the direct costs of £150.*

4 *The computer was only available for 3 months of 2013/14 so the benefit is time apportioned.*

Working: Benefit for the sale of the television

Greater of

		£	£
(i)	MV at date of transfer	250	
	Less: Amount paid	(150)	
			100
(ii)	Original cost	800	
	Less: Annual value for 2011/12 and 2012/13 (20% × £800 × 2 years)	(320)	
		480	
	Less: Amount paid	(150)	
			330

(c) **Income tax liability in respect of assessable benefits**

- The income tax on recurring benefits, such as company motor cars, will normally be collected through the PAYE system by a reduction in the employee's tax coding.
- Tax not collected on this basis will be due under the self-assessment system.
- However, tax of less than £3,000 can be collected by an adjustment to an employee's tax coding for a subsequent tax year, whilst tax on minor benefits may be paid under an employer's PAYE settlement agreement.

3 ALI PATEL (ADAPTED) 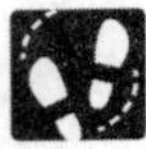 *Walk in the footsteps of a top tutor*

Key answer tips

A common style question requiring the comparison of two remuneration packages and the impact on the income tax computation and national insurance liabilities.

Part (b) requires a decision to be made based on the net cash flow position after taking account of all costs including income tax and national insurance.

Tutor's top tips

Part (a) of this question involves some fairly straightforward income tax computations.

Don't forget that there will be no car benefit if Ali uses his own car for business purposes!

You also need to calculate Class 1 NICs. Remember that for the employee, only cash earnings are subject to national insurance.

(a) **Income tax and Class 1 NICs**

(i) **First remuneration package**

Ali's income tax liability – 2013/14

	£
Salary (£29,000 + (£500 × 12))	35,000
Mileage allowance (W)	496
Employment income	35,496
Less: Personal allowance	(9,440)
Taxable income	26,056
Income tax liability (£26,056 × 20%)	5,211
Class 1 primary NIC – 2013/14	
(£35,000 – £7,755) × 12%	3,269

Working: Mileage allowance

The relocation is not expected to last for more than 24 months, so the branch office will be treated as a temporary workplace.

Mileage for the year = (1,600 × 12) = 19,200 miles

Ali will therefore be taxed on the mileage allowance paid by Box plc as follows:

	£	£
Mileage allowance received (19,200 at 38p)		7,296
Authorised mileage allowance:		
10,000 miles at 45p	4,500	
9,200 miles at 25p	2,300	
		(6,800)
Taxable benefit		496

Tutorial note

For NIC purposes only the excess mileage allowance above 45p per mile is subject to NIC. As Ali will be paid 38p per mile, none of the mileage allowance is charged to NIC.

(ii) **Second remuneration package**

Ali's income tax liability – 2013/14

	£
Salary	29,000
Living accommodation (W)	9,600
Property business profit	6,000
Total income	44,600
Less: Personal allowance	(9,440)
Taxable income	35,160

Income tax	
£	
32,010 at 20%	6,402
3,150 at 40%	1,260
35,160	
Income tax liability	7,662

Class 1 primary NIC – 2013/14	
(£29,000 – £7,755) × 12%	2,549

Working: Living accommodation

The benefit of living accommodation will be the greater of:

(i)	Annual value	£4,600
(ii)	Rent paid by the employer (£800 × 12)	£9,600

(b) **Most beneficial remuneration package**

Tutor's top tips

When calculating the net disposable income think just in terms of cash and identify all cash coming in and all cash payments going out. Cash payments obviously include the tax liabilities calculated in part (a), but also include other expenses such as commuting costs.

Even if you made some mistakes in part (a), as long as you include your tax figures here in this part you will be awarded full marks.

The question specifically asks you to advise Ali as to which remuneration package is most beneficial, so make sure that you do this. A statement of which package should be accepted is therefore needed.

You will be given full marks here if your advice is consistent with your analysis, even if it is the wrong advice!

	Package (1)	*Package (2)*
	£	£
Salary	35,000	29,000
Property business income	Nil	6,000
Mileage allowance received	7,296	Nil
Commuting costs	(1,800)	Nil
Class 1 NIC	(3,269)	(2,549)
Income tax	(5,211)	(7,662)
Net disposable income	32,016	24,789

If he chooses the first remuneration package, Ali will be £7,227 (£32,016 – £24,789) better off.

4 PETER CHIC (ADAPTED)  *Walk in the footsteps of a top tutor*

Key answer tips

A classic individual income tax computation, covering several aspects of employment income, together with a small element covering other types of income.

Initially, due to the amount of information given in the scenario, this question looks very daunting. However, there was nothing that should have caused significant problems.

The child benefit element of this question has been added as these rules were introduced after the question was set.

Tutor's top tips

Part (a) of this question was straight forward if approached logically. Remember to run down each line of the question in turn and consider the implications of each piece of information. Remember not to get held up on any one calculation.

Always ensure that you read the question carefully. The requirement is to calculate income tax payable. Ensure you do not drop easy marks by only calculating the income tax liability.

Make the marker your friend, if you keep your calculations clear and easy to read you will score much higher marks. Always ensure your workings are clearly labelled.

(a) **Peter**

Income tax computation – 2013/14

	Total income	*Other income*	*Savings income*	*Dividend income*
	£	£	£	£
Employment income (W1)	131,775	131,775		
Property income (W4)	13,660	13,660		
Building society interest				
(£4,760 x 100/80)	5,950		5,950	
Dividends (£2,700 × 100/90)	3,000			3,000
Premium bond prize	Exempt			
Total income	154,385	145,435	5,950	3,000
Less: Adjusted PA (W5)	(Nil)	(Nil)		
Taxable income	154,385	145,435	5,950	3,000

	£		£
Income tax:			
Other income – Basic rate (W6)	34,935	× 20%	6,987
Other income – Higher rate	110,500	× 40%	44,200
	145,435		
Savings income – Higher rate	5,950	× 40%	2,380
Dividends – Higher rate	1,540	× 32.5%	500
	152,925		
Dividends – Additional rate	1,460	× 37.5%	547
	154,385		
Add: child benefit charge (W7)			1,056
Income tax liability			55,670
Less: Tax deducted at source			
Dividends (£3,000 × 10%)			(300)
Building society interest (£5,950 × 20%)			(1,190)
PAYE			(42,000)
Income tax payable			12,180

Tutorial note

The premium bond prize is exempt from income tax.

Workings

(W1) **Employment income**

	£	£
Salary		75,600
Bonus – Paid 30 April 2013 (Note 1)		14,300
Bonus – Paid 31 March 2014 (Note 1)		13,700
		103,600
Assessable benefits:		
Car Benefit (W2)	7,175	
Fuel Benefit (W2)	7,385	
Living accommodation		
– Annual value	9,645	
– Additional benefit (W3)	3,920	
Mobile phone (£250 × 20%) (Note 2)	50	
Overnight allowance (Note 3)	Nil	
		28,175
Employment income		131,775

Tutorial note

1 *Entitlement to, and the payment of, both bonuses occurred in 2013/14, therefore both amounts are assessable in that tax year.*

2 *The exemption for mobile telephones does not apply to the second telephone. The normal 20% use of assets benefit applies.*

3 *Payments for private incidental expenses are exempt up to £10 per night when spent outside the UK.*

(W2) **Car and fuel benefit**

CO_2 emissions = 212 g/km (rounded down to 210 g/km), available all year

	%	
Diesel	14	
Plus: (210 – 95) × $^1/_5$	23	
Appropriate percentage	37	Restricted to 35%

	£	£
List price	22,500	
Less: Capital contribution	(2,000)	
	20,500	
Car benefit (£20,500 × 35%)		7,175
Fuel benefit (£21,100 × 35%)		7,385

(W3) **Living accommodation – Additional benefit**

The living accommodation cost is in excess of £75,000 so there will be an additional benefit.

Since the property was not purchased more than six years before first being provided to Peter, the benefit is based on the cost of the property plus subsequent improvements.

The additional benefit is therefore:

(£160,000 + £13,000 – £75,000) × 4% = £3,920

(W4) **Property income**

	£	£
Income		
Rent receivable – Property 1 (£500 × 5)		2,500
– Property 2 (£2,820 × 8)		22,560
		25,060
Allowable expenses		
Irrecoverable rent (£500 × 2) (Note 1)	1,000	
Repairs	600	
Advertising	875	
Loan interest	7,800	
Insurance ((£660 x 3/12) + (£1,080 × 9/12))	975	
Wear and tear allowance (Note 2)		
(£2,500 – £1,000) × 10%	150	
		(11,400)
Property business profit		13,660

Tutorial note

1 All rents accrued must be included in the computation. However, where all attempts have been made to collect the rent from the tenant, but it is not recoverable, relief is available by deducting the irrecoverable amount as an allowable deduction.

2 The wear and tear allowance can only be claimed in respect of the first property since the second property is not let out furnished.

The wear and tear allowance on Property 1 is based on the rents actually received of £1,500 (£2,500 rents receivable – £1,000 irrecoverable debts).

*Note that on the subject of the calculation of the wear and tear allowance, HMRC manuals refer to "net rents" as the start position and this has been interpreted to mean "rents receivable **after** irrecoverable debts have been deducted".*

However, credit was also given in the exam if the allowance was calculated based on the rents receivable without a deduction for irrecoverable debts.

(W5) **Adjusted Personal Allowance**

	£
Total income = Net income	154,385
Less: Gross Gift Aid donation (£2,340 x 100/80)	(2,925)
Adjusted net income (ANI)	151,460

As ANI is above £118,880, the personal allowance is reduced to £Nil.

(W6) **Extension of basic and additional rate band**

	Basic rate	*Additional rate*
	£	£
Basic rate band threshold	32,010	150,000
Plus: Gross Gift Aid donation (as above)	2,925	2,925
Extended basic and additional rate bands	34,935	152,925

(W7) **Child benefit tax charge**

Tutor's top tips

The child benefit tax charge is a new rule in FA13 and is therefore very topical. It is important that you can identify the situation where this charge may apply, and that you know how to calculate the tax charge.

Remember that it is adjusted net income (ANI) which is compared with the limits provided in the tax tables, so you must adjust net income for any gift aid donations or personal pension contributions. The charge will be the full amount of the child benefit if the ANI exceeds £60,000, but will be based on a percentage of the benefit where the ANI is between £50,000 and £60,000. The percentage and the tax charge itself will always be rounded down.

	£	£
Child benefit received		1,056
Adjusted net income (W5 above)	151,460	
Since Peter's ANI exceeds £60,000, the child benefit charge will be the full child benefit received		1,056

(b) **National Insurance Contributions**

Tutor's top tips

Part (b) required a little care. As long as you remember that NIC is payable on cash earnings only by the employee, and that the employer pays NICs on both the cash earnings (Class 1 secondary) and assessable benefits (Class 1A), then there should not be too many problems.

Note that it does not matter if you have calculated the employment income incorrectly in part (a) as long as you calculate the NIC correctly on whatever figure you have, you will still score maximum marks on this part.

Payable by Peter

	£
(£41,450 – £7,755) × 12%	4,043
(£103,600 – £41,450) × 2%	1,243
Class 1 Primary NICs	5,286

Payable by Haute-Couture Ltd

	£
Class 1 Secondary NIC	
(£103,600 – £7,696) × 13.8%	13,235
Class 1A NICs	
(£28,175 (part (a) (W1)) × 13.8%)	3,888
	17,123

Examiner's report

This question was very well answered by the majority of candidates.

In part (a) a few candidates did not appreciate that both bonuses were to be treated as earnings, whilst the basis of assessing the second mobile telephone was not always known. Some candidates deducted the Gift Aid donation rather than extending the basic rate tax band.

In part (b) the most common mistake was to include taxable benefits when calculating Class 1 National Insurance contributions.

ACCA marking scheme		
		Marks
(a)	Salary	0.5
	Bonus payments	1.0
	Car benefit – Relevant percentage	1.0
	– Capital contribution	0.5
	– Calculation	0.5
	Fuel benefit	1.0
	Living accommodation – Annual value	1.0
	– Additional benefit	2.0
	Mobile telephone	1.0
	Overseas allowance	0.5
	Property business profit – Rent receivable	1.0
	– Impairment losses	0.5
	– Repairs	0.5
	– Advertising	0.5
	– Loan interest	1.0
	– Insurance	1.0
	– Wear and tear allowance	1.0
	Building society interest	0.5
	Dividends	0.5
	Premium bond prize	0.5
	Personal allowance	0.5
	Extension of basic rate and additional rate band	1.0
	Income tax	1.5
	Child benefit charge	0.5
	Tax suffered at source	1.5
		21.0
(b)	Employee Class 1 NIC	1.5
	Employer Class 1 NIC	1.5
	Employer Class 1A NIC	1.0
		4.0
Total		25.0

5 JOE JONES (ADAPTED)  *Walk in the footsteps of a top tutor*

Key answer tips

This question covered various aspects of employment income in quite a high level of detail. It is important to be familiar with both how to calculate taxable benefits and which benefits are exempt.

There were many aspects of part (a) which should not have caused concern and on which easy marks could be obtained. However, some aspects were more peripheral to the syllabus and some students may not have been confident in the treatment of some of the benefits.

Part (b) covered administration in relation to certain PAYE forms in some detail, which was quite demanding and this area is difficult to answer if the rules have not been learnt. There were still some easy marks for common sense comments here though, and all students should be familiar with the contents of a P11D form. This part of the question has been added to following the introduction of PAYE real time reporting, and now tests the new rules.

(a) **Taxable income – 2013/14**

Tutor's top tips

Remember to read the requirement carefully. You have not been asked to calculate the income tax payable, only the taxable income - do not go further than you have been asked to do as there are no additional marks available.

Although the majority of marks in this question come from part (a), don't overrun on time and lose the ability to score some easy marks on part (b).

There are some aspects of this part about which you may not be confident, but it is important to make a quick decision and move on. You can't afford to waste time debating whether a benefit is taxable and miss out on marks elsewhere. You should just make an assumption, state it and then forget about it! Remember if you make a mistake you will still get follow through marks for the remainder of your answer.

There is a degree of flexibility over the presentation of the answer, as there is no strict order for the calculation of the employment income and some of the workings could be done on the face of the computation or in a separate referenced working. Whichever way you present your answer you should ensure that all the figures are clearly labelled and all your workings are clear, wherever they appear. It is important not to cram in a working on the face of the computation if it will make it hard to read. Workings enable the marker to give you credit for your thought process even if your final answer is wrong.

You also need to be careful when thinking about the personal allowance as Joe has income in excess of £100,000. You need to consider the adjusted net income and compare it with the income limit for the reduction of the personal allowance.

	£
Employment income – Firstly plc	
Salary (£11,400 × 9)	102,600
Bonus (Note 1)	Nil
Less: Pension contributions (£102,600 × 6%) (Note 2)	(6,156)
	96,444
Beneficial loan (W1)	2,367
Workplace nursery (Note 3)	Nil
Gym membership (Note 4)	1,050
Home entertainment system – use (W2)	660
Home entertainment system – gift (W3) (Note 5)	3,860
Employment income – Secondly plc	
Salary (£15,200 × 3)	45,600
Living accommodation (W4) (Note 6)	6,750
Childcare vouchers (W5)	585
Company gym (Note 7)	Nil
Mobile telephone (Note 8)	Nil
	157,316
Less: PA (W6)	Nil
Taxable income	157,316

Workings

(W1) Beneficial loan

	£	£
Average method		
Loan when first made available	120,000	
Loan balance before end of loan	70,000	
	190,000	
Average loan (£190,000 ÷ 2)	95,000	
Assessable benefit (£95,000 × 4% × 8/12)		2,533
Precise method		
(£120,000 × 4% × 3/12)	1,200	
(£70,000 × 4% × 5/12)	1,167	
		2,367

Joe will elect for the precise method and the benefit will therefore be £2,367.

(W2) Home entertainment system – use

Benefit = 20% × M.V. of asset when it is first made available to the employee, time apportioned for the short period:

£4,400 × 20% × 9/12 = £660

(W3) Home entertainment system – gift

Greater of:

		£
(i)	MV at date of transfer	3,860
(ii)	Original cost	4,400
	Less: Annual value for 2013/14 for use of asset	(660)
		3,740

(W4) Living accommodation

Greater of:

	£
Annual value (£10,400 × 3/12)	2,600
Rent paid by employer (£2,250 × 3)	6,750

(W5) Childcare vouchers

The first £25 per week of childcare vouchers are exempt for additional rate taxpayers, therefore the taxable amount is the excess above this amount:

(£70 – £25) × 13 = £585

(W6) **Personal allowance**

As Joe's income exceeds £100,000, it is necessary to calculate adjusted net income (ANI) and compare this with the income limit for the reduction of the personal allowance.

	£
Net income	157,316
Less: Personal pension contributions	(3,000)
ANI	154,316
Less: Income limit	(100,000)
Excess	54,316

As the ANI exceeds the income limit by more than twice the personal allowance, it will be reduced to nil.

Tutorial notes

1 *Salaries and bonuses are taxable on the earlier of the date of receipt and the date the employee becomes entitled to the payment. The £12,000 bonus was therefore taxable in 2012/13 as Joe became entitled to it on 22 March 2013.*

2 *Occupational pension contributions are deducted from the salary in calculating taxable employment income. Personal pension contributions extend the basic and higher rate bands when calculating the tax liability (see below) and are deducted in the calculation of ANI when calculating the reduction of the personal allowance as in working 6 above.*

3 *The provision of a place in a nursery based at the workplace is exempt.*

4 *All benefits for which there is no specific rule to calculate the benefit will be taxable based on the cost to the employer. Therefore the taxable benefit in respect of the gym membership is simply £1,050.*

5 *When an employee has use of an asset followed by an outright gift of the asset, it is possible (although unusual) to be taxed on a higher total amount than original cost of the asset, as is the case here.*

6 *Unless indicated otherwise, always assume accommodation is not job related. When property is rented by the employer the assessable benefit is the higher of the annual value and the rent paid by the employer, there is no expensive accommodation charge.*

7 *The use of a company gym is exempt provided that it is available for use by all employees and it is not available to the general public.*

8 *The provision of one mobile telephone is exempt even if the employer pays for private calls.*

9 *Although you were not asked to calculate the income tax liability, you may find it good practice to attempt the calculation as Joe is an additional rate taxpayer and has made personal pension contributions. You need to remember that the basic rate and higher rate bands will be extended by the gross personal pension contributions, therefore the basic rate band will be £35,010 (£32,010 + £3,000) and the upper limit of the higher rate band will be £153,000 (150,000 + £3,000).*

The calculation should therefore be as follows:

	£
£35,010 × 20%	*7,002*
£117,990 × 40%	*47,196*
£4,316 × 45%	*1,942*
Income tax liability	*56,140*

(b) (i) **PAYE forms**

Tutor's top tips

Part (b)(i) tests some of the rules regarding the PAYE system in quite a lot of detail. If you don't know these rules many parts of this question will be hard to answer, and there is no point wasting time dwelling on something you simply don't know!

It is likely that you at least know the circumstances in which someone is given a P45 however, and you should certainly know what form P11D is used to report. You can also probably make a sensible guess at who is supposed to provide these forms, and you may be able to state something about what should be included on them. If you don't know the dates the forms should be provided then you have little hope at guessing them.

Form P45

- Form P45 should be completed by Firstly plc when Joe leaves the company's employment. It will show his taxable earnings, income tax deducted in the tax year, and his tax code at the date of leaving.
- Firstly plc should have provided this form to Joe immediately after he left employment with the company.

Form P60

- Form P60 is a year-end summary which should be prepared by Secondly plc. It will show Secondly plc's name and address, Joe's taxable earnings for the year, income tax and NICs deducted, and his final PAYE code.
- Secondly plc should have provided this form to Joe by 31 May 2014.

Form P11D

- A form P11D should have been prepared by both Firstly plc and Secondly plc, including details of the cash equivalents of the benefits provided to Joe.
- Both companies should have provided a form to Joe by 6 July 2014.

(ii) **Real time reporting**

Tutor's top tips

Part (b)(ii) tests the administration of PAYE for an employer. Although the term is not mentioned in the question, you should recognise that the system being tested is real time reporting, A basic awareness of the system should achieve the mark for the monthly reporting, however, the second mark cannot be achieved unless you have learnt the date for the final submission of the year.

- Secondly plc must submit income tax and NIC information to HMRC electronically when or before Joe is paid each month.
- A year end summary of all the tax and NICs deducted must be submitted to HMRC by 19 May 2014.

Examiner's report

Part (a) of this question was reasonably well answered, but **part (b)** caused problems for virtually all candidates.

In **part (a)** there were no areas that consistently caused difficulty, although a surprising number of candidates did not appreciate that a bonus would have been assessed in the previous tax year as the taxpayer was entitled to it in that year.

When calculating the beneficial loan using the average method, many candidates used a nil figure rather than the balance at the date of repayment.

Candidates should try not to repeat their answers. For example, exempt benefits were often shown as such in the computation of taxable income, but were then shown again in subsequent notes. There is no need to do this.

It was surprising in part (b) that very few candidates knew much about the PAYE forms. This just seems to be an area of the syllabus that was not revised. A bit of common sense together with the knowledge that form P45 is given when employment ceases, form P60 is given at the end of the tax year, and form P11D is in respect of the benefits provided to a taxpayer, would have meant that most of the marks were easily obtainable.

ACCA marking scheme

			Marks
(a)	Salary – Firstly plc		0.5
	Bonus		0.5
	Occupational pension scheme contributions		1.0
	Beneficial loan – average method		1.5
	Beneficial loan – strict method		1.5
	Workplace nursery		1.0
	Gym membership		0.5
	Home entertainment system – use		1.5
	Home entertainment system – gift		1.5
	Salary – Secondly plc		0.5
	Living accommodation		2.0
	Childcare vouchers		1.0
	Company gym		0.5
	Mobile telephone		0.5
	Personal pension contributions – deducted from ANI		0.5
	Personal allowance		2.5
			17.0
(b)	(i)	**Form P45**	
		By Firstly plc when employment ceases	0.5
		Details	1.0
		Date provided	0.5
		Form P60	
		By Secondly plc at end of tax year	0.5
		Details	1.0
		Date provided	0.5
		Form P11D	
		Both employers	0.5
		Details	1.0
		Date provided	0.5
			6.0
	(ii)	Monthly real time reporting	1.0
		Deadline for end of year summary	1.0
			2.0
Total			25.0

6 SAMMI SMITH (ADAPTED)  *Walk in the footsteps of a top tutor*

Key answer tips

This was a very unusual style of question for the F6 exam, which would probably challenge many students. However, we can expect more questions like this in the future.

The question required the comparison of two remuneration options, and consideration of the tax consequences from both the employee and the employer's perspective.

It therefore required four separate calculations (each option from each party's perspective), covering income tax, corporation tax and NICs.

The requirements here were very clear and easy marks could be gained from some very basic tax calculations, provided students were not scared off by the style of the question.

The final part of the question, which required the calculation of "after tax net costs" of either option, may have thrown some students. It is helpful to sit back and think through all the tax and other cash consequences of both options before attempting to answer this part.

Tutor's top tips

The key when you are challenged by a style of question you have not seen before is not to panic!

The F6 examiner will often lead you through the more challenging questions through the order of the requirements and in guidance within the requirements themselves. That is the case here, and if you consider the requirements carefully and work through them systematically you will find that the tax calculations themselves are actually very straightforward and it is possible to score very highly on parts (a) and (b).

A comparison of the choices of the provision of a car or remuneration to fund a car is a classic exam scenario. Bear in mind that you already know how to calculate the taxable benefit on a car, you know how to tax employee remuneration and you know the tax consequences for a company of providing a car to an employee or of paying an employee. This question simply combines those calculations.

Ensure that you use clear headings, showing which calculation you are doing, so that the marker can more easily give you credit.

Part (c) may cause more difficulty as it is unfamiliar, but again not technically demanding. Ensure you pick up your figures from parts (a) and (b) as well as any other costs mentioned in the question.

(a) **Sammi Smith – Company car**

CO_2 emissions = 310 g/km, available all year

	%
Petrol	11
Plus: (310 – 95) × 1/5	43
Appropriate percentage	54
Percentage restricted to	35
	£
List price of car	81,858
Car benefit (£81,858 × 35%)	28,650
Income tax at marginal rate (£28,650 × 40%)	11,460

There are no NIC implications for an employee in receipt of a benefit.

Sammi Smith – Additional remuneration

	£
Income tax at marginal rate (£26,000 × 40%)	10,400
NICs at marginal rate (£26,000 × 2%)	520
Total tax cost	10,920

Tutorial notes

1 *The maximum amount for the car benefit percentage (35%) is not listed in the tax tables and must be learnt.*

2 *The list price of the car is £81,858 and this is used to calculate the car benefit.*

3 *There is no fuel benefit to calculate here as Sammi has not been provided with any private fuel.*

4 *It is not necessary to do a full income tax computation in order to calculate the income tax implications of either option. Instead you need to establish Sammi's marginal rate of tax, which is the rate at which additional income will be taxed. As Sammi already receives director's remuneration in excess of £45,000, she is already a higher rate taxpayer, and neither option will take her near the threshold for the reduction in the PA or for tax at the additional rate. Therefore her marginal rate of income tax is 40%.*

5 *Benefits are not subject to NICs for the employee unless they are readily convertible into cash (in which case they form part of earnings and are subject to Class 1 NICs).*

6 *Sammi's marginal rate for NICs can be established in the same way as for income tax. As Sammi's remuneration is in excess of £45,000 she has already exceeded the upper earnings limit and any further income will be taxable at 2%.*

(b) **Smark Ltd – Company car**

Tutor's top tips

This part is slightly more challenging than the previous part as the NICs payable by the company have an impact on the corporation tax payable. It is therefore important that you calculate the NICs before the corporation tax in both cases.

You should also be careful when considering whether all of the lease costs are an allowable deduction for corporation tax purposes.

	£
Annual lease cost	26,540
Disallowance – high emission car (£26,540 × 15%)	(3,981)
	22,559
Class 1A NICs payable (£28,650 × 13.8%)	3,954
Total tax allowable costs	26,513
Corporation tax reduction (£26,513 × 23%)	6,098

Smark Ltd – Additional remuneration

	£
Additional remuneration	26,000
Class 1 secondary NICs (£26,000 × 13.8%)	3,588
Total costs	29,588
Corporation tax reduction (£29,588 × 23%)	6,805

Tutorial notes

1 *Cars with CO_2 emissions in excess of 130 g/km are considered 'high emission' cars and 15% of the lease cost will be disallowed.*

2 *Class 1A NICs are payable on the taxable benefit. You therefore need to use the figure you have calculated in part (a).*

3 *Once you have calculated the relevant allowable costs for tax purposes (including the Class 1A NICs) you can calculate the reduction in the corporation tax liability at the company's marginal rate, which is 23% as you are told in the question that the company pays tax at the main rate.*

(c) **Most beneficial choice for Sammi Smith**

Tutor's top tips

This is the part of the question you may find most difficult, as rather than involving a tax calculation, you need to pull together the tax figures you have already calculated as well as the costs per the question to recommend which option Sammi and Smark Ltd will prefer.

You need to remember to include all the relevant costs in your calculations – the cost of providing the car or the remuneration, the IT costs, the NIC costs (for both Sammi and Smark Ltd) and the CT saving.

If you have made an error in your calculations earlier in the question, you will still get follow through marks provided you use your own figures correctly in this part.

- If Sammi is provided with a company car the only cost will be the additional income tax of £11,460.
- If Sammi chooses the director's remuneration the net after tax cost will be:

	£
Cost of leasing car	26,540
Additional tax cost	10,920
Additional remuneration	(26,000)
Net after tax cost	11,460

- The net costs are exactly the same; it therefore shouldn't matter to Sammi which option is chosen.

Most beneficial choice for Smark Ltd

- If Smark Ltd provide Sammi with a company car, the net after tax cost will be:

	£
Cost of leasing car	26,540
Additional NIC cost	3,954
Corporation tax saving	(6,098)
Net after tax cost	24,396

- If Smark Ltd provide Sammi with additional director's remuneration, the net after tax cost will be:

	£
Remuneration cost	26,000
Additional NIC cost	3,588
Corporation tax saving	(6,805)
Net after tax cost	22,783

- Smark Ltd would therefore prefer to provide Sammi with additional remuneration, as this option costs less overall.

Examiner's report

This question was generally answered quite badly, with the main problem being that candidates simply did not spend enough time thinking and planning their answers, but just plunged straight in performing every calculation that they could think of.

In **part (a)** the answer was in fact very straightforward, with a fairly simple car benefit calculation and then income tax and NIC calculations at the director's marginal rates of 40% and 2% respectively.

Far too many candidates calculated a fuel benefit despite being told that fuel was not provided for private journeys.

In **part (b)** many candidates stated that capital allowances would be available despite the motor car being leased.

Candidates often stated that the company's corporation tax liability would be increased rather than reduced as a result of the additional expenditure, and very few candidates appreciated that NIC was a deductible expense.

Part (c) was more difficult, although credit was given for any sensible approach such as comparing the tax liabilities under each alternative.

ACCA marking scheme

		Marks
(a)	Company car	
	Car benefit	2.0
	Income tax	1.0
	NIC implications	0.5
	Additional director's remuneration	
	Income tax	0.5
	Class 1 NIC	1.0
		5.0
(b)	Company car	
	Class 1A NIC	1.0
	Allowable leasing costs	1.0
	Corporation tax saving	1.0
	Additional director's remuneration	
	Class 1 NIC	1.0
	Corporation tax saving	1.0
		5.0
(c)	Sammi	
	Director's remuneration – net cost	2.0
	Smark Ltd	
	Director's remuneration – net cost	1.0
	Company car – net costs	1.0
	Conclusion	1.0
		5.0
Total		15.0

7 PHILIP, CHARLES AND WILLIAM (ADAPTED)  *Walk in the footsteps of a top tutor*

Key answer tips

This question involved preparing three separate income tax computations which covered a broad spectrum of income tax topics, tested knowledge of NIC and some basic tax planning.

The requirements and mark allocation are very clear.

Although there is a wide coverage of the syllabus, all the topics are covered at a basic level and should therefore have been manageable.

The first individual is an elderly taxpayer eligible for the personal age allowance (PAA), but this needs abatement due to the level of his net income.

The second individual is a high earner requiring abatement to his standard personal allowance due to the level of his net income.

The third individual is an additional rate taxpayer with no personal allowance entitlement.

Tutor's top tips

For part (a) a systematic approach is needed, taking one individual at a time, and therefore breaking up the information given into smaller, manageable chunks.

As you read the question it is useful to highlight all the information you will need for the income tax computations, and then as you use this information tick each item, so you can easily check you have included everything.

Always ensure that you read the question carefully. The requirement is to calculate income tax liability. Therefore do not waste time calculating income tax payable as this will not gain you any additional marks.

Make the marker your friend, if you keep your calculations clear and easy to read you will score much higher marks. Always ensure your workings are clearly labelled.

(a) (i) **Philip Wind**

Income tax computation – 2013/14

	Total	*Other income*	*Savings income*
	£	£	£
Pensions	11,600	11,600	
Building society interest (£14,880 × 100/80)	18,600		18,600
Total income/net income	30,200	11,600	18,600
Less: PAA (W)	(8,610)	(8,610)	
Taxable income	21,590	2,990	18,600

Income tax		£
£		
2,990	at 20%	598
18,600	at 20%	3,720
21,590		
Income tax liability		4,318

Working: Personal age allowance

	£		£
PAA (born before 6.4.1938)			10,660
Less: Abatement			
Net income	30,200		
Less: Income limit	(26,100)		
Excess	4,100	× 50%	(2,050)
			8,610

Tutorial note

Other income (£2,990) exceeds £2,790, so the starting rate of 10% does not apply to the savings income.

Tutor's top tips

Whenever you are given the date of birth of a taxpayer you need to think why this may be relevant. The two areas where date of birth is relevant are the personal age allowance and NIC. Philip was born before 6 April 1938 so is entitled to the higher age allowance (subject to abatement for his income) and he is over retirement age so pays no NIC.

(ii) **Charles Wind**

Income tax computation – 2013/14

	£
Trading profit/total income/net income	109,400
Less: Adjusted PA (W1)	(5,140)
Taxable income	104,260

Income tax		
£		£
32,810	at 20% (W2)	6,562
71,450	at 40%	28,580
104,260		
Income tax liability		35,142

Workings

(W1) **Adjusted personal allowance**

	£		£
Personal allowance			9,440
Total income = net income	109,400		
Less: Gross Gift Aid	(800)		
ANI	108,600		
Less: Limit	(100,000)		
	8600	× 50%	(4,300)
Adjusted PA			5,140

Tutorial note

1 *Charitable donations under Gift Aid are grossed up before being used in the adjusted personal allowance computation and to extend the basic rate band. The gross figure is given in the question, therefore there is no need to gross up the figure given.*

2 *As the adjusted net income exceeds £100,000 the allowance is reduced by £1 for every £2 it exceeds the limit. Net income for these purposes is adjusted (i.e. reduced) for both gross Gift Aid and gross Personal Pension Contributions (PPCs) made in the year.*

(W2) **Extension of basic rate band**

	£
Basic rate band threshold	32,010
Plus: Gross Gift Aid	800
Extended basic rate band	32,810

Tutor's top tips

Always check carefully whether you have been given income or payments gross or net.

(iii) **William Wind**

Income tax computation – 2013/14

	£
Employment income	
Salary	182,700
Less: Pension contributions	(7,300)
	175,400
Car benefit (W)	24,285
Fuel benefit (W)	7,385
	207,070
Less: Adjusted PA (Note)	(Nil)
Taxable income	207,070

Income tax

£		£
32,010	at 20%	6,402
117,990	at 40%	47,196
150,000		
57,070	at 45%	25,681
207,070		
Income tax liability		79,279

Tutorial note

William is not entitled to a personal allowance as his adjusted net income of £207,070 exceeds £118,880.

Working: Car and fuel benefit

CO_2 emissions = 222 g/km (rounded down to 220 g/km), available all year

	%	
Petrol	11	
Plus: (220 – 95) × $^1/_5$	25	
Appropriate percentage	36	Restricted to 35%

	£	£
Car benefit (£83,100 × 35%) (Note)	29,085	
Less: Contribution (use of car)	(4,800)	
		24,285
Fuel benefit (£21,100 × 35%)		7,385

Tutorial note

1 *The manufacturer's list price (MLP) is used to calculate the car benefit, not the actual cost of the car.*

2 *The contribution of £4,800 made by William towards the provision of the car is an allowable deduction.*

3 *The private fuel benefit is not reduced by the contribution of £3,200 made by William. There is no reduction in the fuel benefit for employee contributions unless the full cost of fuel for private journeys is reimbursed, in which case no private fuel benefit arises.*

(b) **National Insurance Contributions – 2013/14**

Philip Wind

- No national insurance contributions (NIC) are payable by Philip.
- This is because NICs are not payable on pension income or building society income, and he is over the state pension age so would not pay NIC in any case.

Charles Wind

- As Charles is self-employed; Class 2 and Class 4 NICs are payable.
- Class 2 NICs payable:

(£2.70 × 52 weeks)	£140

- Class 4 NICs payable:

	£
(£41,450 – £7,755) = £33,695 at 9%	3,033
(£109,400 – £41,450) = £67,950 at 2%	1,359
	4,392

William Wind

- As William is an employee; Class 1 primary contributions are payable.
- Class 1 primary NICs payable:

	£
(£41,450 – £7,755) = £33,695 at 12%	4,043
(£182,700 – £41,450) = £141,250 at 2%	2,825
	6,868

Tutorial note

Pension contributions are ignored, and benefits are not subject to employee Class 1 primary NIC.

Tutor's top tips

You are not asked to calculate the employer's NIC for William so do not waste time calculating it!

(c) **Reduction in income tax liabilities**

Key answer tips

This part of the question will require some thought and planning before answering.

It is important to consider **all** the implications of personal pension contributions – remember that they are taken into account in the ANI calculation in relation to the reduction of the basic personal allowance as well as extending the basic rate band.

In relation to the company car contributions, if you refer back to your answer to part (a) you will hopefully spot how the contributions have been used inefficiently, however, you should consider carefully how they could be reallocated as the best answer may not be as obvious as you would first think.

(i) **If Charles had contributed £8,600 into a personal pension scheme**

- Charles' adjusted net income will now be reduced to £100,000 (£108,600 – £8,600). He will therefore be entitled to the full personal allowance, and it will not be restricted by £4,300 as shown above.
- The personal pension scheme contribution will also further extend the basic rate tax band by £8,600.
- Charles' income tax liability for 2013/14 would therefore have been reduced as follows:

	£
Extra personal allowance (as no restriction)	
(£4,300 at 40%)	1,720
Extension of the basic rate band (Note)	
(£8,600 at (40% – 20%))	1,720
	3,440

Tutorial note

The extension of the basic rate band ensures that income formerly taxable at the higher rate of 40% is now taxable at the basic rate of 20%, and therefore saves income tax at 20%.

(ii) **If William's contributions towards the car and fuel was allocated differently**

- William and Crown plc should have allocated £4,400 of the contributions towards the fuel for private use, as there will then be no private fuel benefit assessed on William.

- The allocation should therefore be adjusted as follows:

	Original allocation	*Adjustment*	*Recommended allocation*
	£	£	£
Car	4,800	– 1,200	3,600
Private fuel	3,200	+ 1,200	4,400
	8,000		8,000

- William's income tax liability for 2013/14 would therefore have been reduced as follows:

	£	£
No fuel benefit assessed	7,385	
Increase in car benefit	(1,200)	
Net decrease in taxable income	6,185	
Income tax saved (Note)	× 45%	2,783

Tutorial note

The total cost to the employer for private fuel used is £4,400. When the employee reimburses the employer with the full cost of ALL private fuel consumed, there is no assessable private fuel benefit.

As William is an additional rate taxpayer, income tax is saved at 45%.

Students may have been tempted to recommend that all of the £8,000 should be allocated to the car benefit. This is because all contributions towards the provision of the car are allowable deductions against the car benefit, but partial contributions towards private fuel are not deductible from the fuel benefit.

However, if this strategy were adopted, it would only save £1,440 (£3,200 × 45%). The increased allowable deduction to the car benefit of £3,200 (£8,000 – £4,800) would reduce the car benefit and save tax at 45%, but the private fuel benefit would remain unchanged.

It is therefore more beneficial to eliminate the private fuel benefit charge by allocating contributions first to the full cost of the private fuel, and the rest to the car. See the examiner's report below for his comments on this approach.

Examiner's report

Part (a) was very well answered, particularly for the second and third taxpayers. The only aspect which sometimes caused problems was the benefit calculations.

For the car benefit it was not always appreciated that the list price was restricted to a maximum figure of £80,000. *(Tutorial note: the maximum upper limit restriction on the manufacturer's list price for the car benefit has been removed in FA2012 and therefore this point is no longer valid).*

For the fuel benefit, the contribution towards the cost of fuel was often incorrectly deducted.

There were few problems in part (b) as regards the calculation of the national insurance contributions.

Part (c) was the most difficult aspect on the paper, and it was pleasing to see several good attempts.

For the second taxpayer most candidates appreciated that the basic rate tax band would be extended by the amount of the pension contribution, and several candidates realised that the amount of contribution was the exact amount required so that the personal allowance was not restricted.

For the third taxpayer several candidates stated that tax could be saved if the whole of the contributions were set against just the car benefit, and marks were awarded for this approach.

However, the most beneficial basis was to allocate additional contributions towards the fuel benefit so as to cover the full cost of fuel for private journeys – and a few candidates did take this approach.

ACCA marking scheme	
	Marks
(a) (i) **Philip Wind**	
Pensions	0.5
Building society interest	0.5
Personal allowance	2.0
Income tax	1.0
	4.0
(ii) **Charles Wind**	
Trading profit	0.5
Personal allowance	2.0
Extension of basic rate band	0.5
Income tax	1.0
	4.0
(iii) **William Wind**	
Salary	0.5
Pension contributions	1.0
Car benefit – List price	0.5
– Relevant percentage	1.0
– Contribution	0.5
– Calculation	0.5
Fuel benefit	1.0
Personal allowance	1.0
Income tax	1.0
	7.0
(b) **Philip Wind**	
No NIC	0.5
Charles Wind	
Class 2 NIC	0.5
Class 4 NIC	1.5
William Wind	
Class 1 NIC	1.5
	4.0
(i) **Charles Wind**	
Personal allowance	1.0
Basic rate band	1.0
Income tax liability	1.0
	3.0
(ii) **William Wind**	
Allocation	1.0
Contributions for use of motor car	1.0
Income tax liability	1.0
	3.0
Total	25.0

8 LETICIA STONE  *Walk in the footsteps of a top tutor*

Key answer tips

This question required the calculation of property losses – one for a furnished holiday letting property and one for the other let properties.

The calculations are not difficult provided you remember the following:

1. Property income is assessed on an accruals basis as if the individual had a trade with a 5 April year end.
2. Separate calculations are required for furnished holiday lettings, but all other property income and expenses are pooled into one calculation
3. One of the advantages of furnished holiday lettings is that they are entitled to capital allowances rather than the wear and tear allowance.

Two easy marks were available in part (b) for explaining what an individual can do with property losses.

(a) **Furnished holiday letting loss – 2013/14**

	£	£
Rent receivable (£425 × 22)		9,350
Loan interest	12,700	
Repairs (£12,200 – £10,900)	1,300	
Mileage allowance (W)	454	
Other expenses	3,770	
Capital allowances (£4,600 × 100%)	4,600	
		(22,824)
Furnished holiday letting loss		(13,474)

Working: Mileage allowance

The mileage that Leticia drove in respect of the property purchase is capital in nature, and therefore does not qualify.

Her mileage allowance is therefore:

(880 + 130) = 1,010 at 45p = £454

Tutor's top tips:

You are told in the question that property one qualifies as a trade under the furnished holiday letting rules. Hence you will not receive any marks for writing out the conditions for a property to be a furnished holiday let and trying to apply them to any of the properties.

Property business loss – 2013/14

	Notes	£	£
Premium received for sub-lease			45,000
Less: £45,000 × 2% × (5 – 1)			(3,600)
	1		41,400
Rent receivable	2		
– Property 2 (£2,160 × 4 × 11/12)	3		7,920
– Property 3 (£580 × 10)	4		5,800
– Security deposit	5		Nil
			55,120
Rent payable (£1,360 × 11)		14,960	
Impairment loss		580	
Loan interest		9,100	
Other expenses		36,240	
			(60,880)
			(5,760)
Furnished room (£3,170 – £4,840)	6		(1,670)
Property business loss			(7,430)

Tutorial note

1 *An alternative calculation of the assessment of the premium received on the granting of a short lease is as follows:*

P × (51 – D) / 50

= £45,000 × (51 – 5) / 50 = £41,400

2 *Rents are assessed on an accruals basis. Therefore the rents receivable between 6 April 2013 and 5 April 2014 are required.*

3 *Property 2 is rented out for 11 months of the tax year, but the rents are quoted in the question on a quarterly basis. Therefore the annual rents needs to be calculated and 11/12ths of the annual rents are assessed in 2013/14.*

4 *Property 3 is only rented out for 10 months of the tax year, but the information is given in monthly terms, so the calculation is straightforward.*

5 *The security deposit relating to Property 3 is received in the tax year, but it relates to the tenancy of the property in 2014/15 (commencing 15 April 2014). Therefore it will not be assessed in 2013/14.*

6 *Leticia would use the normal basis of assessment in respect of the furnished room since this allows a loss to be generated.*

(b) **Relief for property losses**

- The furnished holiday letting loss will be carried forward and relieved against Leticia's future profits from furnished holiday lettings only.
- The property business loss will be carried forward and relieved against the first available future property business profits only.

Examiner's report

Part (a) of this question was very well answered, with no aspect causing significant problems. However, several candidates claimed the wear and tear allowance for the furnished holiday letting rather than capital allowances.

Although candidates were not penalised if they combined the property losses into just one calculation, not separating out the furnished holiday letting loss invariably meant that marks were then lost in part (b) as marks were not awarded for vague details on loss relief if it was not clearly stated as to which reliefs were available for which type of loss.

ACCA marking scheme

			Marks
(a)	**Furnished holiday letting loss**		
	Rent receivable		0.5
	Loan interest		1.0
	Repairs		1.0
	Mileage allowance		1.5
	Other expenses		0.5
	Capital allowances		1.0
	Business property loss		
	Lease premium received		1.0
	Rent receivable	– Property 2	1.0
		– Property 3	1.0
		– Security deposit	0.5
	Rent payable		1.0
	Impairment loss		1.0
	Loan interest		0.5
	Other expenses		0.5
	Furnished room		1.0
			13.0
(b)	Furnished holiday letting loss		1.0
	Property business loss		1.0
			2.0
Total			15.0

INCOME TAX BASICS AND INCOME FROM SELF-EMPLOYMENT

9 CAROL COURIER

Key answer tips

A straight forward purely computational question dealing with the income tax and national insurance consequences of being employed and self-employed.

Part (c) requires a comparison of the net disposable income arising from the two options.

(a) **Carol continues to be employed**

Carol's income tax liability – 2013/14

	£
Salary	37,500
Less: Pension contributions (£37,500 × 5%)	(1,875)
Employment income	35,625
Less: PA	(9,440)
Taxable income	26,185
Income tax liability (£26,185 × 20%)	5,237
Class 1 NICs – Primary contributions	
(£37,500 – £7,755) × 12%	3,569

(b) **Carol accepts self-employed contract**

Carol's income tax liability – 2013/14

	£
Income (£43,500 + £8,000)	51,500
Less: Expenses (£4,400 + £2,800)	(7,200)
Trading income	44,300
Less: PA	(9,440)
Taxable income	34,860
Income tax liability (£34,860 × 20%) (Working)	6,972
Class 4 NICs	
(£41,450 – £7,755) × 9%	3,033
(£44,300 – £41,450) × 2%	57
	3,090
Class 2 NICs	
(£2.70 for 52 weeks)	140

Working: Extension of the basic rate band

	£
Basic rate band	32,010
Plus: Gross pension contributions	3,000
Extended basic rate band	35,010

All of Carol's taxable income of £34,860 falls into this extended basic rate band and is therefore taxed at 20%.

(c) **Benefit of accepting self-employed contract**

	Employed	*Self employed*
	£	£
Salary	37,500	Nil
Trading income	Nil	44,300
Pension contributions paid (Note)	(1,875)	(2,400)
NIC – Class 1 and Class 4	(3,569)	(3,090)
NIC – Class 2	Nil	(140)
Income tax	(5,237)	(6,972)
Net disposable income	26,819	31,698

It is therefore beneficial for Carol to accept the offer to work on a self-employed basis as her net income will increase by £4,879 (£31,698 – £26,819).

Tutorial note

Carol will pay personal pension contributions net of basic rate tax. If self-employed she will therefore pay £2,400 (£3,000 × 80%).

Key answer tips

When calculating the net disposable income think just in terms of cash and identify all cash coming in and all cash payments going out.

Cash payments obviously include the tax liabilities but also include other expenses such as pension contributions.

10 IDRIS WILLIAMS  *Walk in the footsteps of a top tutor*

Key answer tips

This question has been written to test the new rules introduced in Finance Act 2013 on the cash basis as well as the choice of accounting date.

Students should be familiar with the factors that influence the choice of accounting date and the advantages and disadvantages of choosing an accounting date early or late in the tax year.

The new cash basis rules are examinable in F6 to a limited extent. This question tests all the rules which could be examined.

Tutor's top tips

There are four marks available for part (a), therefore four clear points should be made.

(a) **Advantages of a 5 April accounting date**

- If Idris chooses to prepare his accounts to 5 April, the application of the basis period rules will be simplified.
- Idris will not have any overlap profits on the commencement of trade. If he prepares his accounts to 30 June, nine months of overlap profits will arise and these would not be relieved until the cessation of trading.

Advantages of a 30 June accounting date

- If Idris prepares his accounts to 30 June the interval between earning profits and paying the related tax liability will be 9 months longer than with an accounting date of 5 April.
- An accounting date of 30 June would make it easier to implement tax planning measures as there is a longer period over which to plan.

(b) (i) **Tax adjusted trading profit – accruals basis – year ended 5 April 2014**

Tutor's top tips

This question does not specifically request that you start with the net profit figure and adjust for any disallowable items, but this was the most obvious approach to take.

Always show your workings if the figure you are adjusting for is not clear from the question.

When using the normal accruals basis no adjustment should be made for any receivables or payables.

	£	£
Net profit	20,175	
Depreciation	1,250	
Property expenses (£7,600 × 50%)	3,800	
Motor expenses (£9,340 × 7,000/20,000)	3,269	
Capital allowances (W)		4,553
	28,494	4,553
	(4,553)	
Tax adjusted trading profit	23,941	

Tutorial note

The usual presentation of an adjustment of profits is produced above. However, an alternative method of calculating the same taxable trading profit figure is to reproduce the accounts just deducting the expenses which are allowable, as opposed to adding back those that are not allowable to the net profit. This alternative presentation is given below as it provides a more direct comparison of the difference in the treatment when the cash basis is used.

	£	*£*
Revenue		*57,510*
Cost of sales		*(17,660)*
		39,850
Depreciation	*Nil*	
Property expenses (£7,600 × 50%)	*3,800*	
Motor expenses (£9,340 × 13,000/20,000)	*6,071*	
Other expenses	*1,485*	
Capital allowances (W)	*4,553*	
		(15,909)
		23,941

Working: Capital allowances

		General pool	Private use car		Allowances
	£	£	£		£
Additions (no AIA)					
Car (96 – 130 g/km)			9,000		
Additions (with AIA)					
Equipment	3,500				
Less: AIA	(3,500)				3,500
		Nil			
WDA (18%) (Note)			(1,620)	× 65%	1,053
TWDV c/f		Nil	7,380		
Total allowances					4,553

Tutorial note

Capital allowances on new car purchases are calculated based on the CO_2 emissions.

As the car purchased in this question has CO_2 emissions of between 96 – 130 g/km, it is eligible for a WDA at 18%. The WDA then needs to be adjusted for the private use by Idris, as only the business use proportion of the allowance can be claimed.

The business mileage is 13,000 out of 20,000 miles, i.e. 65%.

(b) (ii) **Cash basis**

Idris is entitled to use the cash basis as his revenue is below the VAT registration threshold of £79,000.

Tutor's top tips

When operating the cash basis adjustments need to be made for any receivables and payables. The motor expenses deduction should be calculated on the basis of the approved mileage allowances and property expenses are subject to a flat rate adjustment for private use.

Capital purchases are deductible in full in the year of purchase, however, no deduction is available for the purchase of a motor car.

	£	£
Revenue (£57,510 – £8,275)		49,235
Less: Purchases (£17,660 × 95%)		(16,777)
		32,458
Depreciation	Nil	
Capital expenditure	3,500	
Property expenses (£7,600 – £4,200)	3,400	
Motor expenses (W)	5,250	
Other expenses (£1,485 – £400)	1,085	
		(13,235)
Tax adjusted trading profit		19,223

Working: Motor expenses

Idris is entitled to claim a deduction for his business mileage of 13,000 miles at the approved mileage rates.

	£
10,000 miles at 45p	4,500
3,000 miles at 25p	750
	5,250

(iii) **More beneficial basis**

Using the cash basis will result in Idris being taxed on a lower amount in 2013/14, and is therefore preferable. The difference is £4,718 (£23,941 – £19,223).

11 CHATRU (ADAPTED)  *Walk in the footsteps of a top tutor*

Key answer tips

A question in two parts but the parts are not independent.

In part 1 (a) and (b) you have to apply the opening and closing year rules to calculate the trading income assessments.

The 2013/14 assessment is then needed in the income tax computation in part 2 (a), which is a straight forward 'bread and butter' computation that should not have caused problems.

Part 2 (b) requires some thought into tax planning advice for a husband and wife. Typically the solution is to recommend the transfer of some assets generating income from the higher rate taxpayer to the basic rate taxpayer. However, there are other valid points that could have been made.

Tutor's top tips

In part 1 (a), be sure to show each tax year; describe the basis of assessment; and apply the appropriate rule to the question - give the appropriate dates and then show the working to calculate the number.

Just calculating the number will not gain full marks for this type of question.

(1) (a) **Assessable income**

Tax year	*Basis of assessment*		£
2009/10	Actual basis (1.11.09 – 5.4.10)		
	£40,500 × 5/18		11,250
2010/11	Actual basis (6.4.10 – 5.4.11)		
	£40,500 × 12/18		27,000
2011/12	12 months ended 30.4.11		
	£40,500 × 12/18		27,000
2012/13	CYB (y/e 30.4.12)		12,000
2013/14	Year of cessation – 1.5.12 to 31.3.14		
	(£24,000 + £50,000)	74,000	
	Less: Overlap profits (1.5.10 – 5.4.11)		
	£40,500 × 11/18	(24,750)	
			49,250
Total assessable income			126,500

Tutorial note

Check that total assessments = total tax adjusted profits of the business:

(£40,500 + £12,000 + £24,000 + £50,000) = £126,500

(b) **Assessments (cessation 30.4.14)**

Tutor's top tips

You need to show clearly that the effect of trading another month will be that there is another tax year of assessment, and that therefore only the final assessments will be affected.

Make sure that you explain the effect in words as well as in the numbers.

Tax year	*Basis of assessment*	£	£
2009/10	(as above)		11,250
2010/11	(as above)		27,000
2011/12	(as above)		27,000
2012/13	(as above)		12,000
2013/14	CYB (y/e 30.4.13)		24,000
2014/15	Year of cessation – 1.5.13 to 30.4.14		
	(£50,000 + £4,200)	54,200	
	Less: Overlap profits (as above)	(24,750)	
			29,450
			130,700

Tutorial note

Check that total assessments = total tax adjusted profits of the business: (£126,500 + £4,200) = £130,700

Assessments under the current year basis ensure that all profits earned are assessed. If Chatru continues to trade for one extra month, earning an additional £4,200 his total assessments will increase by £4,200.

However, by trading for one extra month, the amount assessed in 2013/14 is reduced from £49,250 to £24,000. This may be an income tax benefit if Chatru has little or no other income, as profits are now covered by the basic rate band.

Tutorial note

The taxpayer can choose his date of cessation, provided the business is solvent. The choice of date is important as there is an opportunity to alter the timing of assessments over the final years.

This may change the rate of tax at which the profits are assessed and the due date of payment.

In practice this is an important tax planning consideration in the closing years of a business.

Tutor's top tips

Strictly there is no need, in part 1 (a) and (b), to provide a proof that total profits earned equals total profits assessed but it is good practice and will uncover any arithmetic mistakes for you to go back and correct.

However, only go back and correct an answer if you have time. Normally it is better to move on and finish the question.

(2) (a) **Income tax computation – 2013/14**

Tutor's top tips

A straightforward income tax computation is required in part 2 (a) and the trading income figure in the income tax computation comes from part 1 (a).

Remember that even if you got that part wrong, you can get all of the marks in part 2 (a) for following through your computation in the correct way using your trading income figure – so keep going!

	Total	*Other income*	*Savings income*	*Dividend income*
	£	£	£	£
Trading income (part 1 (a))	49,250	49,250		
Property business income (W1)	10,000	10,000		
Bank interest (£2,500 × 100/80)	3,125		3,125	
ISA interest (Exempt)	Nil			
Dividends (£33,500 × 100/90)	37,222			37,222
Total income	99,597	59,250	3,125	37,222
Less: PA	(9,440)	(9,440)		
Taxable income	90,157	49,810	3,125	37,222

Income tax		£
£		
38,260	at 20% (W2) (Other income)	7,652
11,550	at 40% (Other income)	4,620
49,810		
3,125	at 40% (Savings)	1,250
37,222	at 32.5% (Dividends)	12,097
90,157		
Income tax liability		25,619
Less: Tax suffered at source		
	Dividends (£37,222 at 10%)	(3,722)
	Bank interest (£3,125 at 20%)	(625)
Income tax payable		21,272

Workings

(W1) **Property business income**

(i) **Rent from the room in house**

The rental income is less than £4,250 per annum and is therefore exempt from income tax under the rent a room scheme.

(ii) **Property business profit**

	£
Furnished property	
Rent received	11,100
Less: Interest paid	(500)
Allowable expenses	(1,600)
Cooker (Note 1)	Nil
Wear & tear allowance (10% × (£11,100 – £800 – £300))	(1,000)
	8,000
Land (£4,000 × 50%) (Note 2)	2,000
Property business profit	10,000

Tutorial note

1 *The purchase of the cooker is capital expenditure and therefore not allowable.*

2 *Income from assets jointly held by husband and wife is split 50:50 between the spouses unless they have elected to have the income taxed in relation to their actual ownership proportions.*

The question states that Chatru and Sandra have not made any elections in relation to their income. The rental income will therefore be split equally between them for tax purposes.

(W2) **Extended basic rate band**

	£
Basic rate band	32,010
Plus: Gross Gift Aid donation (£5,000 × 100/80)	6,250
Extended basic rate band	38,260

(b) **Chatru and Sandra – Ways to reduce joint income tax liability**

Tutor's top tips

The question only required two ways in which the couple could have saved tax. The full answer below is produced for tutorial purposes.

Sandra's only taxable income is from her part-time earnings of £8,000 and rental income from the land of £2,000 p.a. She is therefore a basic rate taxpayer.

Chatru was a higher rate taxpayer in 2013/14 and if the level of his dividend income remains the same he is likely to continue to be so in future years.

Chatru has suffered tax on his property income and savings income at 40% and on his dividend income at 32.5%.

Sandra has an unused basic rate band of £31,450 (W). She would therefore only pay tax at 20% on this income up to the level of her remaining basic rate band.

Chatru and Sandra should therefore have considered the following to reduce their income tax liability:

(1) Electing for the rental income from the land to be taxed in accordance with their actual ownership proportions of 25:75. This would have reduced their joint tax liability by £200 (£1,000 × (40% – 20%)).

(2) Transferring income generating assets such as the shares and the bank account into Sandra's name in order to produce income to fully utilise her basic rate band.

(3) Transferring funds from either the bank account or the shareholdings into an Individual Savings Account in Sandra's name in order to generate tax free income.

Working: Remaining basic rate band

Tutorial note

Remember that to calculate the remaining basic rate band you need to compare £32,010 to Sandra's taxable income which is after deducting her personal allowance.

	£	£
Basic rate band		32,010
Earnings	8,000	
Property income	2,000	
	10,000	
Less: PA	(9,440)	
Taxable income		(560)
Remaining basic rate band		31,450

12 OLIVE GREEN (ADAPTED)  *Walk in the footsteps of a top tutor*

Key answer tips

A classic, straightforward income tax computation for a self-employed individual with some self-assessment points at the end.

The adjustment of profit should not have caused problems but remember to lay out your answer in the way the examiner has specifically asked for it. Remember also to read the private use/business use proportion of Olive's car carefully and adjust both the profits figure and the capital allowances.

The income tax computation was not difficult; the only area of concern may have been the relief for interest on the loan taken out to purchase an asset for use in Olive's employment.

Calculating balancing payments, payments on account and interest for late payment of tax are commonly examined and should not have been problematic.

(a) **Tax adjusted trading profit – year ended 31 March 2014**

Tutor's top tips

In the adjustment to profits calculation it is important to list all the major items indicated in the question requirement, showing a zero (0) for expenditure that is allowable. This is because credit will be given for showing no adjustment where none is needed.

If required, also add notes to show why you have not adjusted for an item, or why you have added it back. However, lengthy explanations are not required where the requirement is just to 'calculate' the adjusted profits, rather than to explain them.

Always show your workings if the figure you are adjusting for is not clear from the question.

	£	£
Net profit	30,050	
Depreciation	2,350	
Private accommodation (£1,980 + £5,920) × 30%	2,370	
Motor expenses (£4,700 × 12,000/20,000)	2,820	
Lease costs – high emission car (£3,000 × 15%)	450	
Fine (Note 1)	220	
Theft by employee (Note 2)	0	
Donation to political party	100	
Trade subscription (Note 3)	0	
Excessive salary (Note 4) (£14,000 – £10,500)	3,500	
Own consumption (Note 5) (52 × £45)	2,340	
Patent royalties (£150 × 4) (Note 6)		600
Capital allowances (W)		1,138
	44,200	1,738
	(1,738)	
Tax adjusted trading profit	42,462	

Tutorial note

1 *Fines are not allowable except for parking fines incurred by an employee.*

2 *Theft is allowable provided it is by an employee rather than the business owner.*

3 *Trade subscriptions are allowable as they have been incurred wholly and exclusively for the purposes of the trade.*

4 *A salary to a family member must not be excessive. Since Olive's daughter is paid £3,500 more than the other sales assistants, this amount is not allowable.*

5 *Goods for own consumption are valued at selling price. It is assumed that no adjustment has been made in the accounts for these goods. If the goods taken out had already been correctly accounted for, only the profit element of £15 per week would be adjusted for.*

6 *Patent royalties are allowable deductions from trading profit if they are for the purposes of the trade. As they have not yet been deducted in arriving at the profit, a deduction is required.*

Read the question carefully as normally they have already been accounted for and therefore no adjustment is required.

Working: Capital allowances

	Private use car	*Business use*	*Allowances*
	£		£
TWDV b/f	15,800		
WDA × 18%	(2,844)	× (8,000/20,000)	1,138
TWDV c/f	12,956		

Tutor's top tips

A familiar full blown capital allowances computation is given in the workings to this answer to show how the allowances are calculated.

However, where there are not many transactions it is perfectly acceptable to do one or two lines and just calculate the allowances available on each asset acquired rather than a full computation.

If you do this however, be careful and make sure you explain your calculations clearly.

(b) **Income tax computation – 2013/14**

Tutor's top tips

A straightforward income tax computation is required.

Note that you would still get full marks for this part, even if your trading income from part (a) is incorrect.

	Total	*Other*	*Savings*	*Dividends*
	£	£	£	£
Trading income (part (a))	42,462	42,462		
Employment income	6,000	6,000		
Building society interest (£1,440 × 100/80)	1,800		1,800	
Dividends (£1,080 × 100/90)	1,200			1,200
Total income	51,462	48,462	1,800	1,200
Less: Reliefs				
Loan interest (Note)	(220)	(220)		
Net income	51,242	48,242	1,800	1,200
Less: PA	(9,440)	(9,440)		
Taxable income	41,802	38,802	1,800	1,200

Tutorial note

The interest on the loan to purchase equipment for employment qualifies as a relief deductible from total income since the loan was used by Olive to finance expenditure for a qualifying purpose. Note that the interest is quoted gross and is paid gross.

Income tax		£
£		
34,610	at 20% (Other income) (W)	6,922
4,192	at 40% (Other income)	1,677
38,802		
1,800	at 40% (Savings)	720
1,200	at 32.5% (Dividends)	390
41,802		
Income tax liability		9,709
Less: Tax suffered at source		
	Dividends (£1,200 at 10%)	(120)
	PAYE	(1,195)
	Building society interest (£1,800 at 20%)	(360)
Income tax payable		8,034

Capital gains tax liability – 2013/14

	£
Chargeable gain	12,800
Less: AE	(10,900)
Taxable gain	1,900
Capital gains tax (£1,900 × 28%)	532

Tutorial note

Capital gains tax is calculated at 28% because capital gains are taxed as the top slice of taxable income and Olive is a higher rate taxpayer.

Balancing payment for 2013/14 – due on 31 January 2015

	£
Total income tax and CGT (£8,034 + £532)	8,566
Less: Payments on account	(4,900)
Balancing payment	3,666

Payments on account – 2014/15

Payments on account are not required for capital gains tax, so the payments on account for 2014/15 will be £4,017 (£8,034 × 50%).

These will be due on 31 January 2015 and 31 July 2015.

Working: Extension of basic rate band

	£
Basic rate band	32,010
Plus: Gross pension contributions	2,600
Extended basic rate band	34,610

(c) **Consequences of paying balancing payment late**

Tutor's top tips

Interest calculations should be made to the nearest month in the examination, unless the question says otherwise.

- Late payment interest is charged where a balancing payment is paid late.

  This will run from 31 January 2015 to 30 April 2015.
- The interest charge will be: (£3,666 × 3% × 3/12) = £27
- In addition, a late payment penalty of £183 (£3,666 at 5%) will be imposed as the balancing payment is more than one month late (but less than six months late).

13 FOO DEE (ADAPTED)

Key answer tips

Part (a) requires a simple adjustment of profit and capital allowances computation which should not have caused any problems if you remembered that it is a 9 month accounting period and therefore the maximum AIA and WDAs are time apportioned.

In part (b) the opening year basis of assessment rules have to be applied to calculate the trading income assessment for 2013/14 for inclusion in the income tax computation.

The employment income computation was complicated in working out the business mileage claim allowance to be deducted. Knowledge of the ordinary commuting rules and temporary workplace rules are tested.

The child benefit aspect of this question has been added since it was written to test these new rules.

Otherwise the income tax, capital gains tax and self-assessment parts were straightforward.

This style of question is often examined, so you need to make sure you know the approach and techniques required.

(a) **Trading profit – period ended 30 September 2014**

	£	£
Net profit	130,854	
Depreciation	3,500	
Motor expenses (£4,200 × 2,000/6,000)	1,400	
Private accommodation (£12,800 × 1/4)	3,200	
Capital allowances (W)		82,514
	138,954	82,514
	(82,514)	
Trading profit	56,440	

Working: Capital allowances – nine months ended 30 September 2014

	£	General pool £	Private use car £		Allowances £
Additions (no AIA)					
Car (96 – 130 g/km)			14,600		
Additions (with AIA)					
Equipment	81,200				
Less: AIA (Note 1)	(81,200)				81,200
		Nil			
WDA (18% × 9/12)(Note 2)			(1,971)	× 4/6	1,314
TWDV c/f		Nil	12,629		
Total allowances					82,514

Tutorial note

1 *Both the WDA and the AIA available are time apportioned by 9/12 as the accounting period is only 9 months long. The maximum AIA available is therefore £187,500 (£250,000 × 9/12). The remainder is then subject to the WDA.*

2 *Capital allowances on new car purchases are calculated based on the CO_2 emissions.*

As the car purchased in this question has CO_2 emissions of between 96 – 130 g/km, it is eligible for a WDA at 18%. The WDA then needs to be adjusted for the short accounting period and for the private use by Foo Dee, as only the business use proportion of the allowance can be claimed.

The business mileage is 4,000 out of 6,000 miles.

(b) **Income tax computation – 2013/14**

	Total	Other	Savings	Dividends
	£	£	£	£
Salary	38,000			
Less: Pension contributions (6%)	(2,280)			
	35,720			
Relocation costs (W1)	4,900			
Expense claim (W2)	(2,048)			
Employment income	38,572	38,572		
Trading profit (W3)	18,813	18,813		
Building society interest (£640 × 100/80)	800		800	
Dividends (£360 × 100/90)	400			400
Total income	58,585	57,385	800	400
Less: PA	(9,440)	(9,440)		
Taxable income	49,145	47,945	800	400

Income tax

£		£
34,010	at 20% (Other income) (W4)	6,802
13,935	at 40% (Other income)	5,574
47,945		
800	at 40% (Savings income)	320
400	at 32·5% (Dividend income)	130
49,145		

	£
Add: child benefit charge (W5)	1,138
Income tax liability	13,964
Less: Tax suffered at source	
Dividends (£400 at 10%)	(40)
PAYE	(5,600)
Building society interest (£800 at 20%)	(160)
Income tax payable	8,164

Capital gains tax liability – 2013/14

	£
Chargeable gain	17,600
Less: AE	(10,900)
Taxable gain	6,700
Capital gains tax (£6,700 × 28%) (Note)	1,876

Tutorial note

Capital gains tax is calculated at 28% as capital gains are taxed as the top slice of taxable income and Foo Dee is a higher rate taxpayer.

Balancing payment

- No payments on account have been made, so the balancing payment for 2013/14 due on 31 January 2015 is £10,040 (£8,164 + £1,876).

Workings

(W1) **Relocation expenses**

Only £8,000 of relocation costs is exempt, and so the taxable benefit is £4,900 (£12,900 – £8,000).

(W2) **Expense claim**

Ordinary commuting (i.e. travel between home and the permanent workplace, including journeys to turn off the fire alarm) and private travel do not qualify for relief.

The travel to a temporary workplace qualifies as business mileage as it is for a period lasting less than 24 months.

Therefore, business mileage = (750 + 3,800) = 4,550 miles

As the company does not reimburse Foo Dee for any mileage, she is allowed to claim an allowable deduction based on the HMRC authorised mileage allowance payments.

Expenses claim = (4,550 miles × 45p) = £2,048

(W3) **Trading income assessment – 2013/14**

9 months ended 30 September 2014		
Trading profit		£56,440
Tax year	*Basis of assessment*	
2013/14	Opening year rules apply	
	Actual basis (1.1.2014 – 5.4.2014)	
	(£56,440 × 3/9)	£18,813

(W4) **Extension of basic rate band**

	£
Basic rate band threshold	32,010
Plus: Personal pension contribution (£1,600 × 100/80)	2,000
Extended basic rate band	34,010

(W5) **Child benefit tax charge**

Tutor's top tips

The child benefit tax charge is a new rule in FA13 and is therefore very topical. It is important that you can identify the situation where this charge may apply, and that you know how to calculate the tax charge.

Remember that it is adjusted net income (ANI) which is compared with the limits provided in the tax tables, so you must adjust net income for any gift aid donations or personal pension contributions. The charge will be the full amount of the child benefit if the ANI exceeds £60,000, but will be based on a percentage of the benefit where the ANI is between £50,000 and £60,000. The percentage and the tax charge itself will always be rounded down.

	£	£
Child benefit received		1,752
Total income	58,585	
Less: Gross personal pension contributions	(2,000)	
Adjusted net income	56,585	
Less: Lower limit	(50,000)	
	6,585	
1% per £100 of £6,585 = 65.85% rounded down to 65%		
Child benefit charge = 65% of £1,752 (rounded down)		1,138

(c) **Consequences of not paying the balancing payment**

Tutor's top tips

Interest calculations should be made to the nearest month in the examination, unless the question says otherwise.

- Late payment interest is charged where a balancing payment is paid late.
  This will run from 31 January 2015 to 31 May 2015.
- The interest charge will be £100 (£10,040 × 3% × 4/12).
- In addition, a late payment penalty of £502 (£10,040 × 5%) will be imposed as the balancing payment is more than one month late (but less than six months late).

14 SAM AND KIM WHITE (ADAPTED)  *Walk in the footsteps of a top tutor*

Key answer tips

A classic husband and wife scenario; one employed, the other self-employed and some joint income.

The adjustment of profits was straightforward, except that some may not have known what to do with the patent royalties. In fact, if you did nothing – that was the right thing to do!

Be careful with the calculation of the private use/business use proportion of the car and remember the impact private use has on both the adjustment of profits computation and capital allowances.

Part (c) requires some thought about tax planning advice for a husband and wife; investing in ISAs and transferring assets generating income from the higher rate taxpayer to the basic rate taxpayer.

The highlighted words in the written sections are key phrases that markers are looking for.

Tutor's top tips

The key to success when you are doing an adjustment of profits is to think about what, if anything, has already been included in the statement of profit or loss.

If an expense is disallowable and it has been deducted, you need to add it back. If it hasn't been deducted you do nothing.

Conversely, if an expense is allowable and it has been deducted, you include it with a zero adjustment. If it hasn't been deducted, you need to deduct it.

Read the question carefully here!

As the question just asks you to 'calculate', you do not need to explain why you are making adjustments, although you do need to make sure you label your answers so that the marker can see which expenses you are adding back or deducting.

It is also important to include all the major items of expenditure in the question, showing a zero for the adjustment figure where the expenditure is allowable.

Always show your workings if the adjustment figure is not clear from the question.

(a) **Sam White**

Trading profit – year ended 5 April 2014

	£	£
Net profit	100,000	
Depreciation	7,600	
Motor expenses (£8,800 × 20%) (W1)	1,760	
Patent royalties (Note 1)	0	
Breach of contract fees (Note 2)	0	
Accountancy fees (Note 2)	0	
Personal capital gains tax advice	320	
Gifts to customers (£560 + £420) (Note 3)	980	
Use of office (£5,120 × 1/8)		640
Private telephone (£1,600 × 25%)		400
Own consumption (Note 4)	1,480	
Capital allowances (W2)		3,957
	112,140	4,997
	(4,997)	
Trading profit	107,143	

Tutorial note

1 *Patent royalties are allowed as a deduction when calculating the trading profit, because they are for the purposes of the trade. As they have already been deducted in arriving at the profit, no adjustment is required.*

2 *The fees incurred for accountancy and the breach of contract defence are allowable as incurred wholly and exclusively for the purposes of the trade.*

3 *Gifts to customers are an allowable deduction if they cost less than £50 per recipient per year, are not of food, drink, tobacco or vouchers exchangeable for goods and carry a conspicuous advertisement for the company making the gift.*

4 *Goods for own consumption must be treated as a sale at full market value. As no entries have been made in the accounts, the full sale proceeds are adjusted for. Had the goods been accounted for already, only the profit element would need to be adjusted for.*

Workings

(W1) **Private/business mileage**

	Total	*Private*	*Business*
Total miles	25,000		
Visiting suppliers	(5,000)		5,000
Allocate (25:75)	20,000	5,000	15,000
		5,000	20,000
(5,000/25,000)		20%	
(20,000/25,000)			80%

Tutor's top tips

A familiar full blown capital allowances computation is given in the workings to this answer to show clearly how the allowances are calculated.

However, where there are not many transactions it is perfectly acceptable to do one or two lines and just calculate the allowances available on each asset acquired rather than a full computation.

If you do this however, be careful and make sure you explain your calculations clearly.

(W2) **Capital allowances**

	General pool	*Private use car*		*Allowances*
	£	£		£
TWDV b/f	14,800	20,200		
WDA (18%)	(2,664)			2,664
WDA (8%)(W1)		(1,616)	× 80%	1,293
TWDV c/f	12,136	18,584		
Total allowances				3,957

Tutorial note

The motor car is a high emission car (CO_2 emissions exceed 130 g/km) and is eligible for a WDA at 8%.

(b) **Sam White**

Income tax computation – 2013/14

Tutor's top tips

As long as your calculation of Sam's income tax is based on your trading profit from part (a), you can still score full marks here in this part.

However, it is very important that you show your workings clearly so that the marker can see that you have applied the correct rates to each type of income.

	Total	*Other income*	*Savings income*
	£	£	£
Trading profit	107,143	107,143	
Interest (£1,200 × 100/80) x 1/2	750		750
Total income	107,893		
Less: Adjusted PA (W)	(5,494)	(5,494)	
Taxable income	102,399	101,649	750

	£		£
Income tax:			
On Other income	32,010	@ 20%	6,402
On Other income	69,639	@ 40%	27,856
	101,649		
On Savings income	750	@ 40%	300
	102,399		
Income tax liability			34,558

Working: Adjusted personal allowance

	£		£
Personal allowance			9,440
Total income = net income = ANI	107,893		
Less: Limit	(100,000)		
	7,893	× 50%	(3,946)
Adjusted PA			5,494

Kim White

Income tax computation – 2013/14

Tutor's top tips

Another straightforward income tax computation, but watch the dates very carefully here!

Where a benefit has only been available for part of the tax year, it must be time apportioned.

However, if you forget to do this, you will only be penalised once and could still score full marks for the calculation of tax, as explained above.

	Total		Other income	Savings income
	£		£	£
Salary	21,600			
Beneficial loan (£14,250 × 4% × 10/12)	475			
Less: Expense claim (W)	(5,125)			
Employment income	16,950		16,950	
Interest (£1,200 × 100/80) × 1/2	750			750
Total income	17,700		16,950	750
Less: Relief for interest paid (Note)	(140)		(140)	
Net income	17,560		16,810	750
Less: PA	(9,440)		(9,440)	
Taxable income	8,120		7,370	750
	£			£
Income tax:				
On Other income	7,370	@ 20%		1,474
On Savings income	750	@ 20%		150
	8,120			
Income tax liability				1,624

Tutorial note

The loan interest paid of £140 is eligible for relief since the loan was used by Kim to finance expenditure for a relevant purpose. The interest is quoted gross and is paid gross.

Working: Expense claim

Ordinary commuting (i.e. travel between home and the permanent workplace) does not qualify for relief. The travel to a temporary workplace qualifies as it is for a period lasting less than 24 months.

Business mileage is therefore 12,500 miles (11,200 + 1,300)

Expense claim is therefore:

	£
10,000 miles at 45p	4,500
2,500 miles at 25p	625
	5,125

(c) **Husband and wife tax planning suggestions**

Tutor's top tips

It should be clear from your answer to part (b) that Sam is a higher rate taxpayer and Kim is a basic rate taxpayer.

Make sure you set out the rates of tax that each will be subject to, and have a go at calculating the tax saving that could be achieved here.

Individual savings accounts

- Sam and Kim can both invest up to a maximum of £5,760 each tax year into a cash ISA.
- Interest received from ISAs is exempt from income tax, so Sam will save tax at the rate of 40%. Kim will save tax at the rate of 20%.
- They received a 6% gross interest rate of return on their investment in the building society, calculated as:

  Gross interest = £1,200 × 100/80 = £1,500

  Gross rate of interest = £1,500/£25,000 = 6%
- Sam and Kim will therefore each save tax on gross interest of £346 (£5,760 × 6%) if they invested in ISAs.

  This is assuming that the interest that will be received on the ISA will be the same rate of interest as their existing investment.

Transfer to Kim's sole name

- Sam pays income tax at the rate of 40%, whilst Kim's basic rate tax band is not fully utilised.
- Transferring the building society deposit account into Kim's sole name would therefore save tax of £150 (£750 × (40% – 20%)).

Tutorial note

The original question just asked for consideration of the ISA and transfer of assets to Kim.

However, there is another tax planning opportunity in respect of Kim's Gift Aid donations as follows:

- *Kim is making a regular contribution to charity of £1,000 gross.*
- *If Sam made this payment instead, it would reduce his income for the calculation of the personal allowance restriction.*

  This would save £200 (£1,000 reduction would reduce the restriction by £500, and the income is being taxed at 40%).
- *In addition, Sam's basic rate band would be extended by £1,000, reducing the amount of income taxed at 40% and taxing it at 20% instead.*

  This would save a further £200 (£1,000 × (40% – 20%)).

Examiner's report

This question was very well answered by the majority of candidates.

In part (a) the adjustments for use of office, business use of a private telephone and own consumption caused the most problems, with a number of candidates being unsure as to whether adjustments should be added or subtracted in order to arrive at the tax adjusted trading profit.

Part (b) was also well answered, with only the expense claim for the business mileage causing any difficulty. This was often treated as a benefit rather than as an expense.

Part (c) was answered reasonably well, especially the transfer into the spouse's sole name. Many candidates correctly calculated the amount of income tax saving.

ACCA marking scheme

			Marks
(a)	Net profit		0.5
	Depreciation		0.5
	Motor expenses		1.5
	Patent royalties		1.0
	Professional fees		1.5
	Gifts to customers		1.0
	Use of office		1.0
	Private telephone		1.0
	Own consumption		1.0
	Capital allowances	– Pool	1.0
		– Motor car	1.0
			11.0
(b)	Sam White		
	Trading profit		0.5
	Building society interest		0.5
	Personal allowance		1.5
	Income tax		1.0
	Kim White		
	Salary		0.5
	Beneficial loan		1.0
	Expense claim		1.5
	Building society interest		0.5
	Loan interest		1.0
	Personal allowance		0.5
	Income tax		1.5
			10.0
(c)	Individual savings accounts		
	Limit		1.0
	Tax saving		1.0
			2.0
	Transfer to Kim's sole name		
	Tax rates		1.0
	Tax saving		1.0
			2.0
Total			25.0

15 GOMEZ BROTHERS (ADAPTED)  *Walk in the footsteps of a top tutor*

Key answer tips

This question involved preparing three separate income tax computations which covered a broad spectrum of income tax topics, tested compliance knowledge of self-assessment and due dates of payment of tax.

The requirements and mark allocation are very clear.

Although there is a wide coverage of the syllabus, all the topics are covered at a basic level and should therefore have been manageable.

Tutor's top tips

For part (a) a systematic approach is needed, taking one individual at a time, and therefore breaking up the information given into smaller, manageable chunks.

As you read the question it is useful to highlight all the information you will need for the income tax computations, and then as you use this information tick each item, so you can easily check you have included everything.

Remember not to ignore exempt income, as credit is given for stating that it is exempt, even though you do NOT include the figure in your computation. Remember not to get held up on any one calculation.

Always ensure that you read the question carefully. The requirement is to calculate income tax liability. Therefore do not waste time calculating income tax payable as this will not gain you any additional marks.

Make the marker your friend, if you keep your calculations clear and easy to read you will score much higher marks. Always ensure your workings are clearly labelled.

(a) (i) **Domingo Gomez**

Income tax computation – 2013/14

	£
Pensions (£4,500 + £3,300)	7,800
Building society interest (£15,200 × 100/80)	19,000
Interest from savings certificate (exempt)	Nil
Total income	26,800
Less: PAA (W)	(10,150)
Taxable income	16,650

Tutorial note

Interest from savings certificates is always exempt from tax.

This income is not the same as interest from a National Savings and Investment Bank account, which is taxable and would be received gross.

Make sure you read the question carefully and have identified the income correctly.

Income tax:

£		£
2,790	at 10% (Note)	279
13,860	at 20%	2,772
16,650		
Income tax liability		3,051

Tutorial note

1 *The non-savings income is fully covered by the personal allowance, so the first £2,790 of savings income is taxed at the starting rate of 10%.*

2 *No tax relief is available in respect of the donations as they were not made under the Gift Aid scheme.*

If Domingo had made the donation under the Gift Aid scheme it would have enabled the charity to claim an additional £75 (£300 × 20/80) with no additional cost to Domingo. The amount paid of £300 (i.e. gross £375) would be deemed to have had basic rate tax deducted at source and as a basic rate taxpayer no additional tax relief would be due.

In addition if the donations had been made under the Gift Aid scheme the gross amount (£375) would have been deducted from Domingo's total income for the purposes of calculating the personal age allowance thus decreasing the restriction and increasing the age allowance by £188 (£375 × 50%).

Working: Personal age allowance

	£		£
PAA (born between 6.4.1938 and 5.4.1948)			10,500
Less: Abatement			
Total income	26,800		
Income limit	(26,100)		
Excess	700	× 50%	(350)
Reduced PAA			10,150

(ii) **Erigo Gomez**

Income tax computation – 2013/14

	£
Salary	36,000
Relocation costs (W1)	3,400
Pension contributions (£36,000 × 6%)	(2,160)
Charitable payroll deductions (£12 × 100)	(1,200)
Mileage allowance (W2)	(2,900)
Employment income	33,140
Less: PA	(9,440)
Taxable income	23,700
Income tax liability (£23,700 at 20%)	4,740

Workings

(W1) **Relocation costs**

Only £8,000 of relocation costs is exempt, and so the taxable benefit is £3,400 (£11,400 – £8,000).

(W2) **Mileage allowance**

The mileage allowance received will be tax-free as it falls below the AMAP, and Erigo can make the following expense claim:

	£
10,000 miles at 45p	4,500
8,000 miles at 25p	2,000
AMAP	6,500
Mileage allowance received (18,000 at 20p)	(3,600)
Allowable deduction	2,900

Tutorial note

Charitable donations via a payroll deduction scheme receive full tax relief at source as they are deducted from employment income before it is taxed.

This is exactly the same treatment as pension contributions into an employer's occupational scheme.

(iii) **Fargo Gomez**

Income tax computation – 2013/14

	£
Trading profit (£112,800 – £2,600)	110,200
Less: Capital allowances (W1)	(990)
Total income	109,210
Less: Adjusted PA (W2)	(8,935)
Taxable income	100,275

Income tax

£		£
40,210	at 20% (W3)	8,042
60,065	at 40%	24,026
100,275		
Income tax liability		32,068

Tutorial note

1. *The advertising expenditure incurred during May 2013 is pre-trading, and is treated as incurred on 6 July 2013. An adjustment is therefore required.*
2. *Although Fargo's business had commenced during the year, there is no adjustment required under the opening year rules.*

   This is because Fargo has selected a year end of 5 April, which is the only date that will avoid any overlap profits arising.

Workings:

(W1) **Capital allowances**

Fargo's period of account is nine months' long so the capital allowances in respect of his motor car are:

(£11,000 × 18% × 9/12) = £1,485 before adjustment for private use

Capital allowances = £1,485 × (16,000/24,000) = £990

Tutorial note

Capital allowances on new purchases of cars are calculated based on their CO_2 emissions. As Fargo's car has CO_2 emissions of between 96 – 130 g/km the car is eligible for a writing down allowance at 18%. This then needs to be adjusted for the short accounting period and for the private use by Fargo.

(W2) **Adjusted personal allowance**

	£		£
Personal allowance			9,440
Total income = net income	109,210		
Less: Gross PPC	(5,200)		
Gross Gift Aid (£2,400 × 100/80)	(3,000)		
ANI	101,010		
Less: Limit	(100,000)		
	1,010	× 50%	(505)
Adjusted PA			8,935

Tutorial note

1. *Charitable donations under Gift Aid are grossed up before being used to reduce the personal allowance and extend the basic rate band. This is exactly the same treatment as pension contributions to a personal pension scheme.*
2. *As the adjusted net income exceeds £100,000 the allowance is reduced by £1 for every £2 it exceeds the limit. Net income for these purposes is adjusted (i.e. reduced) for both Gift Aid and personal pension contributions made in the year.*

(W3) **Extension of basic rate band**

	£
Basic rate band threshold	32,010
Plus: Gross PPC	5,200
Gross Gift Aid (£2,400 × 100/80)	3,000
Extended basic rate band	40,210

(b) **Self-assessment deadlines**

Tutor's top tips

There are easy marks to be had in part (b), provided you have learnt the filing deadlines.

It is very important that you learn the self-assessment rules and key dates for filing and payments of tax, as these are very often examined.

- Unless the return is issued late, the latest date that Domingo and Erigo can file paper self-assessment tax returns for 2013/14 is 31 October 2014.
- If Domingo completes a paper tax return by 31 October 2014 then HM Revenue and Customs will prepare a self-assessment tax computation on his behalf.
- Fargo has until 31 January 2015 to file his self-assessment tax return for 2013/14 online.

(c) **Retention of records**

Tutor's top tips

Again these are easy marks if you have learnt the rules.

As there are three marks available, it is clear that 3 separate points must be made, which gives you a clue that the filing deadlines are not the same for all three brothers.

- Domingo and Erigo were not in business during 2013/14, so their records must be retained until one year after 31 January following the tax year, which is 31 January 2016.
- Fargo was in business during 2013/14, so all of his records (both business and non-business) must be retained until five years after 31 January following the tax year, which is 31 January 2020.
- A failure to retain records for 2013/14 could result in a penalty of up to £3,000. However, the maximum penalty will only be charged in serious cases.

Examiner's report

This question was very well answered by the majority of candidates.

In part (a) many candidates did not appreciate that donations to charity not made under Gift Aid are simply ignored, and some candidates missed the income limit for the age-related personal allowance. The expense claim in respect of the business mileage driven by the employed brother often caused problems. Either it was incorrectly calculated, or it was treated as a benefit.

Part (b) was well answered.

In part (c) few candidates appreciated that the period of retention differs between taxpayers in business and those not in business. However, virtually all candidates were aware of the £3,000 penalty.

ACCA marking scheme		
		Marks
(a)(i)	**Domingo Gomez**	
	Pensions	1.0
	Building society interest	1.0
	Interest from savings certificates	0.5
	Donations	0.5
	Personal allowance	2.0
	Income tax	1.0
		6.0
(ii)	**Erigo Gomez**	
	Salary	0.5
	Pension contributions	1.0
	Charitable payroll deductions	1.0
	Relocation costs	1.0
	Mileage allowance	1.5
	Personal allowance	0.5
	Income tax	0.5
		6.0
(iii)	**Fargo Gomez**	
	Trading profit	0.5
	Pre-trading expenditure	1.0
	Capital allowances	1.5
	Personal allowance	2.0
	Extension of basic rate band	1.0
	Income tax	1.0
		7.0
(b)	Paper returns	2.0
	Return filed online	1.0
		3.0
(c)	Domingo and Erigo	1.0
	Fargo	1.0
	Penalty	1.0
		3.0
Total		25.0

16 ANDREW ZOOM  *Walk in the footsteps of a top tutor*

Key answer tips

A classic tax exam question on self-employed versus employed which was not difficult, but presented in a scenario requiring the application of knowledge to the particular situation given.

This is a newer style of question for F6 students, but is useful preparation for those planning to move on to P6.

Tutor's top tips

It is important to learn the rules for determining whether an individual is self-employed.

However, it is not enough here to simply state those rules, instead they must be applied to the situation given.

The question requirement specifically asks only for those factors that indicate employment rather than self-employment.

The answer must therefore focus on those factors, not any factors you can remember and not those that would clearly suggest self-employment rather than employment.

Even without detailed knowledge of the rules here, common sense suggestions should enable students to pick up some marks.

(a) **Factors indicating employment**

- Andrew is under the control of Slick-Productions Ltd.
- Andrew is not taking any financial risk.
- Andrew works a set number of hours, is paid by the hour and is paid for overtime.
- Andrew cannot profit from sound management.
- Andrew is required to do the work personally.
- There is an obligation to accept work that is offered.
- Andrew does not provide his own equipment.

(b) (i) **Treated as an employee**

Tutor's top tips

Part (b) involves straightforward income tax and NIC calculations, which you should be able to score well on, regardless of your answer to part (a).

Don't miss the opportunity to gain these easy marks by being put off by the first part of the question, or by running out of time.

Andrew's income tax liability for 2013/14 will be:

	£	£
Employment income		50,000
Less: PA		(9,440)
Taxable income		40,560
Income tax		
£		£
32,010 at 20%		6,402
8,550 at 40%		3,420
40,560		
Income tax liability		9,822
Class 1 NIC for 2013/14 will be:		
(£41,450 – £7,755) × 12%	4,043	
(£50,000 – £41,450) × 2%	171	
		4,214
Total income tax and NICs		14,036

(ii) **Treated as self-employed**

	£	£
Andrew's trading profit for 2013/14 will be £50,000, so his income tax liability will be unchanged (as above)		9,822
Class 2 NIC for 2013/14 (52 weeks × £2.70)		140
Class 4 NIC for 2012/13:		
(£41,450 – £7,755) × 9%	3,033	
(£50,000 – £41,450) × 2%	171	
		3,204
Total income tax and NICs		13,166

Examiner's report

This question was very well answered by the majority of candidates.

However, in part (a) only a few candidates pointed out that the taxpayer did not take any financial risk or profit from sound management.

The only common mistake in part (b) was that candidates often based their NIC calculations on the taxable income figure rather than on employment income or trading profit.

ACCA marking scheme

		Marks
(a)	Control	0.5
	Financial risk	0.5
	Basis of remuneration	1.0
	Sound management	0.5
	Required to do the work personally	0.5
	Obligation to accept work offered	0.5
	Equipment	0.5
		4.0
(b)(i)	**Treated as an employee**	
	Employment income	0.5
	Personal allowance	0.5
	Income tax liability	0.5
	Class 1 NIC	1.5
		3.0
(ii)	**Treated as self employed**	
	Income tax liability	0.5
	Class 2 NIC	1.0
	Class 4 NIC	1.5
		3.0
Total		10.0

17 NA STYLE  *Walk in the footsteps of a top tutor*

Key answer tips

This question is a classic self-employed individual scenario, testing the rules on the adjustment of profits, opening year's basis of assessment and the compilation of an income tax computation. There is also an element of self-assessment at the end.

The first three parts are relatively easy to score highly on.

Part (d) was straightforward provided the self-assessment rules had been learnt and applied to the information given.

Tutor's top tips

Remember to read the requirement carefully.

This question has clear mark allocations, which should be used to allocate the time spent on each section. You need to adopt a logical approach, using the requirements to break down the information and plan your answer.

It is possible to score very well on this sort of question, which is not technically difficult, as long as you do not panic over the quantity of information.

The first part just requires the application of the opening year rules to figures given in the question.

Be sure to explain your answer; clearly showing the tax year, basis of assessment and calculation so that method marks can be given even if the maths goes awry!

Don't forget to highlight the overlap profits as they are specifically asked for and will therefore be mark earning.

(a) **Assessable trading profits – first three tax years**

Tax year	*Basis of assessment*	£
2010/11	Actual basis (1 January 2011 to 5 April 2011) (£25,200 × 3/6)	12,600
2011/12	First 12 months trading (1 January 2011 to 31 December 2011) £25,200 + (£21,600 × 6/12)	36,000
2012/13	Current year basis (Year ended 30 June 2012)	21,600

Overlap profits

Tax year	*Profits taxed twice*	£
2011/12	(1 January 2011 to 5 April 2011) (£25,200 × 3/6)	12,600
2012/13	(1 July 2011 to 31 December 2011) (£21,600 × 6/12)	10,800
		23,400

Tutorial note

The assessment for 2011/12 is the first 12 months of trading as the accounting period ending in that year is less than 12 months from the commencement of trading.

(b) **Tax adjusted trading profit for the year ended 30 June 2013**

Tutor's top tips

Part (b) gives you clear guidance on the approach that is needed, and you should follow this – starting with the net profit and then making the necessary adjustments.

Work through the notes in order, and ensure you have dealt with every single item, as credit is given for showing nil where an adjustment is not necessary, as stated in the requirement.

If you are not sure of how to deal with an item, make a sensible assumption and move on, but do not ignore it, or waste unnecessary time.

Note that as the question has asked you to 'calculate' the adjusted profits you do not need to explain each adjustment that you make, but you should show any workings.

As you read the question it is useful to highlight all the information you will need for the computation, and then as you use this information tick each item, so you can easily check you have included everything.

	£	£
Net profit	22,000	
Depreciation	1,300	
Motor expenses (£2,200 × 7,000/8,000)	1,925	
Accountancy	0	
Legal fees in connection with the grant of a new lease	1,260	
Property expenses (£12,900 × 1/3)	4,300	
Own consumption	450	
Fine	400	
Donation to political party	80	
Trade subscription	0	
Private telephone (£1,200 × 20%)		240
Capital allowances		810
	31,715	1,050
	(1,050)	
Tax adjusted trading profit	30,665	

Tutorial note

1. *The legal cost relating to the grant of a new lease (short or long) is not allowable. Only the legal costs relating to the renewal of a short lease is specifically allowable.*
2. *Goods for own consumption are treated as if Na Style has sold the goods to herself at full market value.*

   As no entries have been made in the accounts for the withdrawal of the items, the full selling value must be adjusted for.

   If the withdrawal had been correctly accounted for at cost, only the profit element would need to be added in the adjustment of profits computation.
3. *Business expenses paid for out of Na Style's own bank accounts are still allowable deductions in her adjustment of profits computation.*

(c) (i) **Income tax computation – 2013/14**

Tutor's top tips

For part (c) a systematic approach is needed.

Remember not to ignore exempt income, as credit is given for stating that it is exempt, even though you do NOT include the figure in your computation.

Always ensure that you read the question carefully – make sure you understand whether you have to compute income tax liability or payable.

The requirement for part (c)(i) is to calculate income tax payable; therefore you need to calculate the liability and deduct the tax credits for tax already suffered at source.

Part (c)(ii) goes on to require the balancing payment after taking account of payments on account (POAs) already paid, and then requires the POAs to be paid in the following year.

	£
Trading profit	30,665
Building society interest (£560 × 100/80)	700
Interest from Individual Savings Account (exempt)	Nil
Interest from National Savings Certificate (exempt)	Nil
Interest from government stocks (received gross)	370
Dividends (£1,080 × 100/90)	1,200
Total income	32,935
Less : PA	(9,440)
Taxable income	23,495

Analysis of income (Note)

Dividends = £1,200;

Savings (£700 + £370) = £1,070;

Other income (£23,495 – £1,200 – £1,070) = £21,225

Income tax

£		
21,225	× 20% (other income)	4,245
1,070	× 20% (savings income)	214
1,200	× 10% (dividend income)	120
23,495		
Income tax liability		4,579
Less: Tax suffered at source		
Dividends (£1,200 at 10%)		(120)
Building society interest (£700 at 20%)		(140)
Income tax payable		4,319

Tutorial note

There is nothing wrong in presenting your computation in columnar form if you prefer to, however there is also no need to do so if you do not want to.

However, you do need to be able to break down the taxable income into the different types of income, namely: dividends, savings and other income, in order to apply the correct rates of tax to each type of income.

(ii) **Tax payments**

- Na's balancing payment for 2013/14 due on 31 January 2015 is £1,119 (£4,319 – £3,200).
- Her payments on account for 2014/15 will be £2,160 and £2,159 (£4,319 × 50%). These will be due on 31 January 2015 and 31 July 2015.

(d) **Late payment of balancing payment**

Tutor's top tips

Part (d) carries only 3 marks, so there are likely to be three clear bullet points to make.

You have either learnt these rules or not, but even if you cannot remember the exact rules, do not ignore this part.

Remember that an educated guess should have enabled you to write something worthy of a mark!

Note that there is usually interest to pay on late tax and a penalty, depending on the timing.

Calculations of interest should be to the nearest month unless the question says otherwise.

- Late payment interest is charged where a balancing payment is paid late.

  This will run from 31 January 2015 to 31 May 2015.
- The interest charge will be £11 (£1,119 × 3% × 4/12).
- In addition, a late payment penalty of £56 (£1,119 at 5%) will be imposed as the balancing payment is made more than one month late (but less than six months late).

Examiner's report

This question was very well answered, and there were many high scoring answers.

In part (a) some candidates lost marks because they did not show the relevant tax years in which profits were assessable.

There were few problems as regards the calculation of the trading profit or the income tax payable, although many candidates did not appreciate that interest from government stocks is received gross and is taxable.

As regards the balancing payment and payments on account, candidates were often not aware of the relevant dates.

In part (d) many candidates did not appreciate that a late payment penalty would be imposed in addition to the interest charge.

ACCA marking scheme				*Marks*
(a)	2010/11			1.0
	2011/12		– Assessment	1.5
			– Overlap profits	1.0
	2012/13		– Assessment	0.5
			– Overlap profits	1.0
				5.0
(b)	Net profit			0.5
	Depreciation			0.5
	Motor expenses			1.0
	Accountancy			0.5
	Legal fees			0.5
	Property expenses			1.0
	Own consumption			1.0
	Fine			0.5
	Donation to political party			0.5
	Trade subscription			0.5
	Private telephone			1.0
	Capital allowances			0.5
				8.0
(c)	(i)	Income tax computation		
		Trading profit		0.5
		Building society interest		0.5
		Individual Savings Account		0.5
		Interest from National Savings Certificate		0.5
		Interest from government stocks		1.0
		Dividends		0.5
		Personal allowance		0.5
		Income tax		1.0
		Tax suffered at source		1.0
				6.0
	(ii)	Tax payments		
		Balancing payment		1.5
		Payments on account		1.5
				3.0
(d)	Interest			1.0
	Calculation			1.0
	Penalty			1.0
				3.0
Total				25.0

18 SIMON HOUSE (ADAPTED)  *Walk in the footsteps of a top tutor*

Key answer tips

A very familiar style question covering the Badges of Trade and requiring the calculation of the tax consequences of a transaction being deemed to be a trading transaction or a capital event.

Easy marks should have been picked up in this question.

Tutor's top tips

Usually these questions start with the requirement for you to list and then apply the Badges of Trade. However, this question is unusual in that it kindly gives you the Badges of Trade that it requires you to consider and asks you to explain the ***meaning*** *of each for only 3 marks.*

It is fairly certain that half a mark will be allocated to each explanation and so therefore it is not possible, or necessary, to write huge amounts on any one explanation. Note also that it only requires an explanation of the badges of trade listed. Do not waste time explaining other badges of trade that are used by HM Revenue & Customs as you will not gain an extra marks.

Try to be clear and succinct and to the point and move on!

(a) **Badges of trade**

- Trading is indicated where the property (subject matter) does not yield an ongoing income or give personal enjoyment to its owner.
- The sale of property within a short time of its acquisition is an indication of trading.
- Trading is indicated by repeated transactions in the same subject matter.
- A trading motive is indicated where work is carried out to the property to make it more marketable, or where steps are taken to find purchasers.
- A forced sale to raise cash for an emergency is an indication that the transaction is not of a trading nature.
- If a transaction is undertaken with the motive of realising a profit, this is a strong indication of trading.

(b) **Treated as carrying on a trade**

Tutor's top tips

If the transaction is treated as a trade transaction, a straightforward trading profit computation is required.

Simon is then liable to income tax and Class 4 NICs on the trading profit and Class 2 NICs as he will be self-employed.

Make sure you show your calculations for each liability clearly.

Income tax – 2013/14

	£	£
Income		260,000
Cost of property	127,000	
Renovation costs	50,600	
Loan interest (£150,000 × 6% × 4/12)(Note)	3,000	
Legal fees (£1,800 + £2,600)	4,400	
		(185,000)
Trading profit		75,000
Less: PA		(9,440)
Taxable income		65,560
£		
32,010 × 20%		6,402
33,550 × 40%		13,420
65,560		
Income tax liability		19,822

Tutorial note

If treated as a trade, all costs incurred wholly and exclusively for the purposes of the trade are allowable deductions – including interest on the loan to purchase the house.

National Insurance – 2013/14

	£
Class 2 NIC (18 weeks × £2.70)	49
Class 4 NIC	
(£41,450 – £7,755) × 9%	3,033
(£75,000 – £41,450) × 2%	671
	3,704

(c) **Treated as a capital transaction**

Tutor's top tips

You should know that the consequences of applying the Badges of Trade are to determine whether or not the transaction is a trading one, or a capital event.

However, you did not necessarily need to remember that in this question as the examiner has kindly told you to what to do (i.e. calculate the capital gains tax liability).

Capital gains tax liability – 2013/14

	£	£
Proceeds		260,000
Less: Incidental costs – legal fees		(2,600)
		257,400
Less: Cost	127,000	
Enhancement expenditure	50,600	
Loan interest (Note)	Nil	
Incidental costs	1,800	
		(179,400)
Chargeable gain		78,000
Less: AEA		(10,900)
Taxable gain		67,100
£		
32,010 × 18%		5,762
35,090 × 28%		9,825
67,100		
Capital gains tax liability		15,587

Tutorial note

If it is treated as a capital transaction, no relief is available for the interest on the loan used to finance the transaction.

PPR and letting relief are not available as the property has never been his principal private residence.

Entrepreneurs' relief is not available as the house is an investment property, not a business, and it has been owned for less than 12 months.

The gain is taxed at 18% to the extent that it falls in the basic rate band and 28% on the excess. As Simon has no other income or gains, the first £32,010 is taxed at 18%.

Examiner's report

This question was very well answered, and often helped marginal candidates to achieve a pass mark.

In part (a) a number of candidates failed to score any marks because they did not state what did or did not indicate trading. For example, stating that the 'length of ownership' means how long an item has been owned did not score any marks. It was necessary to explain that the sale of property within a short time of its acquisition is an indication of trading.

Part (b) presented no problems for most candidates. In this type of question it is always best to produce full computations for each option. This will maximise marks if any mistakes are made.

It was pleasing to see that many candidates correctly restricted the Class 2 NIC to 18 weeks' contributions.

ACCA marking scheme

		Marks
(a)	The subject matter	0.5
	Length of ownership	0.5
	Frequency	0.5
	Work done	0.5
	Circumstances responsible for realisation	0.5
	Motive	0.5
		3.0
(b)	Income	0.5
	Cost of property	0.5
	Renovation costs	0.5
	Loan interest	1.0
	Legal fees	1.0
	Personal allowance	0.5
	Income tax liability	1.0
	Class 2 NIC	1.5
	Class 4 NIC	1.5
		8.0
(c)	Proceeds	0.5
	Cost	0.5
	Enhancement expenditure	0.5
	Incidental costs	0.5
	Loan interest	0.5
	Annual exempt amount	0.5
	Capital gains tax	1.0
		4.0
Total		15.0

19 BAYLE DEFENDER (ADAPTED)  *Walk in the footsteps of a top tutor*

Key answer tips

A long, time pressured question on self-employment, involving income tax, self-assessment and NICs.

Part (a) firstly requires a straightforward adjustment of profits computation which should not have caused problems.

The subsequent income tax computation tests the reduction of the personal allowance for high earners and the additional rates of tax.

The third part covers self-assessment payments, interest and penalties. These areas are often tested and should be straightforward provided the rules have been learnt.

Part (b) is more complicated as it involves a new person joining a sole trader part way through the accounting period and tax year, either as an employee or a partner.

The employment NIC calculations were not straightforward as the annual basis cannot be applied to the 4 months of earnings. In addition the trading income assessments need to be very carefully calculated by allocating the partnership profits first, then applying the opening year rules.

The self-employment NIC calculations are however straightforward and should not cause difficulties.

Many of the sub-parts in this question require figures brought forward from previous parts. However it is important to remember that full credit will still be given for subsequent parts even if the earlier part is calculated incorrectly.

(a) (i) **Trading profit – year ended 30 September 2013**

	£
Net profit	172,400
Impairment loss (Note 1)	0
Gifts to customers – Clocks (Note 2)	3,300
– Bottles of champagne (Note 2)	2,480
Donations to political parties	2,900
Lease of motor car (£10,360 × 15%) (Note 3)	1,554
Personal tax advice (Note 4)	600
Property expenses (£46,240 × 2/5)	18,496
Parking fines (Note 4)	520
Professional subscription	0
Golf club membership fee (Note 4)	960
Trading profit	203,210

Tutorial note

1. *The recovered impairment loss will have been allowed as a deduction when originally written off, so the recovery is now taxable. As it is already included in the revenue figure given, there is no adjustment required.*

2. *Gifts to customers are only an allowable deduction if they cost less than £50 per recipient per year, are not of food, drink, tobacco or vouchers exchangeable for goods and carry a conspicuous advertisement for the company making the gift.*

   Therefore the clocks are not allowable as they cost in excess of £50, and the champagne is drink and not allowable.

3. *The leased motor car has a CO_2 emission rate in excess of 130 grams per kilometre, therefore 15% of the leasing costs are not allowed.*

4. *Personal expenditure is not allowable. Therefore the tax advice, the golf membership and the parking fines of Bayle are not allowable and need to be adjusted for. Note that parking fines incurred by employees whilst on business activity would be allowable, but not fines incurred by the owner of the business.*

(ii) **Income tax computation – 2013/14**

	Total	*Other*	*Savings*	*Dividends*
	£	£	£	£
Trading profit (part (a)(i)) (Note 1)	203,210	203,210		
Employment income				
Director's remuneration	42,000	42,000		
Bonus payment (Note 2)	6,000	6,000		
NSC interest (Note 3)	Exempt			
Government stock interest (Note 4)	3,600		3,600	
Dividends (£9,900 × 100/90)	11,000			11,000
Total income	265,810	251,210	3,600	11,000
Less: PA (Note 5)	(Nil)			
Taxable income	265,810	251,210	3,600	11,000

Income tax		
£		£
32,010 at 20%	(other)	6,402
117,990 at 40%	(other)	47,196
150,000		
101,210 at 45%	(other)	45,544
251,210		
3,600 at 45% (savings)		1,620
11,000 at 37·5% (dividends)		4,125
265,810		
Income tax liability		104,887
Less: Tax suffered at source		
Dividends (£11,000 at 10%)		(1,100)
PAYE ((£42,000 + £6,000) = £48,000 at 45%)		(21,600)
Income tax payable		82,187

Tutorial note

1 *The trading income figure comes from part (a)(i). However, full credit would be given for this part, even if the previous part was calculated incorrectly, provided you calculate the income tax correctly based on your figure.*

2 *The bonus payment of £6,000 that Bayle became entitled to on 10 March 2013 will have been taxed already as it would have been treated as received during 2012/13.*

3 *Interest received on the maturity of savings certificates issued by National Savings & Investments is exempt income. Note that in the examination, do not ignore exempt income. Instead, make sure you clearly show that you know it is exempt income.*

4 *Interest received on government stocks (gilts) is received gross.*

5 *Bayle's total income = net income = adjusted net income (ANI) as she has no reliefs and has not made any Gift Aid donations or personal pension contributions in the tax year. Accordingly, there is no personal allowance available to Bayle as her ANI of £265,810 exceeds £118,880.*

(iii) **Tax payment due on 31 January 2015**

	£	£
Balancing payment for 2013/14:		
Income tax payable (part (a)(ii))	82,187	
Less: Payments on account (POAs)	(53,400)	
		28,787
First POA for 2014/15:		
(£82,187 × 50%)		41,094
Payment due on 31 January 2015		69,881

Tutor's top tips:

The income tax payable figure comes from part (a)(ii). However, full credit would be given for this part, even if the previous part was calculated incorrectly, provided you calculated the balancing payment and first POA correctly based on your figures.

Interest and penalties

- Interest is charged where payments are made late, from the date the tax was due to be paid to the date of payment.
- Interest will be calculated from 31 January 2015 to 31 August 2015.
- The interest charge will be £1,223 (£69,881 × 3.0% × 7/12).
- Two penalties of £1,439 (£28,787 at 5%) will be imposed on the balancing payment, one when it is one month late and the other when it is six months late.

Tutorial note

Note that penalties for late payment do not apply to payments of account so that in the above answer the penalties only apply to the late balancing payment for 2013/14.

Tutor's top tips:

The payment due on 31 January 2015 and the balancing payment figures come from the previous part. However, full credit would be given for this part, even if the previous part was calculated incorrectly, provided you calculated the interest at the appropriate rate and for the correct period of time based on your figures, and the penalty at the correct rate.

Note that technically the penalties for late payment apply if the tax is paid more than 30 days late and 5 months and 30 days late. However the examiner has given dates to the nearest month and it is acceptable for you to do so in the examination.

(b) **National insurance – if Fyle is employed**

Class 1 – primary employee contributions – paid by Fyle

(£3,300 – £646 (W)) × 12% × 4 months = £1,274

Class 1 – secondary employer contributions – paid by Bayle

(£3,300 – £641) × 13.8% × 4 months = £1,468

Working:

The monthly earnings thresholds are as follows:

Employee Class 1 NIC

Primary earnings threshold (PET) = (£7,755 × 1/12) = £646

Upper earnings limit = (£41,450 × 1/12) = £3,454

Fyle's monthly earnings are £3,300 which falls in between these limits.

For each month that Fyle is employed, he is therefore liable to Class 1 NICs at 12% on the excess over the PET of £646.

Employer Class 1 NIC

Secondary earnings threshold (SET) = (£7,696 × 1/12) = £641

Bayle, as Fyle's employer, is liable to Class 1 NICs at 13.8% on the excess over the SET of £641.

Fyle will be employed for 4 months of the tax year (December to March inclusive).

Tutor's top tips:

Usually at F6, for simplicity, NICs are calculated on an annual basis using the annual limits. In this question however the individual has only been employed for four months in the tax year. Accordingly, the annual limits need to be time apportioned.

This is because NICs are actually calculated on a payment period basis. This means that if an individual is paid monthly, the monthly limits are used (e.g. for primary Class 1 NICs, £646 and £3,454). If they are paid on a weekly basis, the weekly limits are used. For primary Class 1 NICs these are £149 (£7,755 × 1/52) and £797 (£41,450 × 1/52).

The examiner has confirmed that the alternative approach of using the annual earnings threshold and then taking 4/12ths of an annual NIC figure was acceptable in the exam.

(ii) **Trading income assessments**

Allocation of partnership profits

	Total	*Bayle*	*Fyle*
	£	£	£
y/e 30.9.14			
1.10.13 to 30.11.13 (2 mths)			
All profits to Bayle	36,000	36,000	
1.12.13 to 30.09.14 (10 mths)			
PSR (80%:20%)	180,000	144,000	36,000
	216,000	180,000	36,000
y/e 30.9.15			
PSR (80%:20%)	240,000	192,000	48,000

Applying basis of assessment rules

If Fyle joins the partnership on 1 December 2013, the opening year rules will apply to his profit share as follows:

Tax year	*Basis of assessment*		
		£	£
2013/14	Actual basis		
	(1.12.13 to 5.4.14)		
	(£36,000 × 4/10) (Note)		14,400
2014/15	First 12 months trading		
	(1.12.13 to 30.11.14)		
	10 m/e 30.9.14	36,000	
	y/e 30.9.15 × 2/12 (£48,000 × 2/12)	8,000	
			44,000

Tutorial note

The partnership profits should be allocated to the partners according to the partnership agreement in the accounting period.

The basis of assessment rules are then applied to each partner's share of profits separately.

Bayle was a sole trader and becomes a partner. However she will continue to be assessed on a current year basis (CYB).

The commencement rules will apply to Fyle's share of profits from 2013/14 since he will join as a partner on 1 December 2013.

NICs – 2013/14

Paid by Fyle – self employed

Class 2 NICs (Note 1) = (18 weeks × £2.70) = £49

Class 4 NICs (Note 2) = (£14,400 – £7,755) × 9% = £598

Paid by Bayle

There are no NIC implications for Bayle in relation to Fyle's trading income assessments (Note 3).

Tutorial note

1 *Class 2 NICs are £2.70 per week. If Fyle joins the partnership on 1 December 2013, he will be a partner for the period 1 December 2013 to 5 April 2014 which is 126 days (31 + 31 + 28 + 31 + 5), which is 18 weeks (126 days ÷ 7).*

2 *Class 4 NICs are calculated using the full annual lower profits limit (£7,755 in 2013/14), they are not time apportioned, as the opening year rules produce an assessment for the full tax year 2013/14.*

This trading income assessment figure comes from the previous part. However, full credit would be given for this part even if the assessment was calculated incorrectly provided you calculated the NICs correctly based on your figure.

3 *The question asks for the NICs to be paid by Bayle, but only in relation to Fyle's trading income assessment. The question specifically says that her own NICs are not to be calculated.*

Examiner's report

Parts (a)(i), (a)(ii) and (b)(i) were generally well answered, but candidates had more difficulty with the other sections.

In part (a)(i) the only consistent problem was the revenue received in respect of a previously written off impairment loss. Most candidates did not appreciate that no adjustment was necessary.

In part (a)(ii) it was often not appreciated that one of the bonuses was treated as being received in the previous tax year, and often bonuses were included or excluded without any explanation as to why. It should have been obvious that with income of over £250,000 no personal allowance was available, yet many candidates wasted time by showing a calculation for this.

Many candidates simply ignored part (a)(iii), and very few appreciated that both the balancing payment for 2013/14 and the first payment on account for 2014/15 were due on 31 January 2015.

In part (b)(i) it was pleasing to see several candidates correctly restricted NIC contributions to the four months of employment.

Although there were also many good answers to part (b)(ii), there were also a lot of candidates who wasted time by doing NIC calculations for both the taxpayer and the new person, or NIC calculations for both years, instead of just the one required.

ACCA marking scheme			
			Marks
(a)	(i)	Impairment loss	0.5
		Gifts to customers	1.0
		Donations to political parties	0.5
		Lease of motor car	1.0
		Personal tax advice	0.5
		Property expenses	1.0
		Parking fines	0.5
		Professional subscription	0.5
		Golf club membership fee	0.5
			6.0
	(ii)	Trading profit	0.5
		Director's remuneration	0.5
		Bonus payments	1.0
		Interest from government stocks	0.5
		Interest from savings certificate	0.5
		Dividends	0.5
		Personal allowance	1.0
		Income tax	2.0
		Tax suffered at source	1.5
			8.0
	(iii)	Balancing payment	1.0
		Payment on account	1.0
		Interest	1.5
		Penalties	1.5
			5.0
(b)	(i)	Monthly earnings threshold	1.0
		Employee Class 1 NIC	1.5
		Employer Class 1 NIC	1.5
			4.0
	(ii)	Trading income assessments	
		2013/14	1.5
		2014/15	2.5
			4.0
		NIC re Fyle	
		Class 2 NIC	1.5
		Class 4 NIC	1.0
		Bayle	0.5
			3.0
Total			30.0

TRADING LOSSES

20 NORMA (ADAPTED)

Key answer tips

The first part required the computation of taxable income for five tax years before considering loss relief.

Marks should have been gained here in laying out pro forma computations and filling in the easy numbers before applying the opening and closing year rules to establish the trading income assessments. A loss arises in the final tax year and so the trading income assessment in that year will be £Nil.

The second part involved consideration of the options available for loss relief, including a terminal loss.

It is important to communicate to the examiner that you know the loss relief rules, however you must apply the knowledge to the specific facts of the question.

(a) **Taxable income and gains before loss relief**

	2009/10	*2010/11*	*2011/12*	*2012/13*	*2013/14*
	£	£	£	£	£
Trading income (W)	25,250	17,000	15,500	7,835	Nil
Employment income (£11,400 × 10/12)					9,500
Interest income	2,000	2,000	2,000	2,000	2,000
Total income	27,250	19,000	17,500	9,835	11,500
Less: PA	(9,440)	(9,440)	(9,440)	(9,440)	(9,440)
Taxable income	17,810	9,560	8,060	395	2,060
Taxable gain				35,000	

Working: Trading income

Tax year	*Basis of assessment*	£	£
2009/10	Actual basis (1.5.09 – 5.4.10)		
	Period to 31.12.09	21,000	
	1.1.10 – 5.4.10 (£17,000 × 3/12)	4,250	
			25,250
2010/11	Year ended 31.12.10		17,000
2011/12	Year ended 31.12.11		15,500
2012/13	Year ended 31.12.12		7,835
2013/14	Year of cessation		
	Period to 31 May 2013	(11,000)	
	Less: Overlap profits (1.1.10 – 5.4.10) (£17,000 × 3/12)	(4,250)	
	Trading loss/Trading assessment	(15,250)	Nil

Tutorial note

If the trader does not have a 31 March (or 5 April) year end you should be looking for overlap relief. The overlap relief increases the loss of the final year and is included in the calculation of the terminal loss.

(b) **Options available to utilise loss arising in period ended 31 May 2013**

(1) **Relief against total income**

The loss arising in 2013/14 can be set against total income in 2013/14 and/or 2012/13.

(i) Setting the loss against total income of 2013/14 (i.e. employment income and bank interest) would reduce total income to £Nil, would waste the personal allowance and save tax at 10% on £2,000 and 20% on £60.

The remaining loss of £3,750 (£15,250 – £11,500) could be offset against total income of 2012/13, wasting part of the personal allowance and saving tax at 10% on £395 (see Tutorial Note).

(ii) Setting the loss against total income of 2012/13 would reduce total income to £Nil, would waste the personal allowance and save tax at 10% on £395.

The remaining loss of £5,415 (£15,250 – £9,835) could be offset against total income of 2013/14, which would waste part of the personal allowance and save tax at 10% on £2,000 and 20% on £60.

Tutorial note

The rate of tax saving in 2012/13 on £395 and in 2013/14 on £2,000 is 10% because Norma's taxable income includes savings income which will fall into the first £2,790 of taxable income in those years.

(2) **Relief against chargeable gains**

Alternatively, once a claim has been made to offset trading losses against total income in 2012/13, a claim can be made to offset any remaining losses against chargeable gains in 2012/13 instead of total income in 2013/14.

Accordingly, the £5,415 loss remaining after the offset against total income in 2012/13 could be set against the chargeable gain arising in that year.

Assuming that the current tax rates apply throughout this question, this will save tax at 18% on some of the gain and 28% on the remaining gain (see note).

Tutorial note

Currently, before loss relief, there is £31,615 (£32,010 – £395) of gain in the basic rate band and £3,385 (£35,000 – £31,615) in the higher rate band.

So using £5,415 of loss against the gain would save 28% on the top £3,385 of the gain, and 18% on £2,030 (£5,415 – £3,385).

(3) **Terminal loss relief**

The loss arising in the final 12 months of trading can be set against:

- available trading profits
- in the year of cessation, and
- the three preceding tax years
- on a last-in-first-out (LIFO) basis.

Calculation of terminal loss			£
(1) 6 April before cessation to date of cessation (6.4.13 – 31.5.13) (£11,000 loss × 2/5)			4,400
(2) 12 months before cessation to 5 April before cessation	£		
1.6.12 – 31.12.12 (£7,835 profit × 7/12)	4,570	Profit	
1.1.13 – 5.4.13 (£11,000 loss × 3/5)	(6,600)	Loss	
	(2,030)	Net Loss	2,030
(3) Overlap relief 1.1.10 – 5.4.10 (£17,000 × 3/12)			4,250
Terminal loss			10,680

Utilisation of terminal loss

Norma has no trading profits in 2013/14, the year of cessation.

The terminal loss can therefore be carried back against the trading profits arising in the preceding three years, on a LIFO basis, as follows:

	2010/11	*2011/12*	*2012/13*
	£	£	£
Trading income	17,000	15,500	7,835
Less: Terminal loss relief	(Nil)	(2,845)	(7,835)
	17,000	12,655	Nil
Interest income	2,000	2,000	2,000
Net income	19,000	14,655	2,000
Less: PA	(9,440)	(9,440)	(9,440)
Taxable income	9,560	5,215	Nil

The terminal loss reduces taxable income in 2012/13 to £Nil, wasting the personal allowance and saving tax at 10% on £395.

The remaining loss of £2,845 (£10,680 – £7,835) is then offset against the taxable income in 2011/12, saving tax at 20% on £2,845.

Tutorial note

Taxable income in 2011/12 before loss relief of £2,845 comprises other income of £6,060 (£15,500 – £9,440 PA) and savings income of £2,000. Tax on the loss of £2,845 is therefore saved at 20% on other income.

21 LEONARDO

Key answer tips

An opening year loss relief question, requiring a calculation of the assessments for the first few tax years and consideration of loss claims available.

Part (b) should have provided easy marks in stating due dates for making elections.

(a) **Assessments**

Tax year	*Basis period*		£
2010/11	Actual basis		
	(1.9.10 – 5.4.11)	7/9 × £40,500	31,500
2011/12	First 12 months		
	(1.9.10 – 31.8.11)	£40,500 – (3/12 × £54,000)	27,000
2012/13	CYB (y/e 31.5.12)	Loss	Nil
2013/14	CYB (y/e 31.5.13)	Loss	Nil
2014/15	CYB (y/e 31.5.14)		11,000

Key answer tips

As Leonardo will not be making any significant profits in the foreseeable future there is no point in carrying losses forward, therefore offset the losses as soon as possible.

Note the question does not require any calculation of tax savings, just computations to show how the loss would be utilised.

Loss memoranda

Loss in 2012/13	£
Loss in y/e 31.5.2012	54,000
Less: Relief given in 2011/12 when applying the opening year rules (£54,000 × 3/12)	(13,500)
	40,500
Less: Special opening year loss relief – in 2010/11	(31,500)
– in 2011/12	(9,000)
	Nil

Loss in 2013/14	£
Loss in y/e 31.5.2013	27,000
Less: Special opening year loss relief in 2011/12	(18,000)
Loss carried forward to 2014/15	9,000

Assessments after loss relief claims

	2010/11	*2011/12*	*2012/13*	*2013/14*	*2014/15*
	£	£	£	£	£
Trading income	31,500	27,000	Nil	Nil	11,000
Less: Loss relief b/f	–	–	–	–	(9,000)
	31,500	27,000	Nil	Nil	2,000
Less: Special opening year loss relief:					
– 2012/13 Loss	(31,500)	(9,000)			
– 2013/14 Loss		(18,000)			
Net income	Nil	Nil	Nil	Nil	2,000

Tutorial note

*Under special opening year loss provisions, losses that arise in the **first four tax years** of a trade may be set off against:*

- *the total income*
- *of the three years preceding the tax year of loss*
- *on a first-in-first-out (FIFO) basis.*

(b) **Loss relief time limits**

(i) **Special opening year loss relief and 'normal' loss relief against total income**

For claims to carry back losses in the first four years of a trade against income of the three preceding years, and claims to set-off losses against income of the year of the loss and income of the preceding year, the claim must be made:

– within 12 months from 31 January next following the tax year in which the loss was sustained.

In the case of the loss sustained in the year ended 31 May 2012 (i.e. the loss in 2012/13), the claim must be made:

– by 31 January 2015.

In the case of the loss sustained in the year ended 31 May 2013 (i.e. the loss in 2013/14), the claim must be made:

– by 31 January 2016.

(ii) **Carry forward of losses**

There is no specific statutory time limit on claims to carry forward losses against future trading income.

However, a claim to establish the amount of the loss to be carried forward must be made:

– within four years from the end of the tax year in which the loss was sustained

In the case of the loss sustained in the year ended 31 May 2013 (i.e. the loss in 2013/14)

– by 5 April 2018.

22 DEE ZYNE  *Walk in the footsteps of a top tutor*

Key answer tips

An individual that is employed for part of the year, then sets up a business which is initially loss-making, is a common scenario in examination questions.

The calculation of the adjusted loss was straight forward provided you remembered to time apportion WDAs in the opening period of account.

The employment income computation tested classic benefit rules and you were instructed to utilise the loss against the employment income.

Part (c) required consideration of alternative claims and it was fairly obvious why they would be more beneficial than a current year claim.

The highlighted words in the written sections are key phrases that markers are looking for.

Tutor's top tips

In this question, Dee has 5 April as her year end, so the capital allowances are calculated for the period ended 5 April 2014.

However, where a sole trader chooses a different year end, remember that the capital allowances are always calculated for the period of account before matching profits or losses to tax years.

(a) **Tax adjusted trading loss – 2013/14**

	£
Trading loss	(11,440)
Patent royalties (Note)	(500)
Capital allowances (W)	(5,690)
	(17,630)

Tutorial note

The patent royalties were incurred for the trade purposes and are therefore deductible in computing the tax adjusted trading loss. As the question says they have not been accounted for in arriving at the loss of £11,440, they must be adjusted for and will increase the loss.

Working – Capital allowances		*Main Pool*	*Car*		*Allowances*
	£	£	£		£
Additions (no AIA)					
Car (between 96 – 130 g/km)		10,400			
Car (> 130 g/km) (Note 1)			17,800		
Additions (with AIA)					
Computer	1,257				
Office furniture	2,175				
	3,432				
Less: AIA (Note 2)	(3,432)				3,432
		Nil			
Less: WDA (18% × 9/12)		(1,404)			1,404
Less: WDA (8% × 9/12) (Note 3)			(1,068)	× 80%	854
TWDV c/f		8,996	16,732		
Total allowances					5,690

Tutorial note

1 *Capital allowances on new purchases of cars are calculated based on their CO_2 emissions.*

The car with CO_2 emissions of between 96 – 130 g/km is put in the main pool and is eligible for a writing down allowance at 18%.

The car with CO_2 emissions of > 130 g/km is a private use car, has its own column and is eligible for a writing down allowance at 8%.

2 *The maximum AIA and the WDAs are time apportioned because Dee's period of account is only nine months' in length.*

However, the maximum AIA of £187,500 (£250,000 × 9/12) exceeds the total qualifying expenditure and therefore all of the expenditure is eligible for relief.

3 *Only private use by the owner restricts capital allowances. Private use of the employee's motor car therefore does not affect the capital allowance claim, but will instead result in an assessable employment benefit for that employee.*

(b) **Income tax computation – 2013/14**

Tutor's top tips

Watch the dates carefully here! Where a benefit has only been available for part of the tax year, it must be time apportioned.

If you are leaving out a benefit because it is exempt, it is always a good idea to say so, as there will often be a mark available for this.

Don't worry if your loss calculation in part (a) was not completely right. You could still score full marks in this section if your calculations are correct, based on your figures. Make sure you show your workings, so that the marker can see what rates you have used.

	£
Salary	26,000
Car benefit (W1)	940
Fuel benefit (W1)	1,635
Beneficial loan (W2)	300
Staff canteen (exempt) (Note 1)	Nil
Employment income	28,875
Less: Reliefs	
Loan interest (Note 2)	(110)
Loss relief – current year claim	(17,630)
Net income	11,135
Less: PA	(9,440)
Taxable income	1,695

	£
Income tax liability (£1,695 x 20%)	339
Less: Tax suffered at source – PAYE	(5,400)
Income tax repayable	(5,061)

Tutorial note

1 *The provision of meals in a staff canteen does not give rise to a taxable benefit.*

2 *The loan interest qualifies as a deduction against total income since the loan was used by Dee to finance expenditure for a qualifying purpose.*

The qualifying interest is deducted from total income in priority to the loss relief.

Workings

(W1) Car and fuel benefits

CO_2 emissions = 198 g/km (rounded down to 195 g/km), available 3 months

	%
Petrol	11
Plus: (195 – 95) × $^1/_5$	20
Appropriate percentage	31
	£
List price	17,500
Less: Capital contribution	(1,500)
	16,000
Car benefit (£16,000 × 31% × 3/12)	1,240
Less: Contribution for provision of car (£100 × 3)	(300)
	940
Fuel benefit (£21,100 × 31% × 3/12)	1,635

(W2) Beneficial loan

Tutor's top tips

Where the amount of the loan has changed during the year, you should always show both calculations of the benefit; the average and the precise method.

	£	£
Average method		
Loan at start of year	60,000	
Loan at end of the loan	15,000	
	75,000	
Average loan (£75,000 ÷ 2)	37,500	
Assessable benefit (£37,500 × 4% × 3/12)		375
Precise method		
(£60,000 × 4% × 1/12)	200	
(£15,000 × 4% × 2/12)	100	
		300

Dee will elect for the precise method to apply.

The benefit will be £300.

Tutorial note

Remember that if the average method gives the lower benefit, the taxpayer can use the average method.

However, HMRC can insist that the precise method be used, although they do not usually do so unless the difference between the two methods is material.

(c) **Alternative use of trading loss**

Tutor's top tips

When you are describing use of losses, you must be very specific about exactly what the loss can be set against, and when. For example, don't just say "the loss can be set off in the current year". Specify in which tax year that is, and state that the loss can be set against total income.

The examiner has said that the use of section numbers is not required and is not encouraged at the expense of explaining the relief.

- The loss could have been claimed against total income for 2012/13.
- The loss is incurred within the first four years of trading, so a claim for special opening year loss relief could have been made against total income for the three years 2010/11 to 2012/13, earliest first.
- By claiming loss relief against her total income for 2013/14, Dee has relieved the loss entirely at the basic rate of 20% and reduced her income tax liability by £3,526 (£17,630 at 20%).
- As Dee's total income in the years 2010/11 to 2012/13 was £80,000, either of the alternative loss relief claims would have relieved the loss at the higher rate of 40%, and resulted in an income tax refund of £7,052 (£17,630 at 40%).

23 SAMANTHA FABRIQUE (ADAPTED)

Key answer tips

This is a losses question that requires you to choose the best use of the loss.

Given the information about gains it should be fairly obvious that you need to consider a claim against capital gains. However, remember that this only saves tax at 18% or 28% (for a higher rate taxpayer) and can only happen after a claim against total income has been made first in that year.

Be careful to consider the loss relief restriction which applies to loss claims against total income other than the profits of the same trade. This restriction did not apply in the question as originally set, as these rules did not exist then.

Part (a) should have provided easy marks listing the factors a taxpayer takes into account when deciding what to do with a loss.

(a) **Factors influencing choice of loss relief claims**

- The rate of income tax or capital gains tax at which relief will be obtained, with preference being given to income charged at the higher rate of 40% or additional rate of 45%.
- The timing of the relief obtained, with a claim against total income/chargeable gains of the current year or preceding year resulting in earlier relief than a claim against future trading profits.
- The extent to which personal allowances and the capital gains annual exempt amount may be wasted.

Key answer tips

As long as you addressed the factors influencing the choice of relief, not what the relief options are, you should have scored well here.

(b) **Taxable income and gains**

	2012/13	*2013/14*	*2014/15*
	£	£	£
Trading income	21,600	Nil	10,500
Interest	52,100	3,800	1,500
	73,700	3,800	12,000
Less: Loss relief		(Nil)	
– against trade profits (no restriction)	(21,600)		
– against other income (restricted)	(50,000)		
	2,100	3,800	12,000
Less: PA	(9,440)	(9,440)	(9,440)
Taxable income	Nil	Nil	2,560

	2012/13	*2013/14*	*2014/15*
	£	£	£
Capital gains	53,300	Nil	11,300
Less: Trading loss relief	(10,300)		
	43,000	Nil	11,300
Less: Capital loss b/f	–	–	(400)
	43,000	Nil	10,900
Less: AEA	(10,900)	(wasted)	(10,900)
Taxable gains	32,100	Nil	Nil

Tutorial note

The loss relief in 2012/13 against total income is restricted due to the cap on income tax reliefs. The losses offset against profits from the same trade are not restricted, therefore £21,600 of loss can be set against trading income. A further £50,000 of loss relief is available as this is the higher of £50,000 and 25% of total income – £18,425 (£73,700 × 25%).

Although these two claims are both set off against total income in the computation, you may find it helpful to separate them out to ensure you relieve the correct amount of loss.

Loss memorandum

	£
Loss in 2013/14	81,900
Less: Relief against total income	
2013/14 (no claim as income covered by PA)	(Nil)
2012/13 – total claim	(71,600)
Loss remaining	10,300
Less: Relief against chargeable gains	
2012/13	(10,300)
Loss carried forward	Nil

Utilisation of losses

Trading loss

Loss relief has been claimed:

- against total income for 2012/13,
- then against the chargeable gains of 2012/13.

This gives relief at the earliest date and at the highest rates of tax.

Capital loss

The capital loss for 2013/14 is carried forward and set against the chargeable gains for 2014/15.

The use of brought forward capital losses is restricted to the level that reduces gains down to equal the annual exempt amount (£11,300 – £400 = £10,900).

The balance of the loss £3,000 (£3,400 – £400) is carried forward against future gains.

Tutorial note

For 2012/13, if relief is claimed, the personal allowance is partially wasted in that year and the tax saving will be at 40% and 20% for income tax and 28% for capital gains.

Offsetting losses in 2013/14 however would utilise £3,800 of the loss, would waste the personal allowance and would not save any tax.

A claim against total income must be made before relief against chargeable gains can be considered.

Carrying all of the loss forward would use £10,500 of loss, would waste most of the personal allowance and would only save tax partly at 20% and partly at 10%. The taxable income (before loss relief) of £2,560 represents other income of £1,060 (£10,500 - £9,440) and savings income of £1,500. Tax of £212 (20% × £1,060) would be saved on the other income. All of the savings income falls in the starting rate band of £2,790 and tax of £150 (10% × £1,500) would therefore be saved. The remaining loss would not be relieved until subsequent years.

The optimum relief is therefore to claim against total income for 2012/13, then against the chargeable gains of 2012/13, since this gives relief at the earliest date and at the highest rates of tax.

Examiner's report

This question was generally not answered well.

Although it was technically the most demanding question on the paper, requiring a bit more thought than the other four questions, it was quite short and should not have presented too many difficulties for reasonably well prepared candidates.

In part (a) many candidates explained the loss reliefs that were available rather than the factors that must be taken into account when deciding which loss reliefs to actually claim.

In part (b) it was extremely disappointing to see the vast majority of candidates include the capital gains in their computation of taxable income. The capital gains annual exempt amount was often then deducted against the combined figure of taxable income and taxable gains.

Many candidates claimed loss relief against the total income for the year of the loss despite this income clearly being covered by the personal allowance.

Very few candidates, even if they showed the capital gains separately, claimed loss relief against capital gains.

ACCA marking scheme		
		Marks
(a)	Rate of tax	1.0
	Timing of relief	1.0
	Personal allowance and annual exempt amount	1.0
		3.0
(b)	Trading income	0.5
	Building society interest	0.5
	Loss relief against total income	2.0
	Personal allowance	0.5
	Capital gains	1.5
	Loss relief against capital gains	1.0
	Capital loss carried forward	1.0
	Explanation of most beneficial route	5.0
		12.0
Total		15.0

24 GOFF GREEN (ADAPTED)  *Walk in the footsteps of a top tutor*

Key answer tips

This was a fairly standard and predictable question on income tax losses.

There were no particularly tricky aspects and it should be possible to score well on this question, although part (b) will involve a little more thought.

As with any loss question the key to scoring well is clear presentation and a systematic approach to the use of the losses, showing the different claims and any remaining losses in a loss memo.

This question was originally a 10 mark question, and under the current syllabus and rules, this question would still be worth 10 marks.

However, under the new syllabus this type of question would be 15 marks and therefore would probably have an additional 5 mark section.

Tutor's top tips

Part (a) basically involves a fairly methodical loss relief calculation. You should set up your pro formas for income tax and capital gains (keeping the two separate) and once you have entered the income and gains figures it should be fairly clear which claims will be beneficial.

Part (b) asks why it would not be beneficial to make the claim against gains (telling you that you should have made that claim in part (a)!) if Goff will make trading profits of £37,600 in the following year. The examiner has already told you what conclusions you should draw (that the claim against gains is no longer beneficial), so you simply have to work out why! As he is talking about income in the following period you need to consider the option of carrying forward losses.

(a) **Goff Green – Taxable income and taxable gains**

	2011/12	*2012/13*	*2013/14*
	£	£	£
Trading income	14,800	23,600	Nil
Interest	3,800	3,800	3,800
	18,600	27,400	3,800
Less: Loss relief		(27,400)	(3,800)
	18,600	Nil	Nil
Less: PA	(9,440)	(wasted)	(wasted)
Taxable income	9,160	Nil	Nil

	2011/12	*2012/13*	*2013/14*
	£	£	£
Capital gains	Nil	Nil	19,700
Less: Current year loss relief			(4,800)
	Nil	Nil	14,900
Less: Trading loss relief	–	–	(14,900)
	Nil	Nil	Nil
Less: AEA	(wasted)	(wasted)	(wasted)
Taxable gains	Nil	Nil	Nil

Loss memorandum	£
Loss in 2013/14	55,000
Less: Relief against total income	
2013/14 (claimed to allow extension against gains)	(3,800)
2012/13	(27,400)
Loss remaining	23,800
Less: Relief against chargeable gains	
2013/14	(14,900)
Loss carried forward	8,900

Tutorial notes

1 *The claim against total income in 2013/14 is not beneficial as the income is already covered by the personal allowance; however it is a necessary claim in order to be able to set the remaining loss against chargeable gains.*

2 *It is not possible to claim any loss relief in 2011/12 as losses can only be carried back more than one year under an opening years loss claim or on cessation of trade, neither of which are applicable here.*

(b) **Goff Green – Trading profit of £37,600 in 2014/15**

- In 2013/14 the tax saved by making a claim against chargeable gains is:

	£
Income tax (taxable income covered by PA)	Nil
Chargeable gains	14,900
Less: AEA	(10,900)
Taxable gains	4,000
CGT payable at 18% (gains covered by BR band)	720

- If no claim was made against gains in 2013/14 a further loss would be available to carry forward as follows:

	£
Loss relief against income	3,800
Loss relief against gains	14,900
Loss carried forward	18,700

- This could be set against trading income in 2014/15 and would save tax at 20% as Goff's taxable income will all be covered by the basic rate band (£37,600 + £3,800 – £9,440 = £31,960).

  It will also result in a Class 4 NIC saving at 9% as his trading income is below the upper earnings limit of £41,450.

- The total tax saved on the additional loss carried forward is therefore:

	£
Income tax (£18,700 × 20%)	3,740
Class 4 NICs (£18,700 × 9%)	1,683
Total tax saved	5,423

- There is a delay of only twelve months in order to realise this tax saving.

Tutorial notes

1 *The tax saved in 2013/14 is significantly lower than the potential saving in 2014/15 due to the wastage of the personal allowance and annual exempt amount and the lower rate of tax on chargeable gains.*

2 *The claim against total income in 2013/14 is no longer required, since the income is covered by the personal allowance and the claim was only being made in part (a) to allow the extension against chargeable gains.*

3 *Rather than carrying out a full income tax computation for 2014/15, the potential tax saving has been calculated using Goff's marginal rate of tax. He has sufficient trading income to utilise the carried forward loss in full without any wastage of the personal allowance, but his income does not exceed the basic rate band and therefore the income tax saving will all be at 20%. The Class 4 NIC saving is all at 9% as his income does not exceed the upper earnings limit and the loss relief will not reduce his trading income below the primary earnings threshold.*

Examiner's report

This question was reasonably well answered.

In **part (a)** many candidates did not appreciate that loss relief could be claimed against the chargeable gain, and it was disappointing that so many candidates included the chargeable gain as part of their taxable income computation.

Another common error was to restrict the loss relief claims so as to preserve personal allowances, which of course is not possible.

Part (b) was not so well answered since few candidates appreciated that carrying the loss forward would preserve the annual exempt amount as well as saving income tax at the rate of 20% and Class 4 NIC at the rate of 9%, rather than at 18% if relief was claimed against the chargeable gain.

ACCA marking scheme		
		Marks
(a)	Trading income	0.5
	Building society interest	0.5
	Loss relief – 2013/14	1.0
	– 2012/13	0.5
	Personal allowance	1.0
	Loss relief against chargeable gain	1.0
	Trading loss unrelieved	0.5
		5.0
(b)	Tax saving in 2013/14	2.0
	Additional loss carried forward	1.5
	Tax and NIC saving in 2014/15	1.5
		5.0
Total		10.0

PARTNERSHIPS

25 PETER, QUINTON AND ROGER (ADAPTED)

Key answer tips

A loss making partnership presents a tricky problem and it is important to approach the computation in part (b) with care.

Firstly, profits/(losses) need to be allocated to each partner and then the opening year rules applied for each partner according to the date they joined the firm.

There are many loss relief options available. A brief mention of each is all you have time for in the exam. Be careful not to go into too much detail and there is no need to discuss the relative merits of each option in this question.

It is much better to mention all the reliefs available and applicable to the question succinctly than to talk about any one relief in great detail.

Part (2) concentrates on VAT topics. The VAT rules are not hard, they are however extensive and they will be examined. Emphasis in your revision must therefore be put into learning the VAT rules as there is a guaranteed 10% of the exam on VAT each sitting.

(1) (a) **Basis of assessment – Joining partners**

- Each partner is treated as a sole trader running a business.
- The commencement rules therefore apply when a partner joins the partnership, with the first year of assessment being on an actual basis (i.e. date of commencement to the following 5 April).

(b) **Trading income assessments**

	Peter	Quinton	Roger
	£	£	£
2010/11			
Peter and Quinton			
Actual basis (1 January 2011 to 5 April 2011)			
(£40,000 × 1/2 × 3/12)	5,000	5,000	
2011/12			
Peter and Quinton			
CYB (y/e 31 December 2011)			
(£40,000 × 1/2)	20,000	20,000	
Roger			
Actual basis (1 January 2012 to 5 April 2012)			
(£90,000 × 1/3 × 3/12)			7,500
2012/13			
All partners – CYB (y/e 31 December 2012)			
(£90,000 × 1/3)	30,000	30,000	30,000

Tutorial note

The commencement rules apply to:

- *Peter and Quinton from 2010/11, as the partnership started on 1 January 2011.*
- *Roger from 2011/12, since he joined as a partner on 1 January 2012.*

(c) **Possible methods of relieving trading loss for 2013/14**

- Peter, Quinton and Roger each have a tax adjusted trading loss of £10,000 (£30,000 × 1/3) for 2013/14.
- Peter resigned as a partner on 31 December 2013. His unrelieved overlap profits of £5,000 (1 January 2011 to 5 April 2011) will therefore increase his loss to £15,000 (£10,000 + £5,000).
- Carry forward relief:

  Quinton and Roger can carry their share of the loss forward against their first available future trading profits arising in the same trade.
- Relief against total income:

  Peter, Quinton and Roger can claim relief against their total income for 2013/14 and/or 2012/13.

- Special opening year loss relief:

  Peter, Quinton and Roger can carry back their share of the loss against their total income for 2010/11 to 2012/13, earliest year first.

- Terminal loss relief:

  Peter can carry back his share of the loss of the last 12 months trading against his trading profits for 2012/13.

  He has insufficient losses to carry back the loss any further. If he had more losses, he could carry back the loss and make a claim in respect of 2011/12 and 2010/11, in that order.

Key answer tips

The requirement is to "State the possible ways to relieve the losses". Therefore there will be no marks for discussing in detail the relative merits of each claim and which would be the most beneficial.

Remember that it is much better to mention all the reliefs available and applicable to the question succinctly than to talk about any one relief in great detail.

(2) **VAT interest and penalties**

(a) **Default surcharge**

A 'default surcharge' arises when a VAT return is submitted late, or a late payment of VAT due is made.

The 'surcharge default period' will initially be for 12 months and will only come to an end when no further defaults have occurred for a continuous 12-month period.

(b) **Default interest**

HM Revenue & Customs may assess taxpayers to VAT where:

(i) no returns have been submitted;

(ii) evidence to back up the returns is deficient;

(iii) the returns and/or information are considered to be incorrect.

Such assessments bear 'default interest' which runs from the original due date of payment of the VAT until the payment is made.

(c) **Errors on a VAT return**

If Quentin discovers an error on a previous partnership VAT return, he must disclose the error to HM Revenue & Customs.

How he should notify them depends on the amount of the error.

If the error is up to the de minimis limit, it is acceptable to notify by making the necessary correction of the error on the next VAT return.

However, if the error exceeds the de minimis limit, separate notification is required.

The de minimis limit of error is the greater of:

(i) £10,000, and

(ii) 1% of turnover,

subject to an upper limit of £50,000.

If the error is not notified, the standard penalty for the submission of an incorrect VAT return may be levied. A penalty can also be levied even if disclosure is made, but it will be a lower amount and is likely to be reduced to Nil for an error below the de minimis limit.

Key answer tips

In each part, particularly part 2 (a) your study text contains more detail on the topic of the question. But these were not asked for.

The examiner has clearly spelt out his requirements and they should be followed to the letter. Avoid answering questions with all you know about a topic and make sure you address the specific requirements of each question.

26 AE, BEE, CAE, DEE AND EUE (ADAPTED)  *Walk in the footsteps of a top tutor*

Key answer tips

This question tests the basis of assessment rules, but with the application of the rules to partnerships, and includes the opening year rules, overlap profits and the cessation rules.

A well prepared student should have been able to secure good marks on this question and each part is independent.

Part (b) of this question has been amended due to syllabus changes and part (c) has been adapted to take account of the change in rules for capital allowances.

Tutor's top tips

Part (a) deals with both the partnership profit sharing rules together with straightforward opening year rules. This part should not have caused any problems.

(a) **Ae, Bee & Cae**

Tax year	*Basis of assessment*	*Ae*	*Bee*	*Cae*
		£	£	£
2011/12	Actual basis			
	1 July 2011 to 5 April 2012			
	£54,000 × 9/12 × 1/2	20,250	20,250	
2012/13	CYB (y/e 30 June 2012)			
	£54,000 × 1/2	27,000	27,000	
2013/14	CYB (y/e 30 June 2013)			
	£66,000 × 1/2	33,000	33,000	
	Actual basis			
	1 July 2013 to 5 April 2014			
	£87,000 × 9/12 × 1/3			21,750

Tutorial note

The commencement rules apply for Ae & Bee in the tax year 2011/12 and for Cae in the tax year 2013/14, as this is the tax year in which each partner started to trade.

In the case of Cae, the fact that the partnership had been trading in the years before is not relevant.

(b) (i) **Dee – Relief for losses**

Key answer tips

Part (b) has been rewritten due to syllabus changes since the question was originally set. It now tests the new cap on loss reliefs against total income and loss reliefs in a partnership.

Dee can claim relief against her total income in 2013/14 (the year of the loss), and/or 2012/13 (the previous tax year). As she has no trading profits in either year, any loss relief will be claimed against other income and the cap on income tax reliefs will apply. The maximum claim is therefore £50,000 in each year. The remaining loss must then be carried forward for relief against her share of any future trading profits from the partnership.

It is likely that she will obtain relief for some of the carried forward loss in 2015/16 when she anticipates that the business will become profitable again. The fact that the business will then be a partnership does not prevent the future loss relief.

Loss memorandum

	£
Loss in 2013/14	165,000
Less: Relief against total income	
2013/14 (maximum)	(50,000)
2012/13 (maximum)	(50,000)
Carried forward against future trading profits	65,000

Tutorial note

It is assumed that the £5,000 loss for 2012/13 has been carried back to 2011/12 and set off against the savings income in that year.

Tutor's top tips

Since the question asked you to 'explain' the loss reliefs available, it is important to write narrative describing the loss reliefs as well as calculating the amount of loss relief that will be claimed.

(ii) **Di – relief for losses**

Di will be entitled to claim relief for her share of the partnership's trading loss in the year ended 5 April 2015 as follows.

- The loss could be claimed against total income for 2014/15 (the year of the loss) and/or 2013/14 (the previous tax year).
- Since Di has just joined the partnership, the loss is incurred within the first four years of trading from her perspective, therefore a claim for special opening year loss relief could be made against total income for the three years 2011/12 to 2013/14, starting with the earliest first.

Tutorial note

Since the question refers to a 'small' loss, it can be assumed that the cap on income tax reliefs is not relevant in this part.

(c) **Eue**

Tutor's top tips

Part (c) deals with the cessation of trade. The key rule to remember for cessation is that all profits not yet assessed need to be taxed, before deducting any overlap profits.

Tax year	*Basis of assessment*	£
2013/14	CYB (y/e 30 June 2013)	61,200
	Capital allowances (given)	(2,100)
		59,100
2014/15	Period ended 30 September 2014	72,000
	Balancing allowance (W)	(4,400)
		67,600
	Less: Overlap profits	(19,800)
		47,800

Working: Capital allowances

Period ended 30 September 2014	*General pool* £	*Allowances* £
TWDV b/f	6,300	
Addition – Car (CO_2 between 96 – 130 g/km)	2,400	
	8,700	
Disposal	(4,300)	
Balancing allowance	4,400	4,400

Tutorial note

Note that there is no AIA and no WDA in the final period of trade.

As all of the items in the pool are disposed of for less than the TWDV, there is a balancing allowance arising.

A common error is to give an AIA and calculate a WDA in the final period of trade, then calculate a balancing allowance/charge. The net effect on the total allowances is the same, but the principle is incorrect.

Examiner's report

This question was extremely well answered by the majority of candidates, many of whom scored maximum marks.

One of the main problems in the answers of poorer candidates was not showing the appropriate tax years, thus losing a lot of marks throughout.

The final part of the examiner's report referred to the original part (b) which is no longer examinable following syllabus changes.

ACCA marking scheme

				Marks
(a)	Ae, Bee & Cae – 2011/12			1.5
	– 2012/13			1.0
	– 2013/14 Ae & Bee			1.0
	– 2013/14 Cae			1.5
				5.0
(b)	(i)	Dee	– 2013/14 claim	1.0
			– 2012/13 claim	1.0
			– loss carried forward	1.0
	(ii)	Di	– total income claim	1.0
			– opening years relief	1.0
				5.0
(c)	Eue	– 2013/14 Assessment		1.5
		– 2014/15 Assessment		1.0
		– 2014/15 Capital allowances		1.5
	Relief for overlap profits			1.0
				5.0
Total				15.0

27 AUY MAN AND BIM MEN (ADAPTED)  *Walk in the footsteps of a top tutor*

Key answer tips

This question was unusual in that the scenario was a partnership. However, this should not have caused concern as there were many easy marks to be gained.

Part (a) may have caused some problems if the definition of residence status had not been learnt, however it was only worth 2 marks. The rules regarding the definition of residence have been amended since this question was set and are now more complicated.

Parts (b) and (c), comprising over half of the marks, involved preparing familiar adjustment of profits and capital allowances computations, followed by a straightforward allocation of profits between the partners and Class 4 NIC calculations.

Part (d) was an independent VAT section for 10 marks requiring the statement of some rules and straightforward calculations of VAT payable. Easy to score highly on, provided the rules have been learnt.

Tutor's top tips

Remember to read the requirement carefully.

This question has clear mark allocations, which should be used to allocate the time spent on each section. Don't overrun on parts which carry only a few marks.

The first part required the application of the residence status rules. Note that just stating the rules would not have gained full marks. You must apply the knowledge to the facts of the specific individuals.

(a) **Residence status**

- Auy will be treated as resident in the United Kingdom for 2013/14 as she was present in the United Kingdom for 183 days or more and therefore she meets the first automatic UK residency test.
- Bim will be treated as resident in the United Kingdom for 2013/14 as she was previously resident In the UK, was present here for between 91 and 120 days and she meets two of the sufficient ties tests.

  She has a home in the UK which she makes use of for 100 days during the tax year (the 'accommodation' test) and she has spent 90 days or more in the UK during both of the previous tax years (the 'days in UK' test).

Tutorial note

When considering residence it is important to approach a question systematically.

*You should firstly consider whether the individual meets one of the automatic non-residence tests. However, it is clear that these are not relevant here as the examiner has told you in the question that both individuals **are** resident in the UK.*

Secondly, you should consider whether the individual meets one of the automatic residence tests. This is the case for Auy in this question.

Finally, if neither of the automatic tests are applicable, you should consider how many days the individual has spent in the UK, whether they were resident in the UK within the previous three tax years, and how many of the sufficient ties tests are met. The table showing the number of ties which must be met is provided in the examination.

These rules are now more complex than they were when this question was originally set.

(b) **Tax adjusted trading profit – year ended 5 April 2014**

Tutor's top tips

Part (b) gives you clear guidance on the approach that is needed for an adjustment of profits, and you should follow this – starting with the net profit and then making the necessary adjustments.

Work through the notes in order, and ensure you have dealt with every single item, as credit is given for showing nil where an adjustment is not necessary, as stated in the requirement.

If you are not sure of how to deal with an item, make a sensible assumption and move on, but do not ignore it, or waste unnecessary time.

Note that as the question has asked you to 'calculate' the adjusted profits you do not need to explain each adjustment that you make, but you should show any workings.

As you read the question it is useful to highlight all the information you will need for the computation, and then as you use this information tick each item, so you can easily check you have included everything.

Beware of the information in the question Notes 1 and 2 about VAT. This information could have caused problems for some students – but this information is only required for part (d) of the question. It has no impact on the adjustment of profits statement. The notes are just telling you that the VAT has been correctly accounted for and that sales and expenses correctly appear in the statement of profit or loss net of VAT.

	£	£
Net profit	82,000	
Depreciation	3,400	
Input VAT (Note 1)	0	
Motor expenses (£2,600 × 30%)	780	
Entertaining employees (Note 2)	0	
Appropriation of profit (Note 3)	4,000	
Excessive salary (£15,000 – £10,000) (Note 4)	5,000	
Capital allowances (W1)		13,568
	95,180	13,568
	(13,568)	
Tax adjusted trading profit	81,612	

Tutorial note

1 *No adjustment is required in respect of the input VAT as the expense figures are already exclusive of VAT and therefore the VAT has correctly not been deducted from profit.*

2 *The only exception to the non-deductibility of entertainment expenditure is when it is in respect of employees.*

3 *Salaries paid to a partner are not allowable. They merely represent an agreed form of allocation of the partnership profits in the partnership agreement. Appropriations of profit (i.e. drawings such as partner's salaries) need to be added back to profit.*

4 *Salaries paid to family members are allowable provided the amount is reasonable remuneration for services provided. Where an excessive amount is paid, the excess is not allowable.*

Allocation of profits – 2013/14

Tutor's top tips

Once the net profit of the partnership has been calculated, it must be allocated between the partners in accordance with the partnership agreement in force in the accounting period.

Note that full marks can be obtained for this part in showing clearly how you have allocated the amounts; even if your tax adjusted trading profit figure is incorrect.

	Total	*Auy Man*	*Bim Men*
	£	£	£
Salary	4,000		4,000
Interest (£56,000/£34,000 at 5%)	4,500	2,800	1,700
Balance (80%/20%)	73,112	58,490	14,622
	81,612	61,290	20,322

Trading income assessments – 2013/14

	£
Auy Man	61,290
Bim Man	20,322

Tutorial note

The profit share for each partner must now be assessed in the correct tax year. The basis of assessment rules need to be applied to determine in which tax year the profits are assessed.

However, in this question the partnership has a 5 April year end and therefore the rule is simple: the actual profits for the year ended 5 April 2014 will be assessed in 2013/14.

Working – Capital allowances

Tutor's top tips

A standard capital allowances computation is required; however it is slightly unusual in that the only transactions in the year involve cars. There are no other additions and therefore there is no AIA.

The rules for cars need to be known in detail and applied carefully here. Each of the cars has a different CO_2 emissions rate so these need to be considered carefully to determine the correct available capital allowances. Also watch out for 'private use' adjustments.

		Main pool	*Motor car (1)*	*Motor car (2)*	*Special rate pool*	*Allow-ances*
	£	£	£	£	£	£
TWDV b/f		3,100	18,000	14,000		
Additions (no AIA)						
Motor car (4)		14,200				
Motor car (5)					8,700	
Disposal – Motor car (2)				(13,100)		
		17,300	18,000	900		
Balancing allowance				(900) × 70%		630
WDA (18%)		(3,114)				3,114
WDA (8%)			(1,440) × 70%			1,008
WDA (8%)					(696)	696
Addition (with FYA)						
Motor car (3)	11,600					
FYA (100%)	(11,600) × 70%					8,120
		Nil				
TWDV c/f		14,186	16,560		8,004	
Total allowances						13,568

Tutorial notes

1 *Capital allowances on new car purchases are calculated based on the CO_2 emissions of the car as follows:*

- *CO_2 emissions of ≤ 95 g/km:*
  eligible for a FYA of 100% (i.e. Motor Car (3))
- *CO_2 emissions of between 96 – 130 g/km:*
  put in main pool and eligible for a WDA at 18% (i.e. Motor Car (4))
- *CO_2 emissions of > 130 g/km:*
  put in special rate pool and eligible for a WDA at 8% (i.e. Motor Car (5))

However, cars with an element of private use by a partner (i.e. owner of the business) are given a separate column and only the business use percentage of the allowances can be claimed.

Note that motor car (3) is a de-pooled asset and in practice should be given a separate column and carried forward at a tax written down value of Nil. When it is sold it will result in a balancing charge, but only the business proportion will be taxed.

2 *Motor car (1), which was owned at the beginning of the year, has CO_2 emissions of > 130 g/km and is therefore eligible for a WDA at 8%. This must then be adjusted for private use.*

3 *Motor car (2) was owned at the beginning of the year and has been allocated to its own pool as it has an element of private use by one of the partners. It was disposed of in the year and the sale proceeds are deducted from the TWDV brought forward and a balancing allowance arises.*

Note that the lower of cost and sale proceeds is deducted from the pool. As the TWDV b/f is £14,000, the cost must have been more than £14,000 and therefore the cost is greater than the sale proceeds received.

(c) **Class 4 National Insurance Contributions – 2013/14**

Tutor's top tips

Straightforward computations are required for this part.

Remember that full marks can be obtained for this part, even if your allocation of profit to the partners is incorrect, provided that you use the partners' profit allocations which you have calculated in part (b) as the basis of your national insurance calculations. Just make sure that you clearly show the method of calculation.

Auy Man

	£
(£41,450 – £7,755) × 9%	3,033
(£61,290 – £41,450) × 2%	397
	3,430

Bim Men

(£20,322 – £7,755) × 9%	1,131

(d) (i) **Tax point**

Tutor's top tips

Part (d) of this question is an independent part and could be answered before the other parts.

All of the information required for this part is given in question Notes 1 and 2 and the last paragraph of the question.

Remember that VAT will always feature in the exam for a minimum of 10 marks and the requirements are usually straightforward and easy to score highly on provided you put in the time to learn the rules.

However, even if you are a bit vague on some of the areas, you still need to attempt each part and write something – but be mindful of the mark allocation given to each sub-part.

Part (d)(i) should have been straightforward as it required the application of the basic tax point rules. Note that for 3 marks you would be expected to think of three key valid points.

Part (d)(ii) was a straightforward calculation of VAT payable.

For part (d)(iii) you have either learnt the rules for the flat rate scheme, or you haven't.

You would struggle on this part if you haven't. If you have, a few facts followed by a simple calculation would gain easy marks.

- The basic tax point (BTP) is the date when services are completed.
- If an invoice is issued or payment received before the BTP, then this becomes the actual tax point (ATP).
- If an invoice is issued within 14 days of the BTP, the invoice date will usually replace the BTP date and become the ATP.

(ii) **VAT paid for the year ended 5 April 2014**

- The partnership's output VAT is £28,440 and its total input VAT is £320 (£180 + £140).
- Therefore VAT of £28,120 (£28,440 – £320) will have been paid to HM Revenue & Customs in respect of the year ended 5 April 2014.

Tutorial notes

The partnership input and output VAT is given in Notes 1 and 2 in the question, and all that the examiners required was a deduction of the input VAT from output VAT.

(iii) **Flat rate scheme**

- The partnership can join the flat rate scheme if its expected taxable turnover (excluding VAT) for the next 12 months does not exceed £150,000.
- The partnership can continue to use the scheme until its total turnover (including VAT, but excluding sales of capital assets) for the previous year exceeds £230,000.
- If the partnership had used the flat rate scheme throughout the year ended 5 April 2014 then it would have paid VAT calculated as follows:

  VAT inclusive taxable turnover = (£142,200 + £28,440) = £170,640

  VAT payable = (£170,640 × 14%) = £23,890
- This is a saving of £4,230 (£28,120 part (d)(ii) – £23,890) for the year.

Tutorial notes

To calculate the VAT payable under the flat rate scheme, the flat rate is simply applied to the VAT inclusive taxable turnover for the year, with no deduction for input VAT.

In the first 12 months of VAT registration, if the business joins the flat rate scheme, HMRC allow a 1% reduction in the appropriate percentage for that trade group.

However, knowledge of this is not required in the exam. Therefore, the examiner will give you the rate that should apply in the first 12 months and you do not need to deduct 1%, just use the percentage given.

Examiner's report

This question was well answered, especially parts (b) and (c).

In part (a) several candidates simply repeated the information contained within the question rather than explaining the[rules]. *The examiner's comments on this part related to the old residence rules prior to the change in the legislation in FA13..*

There were generally no problems with part (b) although a number of candidates did not appreciate that they had to deduct the salary and interest on capital before allocating the balance of profits.

Most candidates scored maximum marks for part (c).

In part (d) the tax point was explained reasonably well, although some candidates wasted time by also giving details for the supply of goods.

Some students struggled with the VAT calculation, assuming this to be much more complicated than it actually was. For 2 marks, all that was required was to select the output VAT of £28,440 and input VAT of £140 and £180 from the text, and then calculate the amount payable of £28,120. It was not necessary to calculate any VAT figures.

The main problem as regards the VAT calculation using the flat rate scheme was that candidates incorrectly deducted input VAT.

ACCA marking scheme

			Marks
(a)	Auy Man		1.0
	Bim Men		1.0
			2.0
(b)	**Trading profit**		
	Depreciation		0.5
	Input VAT		0.5
	Motor expenses		1.0
	Entertaining employees		0.5
	Appropriation of profit		0.5
	Excessive salary		0.5
	Deduction of capital allowances		0.5
	Capital allowances – Main pool		2.0
	– Motor car (1)		1.5
	– Motor car (2)		2.0
	– Special rate pool		1.5
	– FYA		1.5
	Trading income assessments		
	Salary		0.5
	Interest on capital		1.0
	Balance of profits		1.0
			15.0
(c)	Auy Man		2.0
	Bim Men		1.0
			3.0
(d)	(i)	**Tax point**	
		Basic tax point	1.0
		Payment received or invoice issued	1.0
		Issue of invoice within 14 days	1.0
			3.0
	(ii)	**VAT paid**	
		Output VAT and input VAT	1.0
		Calculation	1.0
			2.0
	(iii)	**Flat rate scheme**	
		Joining the scheme	1.0
		Continuing to use the scheme	1.5
		VAT payable	2.0
		VAT saving	0.5
			5.0
Total			30.0

PENSIONS AND NIC

28 DUKE AND EARL UPPER-CRUST (ADAPTED)

Key answer tips

Part (a) involves a couple of income tax computations:

- one for an additional rate taxpayer with reduced personal allowances requiring the extension of the basic rate band for pension relief;
- the other is a basic rate taxpayer requiring no entries in the income tax computation in respect of pensions.

Parts (b) and (c) are wholly written, covering the rules on additional pension contributions and the significance of the annual allowance.

(a) **Duke Upper-Crust**

Income tax computation – 2013/14

		£
Employment income (£115,000 + £40,000)		155,000
Less: Adjusted PA (W1)		(4,440)
Taxable income		150,560
	£	
	77,010 at 20% (W2)	15,402
	73,550 at 40%	29,420
	150,560	
Income tax liability		44,822

Net amount paid to pension company

All of Duke's pension contribution of £45,000 qualifies for tax relief as it is less than 100% of his earnings (£155,000).

He will therefore have paid £36,000 (£45,000 less 20%) to his personal pension company.

Workings

(W1) **Adjusted personal allowance**

	£		£
Personal allowance			9,440
Employment income = Total income			
= Net income	155,000		
Less: Gross PPC	(45,000)		
	110,000		
Less: Limit	(100,000)		
	10,000	× 50%	(5,000)
Adjusted PA			4,440

(W2) **Extension of basic rate and additional rate band**

	£	£
Basic rate band threshold	32,010	150,000
Plus: Gross PPC	45,000	45,000
Extended basic rate band	77,010	195,000

As taxable income is £150,560, is all employment income, and falls below £195,000, all of the income in excess of £77,010 will be taxed at 40%.

Earl Upper-Crust

Income tax computation – 2013/14

	£
Trading profit	34,000
Less: PA	(9,440)
Taxable income	24,560
Income tax liability (£24,560 at 20%)	4,912

Tutorial note

As Earl is a basic rate taxpayer there is no need to extend his basic rate band for the pension contribution. Relief for allowable contributions is given at source.

Net amount paid to pension company

Only £34,000 of Earl's pension contribution of £40,000 qualifies for tax relief, since relief is only available up to 100% of his earnings.

The amount of tax relief is therefore £6,800 (£34,000 at 20%), which is given at source, and so Earl will have paid £33,200 (£40,000 – £6,800) to his personal pension company.

(b) **Effect of annual allowance**

- Although tax relief is available on pension contributions up to the amount of earnings for a particular tax year, there is no limit as to the amount of earnings that can qualify for tax relief. However, the annual allowance limit of £50,000 acts as an effective annual limit.
- Any tax relieved contributions paid in excess of the annual allowance are subjected to an additional tax charge for the tax year in which the contributions are paid. The tax charge is calculated at the taxpayer's marginal rate of tax.
- The annual allowance limit (£50,000) is increased by any unused annual allowance from the previous three tax years.
- Although the rules changed and the limit reduced to £50,000 in 2011/12, unused annual allowance is available prior to 2011/12 based on an assumed annual allowance limit of £50,000.

(c) **Maximum additional contributions**

- There is no restriction regarding the amounts that Duke and Earl could have contributed into a personal pension scheme for 2013/14.
- However, tax relief is available on the lower of:
  - (i) Gross contributions paid
  - (ii) Higher of:
    - £3,600
    - 100% of relevant earnings

Duke

- Duke could therefore receive tax relief on additional contributions of up to £110,000 (£155,000 relevant earnings – £45,000 gross contributions paid).
- However, if his gross contributions exceed £65,000 (£50,000 plus unused AA limit of £5,000 (£50,000 – £45,000) in each of the last three years) an annual allowance charge will arise.

Earl

- Earl has already made a pension contribution in excess of his earnings for 2013/14, and so any additional pension contribution would not have qualified for any tax relief.

Due date

- Pension contributions for 2013/14 would have had to have been paid between 6 April 2013 and 5 April 2014, as it is not possible to carry back contributions.

Key answer tips

Remember to state the due date of payment; an easy mark to gain, but easily lost if you are not efficient in making sure you address all parts of a question or run out of time.

This could have been answered early in the answer before getting involved with the computations, to make sure you gain the easy marks as quickly as possible.

29 VANESSA AND SERENE (ADAPTED)  *Walk in the footsteps of a top tutor*

Key answer tips

This question is really like two separate questions.

Part (a) is fairly straightforward, and asks for income tax and national insurance computations for a sole trader and an employee, with advice regarding payments under self-assessment.

Part (b) is all about VAT and the flat rate scheme.

The highlighted words in the written sections are key phrases that markers are looking for.

Tutor's top tips

You should be able to score highly on part (a)(i), although there were a few tricky points.

Where a sole trader has just purchased a single asset, there is no need to do a full capital allowances computation, as long as you show your workings. Remember that only the business proportion of the allowances can be claimed.

The car provided to Serene has CO_2 emissions between 76 g/km and 94 g/km and therefore a special rate applies. Note also that the question specifically says that the company did not provide Serene with any fuel for private journeys, so don't waste time calculating a fuel benefit! (See examiner's comments).

Watch out for the pension contributions:

- *the contribution to the personal pension is paid net, and extra relief is given by extending the basic rate band by the gross amount*
- *the occupational pension is paid gross, and is simply deducted from employment income.*

Try not to get these confused.

Remember that you will score full marks for the calculation of tax if you use the correct rates, even if your taxable income figure is wrong.

(a) (i) **Vanessa Serve**

Income tax computation – 2013/14

	Total	*Other income*	*Savings income*
	£	£	£
Trading income	52,400		
Less: Capital allowances (W1)	(1,310)		
	51,090	51,090	
Interest received (Note)	1,100		1,100
Total income	52,190	51,090	1,100
Less: PA	(9,440)	(9,440)	
Taxable income	42,750	41,650	1,100
Income tax:			
On Other income (W2)	38,410	@ 20%	7,682
On Other income	3,240	@ 40%	1,296
	41,650		
On Savings income	1,100	@ 40%	440
	42,750		
Income tax payable			9,418

Tutorial note

Interest from investment accounts at the National Savings & Investments Bank is taxable and is received gross.

Workings

(W1) **Capital allowances**

The car has CO_2 emissions of between 96 g/km and 130 g/km and is therefore eligible for a WDA at 18%.

Only the business proportion of the allowance can be claimed.

WDA = (£10,400 × 18%) × 14,000/20,000 = £1,310

(W2) **Extension of basic rate band**

	£
Basic rate band threshold	32,010
Plus: Personal pension contribution (gross)	6,400
Extended basic rate band	38,410

Serene Volley

Income tax computation – 2013/14

	£
Salary	26,400
Less: Pension contributions (£26,400 × 5%)	(1,320)
	25,080
Car benefit (W)	3,458
Employment income	28,538
Interest from savings certificate (exempt)	Nil
Total income	28,538
Less: Personal allowance	(9,440)
Taxable income	19,098
Income tax liability (£19,098 at 20%)	3,820
Less: Tax suffered at source – PAYE	(3,710)
Income tax payable	110

Working: Car benefit

CO_2 emissions = 87 g/km, available all year

As the CO_2 emissions are between 76 – 94 g/km, the basic percentage of 10% is used.

However, as it is a diesel car, the appropriate percentage is 13%.

Car benefit (£26,600 × 13%)	£3,458

There is no fuel benefit as private petrol is not provided by the company.

(ii) **National Insurance**

Tutor's top tips

Remember that sole traders pay Class 2 and 4 national insurance, whereas employees pay Class 1 primary contributions.

As long as you calculate Vanessa's Class 4 contributions correctly based on your adjusted trading income figure from part (a)(i), you will be awarded full marks.

Vanessa Serve

Class 2 NICs	£
(£2.70 for 52 weeks)	140

Class 4 NICs	£
(£41,450 – £7,755) × 9%	3,033
(£51,090 – £41,450) × 2%	193
	3,226

Serene Volley

Class 1 NICs	
(£26,400 – £7,755) × 12%	2,237

Tutorial note

Class 1 NICs are based on cash earnings, without any allowable deductions. Therefore, pension contributions are ignored, and benefits are not subject to employee Class 1 NIC.

Benefits are assessed to Class 1A NICs which are payable by the employer only, not the employee. However, the requirement is to calculate the NICs payable by the employee only, not the employer.

(iii) **Payment of tax**

Tutor's top tips

You must learn the rules and key dates for payment of tax under self-assessment, as these are very often examined, and the examiner is repeatedly disappointed when students do not seem to learn these important rules. See examiner's comments to this question, and others.

Don't forget that Vanessa's balancing payment due under self-assessment covers both income tax and Class 4 NICs.

As long as this payment and the instalments for 2014/15 are calculated correctly based on your figures, you will be given full marks.

Vanessa Serve

Balancing payment for 2013/14 – due on 31 January 2015

	£
Income tax liability	9,418
Class 4 NIC	3,226
	12,644
Less: Paid on account	(8,705)
	3,939

Payments on account for 2014/15

		£
Due 31 January 2015	(£12,644 × 50%)	6,322
Due 31 July 2015	(£12,644 × 50%)	6,322

Serene Volley

No payments on account have been made, so the balancing payment for 2013/14 due on 31 January 2015 is £110.

Payments on account for 2014/15 are not required because Serene's income tax payable for 2013/14 was less than £1,000.

Also, more than 80% of her income tax liability (£3,820 × 80% = £3,056) was met by deduction at source.

(b) (i) **VAT Return – Quarter ended 30 June 2014**

Tutor's top tips

Part (b) is a standalone part about VAT which could have been attempted before part (a) if you are confident with your VAT knowledge.

A standard VAT return is required, but be careful to read the question carefully to see whether the figures in the question include or exclude VAT.

In this case, the appropriate rate is as follows:

- *If the figure excludes VAT, the VAT is 20%*
- *If the figure includes VAT, the VAT is 20/120 or 1/6.*

The requirement is to 'calculate' and therefore the explanatory notes are not required as part of the answer.

	£	£
Output VAT		
Sales (£18,000 × 20%)		3,600
Input VAT		
Telephone (£600 × 60% × 20%) (Note 1)	72	
Motor car (Note 2)	Nil	
Motor repairs (£882 × 20/120) (Note 3)	147	
Equipment (£1,760 × 20%) (Note 4)	352	
Other expenses (£2,200 – £400) × 20% (Note 5)	360	
		(931)
VAT payable		2,669

Tutorial note

1 *An apportionment is made where a service such as the use of a telephone is partly for business purposes and partly for private purposes.*

2 *Input VAT cannot be recovered in respect of the motor car as this was not exclusively for business purposes.*

3 *No apportionment is necessary for motor expenses provided there is some business use.*

4 *Vanessa can recover the input VAT in respect of the equipment in the quarter ended 30 June 2014 because the actual tax point was the date that the equipment was paid for.*

5 *Input tax on business entertaining cannot be recovered unless it relates to entertaining staff or overseas customers.*

(ii) **Flat rate scheme**

Tutor's top tips

You need to learn the key rules and features of the VAT schemes, but then you must make sure that you apply them to the specific question.

There was an easy mark available for calculating the VAT saving compared to your VAT payable from part (b)(i).

Conditions

- Vanessa can use the flat rate scheme if her expected taxable turnover for the next 12 months does not exceed £150,000.

Advantages

- The main advantage of the scheme is the simplified VAT administration. Vanessa's customers are not VAT registered, so there will be no need to issue VAT invoices.
- If Vanessa had used the flat rate scheme for the quarter ended 30 June 2014 then she would have paid VAT of £1,836 ((£18,000 + £3,600) × 8.5%).
- This is a saving of £833 (£2,669 – £1,836) for the quarter.

Tutorial note

The flat rate % is applied to the VAT inclusive taxable supplies for the quarter.

In the first 12 months of VAT registration, if the business joins the flat rate scheme, HMRC allow a 1% reduction in the appropriate percentage for that trade group. However, it is not applicable here as Vanessa has been registered for some time and knowledge of this 1% reduction is not required in the exam.

Therefore, the examiner will always give you the rate that you should apply.

Examiner's comments

This question was generally very well answered.

In part (a) many candidates did not appreciate that it was not necessary to gross up the interest received from an investment account at the National Savings & Investment Bank, or that interest from savings certificates is exempt from tax.

The contribution to the occupational pension scheme was often used to extend the basic rate tax band rather than being deducted in calculating employment income.

Many candidates wasted time in calculating a fuel benefit despite the question clearly stating that no fuel was provided for private journeys.

The one aspect of the question that consistently caused problems was the calculation of the balancing payments and the payments on account, and this section was often not answered at all. It was disappointing that many candidates were not aware of the relevant due dates.

The VAT aspects in part (b) were well answered, although far too many candidates incorrectly deducted input VAT when calculating the amount of VAT payable using the flat rate scheme.

ACCA marking scheme			
			Marks
(a)	(i)	**Vanessa Serve**	
		Trading profit	0.5
		Capital allowances	1.5
		Interest from NSI Bank	1.0
		Personal allowance	0.5
		Extension of basic rate band	1.0
		Income tax	1.0
		Serene Volley	
		Salary	0.5
		Pension contributions	1.0
		Car benefit	1.5
		Interest from savings certificate	0.5
		Personal allowance	0.5
		Income tax	1.0
		Tax suffered at source – PAYE	0.5
			11.0
	(ii)	**Vanessa Serve**	
		Class 2 NIC	1.0
		Class 4 NIC	1.5
		Serene Volley	
		Class 1 NIC	1.5
			4.0
	(iii)	**Vanessa Serve**	
		Balancing payment	1.5
		Payments on account	1.5
		Serene Volley	
		Balancing payment	1.0
		Payments on account not required	1.0
			5.0
(b)	(i)	Sales	0.5
		Telephone	1.0
		Motor car	0.5
		Motor repairs	1.0
		Equipment	1.0
		Other expenses	1.0
			5.0
	(ii)	Limit	1.0
		Simplified administration	2.0
		VAT saving	2.0
			5.0
Total			30.0

30 ANN, BASIL AND CHLOE (ADAPTED)  *Walk in the footsteps of a top tutor*

Key answer tips

A question covering the pension relief available to three different individuals. This should be a straightforward question provided the rules had been learnt.

Relief for pension contributions is a key area of the syllabus that is tested regularly.

Note that this question has been adapted in light of the new syllabus and part (b) is a new addition to the question to test new rules introduced in the pension legislation.

Tutor's top tips

This question is classic in style with individuals in different situations contributing to a personal pension scheme.

The key is to:

- *Remember the definition of "relevant earnings"*
- *Compare the gross contributions paid with the "relevant earnings" (or £3,600 if this is higher) to decide the maximum tax allowable amount*
- *Consider the annual allowance limit charge.*

Note that the maximum contribution allowable for a person without any relevant earnings in the tax year (£3,600) and the annual allowance limit are given in the exam.

(a) (i) **Ann Peach**

Amount of pension contributions qualifying for relief

Ann can obtain relief for the lower of:

(1) Gross contributions of £52,000

(2) Higher of:

(i) £3,600

(ii) Relevant earnings of £48,000

Therefore, £48,000 will qualify for tax relief and her basic rate band is extended to £80,010 (W).

Her taxable income falls into the extended basic rate band and is therefore taxed at 20%.

Income tax liability

	£
Trading profit	48,000
Less: PA	(9,440)
Taxable income	38,560
Income tax liability (£38,560 × 20%) (W)	7,712

Working: Extension of basic rate band

	£
Basic rate band	32,010
Plus: Gross allowable pension contributions	48,000
Extended basic rate band	80,010

Tutorial note

The annual allowance charge is not applicable in this question, as although Ann has made pension contributions in excess of £50,000, she has only received tax relief for contributions of £48,000. The annual allowance charge is intended to claw back tax relief for contributions in excess of the limit, which is not applicable here.

(ii) **Basil Plum**

Amount of pension contributions qualifying for relief

Basil can obtain relief for the lower of:

(1) Gross contributions of £50,000

(2) Higher of:

(i) £3,600

(ii) Relevant earnings of £120,000

Therefore, £50,000 will qualify for tax relief and his basic rate band is extended to £82,010 (W2).

Tutorial note

Note that this scenario differs from the treatment for Ann (above) as Ann had contributed more than 100% of her relevant earnings into a scheme, whereas Basil has contributed less than 100% of his relevant earnings into the scheme.

Income tax liability

	£
Employment income	120,000
Less: PA (W1)	(9,440)
Taxable income	110,560
Income tax:	
£	
82,010 × 20% (W2)	16,402
28,550 × 40%	11,420
110,560	
Income tax liability	27,822

Workings

(W1) **Personal allowance**

Although Basil's income is in excess of £100,000, there is no restriction of his personal allowance and he will be entitled to the full personal allowance as his adjusted net income (ANI) is £70,000.

His ANI is calculated as follows:

	£
Employment income = Total income = Net income	120,000
Less: Gross PPC	(50,000)
ANI	70,000

(W2) **Extension of basic rate band**

	£
Basic rate band	32,010
Plus: Gross PPC	50,000
Extended basic rate band	82,010

(iii) **Chloe Pear**

Amount of pension contributions qualifying for relief

Property income does not qualify as relevant earnings.

Therefore, as Chloe has no relevant earnings, she will only receive tax relief on £3,600 of her pension contributions.

Her taxable income falls below the basic rate band even before extension due to pension contributions; therefore her income is taxed at 20%.

Income tax liability

	£
Property income	23,900
Less: PA	(9,440)
Taxable income	14,460
Income tax (£14,460 × 20%)	2,892

(b) **Consequences of Banana Bank plc contributing into Basil's pension fund**

There is no limit on the amount that can be put into a personal pension fund by an individual and his employer.

However, there is a maximum amount of tax relief

- that the individual can obtain on their contributions into the scheme (i.e. the maximum contribution each year), and
- on the total contributions paid into a scheme by the individual and others on their behalf (i.e. the annual allowance).

If Basil's employer contributes into his personal pension scheme, the employer contributions are:

- a tax free benefit
- a tax allowable deduction in Banana Bank's corporation tax computation
- combined with Basil's contributions and compared to the annual allowance of £50,000.

Where the annual allowance is exceeded (as is the case if Banana Bank pays £100,000 into the scheme):

- a tax charge is levied on the individual.

Unused allowances from the previous three tax years can be carried forward.

In Basil's case the maximum contributions that can be made in 2013/14 without incurring the annual allowance charge is £80,000 (£50,000 + (£50,000 – £40,000) × 3).

Basil will therefore pay the annual allowance charge in 2013/14 on contributions of £70,000 (£50,000 + £100,000 – £80,000).

The tax charge is calculated at the taxpayer's marginal rate of tax. In Basil's case this is 40%, as the higher rate band is extended by his gross contribution in 2013/14 to £200,000 (£150,000 + £50,000).

Examiner's report

This question was reasonably well answered, although there were few first-rate answers.

For the first taxpayer the most common mistake was to extend the basic rate tax band by the amount of contributions rather than earnings.

For the second taxpayer the basic rate band was often extended by the amount of annual allowance rather than the contributions.

Very few candidates stated that the third taxpayer would have received tax relief up to £3,600 of her contributions.

Note that this question has been adapted in light of the new syllabus and part (b) is a new addition to the question.

ACCA marking scheme

		Marks
(a)	**Ann Peach**	
	Taxable income	0.5
	Extension of basic rate band	1.0
	Income tax	0.5
	Amount qualifying for tax relief	1.0
		3.0
	Basil Plum	
	Taxable income	0.5
	Personal allowance	1.0
	Extension of basic rate band	1.5
	Income tax	1.0
	Amount qualifying for tax relief	1.0
		5.0
	Chloe Pear	
	Taxable income	0.5
	Income tax	0.5
	Amount qualifying for tax relief	1.0
		2.0
(b)	Employer contributions	
	No limit to contributions	0.5
	Limit to relief for individual	0.5
	Tax free benefit	0.5
	Tax allowable deduction for corporation tax	0.5
	Exceeding annual allowance	0.5
	Unused annual allowance for previous 3 years brought forward	0.5
	Basil's maximum contributions	1.0
	Charged at marginal rate	0.5
	Charged at 40% for Basil	0.5
		5.0
Total		15.0

SELF-ASSESSMENT

31 PI CASSO

Key answer tips

The first part of this question involves detailed calculations to work out the income tax, Class 4 NICs and CGT payable under self-assessment and when the payments are due.

The remaining three parts require wholly written answers on three common self-assessment topics.

These are marks which are easy to gain if you have done your work, but easy to lose if you do not invest the time in learning the self-assessment rules.

(a) **Due dates of payment of tax under self-assessment**

Due date	*Tax year*	*Payment*	£
31 July 2013	2012/13	Second payment on account (W1)	2,240
31 January 2014	2012/13	Balancing payment (W2)	5,980
31 January 2014	2013/14	First payment on account (W3)	1,860
31 July 2014	2013/14	Second payment on account (W3)	1,860
31 January 2015	2013/14	Balancing payment (W4)	Nil
31 January 2015	2014/15	First payment on account (W5)	1,860

Workings

(W1) **Second payment on account – 2012/13**

The second payment on account for 2012/13 is based on Pi's income tax and Class 4 NIC liability for 2011/12 as follows:

	£
Income tax	3,240
Class 4 NICs	1,240
	4,480
Payments on account (50%)	2,240

(W2) **Balancing payment – 2012/13**

	£
Income tax	4,100
Class 4 NICs	1,480
Capital gains tax (see Tutorial Note)	4,880
	10,460
Less: POAs (£2,240 × 2)	(4,480)
Balancing payment	5,980

(W3) **Payments on account – 2013/14**

Pi will make a claim to reduce her total payments on account for 2013/14 as follows:

	£
Income tax	2,730
Class 4 NICs	990
	3,720
Payments on account (50%)	1,860

(W4) **Balancing payment – 2013/14**

	£
Income tax and Class 4 NICs	3,720
Capital gains tax	Nil
	3,720
Less: POAs (£1,860 × 2)	(3,720)
Balancing payment	Nil

(W5) **First payments on account – 2014/15**

The first payment on account for 2014/15 is based on Pi's income tax and Class 4 NIC liability for 2013/14.

	£
Income tax	2,730
Class 4 NICs	990
	3,720
Payments on account (50%)	1,860

Tutorial note

Class 2 NICs are payable twice a year on 31 January in the tax year and 31 July after the end of the tax year. Payments can be made in a number of ways, including six monthly direct debits or following payment requests by HMRC. Note that they are not paid via the self-assessment system.

Capital gains tax is collected via self-assessment and is payable all in one payment on 31 January following the end of the tax year along with the balancing payment for income tax and Class 4 NICs.

Payments on account are not required for CGT.

(b) **Reduction of payments on account to £Nil**

- If Pi's payments on account for 2013/14 were reduced to £Nil, then she would be charged late payment interest on the payments due of £1,860 from the relevant due date to the date of payment.
- A penalty will be charged if the claim to reduce the payments on account to £Nil was made fraudulently or negligently.

(c) **Latest submission date**

- Unless the return is issued late, the latest date that Pi can submit a paper based self-assessment tax return for 2013/14 is 31 October 2014.
- If Pi completes a paper based tax return by 31 October 2014 then HMRC will prepare a self-assessment tax computation on her behalf.
- Alternatively, Pi has until 31 January 2015 to file her self-assessment tax return for 2013/14 online.
- A self-assessment tax computation is then automatically provided as part of the filing process.

(d) **HMRC enquiry**

- If HMRC intend to enquire into Pi's 2013/14 tax return they will have to notify her within twelve months of the date that they receive the return.
- HMRC has the right to enquire into the completeness and accuracy of any return and such an enquiry may be made on a completely random basis.
- However, enquiries are generally made because of a suspicion that income has been undeclared or because deductions have been incorrectly claimed.

Examiner's report

This question was generally not well answered, and the impression given was that candidates had struggled with time management and had a lack of time remaining for this question.

Part (a) caused the most problems, with the vast majority of candidates not being able to demonstrate how payments are calculated and paid under the self-assessment system.

Class 2 national insurance contributions were often incorrectly included, whilst few candidates appreciated that a claim to reduce payments on account was possible.

In part (b) most candidates appreciated that interest would be due, but very few mentioned the potential penalty that could be charged.

It was disappointing that the self-assessment tax return submission dates were often not know in part (c), despite these being covered in the Finance Act article.

The same comment applies to part (d). Candidates often gave a long list of reasons why HMRC could enquire into a return, but failed to mention that an enquiry might be on a completely random basis.

ACCA marking scheme		
		Marks
(a)	Second payment on account for 2012/13	1.5
	Balancing payment for 2012/13	2.0
	Claim to reduce payments on account	1.0
	Payments on account for 2013/14	1.0
	Balancing payment for 2013/14	0.5
	First payment on account for 2014/15	1.0
		7.0
(b)	Interest	1.0
	Penalty	1.0
		2.0
(c)	Paper based return	2.0
	Return filed online	1.0
		3.0
(d)	Notification date	1.0
	Random basis	1.0
	Income/Deductions	1.0
		3.0
Total		15.0

32 ERNEST VADER (ADAPTED)  *Walk in the footsteps of a top tutor*

Key answer tips

This is an unusual and tricky question requiring substantial written explanations and statements about ethical issues and self-assessment.

Detailed knowledge is required to score highly on this question; however the application of some basic common sense would also gain quite a few marks.

No calculations are required except for part (e) (i) which accounts for 2 of the 17 marks.

The highlighted words are key words or phrases that markers are looking for.

The legislation regarding the general anti-abuse rule and dishonest conduct by tax agents did not exist when this question was first written, and have been added since to test these areas. The original part (c) tested HMRC's information powers, which are no longer in the syllabus and this part has therefore been removed. The marks allocated to this question (17) are now higher than those originally available in this question (15).

Tutor's top tips

Remember to read the requirement carefully and allocate the time spent on each section.

Part (a) covers the classic topic of tax evasion and tax avoidance, but care must be taken to apply your knowledge to Ernest's particular problem. This part also tests awareness of the new general anti-abuse rule.

Part (b) requires the application of common sense if the specific guidelines have not been learnt.

Parts (c), (d) and (e) are straightforward if the self-assessment rules have been learnt, difficult if not learnt.

(a) **Tax evasion and tax avoidance**

- Tax evasion is illegal and involves the reduction of tax liabilities by not providing information to which HMRC is entitled, or providing HMRC with deliberately false information.
- In contrast, tax avoidance involves the minimisation of tax liabilities by the use of any lawful means. However, certain tax avoidance schemes must be disclosed to HMRC.
- The general anti-abuse rule is a rule to counter artificial and abusive schemes where arrangements (which cannot be regarded as a reasonable course of action) are put in place deliberately to avoid tax.
- If Ernest makes no disclosure of the capital gain then this will be viewed as tax evasion as his tax liability for 2013/14 will be understated by £18,000.

(b) **Failure to disclose information to HMRC**

- How to deal with the failure to disclose is a matter of professional judgement, and a trainee Chartered Certified Accountant would be expected to act honestly and with integrity.
- Ernest should therefore be advised to disclose details of the capital gain to HMRC.
- If such disclosure is not made by Ernest, you would be obliged to report under the money laundering regulations, and you should also consider ceasing to act for Ernest.

  In these circumstances you would be advised to notify HMRC that you no longer act for him although you would not need to provide any reason for this.

(c) **HMRC entitlement to raise an assessment**

- A discovery assessment can be raised because Ernest's self-assessment tax return did not contain sufficient information to make HMRC aware of the capital gain.
- The normal time limit for making a discovery assessment is four years after the end of the tax year, but this is extended to 20 years where tax is lost due to deliberate behaviour.

(d) **Penalties for tax agent**

- A civil penalty may be payable by the firm if there has been dishonest conduct and they have failed to supply the information HMRC have requested.
- The potential penalty is up to £50,000.

(e) **Interest and penalties**

(i) **Interest payable**

- Late payment interest will run from the due date of 31 January 2015 to the payment date of 31 July 2015.
- The interest charge will therefore be £270 (£18,000 × 3% × 6/12).

(ii) **Penalties**

- The amount of penalty is based on the tax due but unpaid as a result of the failure to notify. The maximum penalty is therefore the CGT liability of £18,000.
- However, the actual penalty payable will be linked to Ernest's behaviour.
- Since Ernest would appear to have deliberately failed to notify HMRC of his capital gain, the actual penalty is likely to be 70% of the tax unpaid which is £12,600 (£18,000 × 70%). This assumes that there is no attempt at concealment.
- The penalty would have been substantially reduced if Ernest had disclosed the capital gain, especially if the disclosure had been unprompted by HMRC prior to discovery. The maximum reduction would be to 20% of the tax unpaid.

Examiner's report

This question was not well answered, with many candidates attempting it as their final question or omitting it altogether. This was disappointing given that several sections covered recent tax management changes which have been covered in my Finance Act articles.

In part (a) most candidates knew the difference between tax evasion and tax avoidance, but many failed to score an easy mark by not stating that the taxpayer's actions would be viewed as tax evasion.

Part (b) caused problems for most candidates but a common sense approach would have gained most of the available marks. Unfortunately, far too many candidates instead just incorrectly explained that it would be necessary to inform HMRC themselves.

The examiner's comments on the original part (c) have been deleted as this related to HMRC's information powers which are no longer in the syllabus.

The time limits for raising an assessment were often not known, and most candidates were unaware of the use of a discovery assessment despite being given help in the wording of the requirement.

There was little excuse for getting the interest calculation wrong in part (e) as candidates were given the tax liability, the due date, the payment date and the rate of interest.

There was little awareness of the new penalty regime.

ACCA marking scheme

			Marks
(a)	Tax evasion		1.0
	Tax avoidance		1.0
	General anti-abuse rule		1.0
	Non-disclosure of disposal		1.0
			4.0
(b)	Professional judgement		1.0
	Advise disclosure		1.0
	Obligation to report		1.0
			3.0
(c)	Lack of sufficient information		1.0
	Time limits		1.0
			2.0
(d)	Civil penalty for dishonest conduct		1.0
	£50,000 penalty		1.0
			2.0
(e)	(i)	Interest period	1.0
		Calculation	1.0
			2.0
	(ii)	Maximum penalty	1.0
		Link to behaviour	1.0
		Actual penalty	1.0
		Disclosure	1.0
			4.0
			17.0

CHARGEABLE GAINS

INDIVIDUALS – CAPITAL GAINS TAX

33 CHANDRA KHAN (ADAPTED)

Key answer tips

This question focuses on the capital gains reliefs available to individuals.

One unusual feature is the factory in part (b) which has been used partly for non-business purposes. The rest of the question covers common situations and should not cause problems.

Note however that the requirement asks for the chargeable gains, not the capital gains tax liability. Therefore you should ignore the annual exempt amount and Entrepreneurs' relief.

The original part (c) of this question has been deleted as the relief tested is no longer in the syllabus.

(a) **Universal Ltd shares – Sale at undervaluation**

	£
Deemed proceeds (Note)	110,000
Less: Cost	(38,000)
	72,000
Less: Gift relief (Balancing figure)	(35,000)
Chargeable gain after gift relief (W)	37,000

Tutorial note

Chandra and her daughter are connected persons, and therefore the market value of the shares sold is used as consideration. The actual sale proceeds received are ignored.

Working: Chargeable gain after gift relief

Where there is a sale at undervalue, a chargeable gain will arise if the actual consideration received exceeds the allowable cost:

	£
Actual proceeds	75,000
Less: Cost	(38,000)
Chargeable gain after gift relief	37,000

Gift relief will be the remaining gain of £35,000 (£72,000 – £37,000)

Tutorial note

The question only requires the calculation of the chargeable gain, therefore Entrepreneurs' relief is not considered.

However, the relief is not available anyway, as Chandra is not employed by Universal Ltd.

(b) **Freehold factory**

	£
Disposal proceeds	146,000
Less: Cost	(72,000)
	74,000
Less: Rollover relief (W)	(55,500)
Chargeable gain	18,500

Working: Rollover relief

The proportion of the gain relating to non-business use is £18,500 (£74,000 × 25%), and this amount does not qualify for rollover relief.

The remaining gain of £55,500 (£74,000 – £18,500) can be rolled over provided:

- the business proportion of the sale proceeds is fully reinvested
- within the relevant time period between 8 November 2012 to 7 November 2016.

The business portion of sale proceeds = (£146,000 × 75%) = £109,500

Amount reinvested in qualifying business assets = £156,000

Reinvested on 10 November 2013

Therefore, rollover relief is available for all of the remaining gain of £55,500.

Tutorial note

Per the question, only the chargeable gain is required, therefore Entrepreneurs' relief need not be considered.

However, Entrepreneurs' relief is not available on this disposal anyway, as the disposal of a factory is not a qualifying disposal.

The whole or substantial part of a business must be disposed of. There is no relief for the disposal of individual assets out of a business.

(c) **Private residence**

	£
Disposal proceeds	350,000
Less: Cost	(75,000)
	275,000
Less: Principal private residence (PPR) exemption (W1)	(240,625)
	34,375
Less: Letting relief (W2)	(34,375)
Chargeable gain	Nil

Workings

(W1) **PPR relief**

Chargeable and exempt periods of ownership

		Total months	*Exempt months*	*Chargeable months*
1.4.06 – 31.3.10	(actual occupation)	48	48	
1.4.10 – 31.3.11	(absent – let out)	12		12
1.4.11 – 1.4.14	(final 36 months)	36	36	
		96	84	12

PPR relief = (£275,000 × 84/96) = £240,625

Tutorial note

After Chandra left her residence to live with a friend she never returned. Consequently the exemption for absence for any reason up to 3 years is not available as there is no actual occupation both before and after the period of absence.

In contrast the exemption for the final 36 months of ownership has no such restriction and is therefore still available.

Make sure that you include a brief explanation for the periods you allow as exempt due to the deemed occupation rules – as the examiner has said that such explanations are required to obtain maximum marks in these questions.

(W2) **Letting relief**

Letting relief = lowest of:

(1) £40,000

(2) PPR = £240,625

(3) Gain on letting = (£275,000 × 12/96) = £34,375

34 MICHAEL CHIN (ADAPTED)  *Online question assistance*

Key answer tips

A typical exam question on capital gains tax with a series of disposals covering a variety of topics. All the disposals are gifts and so you must use the market value as the proceeds in the computation of the gains.

Be careful to distinguish disposals (1) and (2), which do qualify for gift relief, from the remaining disposals which do not.

This question was originally a 20 mark question, but it was set when the rules for CGT were considerably more complicated. Under the current syllabus and rules, this question would now be worth 15 marks.

Capital gains tax liability – 2013/14

Disposal of business (Note 1)

	£	£
Goodwill		
Deemed proceeds = MV	60,000	
Less: Cost	Nil	
	60,000	
Less: Gift relief	(60,000)	
		Nil
Freehold property		
Deemed proceeds = MV	150,000	
Less: Cost	(86,000)	
	64,000	
Less: Gift relief (W1)	(48,000)	
		16,000
Net current assets		Nil
Total chargeable gains on the disposal of the business		16,000
Ordinary shares in Minnow Ltd (Note 2)		
Deemed proceeds = MV	180,000	
Less: Cost	(87,500)	
	92,500	
Less: Gift relief (W2)	(74,000)	
		18,500
Ordinary shares in Whale plc (Note 3)		
Deemed proceeds (18,000 × £6·40) (W3)	115,200	
Less: Cost (W4)	(59,600)	
		55,600
Chargeable gains c/f		90,100

	£	£
Chargeable gains b/f		90,100
Painting (Notes 4 and 5)		
Deemed proceeds = MV	7,500	
Less: Cost	(4,000)	
Gain	3,500	
Chargeable gain restricted to maximum of:		
5/3 × (£7,500 – £6,000)	2,500	2,500
Land (Notes 4 and 6)		
Deemed proceeds = MV	50,000	
Less: Cost (£50,000/(£50,000 + £600,000)) × £500,000	(38,462)	
		11,538
Necklace (Note 5)		
Non-wasting chattel bought and sold for < £6,000 = exempt		Nil
Total chargeable gains		104,138
Less: Capital loss brought forward (W5)		(15,600)
Net chargeable gains		88,538
Less: AEA		(10,900)
Taxable gain		77,638
Capital gains tax (£77,638 × 28%)		21,739

Tutorial note

1 *Disposal of the business*

The disposal of a business is treated as separate disposals of each chargeable asset in the business. A gain must be calculated on each chargeable asset.

However, the net current assets are not chargeable assets for capital gains tax purposes.

Gift relief is available on any gain relating to qualifying business assets disposed of, but not on the portion of the building that had never been used for his business.

Per the question, Entrepreneurs' relief is to be ignored.

However, for tutorial purposes, where the full gain is not covered by gift relief, Entrepreneurs' relief may be available. It will be available on the gift of a qualifying business provided the business has been owned for at least 12 months. If this is the case, the remaining gain would be taxed at 10%.

2 *Minnow Ltd shares*

Gift relief is available as ordinary shares in an unquoted trading company are qualifying assets for gift relief purposes. However full relief is not available as the company holds investments.

Per the question, Entrepreneurs' relief is to be ignored. However, for tutorial purposes, where the full gain is not covered by gift relief, Entrepreneurs' relief may be available.

It will be available on the gift of shares in a personal trading company (i.e. donor owns at least 5% interest), provided the donor works for the company and has owned the shares for at least one year. If this is the case, the remaining gain would be taxed at 10%.

3 Whale plc shares

Gift relief is only available on shares in a quoted company if the donor owns at least 5% of the shares in the company and the company is a trading company. As Michael owns less than 1% in Whale plc, gift relief is not available.

For the same reason, Entrepreneurs' relief would not be available.

4 Painting and Investment land

A painting and investment land are not qualifying assets for gift relief purposes.

5 Chattels

It is important to be able to recognise when an asset is a chattel (i.e. tangible and moveable) and therefore that the disposal is subject to special rules. The painting and antique necklace are both chattels.

6 Part disposal

On a part disposal the cost of the part disposed of is calculated using A/(A+B) where A is the value of the part disposed of and B is the value of the part retained.

Workings

(W1) **Freehold property**

The proportion of the freehold property gain relating to non-business use is £16,000 (£64,000 × 25%), and this amount does not qualify for gift relief.

The remaining gain of £48,000 (£64,000 – £16,000) can be held over (i.e. deferred) with a gift relief claim.

(W2) **Minnow Ltd**

The gift relief in respect of the ordinary shares in Minnow Ltd is restricted because the company has investment assets.

The proportion of gain eligible for gift relief is the proportion of chargeable business assets to chargeable assets, calculated as follows:

Gift relief = (£92,500 × £200,000/£250,000) = £74,000

(W3) **Valuation of the Whale plc shares**

Quarter up method = (£6.36 + $^{1}/_{4}$ × (£6.52 – £6.36)) = £6.40 per share

(W4) **Share pool – Whale plc shares**

		Number of shares	*Cost* £
December 2012	Purchase	15,000	63,000
August 2013	Purchase	12,000	26,400
		27,000	89,400
February 2014	Disposal (£89,400 × 18,000/27,000)	(18,000)	(59,600)
Balance c/f		9,000	29,800

(W5) **Capital loss brought forward**

	£
Capital gain – 2012/13	12,100
Less: Capital loss b/f from 2011/12 – Used (Note)	(1,200)
Net chargeable gains	10,900
Less: AEA	(10,900)
Taxable gain	Nil

Tutorial note

The capital loss brought forward is used in 2012/13 but the offset is restricted to preserve the annual exempt amount.

Loss left to c/f to 2013/14

	£
Capital loss	16,800
Less: Used in 2012/13 (above)	(1,200)
Loss c/f to 2013/14	15,600

35 DAVID AND ANGELA BROOK (ADAPTED)  *Walk in the footsteps of a top tutor*

Key answer tips

A classic question involving the calculation of capital gains tax liabilities of both a husband and his wife, with joint assets and assets held personally.

This question was originally a 20 mark question, and under the current syllabus and rules, this question would still be worth 20 marks.

No attempt has been made to reduce the question as it is still representative of the type of question you will see in the examination and provides good practice for your revision. However, under the new syllabus the question on capital gains will only be 15 marks and therefore will probably have fewer disposals to deal with in the time available than this question has.

Tutor's top tips

Be careful to spot the exempt assets. You don't need to do any calculations for these – just say that they are exempt!

Predictably a husband and wife nil gain/nil loss transfer is included, with the subsequent disposal by the recipient spouse.

Remember also to consider Entrepreneurs' relief on the disposal of shares and gift relief if they have been gifted.

David Brook

Capital gains tax liability – 2013/14

	£
Motor car (exempt)	Nil
House (W1)	20,343
Antique table (W3)	Nil
Shares in Bend Ltd (W4)	Nil
Shares in Galatico plc (W5)	14,850
Total chargeable gains	35,193
Less: AEA	(10,900)
Taxable gain	24,293
Capital gains tax (£24,293 at 18%)	4,373

Tutorial note

David has no taxable income. All of his gains therefore fall into his basic rate band and are taxed at 18%. Entrepreneurs' relief is not available on any of his gains.

Angela Brook

Capital gains tax liability – 2013/14

	£
House (W1)	20,343
Antique clock (W8)	2,000
Ordinary shares in Bend Ltd (W9)	26,400
Chargeable gains	48,743
Less: AEA	(10,900)
Taxable gain	37,843
£	
700 × 18% (W10)	126
37,143 × 28%	10,400
37,843	
Capital gains tax liability	10,526

Tutorial note

Angela has taxable income that uses some of, but not all of, her basic rate band. Therefore part of her taxable gain is taxed at 18% and the majority is taxed at 28%.

There is no Entrepreneurs' relief available on any of her gains therefore the 10% rate does not apply.

Workings

(W1) **House**

Tutor's top tips

If an asset is jointly owned by husband and wife, all you need to do is to calculate the gain as usual and then split it 50:50.

Make sure you show your working for the calculation of principal private residence relief. Even if you can't count months, you will still be given marks for applying the correct principles!

	£
Disposal proceeds	381,900
Less: Cost	(86,000)
	295,900
Less: Principal private residence exemption (W2)	(255,214)
Chargeable gain	40,686

David and Angela will each be assessed on 50% of the chargeable gain:

Chargeable gain each = (£40,686 × 50%) = £20,343

(W2) **Occupation of the house**

The total period of ownership of the house is 240 months (207 + 33), of which 207 months qualify for exemption as follows:

		Total months	*Exempt months*	*Chargeable months*
1.10.93 to 31.3.97	(occupied)	42	42	
1.4.97 to 31.12.00	(working in UK)	45	45	
1.1.01 to 31.12.07	(occupied)	84	84	
1.1.08 to 30.9.10	(unoccupied)	33		33
1.10.10 to 30.9.13	(final 36 months)	36	36	
		240	207	33

PPR relief = (207/240 × £295,900) = £255,214

Tutor's top tips

Make sure that you include a brief explanation for the periods you allow as exempt due to the deemed occupation rules – as the examiner has said that such explanations are required to obtain maximum marks in these questions.

(W3) **Antique table**

Tutor's top tips

As soon as you see the word 'antique', think about the special chattels rules.

This is a chattel bought and sold for no more than £6,000 and hence is exempt.

(W4) **Shares in Bend Ltd – gift by David**

Tutor's top tips

Remember that the market value at the time of the inter-spouse gift is a red herring and irrelevant. The transfer will be at no gain/no loss.

Transfers between husband and wife are no gain-no loss transfers.

David makes no gain and Angela takes over David's cost of £48,000.

(W5) **Shares in Galatico plc**

	£
Proceeds (Market value for a gift) (15,000 × £2.95) (W6)	44,250
Less: Cost (W7)	(29,400)
Chargeable gain	14,850

Tutorial note

There is no gift relief available on these shares as Galatico plc is a quoted company and David has a less than 5% interest.

For the same reason, and because David does not work for the company, Entrepreneurs' relief is not available.

(W6) **Value of Shares in Galatico plc shares**

Quarter up method = £2.90 + ¼ × (£3.10 – £2.90) = £2.95

(W7) **Share pool – Galatico plc**

		Number of shares	Cost £
15.6.12	Purchase	8,000	17,600
24.8.12	Purchase	12,000	21,600
		20,000	39,200
14.2.14	Gift (£39,200 × 15,000/20,000)	(15,000)	(29,400)
Balance c/f		5,000	9,800

(W8) **Antique clock**

	£
Disposal proceeds	7,200
Less: Cost	(3,700)
Gain	3,500

Chargeable gain cannot exceed: 5/3 × (£7,200 – £6,000) = £2,000

Tutorial note

The clock is a chattel sold at a marginal gain, therefore in the answer the gain is compared with the 5/3rds rule.

In fact, HMRC accept that antique clocks are a form of machinery, and are therefore wasting chattels, which will be exempt (if not used in a business). However, the examiner did not expect you to know this.

(W9) **Shares in Bend Ltd – Sale by Angela**

	£
Disposal proceeds	62,400
Less: Cost (£48,000 × 15,000/20,000)	(36,000)
Chargeable gain	26,400

Tutorial note

It is not clear what percentage interest Angela has in Bend Ltd and whether it is her personal trading company (i.e. she holds 5% interest or more). However, even if she does hold at least 5%, Entrepreneurs' relief is not available as Angela does not work for the company.

(W10) **Remaining basic rate band**

	£
Basic rate band	32,010
Less: Taxable income	(31,310)
Remaining basic rate band	700

Examiner's report

Although there were some very good answers to this question from well prepared candidates, it caused problems for many and was often the reason that they failed to achieve a pass mark.

One particular problem was that a lot of time was often spent performing unnecessary calculations for the exempt assets, and then not having sufficient time to deal with the chargeable assets.

Many candidates therefore did a lot of work for this question but scored few marks.

The jointly owned property caused particular difficulty. Only a few candidates correctly calculated the principal private residence exemption.

Some candidates did not allocate the resulting chargeable gain between the couple but instead deducted an annual exempt amount and calculated a separate tax liability.

ACCA marking scheme	
	Marks
Jointly owned property – Motor car	0.5
– House – Proceeds	0.5
– Cost	0.5
– Period of exemption	2.5
– Exemption	1.0
– Division of gain	1.0
David Brook – Antique table	1.0
– Bend Ltd	0.5
– Galatico plc – Deemed proceeds	1.0
– Cost	2.0
– No gift relief	1.0
– No Entrepreneurs' relief	1.0
– Annual exempt amount	0.5
– Capital gains tax	1.0
Angela Brook – Antique clock	2.0
– Bend Ltd – Proceeds	0.5
– Cost	1.0
– No Entrepreneurs' relief	1.0
– Annual exempt amount	0.5
– Capital gains tax	1.0
Total	20.0

36 WILSON BIAZMA (ADAPTED)

Key answer tips

Part (a) relates to the test for residence. This question was originally written before the residence rules changed, and the test became more complex. Don't forget to read all the requirements and state the consequences of the residence on the liability of an individual to capital gains tax. Do not discuss the automatic non-UK residency tests or the sufficient ties tests as the question only asks for the automatic UK residence tests.

Part (b) involved a series of disposals testing the various reliefs available, part disposals and incorporation. This style of question is a regular feature in the Paper F6 exam.

This was, however, the first time the compensation rules for damaged assets were tested.

This question was originally a 20 mark question, and under the current syllabus and rules, this question would still be worth 20 marks.

No attempt has been made to reduce the question as it is still representative of the type of question you will see in the examination and provides good practice for your revision. However, under the new syllabus the question on capital gains will only be 15 marks and therefore will probably have fewer disposals to deal with in the time available than this question has.

(a) **Automatic residence tests**

A person will be treated as automatically UK residence if they meet one of the following tests:

- They are in the UK for at least 183 days in the tax year.
- Their only home is in the UK.
- They work full time in the UK.

Liability to capital gains tax

- A person is liable to capital gains tax (CGT) on the disposal of assets during any tax year in which they are resident in the UK.

(b) **Chargeable gains – 2013/14**

		£	£
Gains not qualifying for Entrepreneurs' relief:			
Office building (W1)		110,000	
Ordinary shares in Gandua Ltd (W4)		8,000	
Antique vase (W6)		Nil	
Land (W7)		17,000	
Gains qualifying for Entrepreneurs' relief:			
Goodwill (W3)			120,000
Total chargeable gains		135,000	120,000
Less: AEA		(10,900)	
Taxable gains		124,100	120,000
Capital gains tax:			£
Qualifying gains	(£120,000 × 10%)		12,000
Not qualifying gains	(£124,100 × 28%)		34,748
CGT payable			46,748

Tutorial note

Wilson is a higher rate taxpayer. Therefore he will pay capital gains tax at 28% on his gains that do not qualify for Entrepreneurs' relief.

Those gains that qualify for Entrepreneurs' relief will be taxed at 10% regardless of whether they fall into the basic rate or higher rate band. If applicable, these qualifying gains are deemed to utilise any remaining basic rate band first before the gains not qualifying for the relief.

Workings

(W1) **Office building**

	£
Disposal proceeds	246,000
Less: Cost	(104,000)
Capital gain before reliefs	142,000
Less: Rollover relief (W2)	(32,000)
Chargeable gain	110,000

Tutorial note

Entrepreneurs' relief is not available as this is the disposal of a single asset, not the whole or part of a business.

(W2) **Rollover relief**

Rollover relief is not available in full because not all the proceeds are reinvested.

The gain remaining chargeable is the lower of:

(i) Total gain of £142,000, or

(ii) Proceeds not reinvested (£246,000 – £136,000) = £110,000

Rollover relief is therefore £32,000 (£142,000 – £110,000).

(W3) **Goodwill**

	£
Disposal proceeds	120,000
Less: Cost	Nil
Chargeable gain qualifying for Entrepreneurs' relief	120,000

Tutorial note

Entrepreneurs' relief is available as Wilson has disposed of a complete business which he has owned for at least one year.

(W4) **Ordinary shares in Gandua Ltd**

	£
Deemed proceeds (Market value)	160,000
Less: Cost	(112,000)
	48,000
Less: Gift relief (W5)	(40,000)
Chargeable gain	8,000

Tutorial note

Although Gandua Ltd qualifies as Wilson's personal company, Entrepreneurs' relief is not available unless he also works for the company.

(W5) **Gift relief on shares in Gandua Ltd**

Gift relief is available on these shares as Wilson owns 100% of the shares (and there is no requirement for him to work for the company for the purposes of gift relief).

However, the gift relief in respect of the ordinary shares in Gandua Ltd is restricted because the company has investment assets.

The proportion of gain eligible for gift relief is the proportion of chargeable business assets to chargeable assets, calculated as follows:

Gift relief = (£48,000 × £150,000/£180,000) = £40,000

(W6) **Antique vase**

The insurance proceeds of £68,000 received by Wilson have been fully reinvested in a replacement antique vase.

The disposal is therefore on a no gain/no loss basis.

The capital gain of £19,000 (insurance proceeds of £68,000 less original cost of £49,000) is set against the cost of the replacement antique vase.

(W7) **Land – part disposal**

	£
Disposal proceeds	85,000
Less: Deemed cost (see below)	(68,000)
Chargeable gain	17,000

Cost of part disposed of = £120,000 × £85,000/(£85,000 + £65,000) = £68,000.

Tutorial note

The cost relating to the ten acres of land sold is calculated as A/(A + B) where:

A = Market value of part disposed of

B = Market value of the remainder

Examiner's report

Part (a) was reasonably well answered, although only a few candidates appreciated that ordinary residence is a matter of where a person habitually resides. *[Ordinary residence is no longer relevant following the changes to the residence rules in FA2013.]*

Many candidates missed an easy mark by not stating that people who are resident or ordinarily resident will be liable to capital gains tax.

Part (b) was also reasonably well answered. The disposal that caused the most problems was the incorporation of the business, with many candidates not appreciating that the gain was simply based on the value of the goodwill transferred. *[Incorporation relief is no longer examinable in the F6 syllabus, therefore this part of the question has now been amended.]*

ACCA marking scheme		
		Marks
(a)	Present in the UK 183 days	1.0
	Only home in the UK	1.0
	Work full time in the UK	1.0
	Liability to CGT	1.0
		4.0
(b)	**Office building**	
	Gain	1.0
	Rollover relief	1.5
	No Entrepreneurs' relief	1.0
	Goodwill	
	Gain	1.0
	Entrepreneurs' relief – need to keep gain separate	1.0
	Ordinary shares in Gandua Ltd	
	Gain	1.0
	Gift relief	1.5
	No Entrepreneurs' relief	1.0
	Antique vase	
	Proceeds fully reinvested	1.0
	No gain no loss	1.0
	Gain reduces base cost	0.5
	Land	
	Proceeds	0.5
	Cost	2.0
	Calculation of CGT payable	
	Annual exempt amount	0.5
	Entrepreneurs' relief rate	1.0
	Rate for remainder of gains	0.5
		16.0
Total		20.0

37 NIM AND MAE LOM (ADAPTED)  *Walk in the footsteps of a top tutor*

Key answer tips

A typical capital gains tax question, requiring the calculation of capital gains tax liabilities for a husband and wife.

Although there is only one requirement, the question can be broken down between the two individuals and then into the different assets sold by each.

This question was originally a 20 mark question, and under the current syllabus and rules, this question would still be worth 20 marks.

No attempt has been made to reduce the question as it is still representative of the type of question you will see in the examination and provides good practice for your revision. However, under the new syllabus the question on capital gains will only be 15 marks and therefore will probably have fewer disposals to deal with in the time available than this question has.

Tutor's top tips

Nim's assets are mostly straightforward. As with any capital gains question, be careful to spot the exempt assets (gilts). You don't need to do any calculations for these – simply state that they are exempt.

There is a classic husband to wife transfer, which from Nim's perspective is simply a no gain/no loss disposal.

When dealing with shares, make sure you consider the matching rules first. There is a purchase within 30 days of the disposal, so this will need to be matched before the shares bought earlier, and these shares will NOT go into the share pool.

Nim Lom

Capital gains tax liability – 2013/14

	£
Ordinary shares in Kapook plc (W1)	13,600
Ordinary shares in Jooba Ltd (Note 1)	Nil
Antique table (W4)	3,500
UK Government securities (Note 2)	Nil
Total chargeable gains	17,100
Less: Capital loss brought forward (see below)	(6,200)
Net chargeable gains	10,900
Less: AEA	(10,900)
Taxable gain	Nil
Capital gains tax	Nil

Capital losses carried forward

The set off of the brought forward capital losses is restricted to £6,200 so that chargeable gains are reduced to the amount of the annual exempt amount.

Nim therefore has capital losses carried forward of £10,500 (£16,700 – £6,200).

Workings

(W1) **Ordinary shares in Kapook plc**

The disposal is first matched against the purchase on 24 July 2013 of 2,000 shares (this is within the following 30 days), and then against the shares in the share pool.

	£	£
Matched with purchases in next 30 days:		
Deemed proceeds (2,000 × £3.70) (W2)	7,400	
Less: Cost	(5,800)	
		1,600
Matched with share pool:		
Deemed proceeds (8,000 × £3.70) (W2)	29,600	
Less: Cost (W3)	(17,600)	
		12,000
		13,600

(W2) **Valuation of ordinary shares in Kapook plc**

The shares in Kapook plc are valued at the lower of:

(i) Quarter up method = £3·70 + ¼ × (£3·90 – £3·70) = £3.75

(ii) Average of highest and lowest marked bargains = (£3·60 + £3·80)/2 = £3.70

(W3) **Share pool – Kapook plc**

The cost of the shares in the share pool is calculated as:

	Number of shares	Cost £
Purchase 19 February 2005	8,000	16,200
Purchase 6 June 2010	6,000	14,600
	14,000	30,800
Disposal 20 July 2013 (£30,800 × 8,000/14,000)	(8,000)	(17,600)
Balance carried forward	6,000	13,200

(W4) **Antique table**

The antique table is a non-wasting chattel (Note 3).

	£
Sale proceeds	8,700
Less: Cost	(5,200)
Chargeable gain	3,500
Chargeable gain is not restricted as the maximum gain is: 5/3 × (£8,700 – £6,000)	4,500

Tutorial note

1. *The transfer of the 5,000 £1 ordinary shares in Jooba Ltd to Mae does not give rise to any gain or loss, because it is a transfer between spouses.*
2. *The disposal of UK Government securities is exempt from CGT.*
3. *Whenever you see the word 'antique' in a question, you should immediately be thinking about the chattel rules.*
4. *It is important to be familiar with the rules for the use of capital losses, which are very regularly tested. Brought forward losses are restricted to utilise the annual exempt amount, but current year losses must be used in full.*

Mae Lom

Capital gains tax liability – 2013/14

Tutor's top tips

Mae has disposed of the shares that she received from her husband. Remember this was a no gain no loss transfer, and in order for Nim to have a gain of nil, he is deemed to have transferred the asset to Mae at original cost.

The house has been Nim and Mae's main residence throughout the period of ownership, so there is no need to consider the absence rules here, however as one room was used exclusively for business purposes, principal private residence relief cannot be given in respect of that part of the gain.

When dealing with business assets make sure you consider their eligibility for Entrepreneurs' relief.

The hardest asset to deal with is the copyright, as this kind of disposal has not been seen in exam questions before. The asset is wasting (it has a useful life of less than 50 years), however it is not a chattel so the £6,000 rules do not apply. Instead the cost must be reduced on a straight line basis for the period of time that the asset has been held by Mae.

	£	£	£
Gains not qualifying for Entrepreneurs' relief:			
Ordinary shares in Jooba Ltd			
Disposal proceeds	30,400		
Less: Cost (£16,000 × 2,000/5,000) (Note 1)	(6,400)		
		24,000	
Principal private residence			
Disposal proceeds	186,000		
Less: Cost	(122,000)		
	64,000		
Less: PPR relief (W)	(56,000)		
		8,000	
Chargeable gains c/f		32,000	

	£	£	£
Chargeable gains b/f		32,000	
Investment property (Note 2)		34,000	
Copyright			
Disposal proceeds	9,600		
Less: Cost (£10,000 × 15/20) (Note 3)	(7,500)		
		2,100	
Gains qualifying for Entrepreneurs' relief:			
Business			
Goodwill	80,000		
Freehold office building	136,000		
			216,000
Total chargeable gains (Note 4)		68,100	216,000
Less: Capital loss brought forward		(8,500)	
Less: AEA		(10,900)	
Taxable gains		48,700	216,000

		£
Capital gains tax (Note 5)		
Qualifying gains	(£216,000 × 10%)	21,600
Non-qualifying gains	(£48,700 × 28%)	13,636
CGT payable		35,236

Tutorial note

1 *Nim's original cost is used in calculating the gain on the disposal of the shares in Jooba Ltd.*

2 *The investment property does not qualify for Entrepreneurs' relief because it was never used for business purposes.*

3 *The copyright is a wasting asset. The cost of £10,000 must therefore be depreciated based on an unexpired life of 20 years at the date of acquisition and an unexpired life of 15 years at the date of disposal.*

4 *The annual exempt amount and capital losses brought forward can be deducted in the most advantageous way. Therefore they are deducted from the gains not eligible for Entrepreneurs' relief, leaving the whole £216,000 to be taxed at 10%.*

5 *Although Mae has taxable income of only £30,000 and £2,010 of the basic rate band remains, gains qualifying for Entrepreneurs' relief are deemed to utilise the remaining basic rate band before non-qualifying gains. Therefore all of the non-qualifying gains are taxed at 28%.*

Capital losses carried forward

There is no capital loss remaining to carry forward as it is all utilised in 2013/14.

Working: Principal private residence relief

One of the eight rooms in Mae's house was always used exclusively for business purposes, so the principal private residence exemption is restricted to £56,000 (£64,000 × 7/8).

Examiner's report

This question was generally well answered.

For the husband, quite a few candidates surprisingly had problems with the valuation rules for quoted shares.

It was also not always appreciated that the transfer between spouses and the sale of the UK Government securities were respectively at no gain, no loss, and exempt. Candidates thus wasted time performing unnecessary calculations.

Many candidates had difficulty with the cost of the quoted shares disposed of, and they incorrectly included the purchase within the following 30 days as part of the share pool.

The restriction of the brought forward capital losses so that chargeable gains were reduced to the amount of the annual exempt amount was often missed.

For the wife, many candidates treated the private portion of the principal private residence as taxable rather than the business portion.

The investment property included within the disposal of the business was sometimes treated as exempt, and sometimes Entrepreneurs' relief was claimed in respect of it.

Only a minority of candidates correctly calculated the cost of the wasting asset.

ACCA marking scheme

			Marks
Nim Lom			
Kapook plc	– Deemed proceeds		2.0
	– Cost		1.0
	– Share pool		2.0
Jooba Ltd			1.0
Antique table			1.5
UK Government securities			0.5
Capital losses brought forward			1.0
Annual exempt amount			0.5
Capital losses carried forward			0.5
Mae Lom			
Jooba Ltd	– Proceeds		0.5
	– Cost		1.0
House	– Proceeds		0.5
	– Cost		0.5
	– Exemption		1.0
Business	– Goodwill		0.5
	– Office building		0.5
	– Investment property		1.0
Copyright	– Proceeds		0.5
	– Cost		1.0
Capital losses brought forward			0.5
Annual exempt amount			0.5
Capital gains tax			2.0
Total			20.0

38 ALICE, BO AND CHARLES (ADAPTED)  *Walk in the footsteps of a top tutor*

Key answer tips

A capital gains tax question requiring the calculation of chargeable gains for three different individuals.

Each scenario covers a different capital gains tax relief: rollover relief, gift relief and principal private residence relief.

In part (a), not all the proceeds of sale of the warehouse are reinvested, so not all of the gain can be rolled over. In part (b) the question requires the consideration of an alternative assumption.

The requirement specifically asked for the chargeable gain, not the capital gains tax liability. Therefore, Entrepreneurs' relief is not relevant, but to make sure the examiner clearly indicated in the notes to the question that you should ignore Entrepreneurs' relief.

Part (a) of this question has been replaced, as the rules previously tested are no longer in the syllabus. This question was originally a 20 mark question, however, following the changes to the question it would now be worth 15 marks.

(a) **Alice Lim**

Chargeable gain – 2013/14

	£	£
Disposal proceeds		152,000
Less: Cost	134,000	
Rolled over gain (W)	(41,000)	
		(93,000)
Chargeable gain		59,000

Working: Rollover relief

The sale proceeds of the warehouse disposed of in April 2012 were not fully reinvested.

Accordingly, a capital gain of £15,000 (£149,000 – £134,000) would have been chargeable at the time.

The amount of gain rolled over must therefore have been £41,000 (£56,000 – £15,000).

Tutorial note

The question says ignore Entrepreneurs' relief.

However, for tutorial purposes, Entrepreneurs' relief is not available anyway as the disposal of the office building is not a qualifying disposal of the whole or part of a business.

There is no relief for the disposal of individual assets out of a business.

(b) (i) **Bo Neptune**

Chargeable gain – 2013/14

Tutor's top tips

Part (b) involves the gift of shares in an unquoted trading company. You should be aware that these shares qualify for gift relief. However even if you couldn't remember the definition of a qualifying asset for gift relief purposes, the question clearly states that an election has been made to holdover (i.e. defer) the gain arising.

Remember that full relief is available for outright gifts of qualifying assets, but there may only be partial gift relief for sales at an undervalue (i.e. where the actual sale proceeds received are less than the market value of the asset at the time of the gift).

Full relief is not available where the actual sale proceeds received exceed the original cost of the asset. This is because, despite selling the asset for less than it is worth now, an actual capital profit has still been made by the owner on the disposal.

- This is a gift, and therefore the market value of the shares sold is used. Bo therefore has a chargeable gain of £116,000 (MV £210,000 – Cost of £94,000).
- Since no consideration has been paid for the shares, all of Bo's chargeable gain can be held over (i.e. deferred) with a gift relief claim.
- The base cost of the son's 50,000 £1 ordinary shares in Botune Ltd will be:

	£
MV of shares acquired	210,000
Less: Gift relief	(116,000)
Base cost of shares	94,000

(ii) **Sale at undervaluation**

- The consideration paid for the shares is less than the market value, but will exceed the allowable cost by £66,000 (£160,000 – £94,000). This amount will be immediately chargeable to capital gains tax.
- The remaining gain of £50,000 (£116,000 – £66,000) can be deferred with a gift relief claim.
- The base cost of the son's 50,000 £1 ordinary shares in Botune Ltd will be:

	£
MV of shares acquired	210,000
Less: Gift relief	(50,000)
Base cost of shares	160,000

Tutorial note

With a sale at undervalue, the chargeable gain will still be calculated using the full market value of the asset, as before.

However, any actual capital profit made by the owner at the time of the sale will be immediately chargeable.

(c) (i) **Charles Orion**

Chargeable gain – 2013/14

Tutor's top tips

Part (c) involves the disposal of Charles' house. It tests the application of the deemed occupation rules and in the second part, letting relief.

This is a classic PPR question which is fairly straightforward but be careful with the dates and identifying the impact of the last 36 months rule.

Charles' chargeable gain on the house is calculated as follows:

	£
Disposal proceeds	282,000
Less: Cost	(110,000)
	172,000
Less: PPR relief (W)	(107,500)
Chargeable gain	64,500

Working: PPR relief

		Total months	*Exempt months*		*Chargeable months*
1.10.01 to 31.3.03	(occupied)	18	18		
1.4.03 to 30.9.10	(unoccupied)	90	36	(Note 1)	54
1.10.10 to 31.12.11	(unoccupied)	15	15	(Note 2)	
1.1.12 to 30.9.13	(occupied)	21	21	(Note 2)	
		144	90		54

PPR exemption = (£172,000 × 90/144) = £107,500

Tutor's top tips

Make sure that you include a brief explanation for the periods you allow as exempt due to the deemed occupation rules – as the examiner has said that such explanations are required to obtain maximum marks in these questions.

Tutorial note

1 *The first 36 months of the "unoccupied" period is a period of "deemed occupation" because 36 months are allowed for no reason provided:*

- *the property is actually occupied at some time before and at some time after the period of absence, and*
- *there was no other PPR at that time.*

2 *The last 36 months are always allowable provided the property was the taxpayer's PPR at some time.*

Note that the last 36 months covers the last 21 months of actual occupation and the last 15 months of the "unoccupied" period.

(ii) **If the property is rented**

- The letting relief exemption will be available if the property is let during periods that are not covered by the PPR exemption.
- The letting relief exemption is the lowest of:
  - (i) PPR exemption = £107,500
  - (ii) the amount of the gain not covered by PPR that is attributable to the period of letting = £64,500 (Note)
  - (iii) Maximum = £40,000.
- Charles' chargeable gain will therefore be:

	£
Gain after PPR relief	64,500
Less: Letting relief	(40,000)
Chargeable gain	24,500

Tutorial note

In this part the house is let for the whole period of Charles' absence.

Therefore, the "amount of the gain not covered by PPR that is attributable to the period of letting" will be the whole of the remaining gain after PPR, as it is let throughout the whole period.

If the property had only been let for a portion of that chargeable period, letting relief would be restricted accordingly.

Examiner's report

This question was not as well answered as would have been expected given that it was effectively three short separate questions on reasonably straightforward areas of capital gains tax.

On an overall note, the question clearly stated that Entrepreneurs' relief was to be ignored, yet some candidates still showed this relief as being claimed.

Base costs were often not shown despite these being required in part (b).

Part (b) was reasonably well answered, although few candidates could correctly calculate the revised base cost following the restriction of holdover relief in the second section.

Although there were some very good answers to part (c), far too many candidates had problems calculating the principal private residence exemption, and often lost marks by not showing detailed workings.

Even when the correct exemption was calculated this was often shown as the amount chargeable rather than the exempt amount. In the second section it was not always appreciated that letting relief was available.

The examiner's comments on the original part (a) have been deleted as this topic is no longer in the F6 syllabus and this part of the question has been replaced.

ACCA marking scheme

			Marks
(a)	Gain rolled over – April 2012		1.0
	Chargeable gain – 2013/14		1.0
			2.0
(b)	(i)	Chargeable gain	1.0
		Gain held over	1.0
		Base cost of shares	1.0
			3.0
	(ii)	Gain chargeable	1.0
		Base cost of shares	1.0
			2.0
(c)	(i)	Proceeds	0.5
		Cost	0.5
		Period of exemption	3.0
		Principal private residence relief	1.0
			5.0
	(ii)	Letting relief	2.0
		Revised chargeable gain	1.0
			3.0
Total			15.0

39 LIM LAM  *Walk in the footsteps of a top tutor*

Key answer tips

This question was somewhat unusual as it tested capital gains for both a company and an individual. However, the gain calculations themselves were not particularly unusual and should not have presented any problems.

Part (a) is a short written question on the availability of Entrepreneurs' relief. It is important that you can express the tax rules in words as well as being able to perform the calculations.

Part (b) involves three gains calculations for an individual, covering a straightforward sale, a trickier gift of shares acquired as a result of a takeover and a sale of shares eligible for Entrepreneurs' relief. These are all key areas which are likely to be regularly tested, although many would find the takeover calculation challenging.

Part (c) required the calculation of the corporation tax liability for a company and this therefore required a part disposal calculation which should not have caused concern.

This question was originally a 20 mark question, and under the current syllabus and rules, this question would still be worth 20 marks.

No attempt has been made to reduce the question as it is still representative of the type of question you will see in the examination and provides good practice for your revision. However, under the new syllabus the question on capital gains will only be 15 marks and therefore will probably have fewer disposals to deal with in the time available than this question has.

Tutor's top tips

Try not to be daunted by the unusual combination of both an individual and company in the same question, this should not be a problem provided the calculations for Lim Lam and Mal-Mil Ltd are kept completely separate.

(a) **Availability of Entrepreneurs' relief**

- Mal-Mil Ltd is a trading company.
- Lim owns more than 5% of the ordinary share capital (185,000/250,000 = 74%).
- Lim works as managing director of the company.
- Lim has owned the shares for 12 months prior to the disposal.

Tutor's top tips

It is crucial to learn the conditions for Entrepreneurs' relief, to be able to explain them in writing and to be able to apply them to a given situation.

(b) **Lim Lam's capital gains tax liability – 2013/14**

Tutor's top tips

When an individual has made a number of gains, some of which qualify for Entrepreneurs' relief, and some of which do not, it is important to separate out the non-qualifying gains. This is because any loss relief available and the annual exempt amount should always be set against those gains first, in order to minimise the overall tax liability.

		£	£
Gains not qualifying for Entrepreneurs' relief:			
Land			
Proceeds (Market value)		260,000	
Less: Cost (Probate value)		(182,000)	
			78,000
Shares in Oily plc			
Proceeds (£7.44 × 5,000) (W1)		37,200	
Less: Cost (W2)		(15,925)	
			21,275
			99,275
Less: Annual exempt amount			(10,900)
Taxable gains			88,375
Gains qualifying for Entrepreneurs' relief:			
Mal-Mil shares			
Proceeds		280,000	
Cost (W3)		(56,000)	
			224,000
Capital gains tax:			
Qualifying for Entrepreneurs' relief	(£224,000 × 10%)		22,400
Not qualifying for Entrepreneurs' relief	(£88,375 × 28%)		24,745
CGT payable			47,145
Due date			31 January 2015

Tutorial notes

You have been told in the question that Entrepreneurs' relief and holdover (gift) relief are not available in respect of the Oily plc shares. You should therefore not spend any time considering these reliefs here.

Although Lim's taxable income is less than the basic rate band all of the gains which do not qualify for Entrepreneurs' relief will be taxed at 28%. This is because the gains eligible for Entrepreneurs' relief are deemed to use the basic rate band first, and there is therefore no basic rate band remaining for the non-qualifying gains.

Workings

(W1) **Value of Oily plc shares**

The shares in Oily plc are valued at the lower of:

(i) Quarter up method = (£7.40 + 1/4 × (£7.56 – £7.40)) = £7.44

(ii) Average of marked bargains = (£7.36 + £7.60) × 1/2 = £7.48

Therefore valued at £7.44 per share.

(W2) **Takeover of Greasy plc**

		£
Consideration received at time of takeover:		
Ordinary shares	(1,000 × 5 × £3.50)	17,500
Preference shares	(1,000 × 2 × £1.25)	2,500
		20,000
Therefore cost of shares gifted in August 2013:		
£18,200 × (£17,500/£20,000)		15,925

Tutorial note

A takeover is a share-for-share exchange. The new shares acquired simply 'step into the shoes' of those originally purchased, and therefore take on the same cost and acquisition date. It is therefore necessary to apportion the original cost of the Greasy plc shares between the two types of shares in Oily plc. This apportionment is done based on the market values of those shares on the date they are acquired.

(W3) **Mal-Mil Ltd shares**

The Mal-Mil Ltd shares sold are all matched with shares in the pool.

Share pool	*Number*	*Cost*
		£
Purchase – 8 June 2005	125,000	142,000
Purchase – 23 May 2007	60,000	117,000
	185,000	259,000
Disposal – 22 March 2014		
Cost × 40,000/185,000	(40,000)	(56,000)
Balance c/f	145,000	203,000

(c) **Mal-Mil Ltd corporation tax liability – year ended 31 March 2014**

Tutor's top tips

You need to remember to include indexation as it is now a company disposal.

This is a part disposal and you need to consider carefully to which cost or costs the part disposal calculation should be applied.

		£	£
Disposal proceeds			162,000
Less: Legal fees			(3,800)
			158,200
Less:	Cost		
	(£162,000/(£162,000 + £254,000)) × £260,000	101,250	
	Enhancement		
	(£162,000/(£162,000 + £254,000)) × £31,200	12,150	
			(113,400)
			44,800
Less:	Indexation allowance		
	(254.6 – 249.9)/249.9 = 0.019 × £113,400		(2,155)
Chargeable gain			42,645
Trading profit			163,000
Taxable total profits			205,645
Corporation tax liability (£205,645 × 20%)			41,129
Due date			1 January 2015

Tutorial notes

1 *The part disposal calculation is Cost × A/A + B. A represents the value of the part sold and B represents the value of the remainder. This formula must be applied to both the cost and the enhancement value as the cost of levelling the land related to the whole plot and not just the part that has been sold.*

2 *The same indexation factor can be applied to both the cost and the enhancement expenditure as both were incurred in July 2013.*

3 *The corporation tax liability is calculated at 20% since the taxable total profits are less than £300,000.*

4 *Corporation tax paid at less than the main rate is due 9 months and 1 day after the end of the accounting period.*

Examiner's report

This question was very well answered, with many perfect answers. It was often the question that made the difference between a pass mark and a fail.

In **part (a)** the fact that the company was a trading company was often not mentioned.

There were few problems in **part (b)**, although for the disposal of land it was not always appreciated that the relevant cost was that when it was inherited by the taxpayer.

Part (c) generally caused a few more problems. Even when the part disposal rules were correctly applied to the cost of the land, many candidates did not appreciate that the same principle applied to the enhancement expenditure.

It was disappointing that the annual exempt amount was often deducted when calculating the corporation tax liability.

ACCA marking scheme

			Marks
(a)	Trading company		0.5
	Shareholding of more than 5%		0.5
	Director		0.5
	Shares owned for one year		0.5
			2.0
(b)	Land	– proceeds	0.5
		– cost	0.5
	Oily plc	– deemed proceeds	2.0
		– value of shares received	2.0
		– cost	1.0
	Mal-Mil Ltd	– proceeds	0.5
		– cost	2.0
	Annual exempt amount		0.5
	Capital gains tax		1.5
	Due date		0.5
			11.0

ACCA marking scheme		
		Marks
(c)	**Chargeable gain**	
	Proceeds	0.5
	Incidental costs of disposal	0.5
	Cost	1.5
	Enhancement expenditure	1.0
	Indexation	1.5
	Corporation tax liability	
	Calculation	1.5
	Due date	0.5
		7.0
Total		20.0

40 ALPHABET LTD  *Walk in the footsteps of a top tutor*

Key answer tips

This is a familiar style capital gains tax question involving four individuals making disposals. All of them had shares in a company which is taken over.

Takeovers can be complicated where there is mixed consideration and many students may have been put off by the opening paragraph. However, in this question, there is no mixed consideration and it is quite straightforward.

They are disposing of their existing shares and have a choice of either cash or shares, but not a mixture of the two.

Of the four individuals, two choose cash and therefore just have a straightforward disposal of shares for cash.

The other two choose shares which are just a share for share exchange with no capital gains tax consequences at that time. The new shares just 'stand in the shoes' of the old shares and are deemed to have been acquired at the same cost and at the same time as the original shares. They then dispose of some of the new shares.

For the first part, detailed knowledge of the Entrepreneurs' relief conditions is required. However, the requirement of part (a) indicates that only Aloi's disposal is eligible for Entrepreneurs' relief. Therefore, even if you could not remember the detailed conditions for part (a), you should have realised that in calculating the capital gains tax liabilities in part (b) the gains for three of the individuals cannot be taxed at 10% whilst some of Aloi's gains would be taxed at 10%.

(a) **Entrepreneurs' relief**

Bon

Bon acquired her shareholding and became a director on 1 February 2013, so the qualifying conditions were not met for the 12 months prior to the date of disposal.

Cherry

Cherry is not, and has never been, an officer or an employee of Alphabet Ltd and therefore does not qualify.

Dinah

Dinah owns 3,000 shares out of the 100,000 shares in the company, which is a 3% shareholding.

This is less than the minimum required holding of 5% to qualify for the relief.

Tutorial note

To qualify for Entrepreneurs' relief, the company must be trading and the individual must:

- *Own 5% or more of the shares, and*
- *Work for the company, and*
- *Must satisfy both of these conditions for 12 months prior to the date of disposal.*

(b) **Aloi**

Capital gains tax liability – 2013/14

	Not qualifying for ER	*Qualifying for ER*
	£	£
Qualifying for Entrepreneurs' relief		
Ordinary shares in Alphabet Ltd		
Disposal proceeds (60,000 × £6)		360,000
Cost (£50,000 + £18,600)		(68,600)
Not qualifying for Entrepreneurs' relief		
Investment property	22,600	
Chargeable gains	22,600	291,400
Less: Annual exempt amount (Note 1)	(10,900)	(Nil)
	11,700	291,400

	£
Capital gains tax liability	
Qualifying for ER (£291,400 at 10%) (Note 2)	29,140
Not qualifying for ER (£11,700 at 28%) (Note 3)	3,276
	32,416

Tutorial note

1 *The annual exempt amount is set against the chargeable gain from the sale of the investment property as it does not qualify for Entrepreneurs' relief and therefore this saves CGT at the higher rate of 28% rather than 10%.*

2 *The gains qualifying for Entrepreneurs' relief have to be taxed first and, if applicable, they utilise any remaining BR band before non-qualifying gains are considered.*

3 *Gains not qualifying for Entrepreneurs' relief are then taxed based on the level of taxable income. As Aloi's taxable income is £60,000 the basic rate band has been utilised and therefore the non-qualifying gains will be taxed at 28%.*

Bon

Capital gains tax liability – 2013/14

	£
Ordinary shares in XYZ plc	
Deemed proceeds (10,000 × £7·12) (W1)	71,200
Less: Cost (W2) (Note 1)	(36,880)
Chargeable gain	34,320
Less: Annual exempt amount	(10,900)
Taxable gain	23,420
Capital gains tax liability	
(£23,420 at 28%) (Note 2)	6,558

Tutorial note

1 *Following the takeover Bon received 25,000 ordinary shares in XYZ plc.*

Where there is a share for share exchange, the cost of the original shareholding is treated as the cost of the new shareholding acquired on the takeover.

The cost of the new shares disposed of is therefore a proportion of the original cost of the Alphabet shares.

2 *As Entrepreneurs' relief is not available, the gain is taxed according to the level of Bon's taxable income. As she has taxable income of £55,000 she is a higher rate taxpayer and the gain will be taxed at 28%.*

Working

(W1) **Value of XYZ plc shares**

The shares in XYZ plc are valued using the quarter up method:

(£7.10 + (£7.18 – £7.10) × 1/4) = £7.12

There is no comparison to an average value as there were no recorded bargains for the date of the gift.

(W2) **Cost of shares**

The cost attributable to the 10,000 shares sold is:

(£92,200 × 10,000/25,000) = £36,880

Cherry

Capital gains tax liability – 2012/13

	£
Ordinary shares in Alphabet Ltd	
Disposal proceeds (12,000 × £6)	72,000
Less: Cost	(23,900)
Chargeable gain	48,100
Less: Annual exempt amount	(10,900)
Taxable gain	37,200
Capital gains tax liability	
(£4,410 at 18%) (W)	794
(£32,790 at 28%)	9,181
	9,975

Working: Remaining basic rate band

	£
Basic rate band	32,010
Plus: Gross PPC	3,400
Extended basic rate band	35,410
Less: Taxable income	(31,000)
Remaining basic rate band	4,410

Dinah

Capital gains tax liability – 2013/14

Disposal of ordinary shares in XYZ plc (Note):

There is no CGT liability on the sale of the XYZ plc shares as:

- the sale proceeds were only £6,600, and
- Dinah had no other disposals

therefore, even if the shares had £Nil cost, the gain is below the annual exempt amount of £10,900.

Transfer of XYZ plc on Dinah's death:

Transfers on death are exempt disposals.

Tutor's top tips:

The gain on the disposal of the XYZ plc shares is:

	£
Proceeds	*6,600*
Less: Cost (£4,800 × 1,000/3,000)	*(1,600)*
Chargeable gain	*5,000*

However, there is no need to do any calculation in this part to conclude that there is no capital gains tax liability (see examiner's report).

Examiner's report

Answers to this question either tended to be very good or quite poor, with many candidates making the calculations far more complicated than they actually were.

In part (a) many candidates simply reproduced the qualifying conditions for entrepreneurs' relief, without relating them to the information given for each of the three shareholders.

In part (b) a number of candidates included taxable income as part of their calculations, and the annual exempt amount was often omitted.

For the fourth shareholder, it should have been obvious that with sales proceeds of just £6,600 there would be no capital gains tax liability, yet the vast majority of candidates wasted time attempting to calculate a liability.

Similarly, there was little awareness that the transfer on death was an exempt disposal.

ACCA marking scheme				
				Marks
(a)	Bon			1.0
	Cherry			1.0
	Dinah			1.0
				3.0
(b)	**Aloi** Alphabet Ltd	– Disposal proceeds		0.5
		– Cost		1.0
	Investment property			0.5
	Annual exempt amount			1.0
	Capital gains tax			1.0
	Bon Deemed proceeds			1.0
	Cost			1.0
	Annual exempt amount			0.5
	Capital gains tax			0.5
	Cherry Disposal proceeds			0.5
	Cost			0.5
	Annual exempt amount			0.5
	Capital gains tax			2.0
	Dinah Sale of shares			1.0
	Exempt disposal on death			0.5
				12.0
	Total			15.0

41 JORGE JUNG  *Walk in the footsteps of a top tutor*

Key answer tips

A fairly involved capital gains question requiring the calculation of the total taxable gains of an individual, but not the capital gains tax liability. There are some easy marks to be gained but also some tricky aspects to watch out for.

The PPR relief calculation is much more involved than in any of the examiner's previous questions. The periods of occupation and non-occupation need careful consideration and an explanation of the treatment of each is required.

The letting relief part is however straightforward as the property was let throughout all of the periods of non-occupation.

Copyrights appear in the question, which has become a more popular disposal and, as always, there are a couple of exempt assets disposed of which need to be identified.

The classic part disposal should not give cause for concern, although the seller had not purchased the asset; he had acquired it via an inter-spouse transfer and his wife had inherited it from her father. Identification of the correct base cost to use is therefore required.

Finally a sale at undervaluation of a qualifying asset tests the gift relief rules.

A lot to deal with in a short space of time.

Tutor's top tips:

Make sure you quickly identify the exempt assets so that you do not waste time trying to calculate gains on those assets.

Note that you only have to calculate taxable gains which are the net chargeable gains less the annual exempt amount. Make sure you get the mark for deducting this and do not waste time trying to calculate the capital gains tax liability.

Taxable gains computation – 2013/14

	Notes	£	£
House			
Disposal proceeds		308,000	
Less: Cost		(98,000)	
Potential gain		210,000	
Less: PPR relief (W1)		(188,000)	
Letting relief (W2)		(22,000)	
			Nil
Copyright			
Disposal proceeds		8,200	
Less: Depreciated cost (£7,000 × 8/10)	1	(5,600)	
			2,600
Painting	2		Exempt
Motor car	3		Exempt
Land – part disposal	4		
Disposal proceeds		92,000	
Less: Cost			
£28,600 × (£92,000/(£92,000 + £38,000))		(20,240)	
			71,760
Ordinary shares in Futuristic Ltd			
Deemed proceeds	5	64,800	
Less: Cost		(26,300)	
		38,500	
Less: Gift relief (W3)		(24,800)	
			13,700
Total chargeable gains			88,060
Less: Annual exempt amount			(10,900)
Taxable gains			77,160

Tutorial note

1 *The copyright is a wasting asset. The cost of £7,000 must therefore be depreciated based on an unexpired life of ten years at the date of acquisition and an unexpired life of eight years at the date of disposal.*

2 *The painting is a non-wasting chattel, but is exempt from CGT because the gross sale proceeds and the acquisition cost were less than £6,000.*

3 *Motor cars are exempt from CGT, so the loss of £3,900 (£14,600 – £10,700) is not allowable.*

4 *The cost of the land is £28,600 which is the value when Jorge's father-in-law died. Remember that where an individual inherits an asset the cost of acquisition is the market value at the date of death (i.e. probate value). Jorge would have taken over this cost when his wife transferred the land to him as transfers between spouses take place at no gain/no loss.*

The cost relating to the two acres of land sold is:

£28,600 × (£92,000/(£92,000 + £38,000)) = £20,240

5 *Jorge and his sister are connected persons, and therefore the market value of the ordinary shares in Futuristic Ltd is used.*

Workings

(W1) **PPR relief**

	Notes	*Total (months)*	*Exempt (months)*	*Chargeable (months)*	*Property let (months)*
Occupied		16	16		
Travelling overseas	1	18	18		
Working overseas	2	24	24		
Occupied		11	11		
Working elsewhere in UK	3	30	30		
Travelling overseas	1	22	18	4	4
Working elsewhere in UK	3	26	18	8	8
Occupied		17	17		
Working overseas	2, 4	12	2	10	10
Travelling overseas	4	13	13		
Living with sister	4	21	21		
		210	188	22	22

PPR relief = £210,000 × 188/210 = £188,000

Tutor's top tips:

The best way to calculate the chargeable and exempt periods is to prepare a table as shown above in (W1).

Tutorial note

The examiner has stated that, in general, lengthy explanations are not required in answers where he asks for a computation to be performed. However he mentioned the explanations regarding deemed occupation for PPR as an exception to this general rule.

It is necessary therefore to provide brief explanations to aid the understanding of your calculation of PPR relief.

The explanation given by the examiner in his model answer is below, but then followed by a fuller explanation for tutorial purposes.

Brief explanatory note (per examiner)

In calculating the principal private residence exemption periods of absence while working overseas, a maximum of four years absence while working elsewhere in the UK and a maximum of three years absence for any reason are treated as deemed occupation.

However, the second period working overseas is not a period of deemed occupation as it was not followed by a period of actual occupation.

Detailed explanatory note (for tutorial purposes)

1 Travelling overseas does not qualify for relief as the taxpayer is not working overseas.

However, the taxpayer has a **maximum period of 36 months in total** which is allowable for **no reason**, provided that there is:

- a period of actual occupation **at some time** before and **at some time** after the period of absence, and
- the property is the taxpayer's principal private residence at that time.

This maximum 36 months will therefore be allowed in this question as follows:

	months
First period travelling overseas	18
Second period travelling overseas	18
Maximum	36

The third period travelling overseas is not allowed under this rule as the 36 months have already been utilised. However, even if the maximum amount had not been utilised, it would not be allowed as the period is not followed by a period of actual occupation.

This third period is however allowed for other reasons, due to the last 36 months rule (see Note 4 below).

2 **Any period working overseas** is allowable provided the same two conditions outlined above apply to these periods.

The first period working overseas is therefore allowed, but the second period is not allowed as the period is not followed by a period of actual occupation.

However, some of this second period is allowed due to the last 36 months rule (see Note 4 below).

3 A **maximum of 48 months in total** is allowable for periods **working elsewhere in the UK**, provided the same two conditions outlined above apply to these periods.

Both periods of working in the UK satisfy these conditions and therefore are allowable. However, they total 56 months and therefore the maximum 48 months will be allowed in this question as follows:

	months
First period working elsewhere in UK	30
Second period working elsewhere in UK	18
Maximum	48

4 The last 36 months of ownership of the property are always allowed, unconditionally. The last 36 months will therefore allow the final period living with his sister, the last period of travelling overseas and 2 months of the last period working overseas.

(W2) **Letting relief**

Lowest of:

(i) PPR relief = £188,000

(ii) Maximum = £40,000

(iii) The amount of gain attributable to the period of letting

= (£210,000 × 22/210) = £22,000

(W3) **Gift relief**

The sale of the Futuristic Ltd shares is a sale at undervaluation (i.e. for less than the full market value).

Gift relief is available, but not for the full gain.

Gain chargeable immediately = Actual sale proceeds received – Original cost

= £40,000 – £26,300 = £13,700

Gift relief = gain less amount chargeable immediately

= (£38,500 – £13,700) = £24,800

Examiner's report

This question was well answered, with only the principal private residence consistently causing problems.

However, quite a few candidates wasted time by calculating the taxpayer's tax liability when the requirement was to just calculate the taxable gains.

The easiest approach to the principal private residence exemption was to start with the total period of ownership and then to deduct the exempt periods.

Most of these were straightforward, being the periods of actual occupation, any period up to 36 months, working elsewhere in the UK up to 48 months, and the final 36 months of ownership.

The only difficult aspect was a period working overseas which was not exempt as it was not followed by a period of actual occupation.

The easy half-mark for deducting the annual exempt amount was often missed.

ACCA marking scheme

			Marks
House	– Proceeds		0.5
	– Cost		0.5
	– Period of exemption		3.0
	– Principal private residence exemption		1.0
	– Letting relief exemption		1.0
Copyright	– Proceeds		0.5
	– Cost		1.5
Painting			0.5
Motor car			0.5
Land	– Proceeds		0.5
	– Relevant cost		1.0
	– Apportionment of cost		1.0
Ordinary shares	– Deemed proceeds		1.0
	– Cost		0.5
	– Gift relief		1.5
Annual exempt amount			0.5
Total			15.0

COMPANIES – CHARGEABLE GAINS

42 FORWARD LTD (ADAPTED)

Key answer tips

This question requires the calculation of the corporation tax liability of a company, however before that can be calculated several chargeable gains need to be calculated.

Remember that disposals by a company are entitled to an indexation allowance and rollover relief for replacement of business assets is a key relief available for companies. No other reliefs are available. Note that the effect of reinvesting in a depreciating asset as in part (b) must be understood as this is an area that is often tested.

This question was originally a 20 mark question, but it was set when the rules for capital gains were considerably more complicated. Under the current syllabus and rules, this question would now be worth 15 marks.

(a) **Corporation tax liability – year ended 31 March 2014**

	£
Trading profit	78,000
Net chargeable gains	
(£30,000 (W1) + £36,388 (W3) + £9,877 (W5))	76,265
Taxable total profits	154,265
Corporation tax liability	
FY 2013 (£154,265 × 20%)	30,853
Due date	1 January 2015

Workings

(W1) **Freehold office building**

	£
Disposal proceeds	290,000
Less: Cost	(148,000)
Unindexed gain	142,000
Less: Indexation allowance	
(250.2 – 144.0)/144.0 = 0.738 × £148,000	(109,224)
Chargeable gain before reliefs	32,776
Less: Roll over relief (W2)	(2,776)
Chargeable gain	30,000

(W2) **Rollover relief**

The sale proceeds of the office building are not fully reinvested.

The chargeable gain cannot be rolled over:

	£
Disposal proceeds	290,000
Less: Reinvested in qualifying business asset	(260,000)
Sale proceeds not reinvested = chargeable now	30,000

The remaining gain of £2,776 (£32,776 – £30,000) can be deferred with a rollover relief claim.

(W3) **Ordinary Shares in Backward plc**

	£
Disposal proceeds	62,500
Less: Cost (W4)	(12,895)
Unindexed gain	49,605
Less: Indexation allowance (£26,112 – £12,895) (W4)	(13,217)
Chargeable gain	36,388

Tutorial note

The gain cannot be rolled over into the acquisition of the shares in Sideways plc as shares are not qualifying assets for the purpose of rollover relief.

(W4) **Share pool – Backward plc**

		Number	*Cost*	*Indexed cost*
			£	£
April 1988	Purchase	9,000	18,000	18,000
Indexation to November 2013 £18,000 × (253.4 – 105.8)/105.8 (do not round indexation factor)				25,112
				43,112
November 2013	Purchase	500	6,500	6,500
		9,500	24,500	49,612
November 2013 Cost × (5,000 / 9,500)	Disposal	(5,000)	(12,895)	(26,112)
Balance c/f		4,500	11,605	23,500

(W5) **Painting**

	£
Deemed proceeds	22,000
Less: Deemed cost (see Tutorial Note)	
£15,000 × (£22,000/(£22,000 + £20,000))	(7,857)
Unindexed gain	14,143
Less : Indexation to February 2014	
(255.5 – 165.6)/165.6 = 0.543 × £7,857	(4,266)
Chargeable gain	9,877

Tutorial note

Where an asset is damaged, compensation is received and the proceeds are not used to restore the asset, there is a part disposal of the asset for capital gains purposes.

The deemed cost is calculated using A/(A+B) where:

A = Insurance proceeds received

B = Value of asset after damage

The date of disposal is the date that the compensation is received not the date that the asset is damaged.

(b) **Reinvestment in leasehold office building**

- The freehold office building's sale proceeds of £290,000 will be fully reinvested, and so the whole of the gain of £32,776 is eligible for rollover relief.
- The leasehold office building is a depreciating asset, so its base cost will not be adjusted.
- The base cost of the 15 year lease will therefore be its actual cost of £300,000.
- The gain will be deferred until the earliest of:
  - ten years from the date of acquisition of the leasehold building,
  - the date that it is disposed of, or
  - the date that it ceases to be used for trading purposes.

43 HAWK LTD  *Walk in the footsteps of a top tutor*

Key answer tips

This question requires the computation of a corporation tax liability for a company, however several chargeable gains need to be calculated before the corporation tax liability computation can be performed.

You need to remember that disposals made by a company will usually have some element of indexation allowance, so you need to be aware of the rules regarding the rounding of the indexation factor.

The only capital gains relief available to companies is rollover relief and therefore it is not surprising to see it here in this question and it is often tested in corporation tax questions.

This question was originally a 20 mark question, and under the current syllabus and rules, this question would still be worth 20 marks.

No attempt has been made to reduce the question as it is still representative of the type of question you will see in the examination and provides good practice for your revision. However, under the new syllabus the question on capital gains will only be 15 marks and therefore will probably have fewer disposals to deal with in the time available than this question has.

Tutor's top tips

Part (a) consisted of a number of reasonably straightforward disposals made by a company. As long as the gains are calculated individually, a good mark can be achieved.

It is important not to get bogged down with any particular computation. If you cannot remember how to deal with a disposal, move on! You will pick up far more marks by moving forward, and if you have time you can revisit the problem area again later.

Part (b) covers rollover relief and requires you to apply your knowledge of the relief.

(a) **Hawk Ltd**

Corporation tax computation – year ended 31 March 2014

	£
Trading profit	125,000
Net chargeable gains (W)	80,296
Taxable total profits	205,296
Corporation tax liability	
FY 2013 (£205,296 × 20%)	41,059

Tutorial note

Hawk Ltd has no associated companies; therefore the taxable total profits of £205,296, which fall entirely in FY 2013, are taxed at 20% as profits fall below the lower limit of £300,000.

Workings: Chargeable gains

	£	£
Office Building		
Proceeds (April 2013)	260,000	
Less: Costs of disposal	(3,840)	
Net disposal proceeds	256,160	
Less: Cost and legal fees (July 1993)		
(£81,000 + £3,200)	(84,200)	
Enhancement (May 2005)	(43,000)	
Unindexed gain	128,960	
Less: Indexation allowance		
On cost (July 1993 to April 2013)		
(250.3 – 140.7)/140.7 = 0.779 × £84,200	(65,592)	
On enhancement (May 2005 to April 2013)		
(250.3 – 192.0)/192.0 = 0.304 × £43,000	(13,072)	
		50,296
Shares in Albatross plc (5,000 shares)		
Proceeds (August 2013)	42,500	
Less: Cost (below) (Note 1)	(17,500)	
		25,000

Share pool – Albatross plc	*Number*	*Cost*
		£
1 August 2013 Purchase	6,000	18,600
17 August 2013 Purchase	2,000	9,400
	8,000	28,000
29 August 2013 Disposal	(5,000)	
(£28,000 × 5,000/8,000)		(17,500)
	3,000	10,500

Shares in Cuckoo (10,000 preference shares)			
Proceeds (October 2013)		32,000	
Less: Cost (below)		(15,000)	
			17,000
Consideration received at time of takeover:			
Ordinary shares	(5,000 × 3 × £4.50)	67,500	
Preference shares	(5,000 × 2 × £2.25)	22,500	
		90,000	
Therefore cost of shares disposed of in October 2013:			
£60,000 × (£22,500/£90,000)		15,000	
			92,296
Land			
Proceeds (March 2014)		120,000	
Less: Cost of part disposed of (Note 2)			
£203,500 × (£120,000/(£120,000 + £65,000))		(132,000)	
Allowable loss			(12,000)
Net chargeable gains			80,296

Tutorial note

1 *There is no indexation allowance available on either of the share disposals, as the purchase and sale occur in the same month.*

2 *There is no indexation allowance available on the disposal of the land, as indexation cannot create or increase a loss.*

The disposal of the land is a part disposal and therefore the allowable cost is calculated by apportioning the original cost to the part disposed of as follows:

Original cost × A / (A + B) *where:* *A = MV of the element disposed of*

B = MV of the element retained

(b) **Rollover relief**

(i) **Minimum amount of reinvestment**

- The only disposal that qualifies for rollover relief is the sale of the freehold office building.
- The office building was sold for £256,160 (net of disposal expenses) and this is therefore the amount that Hawk Ltd will have to reinvest in order to claim the maximum possible amount of rollover relief.

Tutorial note

HMRC allow full rollover relief provided the net sale proceeds are reinvested in qualifying assets within the qualifying time period.

It is not necessary to reinvest the gross sale proceeds. However, the examiner gave credit if the gross sale proceeds were used in this part.

(ii) **Period of reinvestment**

- The reinvestment will have to take place between 1 May 2012 and 30 April 2016 (i.e. one year before and three years after the date of sale).

(iii) **Amount of corporation tax deferred**

- Corporation tax of £10,059 (£50,296 at 20%) will be deferred if the maximum possible amount of rollover relief is claimed.

Examiner's report

Part (a) was reasonably well answered.

As regards the freehold office building, many candidates did not appreciate that indexation would also be available for the incidental costs of acquisition.

For the quoted shares many candidates based their answers on the rules applicable to individuals rather than the pooling rules. The allocation of cost following the reorganisation also caused problems.

Part (b) was also reasonably well answered, with a number of candidates providing perfect answers.

ACCA marking scheme		
		Marks
(a)	**Office building**	
	Disposal proceeds	0.5
	Costs of disposal	0.5
	Cost	0.5
	Costs of acquisition	0.5
	Enhancement expenditure	0.5
	Indexation – Cost	1.0
	– Enhancement	1.0
	Albatross plc	
	Proceeds	0.5
	Cost	2.0
	Cuckoo Ltd	
	Proceeds	0.5
	Value of shares – Ordinary shares	1.0
	– Preference shares	1.0
	Cost	1.5
	Land	
	Proceeds	0.5
	Cost	2.0
	Corporation tax liability	
	Net chargeable gains	1.0
	Calculation	1.5
		16.0
(b)	Qualifying disposal	1.0
	Amount of reinvestment	1.0
	Period of reinvestment	1.0
	Corporation tax saving	1.0
		4.0
Total		20.0

44 PROBLEMATIC LTD  *Walk in the footsteps of a top tutor*

Key answer tips

This is a standard chargeable gains question, based on a company making four disposals.

Part (a) requires the taxable total profits of the company, but as there is only one other source of income, it really requires the calculation of the total net chargeable gains and one number adding to it!

Part (b) is unusual in that it requires advice about the base costs to carry forward in respect of those assets still owned by the company after the disposals.

The two parts are inter-linked and consideration of the remaining base costs is best calculated as each disposal is considered. It is therefore more time efficient to answer both parts (a) and (b) together as you consider each disposal. Make sure that you highlight your answer to part (b) clearly in your answer though.

This question was originally a 20 mark question, and under the current syllabus and rules, this question would still be worth 20 marks.

No attempt has been made to reduce the question as it is still representative of the type of question you will see in the examination and provides good practice for your revision. However, under the new syllabus the question on capital gains will only be 15 marks and therefore will probably have fewer disposals to deal with in the time available than this question has.

Tutor's top tips

There are four disposals to deal with here, some more complicated than others. There is no need for you to calculate the gains in order if you prefer to do the easier computations first – as long as you clearly label each disposal as you attempt it.

(a) **Problematic Ltd**

Taxable total profits – y/e 31 March 2014

	£
Trading profit	108,056
Net chargeable gains (£27,898 + £16,200 + £45,550) (see below)	89,648
Taxable total profits	197,704

Chargeable gain computations:

Easy plc shares

Tutor's top tips

The disposal of shares by a company requires the construction of a share pool and the calculation of the indexation allowance before recording each operative event.

The calculation of the gain is then straightforward.

	£
Disposal proceeds	54,400
Less: Cost (below)	(18,880)
	35,520
Less: Indexation (£26,502 – £18,880) (below)	(7,622)
Chargeable gain	27,898

Share pool – Easy plc	*Number*	*Cost*	*Indexed cost*
		£	£
Purchase – June 1996	15,000	12,600	12,600
Indexation to September 2008			
£12,600 × (218.4 – 153.0)/153.0			5,386
Rights issue – September 2008			
15,000 × 1/3 = 5,000 × £2·20	5,000	11,000	11,000
	20,000	23,600	28,986
Indexation to June 2013			
£28,986 × (249.6 – 218.4)/218.4			4,141
			33,127
Disposal – June 2013			
Cost × 16,000/20,000	(16,000)	(18,880)	(26,502)
Balance c/f	4,000	4,720	6,625

Tutorial note

1. *The movement in the RPI in the share pool of a company is not rounded to three decimal places.*
2. *The "balance carried forward" figures in the share pool are the information required to answer part (b) of this question.*

Office building

Tutor's top tips

This part of the question may have thrown a number of students, who are perhaps less familiar with the rules regarding damage or destruction of an asset.

However, the examiner has given a hint in the question, in saying that Problematic Ltd has made a claim to defer the gain, and this information could be used to make a sensible assumption about the treatment of the insurance proceeds.

If you are ever unsure of how to deal with part of a question it is important to make a sensible guess and move on, rather than wasting time, or potentially missing easy marks by not attempting to answer the part.

- The insurance proceeds of £36,000 received by Problematic Ltd have been fully applied in restoring the office building.
- Therefore, provided an election is made, there is no chargeable gain arising on the receipt of the insurance proceeds.

Tutorial note

Where an asset is damaged, insurance proceeds are received and the proceeds are fully reinvested in restoring the asset, if an election is made to defer the gain; no chargeable gain arises at that time.

Instead, the base cost of the asset is adjusted for the receipt of the insurance proceeds (i.e. the proceeds are deducted from the base cost) and the cost of the restoration is treated as enhancement expenditure and is added.

Freehold factory

Tutor's top tips

A gain on the disposal of the factory needs to be calculated and then rollover relief needs to be considered.

You need to check that the necessary conditions are satisfied to make a claim. Then you need to recognise that the replacement asset is a depreciating asset and know the consequences as a result.

	£
Disposal proceeds	171,000
Less: Indexed cost	(127,000)
Chargeable gain before reliefs	44,000
Less: Rollover relief (£44,000 – £16,200) (Note 1)	(27,800)
Chargeable gain	16,200

Tutorial note

1 *Rollover relief is available as Problematic has:*

Disposed of a qualifying business asset (Freehold factory), and

Replaced with another qualifying business asset (Leasehold factory),

Within the qualifying reinvestment period of 28 January 2013 to 27 January 2017

(i.e. 12 months before and 36 months after the date of disposal).

2 *The sale proceeds are not fully reinvested, and so £16,200 (£171,000 – £154,800) of the gain cannot be held over.*

The rollover relief is therefore £27,800 (£44,000 – £16,200).

3 *The replacement asset is a depreciating asset (i.e. has a life of less than 60 years).*

As a result, the rollover relief is deferred, but the gain is not deducted from the base cost of the replacement asset.

Instead, the gain is "frozen" and becomes chargeable on the earliest of.

- *The disposal of the replacement asset.*
- *The date the replacement asset is no longer used in the business*
- *Ten years after the acquisition of the replacement asset (i.e. in this case, 10 December 2023).*

Land

Tutor's top tips

Part disposals are regularly examined, and it is important to learn the formula for calculating the cost and to know how to apply it. You should not be misled by the size of the parts bought and sold; it is the values which are used in the calculation.

	£
Disposal proceeds	130,000
Less: Incidental costs of disposal	(3,200)
	126,800
Less: Indexed cost (£130,000/(£130,000 + £350,000)) × £300,000	(81,250)
Chargeable gain	45,550

Tutorial note

This standard part disposal computation requires the appropriate proportion of the indexed cost to be calculated using the A / (A + B) formula.

Note however that all of the incidental disposal costs are deducted as they relate entirely to this disposal.

(b) **Indexed base costs carried forward for capital gains tax purposes**

Tutor's top tips

All of the thought processes required to answer this part will have been considered when calculating the gains arising on the individual disposals.

A summary is therefore now required in this part to highlight the remaining base costs for the assets not disposed of.

Easy plc shares

- The 4,000 £1 ordinary shares in Easy plc have an indexed base cost of £6,625 (see part (a) share pool working).

Office building

- The indexed base cost of the office building is:

	£
Original indexed cost	169,000
Less: Insurance proceeds received	(36,000)
Plus: Restoration costs	41,000
Indexed base cost	174,000

(See tutorial note in part (a) for explanation).

Leasehold factory

- The leasehold factory is a depreciating asset, and so there is no adjustment to the base cost of £154,800.

  (See tutorial note in part (a) for explanation).

Remaining three acres

- The indexed base cost of the remaining three acres of land is £218,750 (£300,000 – £81,250 used in the part disposal computation).

Examiner's report

It was pleasing to see that this question was well answered.

On an overall note, it does not create a very good impression when candidates deduct the annual exempt amount when dealing with a company.

The only aspect that consistently caused problems in part (a) was the restoration of the asset. Despite the question telling candidates that a claim to defer the gain had been made, many insisted that such a claim was not possible and instead calculated a capital loss.

Many candidates did not even attempt part (b) despite the fact that this section generally just required them to provide figures already calculated in part (a).

ACCA marking scheme

		Marks
(a)	**Easy plc**	
	Share pool– Purchase	0.5
	– Rights issue	1.5
	– Indexation	2.0
	– Disposal	1.0
	Chargeable gain	1.5
	Office building	
	Proceeds fully reinvested	1.0
	No chargeable gain arising	1.0
	Freehold factory	
	Disposal proceeds	0.5
	Indexed cost	0.5
	Rollover relief	2.0
	Land	
	Proceeds	0.5
	Incidental costs of disposal	1.0
	Cost	2.0
	Taxable total profits	
	Chargeable gains	0.5
	Calculation	0.5
		16.0
(b)	Ordinary shares in Easy plc	0.5
	Office building	1.5
	Leasehold factory	1.0
	Land	1.0
		4.0
Total		20.0

INHERITANCE TAX

45 BRUCE VINCENT

Key answer tips

A classic inheritance tax question involving two lifetime gifts, one CLT and one PET, requiring both lifetime and death tax calculations and a death estate computation.

Be careful to calculate the cumulation of gifts correctly when calculating the available NRB.

Note that there is no set way to present an IHT computation, however the columnar approach avoids repetition of narrative headings and aids the correct allocation of annual exemptions and calculating cumulation totals.

Lifetime tax on lifetime gifts

	CLT – Gift into trust Jan 2009		*PET – Gift to nephew May 2010*	
		£		£
Transfer of value		350,000		100,000
Less: Annual exemption				
Current year	2008/09	(3,000)	2010/11	(3,000)
Previous year	2007/08 b/f	(3,000)	2009/10 b/f	(3,000)
Chargeable amount	Net	344,000		94,000
NRB @ date of gift	£			
2008/09	312,000			
Less: GCTs < 7 years before gift (Jan 2002 – Jan 2009)	(Nil)			
NRB available		(312,000)		
Taxable amount		32,000		Nil
IHT payable (Notes 1 and 2)	@ 25%	8,000		Nil
Paid by		Bruce		
Due date of payment		31.7.2009		
Gross chargeable amount c/f (£344,000 + £8,000)		352,000		94,000

Tutorial notes:

1 *As the question states that Bruce paid the IHT the tax is calculated at 25% and it is necessary to gross up the net gift as the value of the transfer (i.e. the loss to Bruce's estate) is the value of the gift and the related tax.*

2 *The gift to the nephew is a PET; therefore no lifetime IHT is payable.*

The information in the question about the nil rate band in 2010/11 is not relevant. Only the nil rate band at the date of death is required to calculate the tax on death.

Death tax on lifetime gifts

Date of death: August 2013

7 years before: August 2006

	CLT – Gift into trust Jan 2009		*PET – Gift to nephew May 2010*	
	£	£	£	£
Gross chargeable amount b/f		352,000		94,000
NRB @ date of death – 2013/14	325,000		325,000	
Less: GCTs < 7 years before gift				
(Jan 2002 – Jan 2009)	(Nil)			
(May 2003 – May 2010)			(352,000)	
NRB available		(325,000)		(Nil)
Taxable amount		27,000		94,000
IHT payable @ 40%		10,800		37,600
Less: Taper relief				
(Jan 2009 – Aug 2013) (4 – 5 yrs)	(40%)	(4,320)		
(May 2010 – Aug 2013) (3 – 4 yrs)			(20%)	(7,520)
Less: IHT paid in lifetime		(8,000)		(Nil)
IHT payable on death		Nil		30,080
	No refund possible			
Paid by				Nephew
Due date of payment				28 February 2014

Tax on death estate

	£	£
Gross chargeable estate (W)		797,500
Nil rate band at death	325,000	
Less: GCTs in 7 years pre death (August 2006 – August 2013) (£352,000 + £94,000)	(446,000)	
Nil rate band available		(Nil)
Taxable amount		797,500
IHT (£797,500 × 40%)		319,000
Due date		28 February 2014
Paid by		Executors

Working: Estate at death – August 2013

	£
House	450,000
Less: Mortgage (interest only)	(100,000)
	350,000
Holiday cottage	280,000
Quoted shares	145,000
Bank and cash	10,000
Personal chattels	50,000
	835,000
Liabilities: Credit card debts	(12,000)
Outstanding income tax	(8,000)
Funeral expenses	(7,500)
	807,500
Exempt legacy to wife	(10,000)
Chargeable estate	797,500

Tutorial note

The fact that the mortgage is interest only does not mean that it cannot be deducted in the death estate computation. It simply means that during the life of the loan no capital was repaid.

If the mortgage had been an endowment mortgage, then it would not have been deducted from the death estate as it would no longer be outstanding. It would have been repaid by the maturity of the endowment policy attached to the loan.

46 PAUL MASTERS

(a) **IHT liabilities if Paul dies on 31 December 2013**

Lifetime tax on lifetime gifts

Gift 1.7.2011 – The gift to the niece is exempt as a small gift under £250.

	CLT – Gift into trust 1.11.2005		*PET – Gift to son 1.10.2010*	
		£		£
Transfer of value		203,000		150,000
Less: Marriage exemption				(5,000)
Less: Annual exemption				
Current year	2005/06	(3,000)	2010/11	(3,000)
Previous year	2004/05 b/f	(3,000)	2009/10 b/f	(3,000)
Chargeable amount	Gross	197,000		139,000
NRB @ date of gift	£			
2005/06	275,000			
Less: GCTs < 7 years before gift (1.11.1998 – 1.11.2005)	(Nil)			
NRB available		(275,000)		
Taxable amount		Nil		Nil
IHT payable		Nil	(Note)	Nil
Gross chargeable amount c/f		197,000		139,000

Tutorial note

Note that as the gift on 1.10.2010 is a PET, no lifetime IHT is payable, therefore the information in the question about the nil rate band in 2010/11 is not relevant.

Only the nil rate band at the date of death is required to calculate the tax on death.

Death tax on lifetime gifts

Date of death: 31.12.2013

7 years before: 31.12.2006

1 November 2005 – CLT

The gift is more than seven years before the date of Paul's death, and therefore there is no tax due on Paul's death.

It is, however, within seven years of the other lifetime transfer, and will reduce the nil rate band available by £197,000.

		PET – Gift to son 1.10.2010
	£	£
Gross chargeable amount b/f (as above)		139,000
NRB @ date of death – 2013/14	325,000	
Less: GCTs < 7 years before gift (1.10.2003 – 1.10.2010)	(197,000)	
NRB available		(128,000)
Taxable amount		11,000
IHT payable @ 40%		4,400
Less: Taper relief (1.10.2010 – 31.12.2013) (3 – 4 yrs)	(@ 20%)	(880)
Less: IHT paid in lifetime		(Nil)
IHT payable on death		3,520
Due date of payment		30.6.2014

Tax on death estate

	£	£
Gross chargeable estate		580,000
Nil rate band at death	325,000	
Less: GCTs in 7 years pre death (31.12.06 – 31.12.13) (first gift is too old, but include PET as it became chargeable))	(139,000)	
Nil rate band available		(186,000)
Taxable amount		394,000
IHT (£394,000 × 40%)		157,600
Due date of payment		30.6.2014

Tutorial note

The tax payable on the PET would be paid by Paul's son, and the tax payable on the death estate would be paid by the executors.

(b) (i) **Main advantages in lifetime giving for IHT purposes**

Possible advantages of lifetime giving include:

- Making use of lifetime IHT exemptions (e.g. marriage exemption, small gifts and annual exemption) in reducing a taxpayer's chargeable estate at death. In particular, gifts between individuals will not become liable to IHT unless the donor dies within seven years of making the gift.
- If the donor dies prematurely there may still be an IHT advantage in lifetime giving because usually:
  - The value of the asset for calculating any additional IHT arising upon death is fixed at the time the gift is made.
  - The availability of tapering relief (providing the donor survives at least three years) may help reduce the effective IHT rate.

(ii) **Main factors to consider in choosing assets to gift**

The main factors to consider include:

- Whether an asset is appreciating in value.

  Because any additional IHT arising as a result of death will be based on the (lower) value of the asset at the date of gift it may be advantageous to select assets that are likely to significantly appreciate in value.
- Whether the donor can afford to make the gift.

  Whilst lifetime gifting can result in significant IHT savings this should not be at the expense of the taxpayer's ability to live comfortably, particularly in old age.
- Whether or not a significant CGT liability will arise upon making the gift.

  Lifetime gifting may give rise to a capital gains tax liability unless gift relief is available (on qualifying business assets) and/or the annual exempt amount is available.

  However, no capital gains tax liability arises upon death.

  Therefore the availability of gift relief and CGT annual exempt amount is relevant in selecting assets to gift during lifetime.

Tutorial note

The answer to part (b) is included for completeness sake, however this level of detail would not be required to obtain the full 5 marks for this part.

47 HENRY HIGGINS  *Walk in the footsteps of a top tutor*

Key answer tips

This question deals with the calculation of lifetime and death tax on two chargeable lifetime transfers, and the calculation of IHT due on an estate at death.

The computations are straightforward and should not present any particular problems.

However, be careful to note the dates of the events and in particular note that the first gift is more than seven years before Henry's death.

The second part required some standard basic tax planning advice concerning the transfer of the nil rate band.

Tutor's top tips

In the calculations remember to approach the answer in strict date order:

Step 1: Calculate the lifetime tax on the lifetime gifts

Step 2: Calculate the death tax on lifetime gifts

Step 3: Calculate the value of the estate on death

Step 4: Calculate the IHT due on the estate.

Be careful to use the correct nil rate band and to calculate the cumulation period of seven years accurately.

Remember to write down the dates so that the marker can give method marks even if you do not get the numbers right:

For lifetime IHT calculations

- *NRB = at **date of the gift***
- *Cumulation = 7 years **before the gift***
- *include **CLTs only***

For death calculations on lifetime gifts

- *NRB = at **date of death***
- *Cumulation = 7 years **before the gift***
- *include **CLTs and PETs which have become chargeable** (if any)*

For death estate computation

- *NRB = at **date of death***
- *Cumulation = 7 years **before death***
- *Include **all CLTs and PETs** in the 7 year period*

(a) **Inheritance tax liabilities**

Tutorial note

1 *The annual exemptions are allocated to the first gift in each tax year. The current year annual exemption must be deducted before the previous year's unused amount.*

2 *Henry agreed to pay any tax due on the gifts into the trusts, therefore they are net gifts and the appropriate rate of lifetime tax is 25%. Don't forget to add the tax onto the net chargeable amount to carry forward the gross chargeable amount for subsequent computations.*

(i) **Lifetime tax on lifetime gifts**

	CLT – Gift into trust 1.1.2006		*CLT – Gift into trust 1.1.2009*	
		£		£
Transfer of value		193,000		164,000
Annual exemption				
Current year	2005/06	(3,000)	2008/09	(3,000)
Previous year	2004/05 b/f	(3,000)	2007/08 b/f	(3,000)
Chargeable amount	Net	187,000	Net	158,000
NRB @ date of gift	£			
2005/06	275,000			
2008/09			312,000	
Less: GCTs < 7 years before gift				
(1.1.1999 – 1.1.2006)	(Nil)			
(1.1.2002 – 1.1.2009)			(187,000)	
NRB available		(275,000)		(125,000)
Taxable amount		Nil		33,000
IHT payable		Nil	(25%) (Note 2)	8,250
Gross chargeable amount c/f		187,000	(£158,000 + £8,250)	166,250

(ii) **Death tax on lifetime gifts**

Date of death: 5 October 2013

Seven years before: 5 October 2006

1 January 2006 – CLT

This gift is more than seven years before death; therefore there is no IHT payable on death.

	CLT 1.1.2009	
	£	£
Gross chargeable amount b/f		166,250
NRB @ date of death – 2013/14	325,000	
Less: GCTs < 7 years before gift (1.1.2002 – 1.1.2009)	(187,000)	
NRB available		(138,000)
Taxable amount		28,250
IHT payable @ 40%		11,300
Less: Taper relief (1.1.2009 – 5.10.13) (4 – 5 yrs)	(40%)	(4,520)
Less: IHT paid in lifetime		(8,250)
IHT payable on death		Nil
	No refund possible	

Tutorial note

1 *Tax is only due on lifetime gifts within seven years of death. Therefore, any gifts before 5 October 2006 are too old and there will be no tax to pay on those gifts.*

Be careful though: any CLTs are still taken into account in the cumulation for the calculation of tax on later gifts.

2 *Taper relief is available as more than 3 years has elapsed since the gift.*

3 *Lifetime tax can be deducted in the death calculation; however there will never be a repayment of lifetime IHT paid.*

Tax on death estate

	£	£
Gross chargeable estate(W)		41,750
Nil rate band at death	325,000	
Less: GCTs in 7 years pre death (5.10.06 – 5.10.13) (first gift is too old)	(166,250)	
Nil rate band available		(158,750)
Taxable amount		Nil
IHT payable		Nil

Working: Estate at death – 5 October 2013

Tutor's top tips

Note that the estate computation is usually the easiest part of an IHT question as it basically requires you to:

- *copy out the question*
- *present the information in a standard way, and*
- *add it up!*

This part could therefore be calculated first to get the easy marks as soon as possible.

However, note that you cannot calculate the tax on the estate value until the lifetime gifts have been dealt with.

	£
Shares – Petal plc (100,000 × 202p)	202,000
Government stock	20,100
Cash (£25,000 + £18,000)	43,000
Income tax refund due	1,650
Home	450,000
	716,750
Less: Exempt legacy to spouse	(675,000)
Gross chargeable estate	41,750

(b) **Tax implications of transferring unused nil rate band**

Tutor's top tips

In terms of this syllabus there are very limited areas of tax planning that the examiner can ask.

The main areas are:

- *the transfer of unused nil rate band (covered in this question)*
- *making use of lifetime exemptions*
- *gifting appreciating assets as lifetime gifts are frozen in value at the time of the gift.*

It is important that you make sure that you apply the standard advice to the particular circumstances of the question.

Transfer of unused nil rate band

The terms of Henry's will resulted in the majority of the estate being covered by an exempt transfer to his wife. This has left £117,000 (£158,750 – £41,750) of his nil band unused.

Therefore the percentage of unused nil rate band is as follows:

(£117,000/£325,000) × 100% = 36%.

This unused proportion can be transferred to Sally and utilised against her death estate, in addition to her own available nil rate band (i.e. she will be entitled to 136% of the nil rate band available at the date of her death).

The executors of Sally's estate must claim the transferable nil rate band on submission of Sally's IHT return within 2 years of her death.

48 HELGA EVANS  *Walk in the footsteps of a top tutor*

Key answer tips

This question deals with a classic scenario:

Should Helga give assets away now or die owning them?

Calculations of the two options are required and a conclusion of what she should do and how much tax will be saved as a result of the advice.

The calculations are straightforward, but you must read the question carefully to sort out which assets are to be gifted now and which will remain in the estate – and their values at the different points in time.

Tutor's top tips

Dealing with the retention of assets first – a straightforward estate computation is required. Remember to bear in mind that:

- *there has already been a lifetime gift within seven years, and*
- *part of the estate is left to the spouse and is therefore exempt.*

(i) **Helga retains assets until death**

IHT implications

Cash gift – September 2011

The cash gift made to Louise in September 2011 is a PET.

No IHT would have been payable at the time, however the PET will become chargeable if Helga dies within seven years of making the gift.

If Helga therefore dies in four years' time (i.e. June 2017) this gift will be within seven years of death and IHT will become payable on the PET in September 2011 as follows:

	£	£
Gross chargeable transfer (after exemptions per question)		360,000
Nil rate band **at date of death**	325,000	
Less: GCTs in 7 years pre-gift (September 2004 – September 2011)	(Nil)	
		(325,000)
Taxable amount		35,000
IHT (£35,000 × 40%)		14,000
Less: Taper relief (September 2011 – June 2017) (5 – 6 years) (60%)		(8,400)
Less: Lifetime tax paid		(Nil)
IHT payable		5,600

Tutorial note

Note that as the gift is a PET, no lifetime IHT is payable, therefore the information in the question about the nil rate band in 2011/12 is not relevant.

Only the nil rate band at the date of death is required to calculate the tax on death.

There are no other lifetime gifts made in this scenario.

Estate at death – 30 June 2017

	£	£
Residence		600,000
Starling plc shares		200,000
Wren loan stock		25,000
Cash deposits		180,000
Other chattels		20,000
		1,025,000
Less: Exempt legacy to spouse (£600,000 + £20,000)		(620,000)
Gross chargeable estate		405,000
Nil rate band at death	325,000	
Less: GCTs in 7 years pre death (30.6.10 – 30.6.17) (include PET as chargeable on death)	(360,000)	
		(Nil)
Taxable amount		405,000
IHT due on death (£405,000 × 40%)		162,000

(ii) **Helga gifts selected assets to Louise now**

Tutor's top tips

Assuming another lifetime gift is made, the death tax on two PETs is required but no estate tax as the remaining estate is to be left to the husband and will be exempt.

Remember to deal with each gift in date order – and as the PETs become chargeable on death, they are included in cumulation for later computations.

IHT implications

Cash gift – September 2011

The implications for the PET made in September 2011 are as above with £5,600 of IHT becoming payable as a result of Helga's expected death in four years' time.

Gifts to Louise now

Assume the gift is made on 6 July 2013.

The gifts of assets to Louise will be further PETs.

So, no lifetime tax payable, but they are likely to become chargeable on Helga's death, with further IHT arising as follows:

		£	£
Starling plc shares (10,000 × £14.62)			146,200
Wren plc loan stock			25,750
Cash deposits			151,333
			323,283
Less: Annual exemption	– 2013/14		(3,000)
	– 2012/13 b/f		(3,000)
Gross chargeable amount			317,283
Nil rate band at date of death		325,000	
Less: GCTs in 7 years pre-death (30.6.10 – 30.6.17) (include PET as chargeable on death)		(360,000)	
			(Nil)
Taxable amount			317,283

	£
IHT (£317,283 × 40%)	126,913
Less: Taper relief (6.7.13 – 30.6.17) (3 – 4 years) (20%)	(25,383)
	101,530
Less: Lifetime tax paid	(Nil)
IHT payable	101,530

Estate on death

When Helga dies the transfers of the house and personal chattels to Gordon will be exempt under the inter-spouse provisions.

Therefore there is no IHT payable on the estate at death.

Conclusion

The tax payable under both options is as follows:

	£
Retention of assets (£5,600 + £162,000)	167,600
Gifting of assets now (£5,600 + £101,530)	107,130

It would therefore appear that, providing the key assumptions hold (i.e. asset values in four years, Helga survives four years), it is preferable to make the gifts to Louise now giving a tax saving of £60,470 (£167,600 – £107,130).

49 JIMMY  *Walk in the footsteps of a top tutor*

Key answer tips

This is a straightforward IHT question with two lifetime gifts, (one PET and one CLT) and a simple estate. This question should have provided an opportunity to score highly.

(a) **The importance of the distinction between PETs and CLTs**

PETs

- A PET only becomes chargeable to IHT if the donor dies within seven years of making the gift.

CLTs

- A CLT is immediately charged to IHT.
- Additional IHT may arise if the donor dies within seven years of making the gift.

Tutor's top tips:

There are only 2 marks for this part therefore you need to be efficient with time and not take too long on this part. Short, succinct points need to be made.

(b) **Jimmy**

Lifetime tax on lifetime gifts

	PET		*CLT*
	2 August 2012		*14 November 2012*
	£	£	£
Transfer of value	50,000		800,000
Less: Marriage exemption	(2,500)		
AE – 2012/13	(3,000)		(Nil)
– 2011/12 b/f	(3,000)		(Nil)
Chargeable amount	41,500		800,000
NRB at time of gift – 2012/13		325,000	
Less: GCTs in 7 years pre-gift			
(14.11.05 to 14.11.12) Ignore PET		(Nil)	
			(325,000)
Taxable amount in lifetime	Nil		475,000
Lifetime IHT payable (£475,000 × 25%) (Net gift)	Nil		118,750
GCT c/f (£800,000 + £118,750)	41,500		918,750

Tutorial note

1 *For lifetime IHT calculations, never cumulate PETs in calculating the gross chargeable transfers (GCTs) in the 7 years before the gift, as at that stage they are 'potentially' exempt and not chargeable.*

2 *Jimmy paid the IHT on the gift into the trust. It is therefore a net gift and the lifetime IHT is calculated at 25%.*

Death tax on lifetime gifts

		PET *2 August 2012*		*CLT* *14 November 2012*
	£	£	£	£
Chargeable amount		41,500		918,750
NRB at death – 2013/14	325,000		325,000	
Less: GCTs in 7 years pre-gift				
(2.8.05 to 2.8.12)	(Nil)			
(14.11.05 to 14.11.12) Include PET			(41,500)	
		(325,000)		(283,500)
Taxable amount on death		Nil		635,250

	PET *2 August 2012*	*CLT* *14 November 2012*
	£	£
Death IHT payable (£635,250 × 40%)	Nil	254,100
Less: Taper relief (< 3 years)		(Nil)
		254,100
Less: Lifetime IHT payable		(118,750)
IHT payable	Nil	135,350

Tutorial note

1 *For death IHT calculations on lifetime gifts, cumulate PETs in calculating the gross chargeable transfers (GCTs) in the 7 years before the gift if they have become chargeable on death, but not if they have become completely exempt.*

2 *Taper relief is not available as there are less than three years between the date of both gifts and the date of death.*

Death estate

	£	£
Property		260,000
Building society deposits		515,600
Proceeds of life assurance policy		210,000
		985,600
Less: Funeral expenses		(5,600)
		980,000
Less: Exempt legacy – spouse		(300,000)
Gross chargeable estate		680,000
NRB at death – 2013/14	325,000	
Less: GCTs in 7 years pre death (£41,500 + £918,750)	(960,250)	
		(Nil)
Taxable amount		680,000
IHT liability (£680,000 at 40%)		272,000

(c) **Due date for tax on death estate**

The IHT payable on the death estate is paid by the personal representatives by the earlier of:

- 31 August 2014, or
- the date they deliver the account to HMRC.

Tutorial note

*The due date for death tax is six months after the **end** of the month of death, or the date of delivery of account.*

Examiner's report

This question was extremely well answered, with a high number of perfect answers.

In part (a) a number of candidates wrote far too much for what should have been a short answer.

In part (b) the only consistent problem was that the gross figure for the chargeable lifetime transfer was often taken as the tax plus the chargeable portion of the transfer, rather than the tax plus the total net transfer.

In part (c) many candidates stated that tax had to be paid within six months of death rather than six months after the end of the month of death.

ACCA marking scheme			
			Marks
(a)	PET		1.0
	CLT		1.0
			2.0
(b)	**Lifetime transfers**		
	PET	– Recognition as a PET	0.5
		– Marriage exemption	1.0
		– Annual exemptions	1.0
	CLT	– Recognition as a CLT	0.5
		– IHT liability	2.0
	Additional liabilities arising on death		
	PET		1.0
	CL	– IHT liability	1.0
		– IHT already paid	0.5
	Death estate		
	Property		0.5
	Building society deposits		0.5
	Life assurance policy		1.0
	Funeral expenses		1.0
	Spouse legacy		1.0
	IHT liability		0.5
			12.0
(c)	Due date		1.0
Total			15.0

50 BLACK LTD (ADAPTED)  *Walk in the footsteps of a top tutor*

Key answer tips

This question has three distinct parts covering a variety of topics.

Part (a) requires the calculation of the maximum group relief claim possible given various sources of profits and losses for two group companies.

It is important to separate out and distinguish between the different types of losses and to explain what can, and cannot, be group relieved, to obtain full marks in this part.

Part (b) tested a topic which is no longer in the syllabus and has therefore been replaced with a question testing the new cash accounting and flat rate basis rules introduced in FA2013.

Part (c) was a very straightforward IHT question requiring the calculation of the lifetime and death tax on one CLT.

Many candidates were disappointed that there was so little IHT in the exam paper in which this question was set. Note that the examiner has said that IHT will always feature in the exam. It could be the subject of a full 15 mark question (question 4 or 5), or it may, on occasions, only represent a small part of the paper.

Tutor's top tips:

You do not have to answer this question in the order set. Provided you start each part on a separate page and clearly indicate which part you are answering, you can answer in any order. Hence you might prefer to start with part (c) on IHT as this may be more familiar.

However, do take care when attempting a question out of order, as sometimes the answer to part (a) is required in part (b), and so on. This is clearly not the case in this question as each part involves a different company or individual.

(a) **Maximum group relief – year ended 31 March 2014**

Maximum group relief claim

= Lower of

(i) Available loss of White Ltd = £351,300 (W1)

(ii) Available profits of Black Ltd = £355,600 (W2)

The maximum group relief claim is therefore £351,300.

Workings

(W1) **Available loss of White Ltd**

Current year capital loss

White Ltd's current year capital loss of £17,200 cannot be group relieved.

Trading losses

Only current year trading losses can be group relieved, therefore White Ltd's trading losses brought forward of £21,800 cannot be surrendered, but the £351,300 current year losses can be surrendered.

Qualifying charitable donations

Only excess unrelieved qualifying charitable donations (QCDs) can be group relieved. Therefore, White Ltd's QCDs of £5,600 cannot be surrendered as they can be fully relieved against the company's property business profit of £26,700.

Conclusion

Therefore the only available loss for surrender = £351,300 current year trading losses.

(W2) **Available profits of Black Ltd**

Available profits of the claimant company = TTP of that company, after taking account of losses brought forward and qualifying charitable donation.

	£
Trading profits	396,800
Less: Loss relief b/f	(57,900)
	338,900
Property business profit	21,100
Total profits	360,000
Less: QCD relief	(4,400)
TTP before group relief = Available profits	355,600

Tutorial note

Black Ltd must deduct trading losses brought forward in the calculation of the available profits.

Black Ltd's capital loss brought forward of £12,600 is ignored as these losses can only be carried forward and set against Black Ltd's future chargeable gains.

(b) **Ethel Brown – Notes on cash accounting and flat rate expense adjustments**

(1) Business premises used partly for private purposes

- The total payments of £25,000 can be deducted from the trading profit but the flat rate private use adjustment of £7,800 must be added to the trading profit for tax purposes.
- A net deduction from trading profits of £17,200 can therefore be claimed for tax purposes.

(2) Car used for private and business purposes

- The cash payments in respect of the purchase and running costs of the car totalling £17,000 (£14,000 + £3,000) are not deductible from the trading profit and capital allowances are not available.
- Instead a tax deduction for the car is allowed using the approved mileage allowances for the business mileage as follows:

	£
First 10,000 miles at 45p/mile	4,500
1,000 miles at 25p/mile	250
Allowable deduction	4,750

(3) Kitchen equipment

- A tax deduction can be claimed from the trading profits for the full cost of the kitchen equipment when the invoice is paid.
- No tax deduction is therefore allowed in the accounts for the year to 5 April 2014 but Ethel will obtain a tax deduction of £350 from trading profits in the following year to 5 April 2015.

Tutorial notes

(1) The question states that Ethel opts to use the cash basis and the flat rate expense adjustments. Note that the examiner has stated that whilst the use of flat rate expenses is optional it should be assumed in any question involving the cash basis that flat rate expenses are claimed.

(2) Where a business premises is used partly for private purposes a private use adjustment must be made for tax purposes if the full costs of the premises have been included in the accounts. The HMRC flat rate private use adjustments are based on the number of occupants and will be provided as part of the question in the exam. Any information regarding actual private use of the premises is irrelevant.

(3) The flat rate expense adjustment in respect of cars is based on the HMRC approved mileage allowances. These are the same rates that are used to calculate the taxable benefit/allowable deduction where employees use their own cars for business purposes. The rates are given in the tax tables provided in the exam.

(4) Under the cash basis a 100% trading deduction is given for the acquisition cost of items of plant and machinery rather than capital allowances.

(c) **Blue Reddy**

Inheritance tax computation

Lifetime tax on lifetime gift – 15 January 2014

	£	£
Value of shares held before the transfer (300,000 × £4)		1,200,000
Value of shares held after the transfer (100,000 × £2)		(200,000)
Transfer of value (Note 1)		1,000,000
Less: AE (ignore per question)		(Nil)
Chargeable transfer (Net)		1,000,000
NRB at time of gift	325,000	
GCTs in 7 years pre gift (15.1.2007 – 15.1.2014)	(Nil)	
		(325,000)
Taxable amount		675,000
IHT liability (£675,000 × 25%) (Note 2)		168,750
Gross chargeable transfer c/f (£1,000,000 + £168,750)		1,168,750

Additional death tax due on lifetime gift – 15 January 2014 (assuming death occurs 31 May 2018)

	£	£
Gross chargeable transfer		1,168,750
NRB at time of death	325,000	
GCTs in 7 years pre death (31.5.2011 – 31.5.2018)	(Nil)	
		(325,000)
Taxable amount		843,750
IHT liability (£843,750 × 40%)		337,500
Less: Taper relief		
(15.1.2014 – 31.5.2018) (4 – 5 years) (40%)		(135,000)
		202,500
Less: Lifetime IHT paid		(168,750)
Additional IHT payable on death		33,750

Tutorial notes

1 The transfer of value is calculated by reference to the diminution in the value of the donor's estate. The value of the 20% shareholding transferred (i.e. 200,000 shares at £2 for a 20% shareholding) is irrelevant for IHT purposes. This is particularly relevant in this situation, where company shares are involved, where the diminution in value of Blu's estate from reducing his interest in the company from 60% to 40% (i.e. £1,000,000) is far greater than valuing a 20% shareholding in isolation (£400,000).

2 Remember that where the donor pays the tax the appropriate tax rate is 25% as their estate has been diminished not just by the gift but also by the IHT paid. The gross chargeable transfer is the value of the gift plus the tax paid.

Examiner's report

This was the least well answered of the three 15 mark questions, although it was often the last one to be answered with time pressure being an issue.

Part (a) was not as complicated as candidates tried to make it, and remembering basic principles would have eliminated the worst of the errors – only current year losses can be group relieved, with no relief available for capital losses.

Part (b) has been amended to reflect changes to the syllabus and therefore the examiner's comments on this part are no longer relevant.

Candidates were again helped in part (c) by being told to ignore annual exemptions, but many also ignored these instructions.

They were not penalised for this, but it made the calculations a bit more complicated than was necessary.

When calculating the additional liability arising on death many candidates had problems computing the amount of brought forward gross chargeable transfer, and taper relief was often calculated and deducted at the wrong point in the computation.

Candidates should also appreciate that examinations are not quite the same as real life.

With a six mark section it should be obvious that the value of the transfer was more than the annual exemption of £325,000 – many candidates calculating the transfer as (200,000 × £1) = £200,000. Using any of the other values would have enabled some marks to be obtained.

However, there were many perfect answers to part (c), with the six marks obtained often being the difference between a pass and a fail.

ACCA marking scheme

		Marks
(a)	Maximum potential claim	2.0
	Qualifying charitable donations	1.0
	Capital losses	0.5
	Maximum potential surrender	1.0
	Maximum claim	0.5
		5.0
(b)	Business premises used for private purposes	
	Premises payments deductible	0.5
	Less £7,800 flat rate private use adjustment	0.5
	Car	
	Payments re purchase and running costs not deductible	0.5
	No capital allowances available	0.5
	Calculation of deductible amount	1.0
	Equipment	
	Cost of acquisition 100% trading deduction	0.5
	Deductible when payment made i.e. following accounting period	0.5
		4.0
(c)	Lifetime transfer	
	Value transferred	2.0
	IHT liability	1.5
	Additional liability arising on death	
	Gross chargeable transfer	0.5
	IHT liability	0.5
	Taper relief	1.0
	IHT already paid	0.5
		6.0
Total		15.0

CORPORATION TAX

CORPORATION TAX BASICS AND ADMINISTRATION

51 ARABLE LTD (ADAPTED)

Key answer tips

This question deals with the calculation of corporation tax for a short accounting period. You should remember that the length of the period affects the calculation of the maximum AIA and the WDA for capital allowances, and the limits for determining the rate of corporation tax to apply.

Other things to watch out for in this question are the effect of the short period on the lease premium deduction and the fact that the company has associated companies, which affects the small company limits for calculating corporation tax.

Make sure you attempt the administration points in part (b) which should be easy marks to obtain.

(a) **Corporation tax computation – 9 months ended 31 October 2013**

	£	£
Trading profit		414,111
Capital allowances – Plant and machinery (W2)	208,740	
Deduction for lease premium (W1)	2,700	
		(211,440)
		202,671
Property business income (W3)		49,700
Interest income – Loan interest (£6,000 + £3,000)		9,000
Chargeable gain (W4)		25,804
Taxable total profits		287,175
Plus: Franked investment income (£18,000 × 100/90)		20,000
Augmented profits		307,175
Corporation tax (W5)		
FY2012		
£287,175 × 24% × 2/9		15,316
Less: Marginal relief		
1/100 × (£375,000 – £307,175) × £287,175/£307,175 × 2/9		(141)
FY2013		
£287,175 × 23% × 7/9		51,372
Less: Marginal relief		
3/400 × (£375,000 – £307,175) × £287,175/£307,175 × 7/9		(370)
Corporation tax liability		66,177

Workings

(W1) **Deduction for lease premium**

The first office building has been used for business purposes, and so a proportion of the lease premium assessed on the landlord can be deducted.

Assessment on landlord:

	£
Premium received	75,000
Less: 2% × £75,000 × (15 – 1)	(21,000)
Assessment on landlord (Note)	54,000
Allowable deduction for 9 month period (£54,000 ÷ 15 × 9/12)	2,700

Tutorial note

Alternative calculation of the assessment on the landlord:

£75,000 × (51 – 15)/50 = £54,000

(W2) **Plant and machinery**

		Main pool	*Special rate pool*	*Allowances*
	£	£	£	£
Additions (no AIA or FYA) (Note 1)				
Car (CO_2 between 96 – 130 g/km)		11,200		
Car (CO_2 > 130 g/km)			14,600	
Additions (with AIA) (Note 2)				
Machinery	199,750			
Alterations	3,700			
Lorry	22,000			
Computer	5,400			
	230,850			
Less: AIA (£250,000 × 9/12) (Note 3)	(187,500)			187,500
Transfer to pool		43,350		
		54,550		
WDA (18% × 9/12) (Note 3)		(7,364)		7,364
WDA (8% × 9/12) (Note 3)			(876)	876
Additions (with FYA) (Note 1)				
Car (CO_2 < 96 g/km)	13,000			
Less: FYA (100%)	(13,000)			13,000
		Nil		
TWDV c/f		47,186	13,724	
Total allowances				208,740

Tutorial notes

1 *Capital allowances on car purchases are calculated based on the CO_2 emissions of the car as follows:*

CO_2 emissions of < 96 g/km:
eligible for a FYA of 100%.

CO_2 emissions of between 96 – 130 g/km:
put in main pool, eligible for a WDA at 18%.

CO_2 emissions of > 130 g/km:
put in special rate pool, eligible for a WDA at 8%.

The appropriate rates are given in the tax rates and allowances.

2 *The machinery purchased on 5 January 2013 and the related building alterations are incurred pre-trading, but are eligible for capital allowances and are treated as if incurred on 1 February 2013. They are therefore brought into the first capital allowances computation.*

3 *The maximum AIA and WDAs are time apportioned because Arable Ltd's accounting period is nine months long. The maximum AIA is £187,500 (£250,000 × 9/12).*

(W3) **Property business income**

	£
Premium received for lease	50,000
Less: 2% × £50,000 × (5 – 1)	(4,000)
Assessment on premium received (Note)	46,000
Plus: Rent receivable (£14,800 × 3/12)	3,700
Property business income	49,700

Tutorial note

Alternative calculation of the assessment on the sub lease:

£50,000 × (51 – 5)/50 = £46,000

(W4) **Chargeable gain**

Share pool – Ranch plc	*Number*	*Cost*	*Indexed cost*
		£	£
Purchase (February 2013)	15,000	12,000	12,000
Indexation to May 2013			
£12,000 × (250.2 – 247.6)/247.6			126
			12,126
Purchase (May 2013)	5,000	11,250	11,250
	20,000	23,250	23,376
Indexation to September 2013			
£23,376 × (252.0 – 250.2)/250.2			168
			23,544
Disposal (September 2013)			
Cost × 10,000/20,000	(10,000)	(11,625)	(11,772)
Balance carried forward	10,000	11,625	11,772

Tutorial note

The indexation allowance in the share pool is not rounded to three decimal places.

	£
Disposal proceeds	37,576
Less: Cost (see pool working)	(11,625)
Unindexed gain	25,951
Less: Indexation (£11,772 – £11,625) (see pool working)	(147)
Chargeable gain	25,804

(W5) **Corporation tax rates**

		£
Upper limit	(£1,500,000 × 1/3 × 9/12)	375,000
Lower limit	(£300,000 × 1/3 × 9/12)	75,000
Augmented profits		307,175 *Marginal relief applies*

The limits are reduced for a nine month period and there are three associated companies in the group.

The accounting period falls partly within FY2012 (2 months) and partly within FY2013 (7 months).

The limits are the same for both financial years but the tax rates are different so the corporation tax liability must be calculated separately for each financial year.

(b) **Self-assessment corporation tax return**

- Arable Ltd's self-assessment corporation tax return for the period ended 31 October 2013 must be submitted by 31 October 2014.
- It will be possible for Arable Ltd to amend its return at any time before 31 October 2015, being 12 months after the filing date.
- If an error or mistake in a return is subsequently discovered, which results in an overpayment of tax then Arable Ltd can make a claim for overpayment relief before 31 October 2017, being four years from the end of the chargeable accounting period.

52 ZOOM PLC (ADAPTED)  *Online question assistance*

Key answer tips

This question has many of the usual features of corporation tax questions with marks for computing capital allowances and corporation tax.

One unusual aspect however is part (a)(ii) where the examiner gives you the figure of taxable total profits and asks for a reconciliation between that and the profit before tax.

Do not waste time trying to make your reconciliation agree if it doesn't on your first attempt. Since you are given the taxable total profits you can use that figure in part (c) to calculate corporation tax even if your reconciliation does not quite balance.

Knowledge of the quarterly instalment rules is often tested and should give some easy marks if you know the rules.

(a) (i) **Capital allowances for plant and machinery**

y/e 31 March 2014		*General Pool*	*Short life asset*	*Special rate pool*	*Allow -ances*
	£	£	£	£	£
TWDV b/f		19,600	20,200		
Additions (no AIA or FYA) (Note 1)					
Car (CO_2 > 130 g/km)				16,600	
Car (CO_2 between 96 – 130 g/km)		11,850			
Additions (with AIA)					
Equipment	8,600				
Computer (Note 2)	12,300				
	20,900				
Less: AIA (Note 3)	(20,900)				20,900
		Nil			
Disposal proceeds (Note 4)			(19,200)		
(£9,800 + £1,000)		(10,800)			
		20,650	1,000		
Balancing allowance			(1,000)		1,000
WDA (18%)		(3,717)			3,717
WDA (8%)				(1,328)	1,328
Addition (with 100% FYA)					
Car (CO_2 < 96 g/km)	14,200				
Less: FYA (100%)	(14,200)				14,200
		Nil			
TWDV c/f		16,933		15,272	
Total allowances					41,145

Tutorial note

1 *Capital allowances on car purchases are calculated based on the CO_2 emissions of the car as follows:*

CO_2 emissions of < 96 g/km: eligible for a FYA of 100%.

CO_2 emissions of between 96 – 130 g/km:
put in general pool, eligible for a WDA at 18%.

CO_2 emissions of > 130 g/km:
put in special rate pool, eligible for a WDA at 8%.

The appropriate rates are given in the tax rates and allowances.

2 *It is assumed that the election to treat the computer as a short life asset has not been made.*

If it had been made, a separate column would be set up, but the allowances in this year would be identical whether or not the election is made.

3 *There is only one AIA of £250,000 for a group of companies which can be allocated to any of the group companies in whatever proportions the group requires.*

However, this aspect of capital allowances is not examinable, so you should assume that the maximum AIA is claimed by Zoom plc.

4 *The sale proceeds for the short life asset, lorry and the equipment are deducted from the short life asset column and general pool respectively as they are less than the original cost.*

(ii) **Reconciliation of profits – year ended 31 March 2014**

Key answer tips

In the adjustment to profits part of the reconciliation it is important to list all the major items indicated in the question requirement, showing a zero (0) for expenditure that is allowable. This is because credit will be given for showing no adjustment where none is needed. List the adjustments in the order they appear in the question.

If required, also add notes to show why you have not adjusted for an item, or why you have added it back. However, lengthy explanations are not required where the requirement is just to 'calculate' the adjusted profits, rather than to explain them.

Always show your workings if the figure you are adjusting for is not clear from the question.

	£	£
Profit before taxation	910,000	
Depreciation	59,227	
Capital allowances (part (a)(i))		41,145
Patent royalties (Note 1)	0	
Income from investments		127,100
Interest payable (Note 2)	0	
	969,227	168,245
	(168,245)	
Trading profit	800,982	
Interest income – Bank interest	10,420	
– Loan interest	22,500	
Property business profit (W)	29,750	
Taxable total profits	863,652	

Tutorial note

1. *The patent royalties received are included as part of the trading profit, so no adjustment is required.*
2. *The interest on a loan used for trading purposes is deductible in calculating the trading profit and has already been deducted, so no adjustment is required.*

Working – Property business profit

	£	£
Rent receivable – Office 1 (£3,200 × 10 months)		32,000
– Office 2 (£26,400 × 8/12)		17,600
		49,600
Irrecoverable rent (£3,200 × 2)	6,400	
Advertising	4,800	
Decorating	5,200	
Insurance ((£3,360 × 9/12) + (£3,720 × 3/12))	3,450	
		(19,850)
Property business profit		29,750

(b) **Quarterly instalment payments – y/e 31 March 2014**

- Large companies have to make quarterly instalment payments in respect of their corporation tax liability. A large company is one paying corporation tax at the main rate.
- Zoom plc has three associated companies, so the upper limit is reduced to £375,000 (£1,500,000 × 1/4). Corporation tax will therefore be paid at the main rate for the year ended 31 March 2014.
- The exceptions for quarterly instalments do not apply because Zoom plc was also a large company for the year ended 31 March 2013.

(c) **Corporation tax liability – y/e 31 March 2014**

- Zoom plc's corporation tax liability for the year ended 31 March 2014 is £198,640 (£863,652 at 23%).
- The company will have paid this in four quarterly instalments of £49,660 (£198,640 × 1/4) as follows:

	£
14.10.2013	49,660
14.01.2014	49,660
14.04.2014	49,660
14.07.2014	49,660
	198,640

(d) **If Zoom plc had no associated companies**

- Zoom plc's 'augmented profits' for corporation tax purposes for the year ended 31 March 2014 is:

	£
Taxable total profits	863,652
Plus: FII (£49,500 × 100/90)	55,000
Augmented profits	918,652

- Zoom plc is no longer a large company since its profits are below the upper limit of £1,500,000.
- The corporation tax liability will therefore be due in one amount on 1 January 2015 (i.e. nine months and one day after the end of the chargeable accounting period).
- The corporation tax liability will be:

	£
Corporation tax (£863,652 at 23%)	198,640
Less: Marginal relief	
3/400 × (£1,500,000 – £918,652) × £863,652/£918,652	(4,099)
Corporation tax liability	194,541

53 BALLPOINT LTD (ADAPTED)  WALK IN THE FOOTSTEPS OF A TOP TUTOR

Key answer tips

This is a wide ranging corporation tax question involving the adjustment of profits, a capital allowances computation and a chargeable gain to calculate.

The highlighted words in the written sections are key phrases that markers are looking for.

Tutor's top tips

It is important when answering questions as long as this, that you have a good technique for dealing with all the information.

You should read the question carefully and highlight key pieces of information as you go through.

Part (a) should have been a very quick and easy way to earn 3 marks, as long as you broke your answer down into 3 separately identifiable points.

(a) **Residency status**

- Companies that are incorporated overseas are only treated as being resident in the UK if their central management and control is exercised in the UK.
- Since the directors are UK based and hold their board meetings in the UK, this would indicate that Ballpoint Ltd is managed and controlled from the UK, and therefore it is resident in the UK.
- If the directors were to be based overseas and to hold their board meetings overseas, the company would probably be treated as resident overseas since the central management and control would then be exercised outside the UK.

(b) **Trading profit – year ended 31 March 2014**

	£	£
Profit before taxation	520,000	
Depreciation	71,488	
Gifts to customers – pens (Note 1)	0	
Gifts to customers – food hampers (Note 1)	770	
Gifts to employees (Note 2)	0	
Donation to national charity (Note 3)	600	
Donation to local charity (Note 4)	0	
Donation to political party (Note 4)	300	
Replacement roof (Note 5)	0	
Initial repairs to office building (Note 6)	13,900	
Accountancy and audit (Note 7)	0	
Legal fees:		
– issue of share capital (Note 8)	3,100	
– issue of a loan note (Note 8)	0	
– defence of internet domain name (Note 9)	0	
Car lease costs (Note 10)	0	
Entertaining overseas customers (Note 11)	3,700	
Entertaining employees (Note 11)	0	
Counselling services for employees (Note 12)	0	
Fine (Note 12)	2,600	
Dividends		45,000
Disposal of factory		60,000
Interest payable (Note 13)	0	
Capital allowances – plant and machinery (W)		78,222
	616,458	183,222
	(183,222)	
Trading profit	433,236	

Tutor's top tips

In the adjustment to profits calculation it is important to list all the major items indicated in the question requirement, showing a zero (0) for expenditure that is allowable. This is because credit will be given for showing no adjustment where none is needed.

List the adjustments in the order they appear in the question.

If required, also add notes to show why you have not adjusted for an item, or why you have added it back. However, lengthy explanations are not required where the requirement is just to 'calculate' the adjusted profits, rather than to explain them.

Always show your workings if the figure you are adjusting for is not clear from the question.

Tutorial note

1 *Gifts to customers are an allowable deduction if they cost less than £50 per recipient per year, are not of food, drink, tobacco or vouchers exchangeable for goods, and carry a conspicuous advertisement for the company making the gift.*

2 *Gifts to employees are allowable, although the gift might result in a taxable benefit for the employee.*

3 *The donation to a national charity is allowable as a qualifying charitable donation, but is deducted from total profits in the TTP computation; it is not an allowable deduction in the adjustment of profits and therefore needs to be added back. It does not matter whether the donation was made under the gift aid scheme or not.*

4 *Small donations to a local charity are allowable where they are for the benefit of the trade (e.g. free advertising), but political donations are not.*

5 *The replacement of the roof is allowable since the whole structure is not being replaced.*

6 *The repairs to the office building are not allowable, being capital in nature, as the building was not in a usable state when purchased and this was reflected in the purchase price.*

7 *Accountancy and audit fees are allowable as incurred wholly and exclusively for the purposes of the trade.*

8 *Legal fees in connection with the issue of share capital are not allowable, being capital in nature.*

However, under the loan relationship rules all costs associated with loans related to the trade (e.g. loan notes) are deductible in calculating trading profits. The costs of obtaining loan finance (even if abortive) are therefore allowable.

9 *The costs of defending the right to an asset (the internet domain name) are also an allowable trading deduction.*

10 *All of the car leasing costs are allowable as the car has CO_2 emissions of less than 130 g/km. If the CO_2 emissions had exceeded 130 g/km, 15% of the lease costs would be disallowable.*

11 *The only exception to the non-deductibility of entertainment expenditure is when it is in respect of employees.*

12 *The costs of counselling services for redundant employees are allowable, whilst fines are generally not allowable.*

13 *Interest on a loan used for trading purposes is deductible in calculating the trading profit on an accruals basis.*

Working: Plant and machinery

		Main pool	*Special rate pool*	*Allowances*
	£	£	£	£
TWDV b/f		8,200	9,800	
Additions (no AIA)(Note 1):				
Car (CO_2 > 130 g/km)			18,200	
Car (CO_2 between 96 – 130 g/km)		11,400		
Additions (with AIA):				
Equipment	61,260			
Equipment	4,300			
	65,560			
Less: AIA (Max) (Note 2)	(65,560)			65,560
Disposal proceeds				
– Equipment		(2,700)		
– Car (2)		(10,110)		
		6,790	28,000	
WDA (18%)		(1,222)		1,222
WDA (8%)			(2,240)	2,240
Addition with FYA:				
Car (CO_2 < 96 g/km)	9,200			
Less: FYA (100%)	(9,200)			9,200
		Nil		
TWDV c/f		5,568	25,760	
Total allowances				78,222

Tutor's top tips

It is important to look carefully at the CO_2 emissions for the cars. There are three categories, all treated differently. Remember that the appropriate rates of allowances are given to you in the tax rates and allowances in the examination.

Tutorial note

1 *Capital allowances on car purchases are calculated based on the CO_2 emissions of the car as follows:*

CO_2 emissions of < 96 g/km: eligible for a FYA of 100%.

CO_2 emissions of between 96 – 130 g/km:
put in main pool, eligible for a WDA at 18%.

CO_2 emissions of > 130 g/km:
put in special rate pool, eligible for a WDA at 8%.

The appropriate rates are given in the tax rates and allowances.

2 *There is only one AIA of £250,000 for Ballpoint Ltd and its 100% subsidiary, and this AIA can be shared between the two companies in any way they choose. However, this aspect of capital allowances is not examinable, so you should assume that sufficient AIA is claimed by Ballpoint Ltd.*

(c) **Corporation tax computation – year ended 31 March 2014**

Tutor's top tips

Don't worry if you made some mistakes in part (b) as you can still score full marks here for calculating the tax correctly based on your figures.

You must make sure you set out your workings clearly so that the marker can see what you have done.

	£
Trading profit	433,236
Chargeable gain (W1)	16,800
	450,036
Less: QCD relief	(600)
	449,436
Less: Group relief (Note 1)	(42,000)
Taxable total profits	407,436
Plus: FII (£27,000 × 100/90) (Note 2)	30,000
Augmented profits	437,436
Corporation tax (W2) (£407,436 at 23%)	93,710
Less: Marginal relief	
3/400 × (£750,000 – £437,436) × £407,436/£437,436	(2,183)
Corporation tax liability	91,527

Tutorial note

1 *Remember that group relief is set off after qualifying charitable donations (QCD) relief, whereas if a company claims relief for its own loss, the loss is set off before QCDs.*

2 *Group dividends are not included as franked investment income.*

Workings

(W1) **Chargeable gain**

	£
Disposal proceeds	300,000
Less: Cost	(240,000)
Unindexed gain	60,000
Less: Indexation allowance	(43,200)
Chargeable gain	16,800

(W2) **Corporation tax rates**

		£
Upper limit	(£1,500,000 × ½)	750,000
Lower limit	(£300,000 × ½)	150,000
Augmented profits		437,436

Therefore marginal relief applies.

54 DO-NOT-PANIC LTD (ADAPTED)

Key answer tips

Originally this was a short question containing just part (a) for 10 marks involving a long period of account which required knowledge of the rules of how to split income and gains between two chargeable accounting periods.

When the question was set, the capital allowance rules were different and more was involved in the calculation than under the current rules.

This question has been extended to become a 20 mark question and provides good practice on some key examinable areas.

(a) **Corporation tax liabilities – fifteen-month period ended 31 March 2014**

	y/e 31.12.2013	p/e 31.3.2014
	£	£
Trading profit (12/15 : 3/15) (Note 1)	350,000	87,500
Less: Capital allowances (W1)	(Nil)	(24,000)
	350,000	63,500
Net chargeable gains (£42,000 – £4,250) (Note 2)	Nil	37,750
Taxable total profits	350,000	101,250
Plus: Franked investment income (Note 3)	Nil	25,000
Augmented profits	350,000	126,250

	£	£
Corporation tax (W2)		
FY2012: (£350,000 × 24% × 3/12)	21,000	
Less: Marginal relief		
1/100 × (£1,500,000 – £350,000) × 3/12	(2,875)	
FY2013: (£350,000 × 23% × 9/12)	60,375	
Less: Marginal relief		
3/400 × (£1,500,000 – £350,000) × 9/12	(6,469)	
FY2013: (£101,250 × 23%)		23,287
Less: Marginal relief		
3/400 × (£375,000 – £126,250) × £101,250/£126,250		(1,496)
Corporation tax liability	72,031	21,791
Due dates	1 Oct 2014	1 Jan 2015
Total liability	£93,822	

Tutorial note

1 *Trading profits are allocated on a time basis: 12/15 to the year ended 31 December 2013 and 3/15 to the period ended 31 March 2014.*

2 *The capital loss £4,250 for the year ended 31 December 2013 is carried forward and set against the first available future gains in the 3 months ended 31 March 2014.*

3 *The figure provided in the question was franked investment income rather than the dividend received, therefore grossing up by 100/90 is not necessary.*

Workings

(W1) **Capital allowances**

		General pool	*Allowances*
	£	£	£
Year ended 31 December 2013			
No additions in the period			
Period ended 31 March 2014			
Additions (with AIA)			
Equipment	24,000		
Less: AIA (Max £250,000 × 3/12)	(24,000)		24,000
		Nil	
TWDV c/f		Nil	
Total allowances			24,000

Tutorial note

The maximum AIA is time apportioned because the company's accounting period is three months long.

(W2) **Corporation tax rate**

		y/e 31.12.13	*p/e 31.3.14*
		£	£
Upper limit	(Full / 3/12)	1,500,000	375,000
Lower limit	(Full / 3/12)	300,000	75,000
Augmented profits		350,000	126,250
		Marginal relief applies	*Marginal relief applies*

The accounting period ended 31 December 2013 falls partly into FY2012 (3 months) and partly into FY2013 (9 months).

As the tax rates are different in these financial years the liability must be calculated separately for each year.

(b) **Corporation tax liabilities – two sets of account prepared**

	p/e 31.3.2013	*y/e 31.3.2014*
	£	£
Trading profit (3/15 : 12/15) (Note 1)	87,500	350,000
Less: Capital allowances (W1)	(Nil)	(24,000)
	87,500	326,000
Net chargeable gains (£42,000 – £4,250) (Note 2)	Nil	37,750
Taxable total profits	87,500	363,750
Plus: Franked investment income	Nil	25,000
Augmented profits	87,500	388,750
Corporation tax (W2)		
FY2012: (£87,500 × 24%)	21,000	
1/100 × (£375,000 – £87,500)	(2,875)	
FY2013: (£363,750 × 23%)		83,662
Less: Marginal relief		
3/400 × (£1,500,000 – £388,750) × £363,750/£388,750		(7,798)
Corporation tax liability	18,125	75,864
Due dates	1 Jan 2014	1 Jan 2015
Total liability	£93,989	

Tutorial note

1 *Trading profits are assumed to accrue evenly over the fifteen month period.*

2 *The capital loss and the capital gain both fall in the year ended 31 March 2014.*

Workings

(W1) **Capital allowances**

		General pool	*Allowances*
Period ended 31 March 2013	£	£	£
No additions in the period			
Year ended 31 March 2014			
Additions (with AIA)			
Equipment	24,000		
Less: AIA	(24,000)		24,000
		Nil	
TWDV c/f		Nil	
Total allowances			24,000

(W2) **Corporation tax rate**

		p/e 31.3.13	*y/e 31.3.14*
Upper limit	(3/12 / Full)	£375,000	£1,500,000
Lower limit	(3/12 / Full)	£75,000	£300,000
Augmented profits		£87,500	£388,750
		Marginal relief applies	*Marginal relief applies*

The accounting period ended 31 March 2013 falls entirely in FY2012 and the accounting period ended 31 March 2014 falls entirely in FY2013.

(c) **Total tax**

The lower total tax liability is £93,822 which is obtained if a long period of account is prepared, rather than two separate accounts which gives a total liability of £93,989.

Examiner's report

This is the examiner's report for part (a) which was the entire original question as amended for legislation and syllabus changes.

Depending on whether candidates appreciated that the period of account needed to be split into a twelve-month period and a three-month period, this question was either answered very well or quite badly.

Invariably many of the less well prepared candidates calculated corporation tax based on a fifteen-month period.

Even when the correct approach was taken, many candidates did not appreciate that the first twelve month period spanned two financial years.

The due dates were often omitted or incorrect.

ACCA marking scheme

			Marks
(a)	Trading profit		1.0
	Capital allowances	– Year ended 31 December 2013	0.5
		– Period ended 31 March 2014	1.5
	Capital gains		1.0
	Franked investment income		1.0
	Corporation tax	– Year ended 31 December 2013	2.5
		– Period ended 31 March 2014	1.5
	Due dates		1.0
			10.0
(b)	Trading profit		1.0
	Capital allowances	– Period ended 31 March 2013	0.5
		– Year ended 31 March 2014	1.0
	Capital gains		1.0
	Franked investment income		1.0
	Corporation tax	– Period ended 31 March 2013	1.5
		– Year ended 31 March 2014	2.0
	Due dates		1.0
			9.0
(c)	Lower total tax liability		1.0
Total			20.0

55 CRASH BASH LTD (ADAPTED)  WALK IN THE FOOTSTEPS OF A TOP TUTOR

Key answer tips

A standard corporation tax question requiring a capital allowances computation for plant and machinery followed by a corporation tax computation. This part of the question carries the majority of the marks available in part (a).

These areas are often tested and should not have caused many difficulties.

The original question also tested various overseas aspects of corporation tax, which are no longer examinable. This section has been replaced by a question on corporation tax administration, which is an area which is frequently tested and must be learnt.

The separate VAT section for 10 marks at the end is also a classic requirement – easy to score highly on, provided the rules have been learnt!

Tutor's top tips

Be sure to read the requirement carefully and pay attention to the mark allocation.

Part (a)(i) only requires two bullet points to be made, but remember to relate your answer to the specific information given in the question.

Part (a)(ii) is where the time should be spent, however, don't run out of time to attempt part (iii) by spending too long here.

Part (iii) deals with the implications of missing filing deadlines, and is a straightforward test of knowledge retention.

(a) (i) **Residence status**

- Companies that are incorporated overseas are only treated as being resident in the UK if their central management and control is exercised in the UK.
- Since the directors are UK based and hold their board meetings in the UK, this would indicate that Crash-Bash Ltd is managed and controlled from the UK, and therefore it is resident in the UK.

(ii) **Corporation tax liability – period ended 31 October 2013**

Tutor's top tips

Remember to use your time effectively for this part.

Computations for capital allowances are required in workings before the corporation tax computation can be drawn up. Remember to reference your workings clearly to your main answer to the question.

Note that this question is now simpler than the original question set as there are no longer any overseas aspects; however the capital allowances computation is a little more complicated than before.

The mark allocation in this answer has been adjusted accordingly.

	£	£
Trading profit per question		553,434
Advertising expenditure (Note 1)	12,840	
Capital allowances – Plant and machinery (W1)	202,084	
		(214,924)
Tax adjusted trading profit		338,510
Taxable total profits		338,510
Plus: FII (£36,000 × 100/90) (Note 2)		40,000
Augmented profits		378,510
Corporation tax (W1)		
FY2012 (£338,510 at 24% × 2/9)		18,054
Less: Marginal relief		
1/100 × (£562,500 – £378,510) × £338,510/£378,510 × 2/9		(366)
FY2013 (£338,510 at 23% × 7/9)		60,556
Less: Marginal relief		
3/400 × (£562,500 – £378,510) × £338,510/£378,510 × 7/9		(960)
Corporation tax liability		77,284

Tutorial note

1 *The advertising expenditure incurred during January 2013 is pre-trading revenue expenditure. Accordingly it is treated as incurred on the first day of trading (i.e. 1 February 2013) and is therefore an allowable deduction for corporation tax purposes.*

As no adjustment has been made for this expenditure yet, an adjustment is required.

2 *If the dividends are received from a non-associated company, they must be grossed up at 100/90 and included in FII. However, dividends from an associated company are excluded from the definition of FII. Safety Ltd is a 100% subsidiary and therefore it is an associated company and any dividends received are not FII.*

Workings

(W1) **Plant and machinery**

		Main pool	*Allowances*
	£	£	£
Additions (No AIA or FYA):			
Car (Note 1)			
(CO_2 between 96 – 130 g/km)		14,000	
Additions (with AIA):			
Machinery	193,750		
Less: AIA (Maximum) (Note 2)	(187,500)		187,500
		6,250	
Disposal (restricted to cost)		(10,000)	
		10,250	
Less: WDA (Note 2)			
(£10,250 × 18% × 9/12)		(1,384)	1,384
Additions (with FYA):			
Car (CO_2 < 96 g/km)	13,200		
Less: FYA (100%)	(13,200)		13,200
		Nil	
TWDV c/f		8,866	
Total allowances			202,084

Tutorial note

1 *Capital allowances on car purchases are calculated based on the CO_2 emissions of the car as follows:*

CO_2 emissions of < 96 g/km:
eligible for a FYA of 100%

CO_2 emissions of between 96 – 130 g/km:

put in main pool and eligible for a WDA at 18%.

2 *The maximum Annual Investment Allowance is £187,500 (£250,000 × 9/12) because Crash-Bash Ltd's accounting period is nine months long.*

The writing down allowance is similarly restricted to 9/12, however first year allowances are never restricted according to the length of the accounting period.

(W2) **Corporation tax rate**

- The accounting period is nine months long and falls partly in FY2012 (two months) and partly in FY2013 (seven months). The corporation tax computation must therefore be done in two stages.
- Crash-Bash Ltd has one associated company.
- The upper limits are the same in both FY2012 and FY2013.
- The upper and lower limits for corporation tax purposes are:

Upper limit	(£1,500,000 × 9/12 × ½)	£562,500
Lower limit	(£300,000 × 9/12 × ½)	£112,500

- The augmented profits of £378,510 fall in between the limits and therefore Crash-Bash Ltd is a marginal relief company in both financial years.

(iii) **Implications of late filing and payment**

- Crash-Bash Ltd's self-assessment tax return for the period ended 31 October 2013 must be submitted by 31 October 2014.
- If the company submits its self-assessment tax return eight months late, then there will be an automatic fixed penalty of £200, since the return is more than three months late.
- There will also be an additional corporation tax related penalty of £7,728 (£77,284 × 10%) being 10% of the tax unpaid, since the self-assessment tax return is more than six months late.

Tutorial note

The tax geared penalty starts when 18 months or more have passed after the end of the return period (i.e. this is the same as saying 6 months or more after the filing date).

(b) (i) **Compulsory registration**

Tutor's top tips

Part (b) of this question is an independent part and could be answered before part (a) if you want to get it out of the way and have learnt the relevant VAT rules!

Remember that VAT will always feature in the exam for a minimum of 10 marks and the requirements are usually straightforward and easy to score highly on provided you put in the time to learn the rules.

However, even if you are a bit vague on some of the areas, you need to attempt each part and write something – try not to spend too long on part (a) so that you run out of time to do part (b) justice.

Part (b)(i) should have been straightforward as it required the application of the compulsory registration rules.

Part (b)(ii) was a little trickier in computing the recoverability of the pre-registration input VAT, but there are some straightforward points to make and numbers to calculate.

For part (b)(iii) you have either learnt the rules, or you haven't. You would struggle on this part if you haven't.

- Traders must register for VAT if at any time they expect their taxable supplies for the following 30-day period to exceed £79,000.
- Crash-Bash Ltd realised that its taxable supplies for April 2013 were going to be at least £100,000. The company was therefore liable to register from 1 April 2013, being the start of the 30-day period.
- Crash-Bash Ltd had to notify HMRC by 30 April 2013, being the end of the 30-day period.

(ii) **Recovery of pre-registration input VAT**

- Input VAT of £21,720 (£108,600 × 20%) can be recovered on the stock of goods at 1 April 2013.
- The stock was not acquired more than four years prior to registration, nor was it sold or consumed prior to registration.
- Input VAT of £11,000 ((£22,300 + £32,700) × 20%) can be recovered on the services incurred from 1 February to 31 March 2013.
- This is because the services were not supplied more than six months prior to registration.
- The total input VAT recovery is therefore £32,720 (£21,720 + £11,000).

(iii) **Voluntary disclosure of errors in a VAT return**

- If the net errors totalled less than the higher of £10,000 or 1% of the turnover for the VAT period, then they could have been voluntarily disclosed by simply entering them on the VAT return for the quarter ended 30 September 2013.
- If the net errors exceeded the limit, they could have been voluntarily disclosed but disclosure would have been made separately to HMRC.
- Default interest is only charged where the limit is exceeded and it is therefore necessary to make separate disclosure to HMRC.

Examiner's report

Although the numerical aspects of this question were well answered, most candidates achieved lower marks for this question than for question one, despite this question being five marks longer.

In the first section of part (a) most candidates were not aware that the essential point regarding residence is where a company's central management and control is exercised.

Most candidates had little difficulty with the corporation tax computation, and there were many perfect answers to this part of the question. *[The remainder of the examiner's comments on this section related to the overseas aspects which have been deleted as they are no longer examinable.]*

In part (b) the VAT aspects of the question were not so well answered.

Many candidates incorrectly stated that VAT registration was necessary because the company had exceeded the registration limit over the previous 12 months; they even gave the wrong date of registration despite this being given in the question.

A number of candidates prepared the company's VAT return showing output VAT and input VAT, rather than calculating the amount of pre-registration input VAT.

Very few candidates were aware of when default interest is charged.

ACCA marking scheme				
				Marks
(a)	(i)	Central management and control		1.0
		Board meetings held in the UK		1.0
				2.0
	(ii)	Trading profit		0.5
		Advertising expenditure		1.0
		P & M	– AIA	1.5
			– Pool	1.5
			– Disposal restricted to cost	1.0
			– WDA	1.5
			– FYA (100%)	1.5
		Dividend from associate– not included in FII		0.5
		Franked investment income		1.0
		Corporation tax calculation		4.0
				14.0
	(iii)	Due date		1.0
		Fixed penalty		1.5
		Corporation tax related penalty		1.5
				4.0
(b)	(i)	Registration limit		1.0
		Taxable supplies for September 2013		1.0
		Notification		1.0
				3.0
	(ii)	Stock of goods	– Calculation	0.5
			– Explanation	1.0
		Services	– Calculation	1.0
			– Explanation	1.0
		Total input VAT recovery		0.5
				4.0
	(iii)	Net errors less than the limit		1.0
		Net errors exceeding the limit		1.0
		Default interest		1.0
				3.0
Total				30.0

56 QUAGMIRE LTD  *Walk in the footsteps of a top tutor*

Key answer tips

This question covers the quarterly instalment system of payment for large companies. It is not difficult provided the self-assessment rules for companies have been learnt.

In particular you need to know the conditions for determining whether or not a company is large for this purpose, and the key due dates of payment.

Tutor's top tips

Part (a) requires an explanation of why the company has to pay by instalments. The clue that the company is large is therefore in the requirement.

The question itself gives taxable total profits and FII which should trigger alarm bells that the level of 'augmented profits' is an important consideration.

The fact that both this year and last year's information is given should also be a clue that they are both important to determine the status of the company.

(a) **Quarterly instalment payments**

- Large companies have to make quarterly instalment payments in respect of their corporation tax liability. A large company is one paying corporation tax at the main rate.
- Quagmire plc has one associated company, so the upper limit is reduced to £750,000 (£1,500,000 × 1/2). Corporation tax will therefore be at the main rate for the year ended 31 January 2014.
- There is an exception for the first year that a company is large, provided profits do not exceed £10 million (divided by the number of associated companies).

  However, no exception applies in this case because Quagmire plc was also a large company for the year ended 31 January 2013.

Tutorial note

The instalment payment system is not applied if:

1. *The corporation tax liability is less than £10,000, or*
2. *The company is 'large' for the first time and the profits do not exceed £10 million (divided by number of associates if applicable)*

(b) **Corporation tax liability and due dates for payment**

	£
Corporation tax – year ended 31 January 2014	
FY2012 (£1,200,000 × 24% × 2/12)	48,000
FY2013 (£1,200,000 × 23% × 10/12)	230,000
Corporation tax liability	278,000

The accounting period falls partly within FY2012 (2 months) and partly within FY2013 (10 months).

The tax rates are different in each financial year so the corporation tax liability must be calculated separately for each financial year.

- Quagmire plc's corporation tax liability for the year ended 31 January 2014 is £278,000.
- The company will have paid this in four quarterly instalments of £69,500 (£278,000/4).
- The instalments will have been due on the 14th of August 2013, November 2013, February 2014 and May 2014.

Tutorial note

Remember that the corporation tax liability is calculated on taxable total profits, not 'augmented profits'.

The instalments are due on the 14th day of the 7th, 10th, 13th and 16th month after the start of the chargeable accounting period.

(c) **Revised position assuming Quagmire did not have an associated company**

Tutor's top tips

The requirement asks for an explanation of the effect if there is no associate – so make sure that you explain in words and do not just do a calculation.

The revised calculation is worth only 1.5 of the 4 marks available.

- Quagmire plc's augmented profits for the year ended 31 January 2014 is £1,400,000 (£1,200,000 plus franked investment income of £200,000).
- Quagmire plc is no longer a large company since its profits are below the upper limit of £1,500,000. The corporation tax liability will therefore be due in one amount on 1 November 2014.

- The corporation tax liability will be:

	£
Corporation tax	
FY2012	
(£1,200,000 at 24% × 2/12)	48,000
Less: Marginal relief	
1/100 × (£1,500,000 – £1,400,000) × £1,200,000/£1,400,000 × 2/12	(143)
FY2013	
(£1,200,000 at 23% × 10/12)	230,000
Less: Marginal relief	
3/400 × (£1,500,000 – £1,400,000) × £1,200,000/£1,400,000 × 10/12	(536)
	277,321

Tutorial note

The normal due date for corporation tax is 9 months and 1 day after the end of the chargeable accounting period.

Examiner's report

This question was reasonably well answered.

In part (a) very few candidates appreciated that there was a possible exception and that the exception did not apply. This was the reason why figures were given for the previous year, and less well prepared candidates created a lot of problems for themselves by trying to use these figures as part of their calculations.

Candidates had little difficulty in calculating the corporation tax liability in part (b), but they often struggled with the quarterly due dates.

There was a similar problem in part (c) where many candidates failed to score an easy mark by omitting the due date.

ACCA marking scheme

		Marks
(a)	Large companies	1.0
	Associated company	1.0
	No exception	1.0
		3.0
(b)	Corporation tax liability	1.0
	Instalments	1.0
	Due dates	1.0
		3.0
(c)	Profit	1.0
	No longer a large company	0.5
	Due date	1.0
	Corporation tax	1.5
		4.0
Total		10.0

57 MOLTEN METAL PLC (ADAPTED)  *Walk in the footsteps of a top tutor*

Key answer tips

Part (a) requires a corporation tax computation including a partial adjustment of profits, an involved capital allowances computation, and property income, interest income and chargeable gain calculations.

Detailed knowledge of capital versus revenue expenditure, capital allowances and the treatment of interest is needed. However, the gain and property income computations should not cause any problems.

Part (b) tests the quarterly instalment system and is straightforward.

(a) **Corporation tax computation – year ended 31 March 2014**

	£	£
Trading profit per question		2,090,086
Loan stock interest payable (W2) (Note 1)	22,000	
Repairs to office building (Note 2)	0	
Capital allowance – P & M (W1)	274,354	
		(296,354)
Tax adjusted trading profit		1,793,732
Property business profit (W3)		68,400
Interest income (W4)		8,700
Chargeable gain (W5)		156,636
TTP		2,027,468
Corporation tax (£2,027,468 at 23%)		466,318

Tutorial note

1 *Interest paid in respect of a loan used for trading purposes is deductible in calculating the trading profit.*

2 *The repairs to the office building are not deductible as revenue expenditure. They are treated as capital in nature, as the building was not in a usable state when purchased and this fact was reflected in the reduced purchase price.*

Workings

(W1) **Plant and machinery**

		Main pool	*Special rate pool*	*Allowances*
	£	£	£	£
TWDV b/f		87,800		
Additions not qualifying for AIA				
Motor cars (£17,300 × 2) (Note 1)		34,600		
Additions qualifying for AIA				
Integral features (Note 2)				
Ventilation system	83,000			
Lift	10,000			
	93,000			
Less: AIA (Note 3)	(93,000)			93,000
			Nil	
Other plant and machinery				
Machinery	140,000			
Building alterations (Note 4)	7,000			
Wall (Note 5)	Nil			
Partition walls (Note 5)	22,900			
	169,900			
Less: AIA (Note 3)	(157,000)			157,000
		12,900		
		135,300		
Less: WDA (18%)		(24,354)		24,354
TWDV c/f		110,946	Nil	
Total allowances				274,354

Tutorial note

1 *The motor cars have CO_2 emissions between 96 and 130 grams per kilometre, and therefore go in the main pool. They do not qualify for the AIA but do qualify for writing down allowances at the rate of 18%.*

The private use of a motor car is irrelevant for company capital allowances computations, since such usage will be assessed on the employee as an employment benefit.

2 *The purchase of an office building itself is not eligible for plant and machinery allowances.*

However, the ventilation system and lift are both integral to a building and are eligible for plant and machinery allowances as special rate pool items.

3 *It is beneficial to claim the AIA of £250,000 initially against the special rate pool expenditure, as it would otherwise only qualify for writing down allowance at the rate of 8%.*

Any remaining AIA, up to a maximum of £250,000 in total, is set against the plant and machinery expenditure and the balance is put in the main pool.

4 *The building alterations were necessary for the installation of the machinery, and therefore qualify for capital allowances.*

5 *Walls are specifically excluded as qualifying for capital allowances, with the exception of partition walls which are movable and intended to be so moved. The partition walls perform a 'function' (enabling the office space to be changed and used efficiently) unlike the wall which is just decorative and is the 'setting' for the business.*

(W2) **Interest payable**

The loan stock was issued to raise funds for a trading purpose; therefore the interest is an allowable deduction against trading profit, calculated on an accruals basis as follows:

	£
Accrual b/f at 1 April 2013	(4,200)
Loan stock interest paid	22,500
Accrual c/f at 31 March 2014	3,700
	22,000

(W3) **Property business profit**

	£
Premium received	68,000
Less: £68,000 × 2% × (6 – 1)	(6,800)
Premium assessable to income tax	61,200
Rent receivable ((£78,800 – £68,000) = £10,800 × 2/3)	7,200
Property business profit	68,400

Tutor's top tips:

The premium received on the granting of a short lease is deemed to be partly income, and partly a capital receipt.

The income element can be calculated as shown above, or by using the alternative calculation below:

Premium × (51 – n)/50 *where n = number of years of the lease*

= £68,000 × (51 – 6)/50

= £61,200

Note that the question says to ignore the capital element of the premium, as this is outside the F6 syllabus.

(W4) **Interest income**

	£
Loan interest receivable (£9,800 + £3,100)	12,900
Bank interest receivable	2,600
	15,500
Less: Loan interest expense	(6,800)
Interest income	8,700

(W5) **Chargeable gain**

	£
Disposal proceeds	872,000
Less: Incidental costs of disposal	(28,400)
Net disposal proceeds	843,600
Less: Cost	(396,200)
Enhancement expenditure – Extension	(146,000)
– Roof (Note)	(Nil)
Unindexed gain	301,400
Less: Indexation allowance	
Cost (£396,200 × 0·302)	(119,652)
Enhancement expenditure (£146,000 × 0.172)	(25,112)
Chargeable gain	156,636

Tutorial note

The cost of replacing part of the roof is not enhancement expenditure as the office building is simply being restored to its original state prior to the fire.

(b) **Final quarterly instalment payment**

	£
Corporation tax liability	466,318
Less: Quarterly instalments paid	(398,200)
Final instalment payment	68,118
Due date:	14 July 2014

Examiner's report

This question was generally well answered, and there were many very good answers.

In part (a) there was no need to have separate computations for the trading profit and for taxable total profits, since it was quite straightforward to combine everything into one computation.

The accruals for the interest payable and interest income often caused problems, and many candidates did not appreciate that no adjustment to the trading profit was necessary in respect of any of the items debited to the capital expenditure account.

The writing down allowance for a motor car with private use was often restricted, despite such an adjustment only being relevant for an unincorporated business.

The calculations for the property business profit and the chargeable gain were often made much more difficult than they actually were.

Although most candidates correctly calculated the final quarterly instalment in part (b), the due date was generally not known.

ACCA marking scheme			
			Marks
(a)	Trading profit		0.5
	Loan stock interest payable		1.5
	Repairs to office building		1.0
	P & M – Office building		1.0
	– Ventilation system and lift		1.5
	– AIA		1.0
	– Machinery		0.5
	– Building alterations		0.5
	– Wall		0.5
	– Partition walls		1.0
	– AIA		1.0
	– Main pool		2.0
	Property business profit – Premium received		2.0
	– Rent		1.0
	Interest income		2.0
	Chargeable gain – Disposal proceeds		0.5
	– Costs of disposal		0.5
	– Cost		0.5
	– Enhancement expenditure		2.0
	– Indexation allowance		2.0
	Corporation tax liability		0.5
			23.0
(b)	Instalment payment		1.0
	Due date		1.0
			2.0
Total			25.0

WITH VAT ASPECTS

58 STRETCHED LTD (ADAPTED)

Key answer tips

This question deals with the rules for a 15 month period of account which must be split into two accounting periods of 12 months and 3 months.

For ease, use a columnar layout to do the corporation tax computations side by side. Don't forget to pick up the easy marks for stating the due dates of payment.

At least 10 marks of VAT will be included in the examination and it is most likely to appear as part of question 1 or 2. In this case it appears as an independent part (b) to the question.

It is important not to neglect VAT. The points tested in this question are all commonly examined.

(1) (a) **Corporation tax computations**

	y/e 31.12.13	p/e 31.3.14
	£	£
Trading profit (12/15 : 3/15) (Note 1)	264,000	66,000
Less: Capital allowances (W1)	Nil	(62,838)
	264,000	3,162
Less: Loss relief b/f	(23,000)	–
	241,000	3,162
Property business profit (12/15 : 3/15) (Note 1)	36,000	9,000
Chargeable gains (£44,000 – £3,000) (Note 2)	41,000	Nil
	318,000	12,162
Less: QCD relief	–	(5,000)
Taxable total profits	318,000	7,162
Plus: Franked investment income	30,000	–
Augmented profits	348,000	7,162
Corporation tax (W2)		
FY2012		
(£318,000 × 24% × 3/12)	19,080	
Less: Marginal relief		
1/100 × (£1,500,000 – £348,000) × £318,000/£348,000 × 3/12	(2,632)	
FY2013		
(£318,000 × 23% × 9/12)	54,855	
Less: Marginal relief		
3/400 × (£1,500,000 – £348,000) × £318,000/£348,000 × 9/12	(5,921)	
FY2013: (£7,162 × 20%)		1,432
	65,382	1,432
Due dates	1 Oct 2014	1 Jan 2015

Tutorial note

1 *Trading profits and property business profits are allocated on a time basis: 12/15 to the year ended 31 December 2013 and 3/15 to the period ended 31 March 2014.*

2 *The capital loss of £6,700 for the period ended 31 March 2014 is carried forward, it cannot be carried back and set off against previous gains.*

Workings

(W1) Capital allowances

		General pool	Allowances
	£	£	£
3 months ended 31 March 2014			
Additions (with AIA)			
Office equipment	70,000		
Less: AIA (Max £250,000 × 3/12)	(62,500)		62,500
		7,500	
Less: WDA (18%) × 3/12		(338)	338
TWDV c/f		7,162	
Total allowances			62,838

Tutorial note

The AIA and WDA must be time apportioned as the chargeable accounting period is only three months in length.

(W2) Corporation tax rates

		y/e 31.12.13	p/e 31.3.14
		£	£
Upper limit	(Full / × 3/12)	1,500,000	375,000
Lower limit	(Full / × 3/12)	300,000	75,000
Augmented profits		348,000	7,162
		Marginal relief	*Small profits*

The accounting period ended 31 December 2013 falls partly into FY2012 (3 months) and partly into FY2013 (9 months).

As there has been a change in rate of tax the corporation tax liability must be calculated separately for each financial year.

(b) **Advantages of 31 March year end**

- Being aligned with the financial year will make it easier for a company to calculate its corporation tax liability, since the same rates, reliefs and legislation will apply throughout the accounting period.
- For owner-managed companies, alignment with the income tax year (the odd five days can be ignored) will make it easier as regards calculating the most tax efficient method of extracting profits from the company.

(2) (a) **VAT return for quarter to 30 June 2014**

Tutorial note

The appropriate rate of VAT for the quarter to 30 June 2014 is as follows:

- *If the figure excludes VAT, the VAT is 20%*
- *If the figure includes VAT, the VAT is 20/120 or 1/6.*

(i) **Goods**

The basic tax point for sale of the goods is the date of despatch (i.e. 20 June 2014).

Deposit received

Where payment is received before the basic tax point this becomes the actual tax point.

Output VAT of £833 (£5,000 × 1/6) should therefore be accounted for in respect of the deposit in the quarter to 30 June 2014.

Balance of invoice

Where an invoice is issued within 14 days of the basic tax point, the invoice date will become the actual tax point.

The actual tax point in respect of the invoice for the balance due of £25,000 is therefore 1 July 2014.

Output VAT will therefore not be due in respect of the invoice until the quarter ended 30 September 2014.

(ii) **Sales director's cars**

Purchase and sale of cars

As the sale director's new car is to be used partly for private purposes, input VAT is not recoverable in respect of the purchase of this car.

VAT would not have been reclaimed on the purchase of the sales director's old car, as this was also used for private purposes.

No output VAT is therefore charged on the sale of this car.

Fuel costs

The company can reclaim input VAT on the full cost of the fuel.

Input VAT of £100 (£600 × 1/6) should be reclaimed in the quarter to 30 June 2014.

As there is some private use of the cars output VAT, in respect of the private fuel, based on a prescribed scale charge, is payable in the quarter to 30 June 2014.

(iii) **Entertaining costs**

Input VAT of £167 (£1,000 × 1/6) is recoverable in respect of staff entertaining.

Input VAT of £83 (£500 × 1/6) in respect of entertaining UK customers is not recoverable.

(b) **Implications of submitting and paying VAT late**

The late submission of the VAT return for the quarter ended 30 September 2013 will have resulted in HM Revenue & Customs issuing a surcharge liability notice specifying a surcharge period running to 30 September 2014.

The late payment of VAT for the quarter ended 30 June 2014 will be the first default in the surcharge period.

A surcharge of 2% of the VAT due will be charged.

In addition, the surcharge period will be extended to 30 June 2015.

59 SCUBA LTD (ADAPTED)  WALK IN THE FOOTSTEPS OF A TOP TUTOR

Key answer tips

This is a classic question testing your knowledge of corporation tax. There is a great deal of information to deal with and it is essential you have a methodical approach.

First draw up the pro forma for the adjusted profit computation and insert the profit figure. Include in your computation both the items that need adjustment, with the relevant figure, **and** the items that do not need adjustment with a zero (0).

Before you can complete the adjusted profit computation you need to do workings to calculate capital allowances.

Then you can complete the calculation of taxable total profits and the corporation tax liability. Note carefully the information about associated companies.

Part (b) contains 11 marks for VAT and requires detailed knowledge of the default surcharge and the treatment of errors on a VAT return.

Remember that VAT is an important area in the syllabus and will always appear in the examination for a minimum of 10 marks of the paper.

Tutor's top tips

It is important when answering questions as long as this, that you have a good technique for dealing with all the information.

You should read the question carefully and highlight key pieces of information as you go through.

Part (a) (i) is a standard adjustment of profits computation.

Remember that in the adjustment to profits calculation it is important to list all the major items indicated in the question requirement, showing a zero (0) for expenditure that is allowable. This is because credit will be given for showing no adjustment where none is needed. List the adjustments in the order they appear in the question.

If required, also add notes to show why you have not adjusted for an item, or why you have added it back. However, lengthy explanations are not required where the requirement is just to 'calculate' the adjusted profits, rather than to explain them.

Always show your workings if the figure you are adjusting for is not clear from the question.

(a) (i) **Trading profit – year ended 31 March 2014**

	£	£
Operating profit	198,400	
Depreciation and amortisation of lease	45,200	
Entertaining customers (Note 1)	7,050	
Entertaining employees (Note 1)	0	
Gifts to customers – diaries (Note 2)	0	
Gifts to customers – food hampers (Note 2)	1,600	
Deduction for lease premium (W1)		1,860
Capital allowances (W2)		62,360
	252,250	64,220
	(64,220)	
Trading profit	188,030	

Tutorial note

1 *The only exception to the non-deductibility of entertainment expenditure is when it is in respect of employees.*

2 *Gifts to customers are an allowable deduction if they cost less than £50 per recipient per year, are not of food, drink, tobacco or vouchers exchangeable for goods, and carry a conspicuous advertisement for the company making the gift.*

The gift of diaries is therefore allowable but the gift of hampers is not allowable.

Workings

(W1) **Deduction for lease premium**

The office building is used for business purposes, and so a proportion of the lease premium assessed on the landlord can be deducted.

	£
Premium received	80,000
Less: 2% × £80,000 × (20 – 1)	(30,400)
Assessment on landlord (Note)	49,600

This is deductible over the life of the lease, starting from 1 July 2013, so the deduction for the year ended 31 March 2014:

(£49,600 ÷ 20) × 9/12 = £1,860.

Tutorial note

Alternative calculation of the assessment on the landlord:

£80,000 × (51 – 20)/50 = £49,600

(W2) **Plant and machinery**

		Main pool	Special rate pool	Allowances
	£	£	£	£
TWDV b/f		47,200	22,400	
Addition (no AIA) (Notes 1, 2 and 3):				
Car (CO_2 between 96 – 130 g/km)		10,400		
Car (CO_2 > 130 g/km)			15,400	
Additions (with AIA):				
Machinery	22,800			
Computer	1,100			
Machinery	7,300			
	31,200			
Less: AIA	(31,200)			31,200
		Nil		
Less: Disposal proceeds – Lorry		(12,400)		
		45,200	37,800	
Less: WDA (18%)		(8,136)		8,136
Less: WDA (8%)			(3,024)	3,024
Additions qualifying for FYA:				
Car (CO_2 < 96 g/km)	20,000			
Less: FYA (100%)	(20,000)			20,000
		Nil		
TWDV c/f		37,064	34,776	
Total allowances				62,360

Tutorial note

1 *Car purchases where the CO_2 emissions are between 96 – 130 g/km are put in the main pool, and are eligible for a WDA at 18%.*

2 *The private use of the motor car by the factory manager is irrelevant, full allowances are available. The manager will be assessed to income tax on the private use of the car as an employment benefit.*

3 *Car purchases where the CO_2 emissions are > 130 g/km are put in the special rate pool, and are eligible for a WDA at 8%.*

(ii) **Corporation tax computation – year ended 31 March 2014**

Tutor's top tips

A straightforward corporation tax computation is required in part (a) (ii) but first a property income computation must be calculated.

These should have been easy marks to gain and full credit would be given for this part even if your trading profit computation in part (a) (i) is incorrect.

	£
Trading profit (part (a) (i))	188,030
Property business profit (W1)	11,570
Interest	430
Taxable total profits	200,030
Corporation tax liability (W2) (£200,030 × 20%)	40,006

Workings

(W1) **Property business profit**

	£
Rent receivable (£7,200 × 1/3) = £2,400 per month × 8 months	19,200
Less: Decorating	(6,200)
Advertisements	(1,430)
Property business profit	11,570

(W2) **Corporation tax rates**

Scuba Ltd has no franked investment income, therefore the taxable total profits = Augmented profits.

Scuba Ltd has no associated companies and therefore augmented profits are compared to the full upper and lower limits of £1,500,000 and £300,000.

As augmented profits are £200,030, the company is a small profits company and therefore the rate of corporation tax is 20%.

(b) (i) **Default surcharge**

Tutor's top tips

This part of the question is an independent part on VAT which could have been answered first, before part (a).

Popular topics were tested, namely the default surcharge rules and errors on a VAT return.

There are easy marks to be gained here if you have learnt the rules, but difficult to score highly on if you have neglected VAT in your studies.

Remember that you will always have a minimum of 10 marks on VAT in the exam.

- The late submission of the VAT return for the quarter ended 30 June 2011 will have resulted in HM Revenue & Customs issuing a surcharge liability notice specifying a surcharge period running to 30 June 2012.
- The late payment of VAT for the quarter ended 30 September 2011 will have resulted in a surcharge of £644 (£32,200 × 2%).
- The late payment of VAT for the quarter ended 31 March 2012 will have resulted in a surcharge of £170 (£3,400 × 5%), but this will not have been collected as it was less than £400.
- Although the VAT return for the quarter ended 30 June 2012 was submitted late, this will not have resulted in a surcharge as Scuba Ltd was due a refund for this period.
- The continued late submission of VAT returns will have resulted in the surcharge period being extended to 30 September 2012, then to 31 March 2013, and finally to 30 June 2013.
- Scuba Ltd then submitted the four consecutive VAT returns during the surcharge period running to 30 June 2013 on time, and so will have reverted to a clean default surcharge record.
- The late submission of the VAT return for the quarter ended 30 September 2013 will therefore result in a surcharge liability notice specifying a surcharge period running to 30 September 2014.

(ii) **Errors on VAT return**

- If the net errors total less than the higher of £10,000 or 1% of turnover (max £50,000), then they can be voluntarily disclosed by simply entering them on the VAT return for the quarter ended 31 March 2014.
- If the net errors total more than this limit, then they can be voluntarily disclosed, but disclosure must be made separately to HM Revenue & Customs.
- Default interest will be charged if the net errors total more than the limit.

Tutorial note

In either case a penalty for submitting an incorrect return can be charged.

However, it is unlikely that a penalty will be charged for an error due to a mistake, rather than a deliberate error, where the mistake is small enough to be disclosed on the next VAT return.

ACCA marking scheme

			Marks
(a)	(i)	Trading profit	
		Operating profit	0.5
		Depreciation and amortisation	0.5
		Entertaining (Staff 0.5 Customers 0.5)	1.0
		Gifts to customers (Diaries 0.5 Food hampers 0.5)	1.0
		Lease premium – Assessable amount	1.5
		– Deduction	1.5
		P & M – Pool	3.0
		– Special rate pool	2.0
		– AIA	2.0
		– Low emission car	2.0
			15.0
	(ii)	Corporation tax computation	
		Trading profit	0.5
		Property business profit	
		– Rent receivable	1.0
		– Expenses	1.0
		Interest	1.0
		Corporation tax	0.5
			4.0
(b)	(i)	Default surcharge	
		Quarter ended 30 June 2011	1.0
		Quarter ended 30 September 2011	1.0
		Quarter ended 31 March 2012	2.0
		Quarter ended 30 June 2012	1.0
		Extension of surcharge period	1.0
		Four consecutive VAT returns on time	1.0
		Quarter ended 30 September 2013	1.0
			8.0
	(ii)	Errors on VAT return	
		Net errors below limit	1.0
		Net errors above limit	1.0
		Default interest	1.0
			3.0
Total			30.0

60 WIRELESS LTD (ADAPTED)  WALK IN THE FOOTSTEPS OF A TOP TUTOR

Key answer tips

This question has two independent parts.

Part (a) involved a classic corporation tax computation with the standard need to compute capital allowances.

Part (b) covers various aspects of VAT, and is mainly written.

The highlighted words in the written sections are key phrases that markers are looking for.

Tutor's top tips

Part (a) (i) should be an easy 2 marks, although you must make sure that you have two separately identifiable points in your answer.

Note that the requirement is only for the definition of when an accounting period starts, not when it ends. Try not to waste time giving information which is not mark earning.

Part (b) on VAT could have been answered next to obtain some more relatively easy marks very quickly.

(a) (i) **Start of an accounting period for corporation tax purposes**

- An accounting period will normally start immediately after the end of the preceding accounting period.
- An accounting period will also start when a company commences to trade or when its profits otherwise become liable to corporation tax.

(ii) **Wireless Ltd**

Tutor's top tips

Most important in this part was the need to read the question carefully and only produce the taxable total profits for the company.

There is no requirement to calculate the tax liability and you should not waste time producing unnecessary computations that will waste time and earn no marks.

There were a few tricky bits, notably the director's remuneration: remember that the employer's NIC is deductible too.

Taxable total profits – period ended 31 March 2014

	£
Trading profit	195,626
Less: Director's remuneration (W1)	(25,112)
Capital allowances – Plant and machinery (W2)	(126,431)
	44,083
Loan interest	1,110
Property income (W3)	12,600
	57,793
Less: QCD relief	(1,800)
Taxable total profits	55,993

Workings

(W1) **Director's remuneration**

The director's remuneration can be deducted as it was paid within nine months of the end of the period of account.

The employer's Class 1 NIC will be:

(£23,000 – £7,696) × 13.8% = £2,112

Total allowable deduction for employing director

(£23,000 salary + £2,112 employer's NIC) = £25,112

(W2) **Capital allowances – plant and machinery**

	£	*General pool* £	*Allowances* £
Additions (no AIA or FYA) (Note 1):			
Car (CO_2 between 96 – 130 g/km)		10,600	
Additions (with AIA):			
Office equipment	10,400		
Machinery	60,200		
Van (Note 2)	15,000		
Computer and software (Note 3)	40,000		
Alterations	4,700		
	130,300		
Less: AIA (£250,000 × 6/12) (Note 4)	(125,000)		125,000
		5,300	
		15,900	
Less: WDA (18% × 6/12) (Note 4)		(1,431)	1,431
TWDV c/f		14,469	
Total allowances			126,431

Tutorial note

1 *Cars purchased with CO_2 emissions of between 96 – 130 g/km are put in the general pool, and are eligible for WDA of 18%.*

2 *The CO_2 emissions are only relevant in relation to cars. A van is always a general pool addition.*

3 *Software is specifically deemed to be plant and machinery for capital allowances.*

4 *The maximum AIA must be time apportioned for a six month period, the maximum AIA is therefore £125,000 (£250,000 × 6/12).*

WDAs are also restricted to 6/12 because of Wireless Ltd's short accounting period.

5 *The private use of the car is irrelevant, full allowances are available. The director will be assessed to income tax on the private use of the car as an employment benefit.*

6 *The office equipment purchased on 20 September 2013 is pre-trading expenditure and is treated as incurred on 1 October 2013.*

(W3) **Property income**

	£
Premium received	10,000
Less: 2% × £10,000 × (10 – 1)	(1,800)
Assessment on premium	8,200
Rent receivable	4,400
Property income	12,600

Tutorial note

Alternative calculation of the assessment on the premium:

£10,000 × (51 – 10)/50 = £8,200

(b) **VAT issues**

Tutor's top tips

The examiner was disappointed with the candidates' lack of VAT knowledge.

The VAT rules are not hard, they are however extensive and they will be examined. Emphasis in your revision must therefore be put into learning the VAT rules as there is a guaranteed 10% of the exam on VAT each sitting.

It is useful to use bullet points for this type of written answer. Try to at least match the number of bullet points with the number of marks available. For part (iv) there is half a mark for each item therefore 6 points are required to earn the full marks available.

(i) **Compulsory registration**

- Wireless Ltd would have been liable to compulsory VAT registration when its taxable supplies during any 12-month period exceeded £79,000.
- This happened on 28 February 2014 when taxable supplies amounted to £87,100 (£9,700 + £18,200 + £21,100 + £14,800 + £23,300).
- Wireless Ltd would have had to notify HMRC by 30 March 2014, being 30 days after the end of the period.
- The company will have been registered from 1 April 2014 or from an agreed earlier date.

(ii) **Input VAT on goods purchased prior to registration**

- The goods must have been acquired for business purposes and not be sold or consumed prior to registration.
- The goods were acquired in the four years prior to VAT registration.

Input VAT on services supplied prior to registration

- The services must have been supplied for business purposes.
- The services were supplied in the six months prior to VAT registration.

(iii) **Advantage of voluntary registration**

- Wireless Ltd's sales are all to VAT registered businesses, so output VAT can be passed on to customers.
- The company's revenue would therefore not have altered if it had registered for VAT on 1 October 2013.
- However, registering for VAT on 1 October 2013 would have allowed all input VAT incurred from that date to be recovered.

(iv) **Additional information for a valid VAT invoice**

The following information is required:

(1) An identifying number (invoice number).

(2) Wireless Ltd's VAT registration number.

(3) The name and address of the customer.

(4) The type of supply.

(5) The rate of VAT for each supply.

(6) The quantity and a description of the goods supplied.

Examiner's report

Although fairly well answered, most candidates scored less marks on this question than on question one, despite it being potentially worth five marks more.

The first section of part (a) caused no problems for well-prepared candidates.

The second section was also well answered, although many candidates were unsure as to what adjustment was necessary for the director's remuneration, and the related national insurance contributions, that had not been taken into account when preparing the draft accounts.

However, the VAT aspects in part (b) were not so well answered.

Few candidates appreciated when VAT registration would have been necessary, with many candidates basing their answer on the future test rather than the historical test.

As regards voluntary VAT registration, few candidates appreciated that the company's revenue would not have altered given that all its customers were VAT businesses.

Very few candidates could provide more than two or three of the six pieces of additional information that the company needed to show on its sales invoices in order for them to be valid for VAT purposes.

ACCA marking scheme			
			Marks
(a)	(i)	End of preceding accounting period	1.0
		Commencement of trading	1.0
			2.0
	(ii)	Trading profit	0.5
		Director's remuneration	1.0
		Employer's Class 1 NIC	1.5
		P & M – Car treated correctly	1.0
		– No Private use adjustment	0.5
		– Office equipment included	0.5
		– Van treated correctly	1.0
		– Software treated as P&M	1.0
		– Alterations treated as P&M	1.0
		– AIA restricted	1.0
		– WDA on balance of additions	0.5
		– WDA	1.0
		Loan interest	0.5
		Property income	2.0
		QCD relief	1.0
			14.0
(b)	(i)	Registration limit	1.0
		February 2014	1.0
		Notification	1.0
		Date of registration	1.0
			4.0
	(ii)	Goods	
		Business purposes/Not sold or consumed	1.5
		Four year limit	1.0
		Services	
		Business purposes	0.5
		Six month limit	1.0
			4.0
	(iii)	Output VAT	1.0
		Revenue	1.0
		Input VAT	1.0
			3.0
	(iv)	An identifying number	0.5
		Wireless Ltd's VAT registration number	0.5
		The name and address of the customer	0.5
		The type of supply	0.5
		The rate of VAT for each supply	0.5
		Quantity and description	0.5
			3.0
Total			30.0

61 STARFISH LTD (ADAPTED)  *Walk in the footsteps of a top tutor*

Key answer tips

This question has two independent topics; the first three parts cover the corporation tax aspects of a loss making company, and the last part covers accounting for VAT on the cessation of the company. It is a demanding time pressured question.

Part (a) required a standard definition of when a chargeable accounting period starts and finishes. This should have provided 4 easy marks as long as the definition had been learnt and clearly stated, but would be difficult to score highly on if not learnt.

Part (b) involved a basic adjustment of profits computation with the standard requirement to calculate capital allowances. However, the period is loss-making and is the period of cessation. Particular care is therefore needed in the calculation of the capital allowances, especially as you are required to deal with the impact of VAT on the additions and disposals.

Part (c) was a little trickier as it involved the need to deal with two trading losses; an opening period loss and a terminal loss in the period of cessation. However, it is a company making the losses, not an individual and the loss relief rules for companies are much more straightforward. There are no special opening year and closing year rules to apply. The terminal loss can just be carried back 36 months rather than 12 months. Make sure you deal with the losses in strict date order.

It is therefore a fairly standard loss question which is largely computational and should not have been too difficult provided the approach to losses questions had been practised. For ease, a columnar format should be used to present the loss offset and remember to show your record of the losses and how they have been relieved in a working.

Part (d) was on VAT accounting. It was unusual in that this part was linked to the same company and previous parts of the question. The information required to produce the final VAT return was scattered throughout the question, rather than being presented as a separate independent part at the end (as in previous exams).

Nevertheless, it was a fairly straight forward VAT return and even if the specific rules on deregistration were not remembered, there were easy marks to be gained by preparing a normal VAT return with the information given.

Tutor's top tips:

This is a long time pressured question and you need to work through it methodically. The requirements are broken down into small parts which help you to structure your answer.

Part (a) is a wholly written question on accounting periods. If you do not know the rules then do not waste time trying to make them up.

There are four marks available for this part. This is usually a clue in written answers that there are either four key points or eight half points required to gain maximum marks.

(a) **When an accounting period starts**

- A chargeable accounting period (CAP) will normally start immediately after the end of the previous accounting period.
- A chargeable accounting period will also start when a company commences to trade, or otherwise becomes liable to corporation tax.

When an accounting period ends

- A chargeable accounting period will normally finish 12 months after the beginning of the accounting period or at the end of a company's period of account (if earlier).
- A chargeable accounting period will also finish when a company ceases to trade, when it otherwise ceases being liable to corporation tax, or on the commencement of winding up procedures.

(b) **Starfish Ltd**

Tax adjusted trading loss – period ended 31 March 2014

	Notes	£	£
Loss before taxation			190,000
Depreciation		25,030	
Donation to political party		300	
Qualifying charitable donation	1	1,350	
Impairment loss		0	
Legal fees			
– Internet domain name	2	0	
– Misleading advertisement	3	2,020	
– Issue of loan notes	4	0	
Entertaining customers	5	3,600	
Entertaining employees	5	0	
Counselling services	6	0	
Capital allowances (W)			2,300
		32,300	192,300
		(192,300)	
Trading loss		(160,000)	

Tutorial note

1 *Qualifying charitable donations (QCDs) made by a company to a charity are allowable deductions, but not from trading profit. They are deductible from total profits in the main corporation tax computation. Therefore, in the adjustment of profits computation they need to be added back to trading profit.*

2 *Legal fees in relation to protecting the company's internet domain are an allowable business expense incurred wholly and exclusively for the purposes of the trade.*

3 *Legal fees in relation to a Court action where it is proved that there was a misleading advertisement campaign by the company (i.e. the company has broken the law) would not be an allowable deduction.*

4 *Under the loan relationship rules all costs associated with loans related to the trade (e.g. loan notes to purchase machinery) are deductible in calculating trading profits. The costs of obtaining loan finance (even if abortive) are therefore allowable.*

5 *The only exception to the non-deductibility of entertainment expenditure is when it is in respect of employees.*

6 *The costs of counselling services for redundant employees are allowable.*

Working – Plant and machinery

	Notes	*Main pool*	*Special rate pool*	*Allowances*
		£	£	£
TWDV b/f		23,600	13,200	
Addition (£3,120 × 100/120)	1, 2	2,600		
		26,200		
Sale proceeds	2			
– Main pool				
(£31,200 + £1,800) × 100/120		(27,500)		
– Motor car	3		(9,600)	
		(1,300)		
Balancing charge		1,300		(1,300)
			3,600	
Balancing allowance			(3,600)	3,600
TWDV c/f		Nil	Nil	
Total allowances				2,300

Tutorial note

1 *The annual investment allowance and writing down allowances are not given for the period in which a trade ceases. Therefore the addition is simply added into the main pool.*

2 *The net cost (excluding VAT) of the addition is added to the main pool as input VAT is recovered on the purchase, and the net sale proceeds (excluding VAT) relating to the sale of main pool items is deducted.*

3 *Input VAT however would not have been recovered in respect of the motor car as it was not used exclusively for business purposes. Therefore, output VAT is not due on the disposal and the gross sale proceeds are deducted in the capital allowances computation.*

Tutor's top tips:

Once you have calculated your trading loss in part (b) you have to use it in the calculation of loss relief in part (c). Remember that even if your answer to part (b) is incorrect you will get marks for applying the rules correctly in part (c).

(c) **Starfish Ltd – Taxable total profits**

	4 m/e 31.3.2010	*y/e 31.3.2011*	*y/e 31.3.2012*	*y/e 31.3.2013*	*9 m/e 31.12.2013*	*3 m/e 31.3.2014*
	£	£	£	£	£	£
Trading profit	Nil	64,200	53,900	14,700	49,900	Nil
Less: Loss relief b/f	(–)	(12,600)	(–)	(–)	(–)	(–)
	Nil	51,600	53,900	14,700	49,900	Nil
Bank interest	600	1,400	1,700	Nil	Nil	Nil
	600	53,000	55,600	14,700	49,900	Nil
Less: Loss relief						
– Current period	(Nil)					(Nil)
– Carry back	n/a	(13,250)	(55,600)	(14,700)	(49,900)	
	600	39,750	Nil	Nil	Nil	Nil
Less: QCD relief	(600)	(1,000)	wasted	wasted	wasted	wasted
TTP	Nil	38,750	Nil	Nil	Nil	Nil

Loss working

	£
Tax adjusted trading loss – 3 m/e 31.3.2014	160,000
Relief given in:	
– 3 m/e 31.3.2014	(Nil)
– 9 m/e 31.12.2013	(49,900)
– y/e 31.3.2013	(14,700)
– y/e 31.3.2012	(55,600)
– y/e 31.3.2011 (3/12 × £53,000)	(13,250)
Loss unrelieved	26,550

Tutorial note

1 *Starfish Ltd would not have made a loss relief claim against total profits for the period ended 31 March 2010 as this would have used £600 of the loss, but wasted the qualifying charitable donations (QCDs) for that period and saved no tax as the QCDs already cover the taxable profits.*

2 *The trading loss for the period ended 31 March 2014 is a terminal loss, and can therefore be relieved against total profits:*

- *firstly for the period of the loss (£Nil in this case), and then*
- *carried back to the previous 36 months prior to the start of the loss-making period, on a LIFO basis.*

As there is a 9 month CAP in the terminal loss carry back period, the loss can be carried back into the year ended 31 March 2011 computation, but can only be set against 3/12 of the total profits in that year.

3 *Note that the terminal loss is offset against total profits (i.e. before QCDs). The relief for QCDs is therefore wasted in each of the last four CAPs. The loss relief is an all or nothing claim and cannot be restricted to preserve relief for the QCDs.*

(d) (i) **Starfish Ltd**

VAT return for the quarter ended 31 March 2014

	Notes	£	£
Output VAT			
Cash sales revenue (£38,520 × 20/120)			6,420
Credit sales revenue			
(£2,200 × 96% × 20%)	1		422
Sale of inventory (£28,800 × 20/120)	2		4,800
Sale of non-current assets			
(£31,200 + £1,800) × 20/120	3		5,500
			17,142
Input VAT			
Expenses			
(£69,960 – £4,320) = £65,640 × 20/120	4	10,940	
Impairment loss (given in question)	5	384	
Purchase of non-current asset			
(£3,120 × 20/120)		520	
			(11,844)
VAT payable			5,298

Tutorial note

1. *The calculation of output VAT on the credit sales revenue takes into account the discount for prompt payment, even for the 40% of customers that did not take it.*
2. *Output VAT on the sale of the remaining inventory based on the sale proceeds (not the original cost) must be accounted for.*
3. *Output VAT on the sale of the non-current assets must also be accounted for, but not on the motor car as input VAT was not recoverable when it was purchased.*
4. *Input VAT on business entertainment is not recoverable.*
5. *Relief for the impairment loss is available because the claim is made more than six months from the time that payment was due, and the debt has been written off in the company's books. The output VAT originally paid in respect of the sale of £384 is recoverable.*

   This amount is given in the question but could have been calculated as:

   (£2,000 × 96% × 20%) = £384

(ii) **If Starfish had sold the business as a going concern**

- A sale of a business as a going concern is not treated as a taxable supply, and therefore output VAT would not have been due on the sale of the inventory or the sale of the non-current assets.
- Instead of VAT being payable, Starfish Ltd would have been due a refund of £5,002 (£5,298 – £4,800 – £5,500).

Examiner's report

Part (a) surprisingly caused quite a few problems, with a number of candidates discussing long periods of account or, even worse, the basis period rules for unincorporated businesses.

Some candidates just stated that an accounting period starts when trading commences, and ends when trading ceases – which would imply that all companies have just one long accounting period.

Part (b) was very well answered, with many very good answers.

The only aspect consistently answered incorrectly was the treatment of a purchased asset. In the final capital allowances computation no allowances are given, so the addition should simply have been added to the main pool.

In part (c) many candidates overlooked the trading loss for the final period of trading.

The VAT calculation in part (d) was generally well answered, although few candidates appreciated that output VAT would not be due on the sale of inventory and non-current assets if the business was sold as a going concern.

Many candidates simply stated that no VAT would be due, which was too vague to score marks.

ACCA marking scheme

		Marks
(a)	When an accounting period starts	2.0
	When an accounting period finishes	2.0
		4.0
(b)	Depreciation	0.5
	Donations	1.5
	Impairment loss	1.0
	Legal fees	1.5
	Entertaining customers	0.5
	Entertaining employees	0.5
	Counselling services	0.5
	P & M – WDV brought forward	1.0
	– Addition	1.5
	– Main pool proceeds	2.0
	– Special rate pool proceeds	1.0
	– Balancing adjustments	0.5
		12.0
(c)	Trading profit	0.5
	Relief for 2010 loss – Period ended 31 March 2010	0.5
	– Carry forward	0.5
	Bank interest	0.5
	Relief for 2014 loss – Year ended 31 March 2011	1.0
	– Other periods	1.0
	Qualifying charitable donations	1.0
		5.0

(d)	(i)	Output VAT	– Cash sales revenue	1.5
			– Credit sales revenue	1.5
			– Inventory	1.0
			– Sale of non-current assets	0.5
		Input VAT	– Expenses	1.0
			– Impairment loss	1.0
			– Purchase of non-current asset	0.5
				7.0
	(ii)	Output VAT not due		1.0
		VAT refund		1.0
				2.0
Total				30.0

RELIEF FOR TRADING LOSSES

62 HALF-LIFE LTD (ADAPTED)

Key answer tips

A loss question which is largely computational but it involves the use of a normal ongoing trading loss, and a terminal loss.

There are two consecutive losses, the first arising from a short three month period. The second is the terminal loss of the last twelve months trading.

Make sure you get the easy marks and give the dates required in part (b).

For ease, use a columnar format to present the loss offset in part (a) and remember to show your record of the losses and their usage.

(a) **Taxable total profits**

	y/e 31.3.11	*y/e 31.3.12*	*y/e 31.3.13*	*p/e 30 .6.13*	*y/e 30.6.14*
	£	£	£	£	£
Trading profit	224,000	67,400	38,200	Nil	Nil
Property income	8,200	12,200	6,500	4,400	–
Chargeable gains	–	–	5,600	–	23,700
	232,200	79,600	50,300	4,400	23,700
Less: Loss relief					
– p/e 30.6.13 loss			(50,300)	(4,400)	
– y/e 30.6.14 loss (W)	(174,150)	(79,600)			(23,700)
	58,050	Nil	Nil	Nil	Nil
Less: QCD relief	(1,200)	wasted	–	–	wasted
Taxable total profits	56,850	Nil	Nil	Nil	Nil

Loss memorandum

Loss for the period ended 30 June 2013	61,700	
Loss for the year ended 30 June 2014		308,800
Losses utilised:		
Current period claim		
– Period ended 30 June 2013	(4,400)	
12 month carry back claim		
– y/e 31 March 2013	(50,300)	
Current year claim		
– y/e 30 June 2014		(23,700)
36 month terminal loss carry back claim		
– y/e 31 March 2012		(79,600)
– y/e 31 March 2011 (W)		(174,150)
Losses unrelieved	7,000	31,350

Working: Terminal loss – set off in y/e 31.3.11

For the year ended 31 March 2011, loss relief is restricted to £174,150 (£232,200 × 9/12) as only 9 months of the year falls into the 36 months carry back period from the start of the final loss making accounting period.

Tutorial note

The trading loss for the period ended 30 June 2013 can be relieved against total profits of the current period and the previous 12 months.

The trading loss for the year ended 30 June 2014 can be relieved against total profits of the current year and the previous 36 months because it is a terminal loss.

Unrelieved Qualifying Charitable Donations

Qualifying charitable donations of £1,000 and £700 for respectively the year ended 31 March 2012 and the year ended 30 June 2014 are unrelieved.

(b) **Due date for loss relief claims**

- The loss relief claims against total profits in respect of the loss for the period ended 30 June 2013 must be made by 30 June 2015.
- The loss relief claims against total profits in respect of the loss for the year ended 30 June 2014 must be made by 30 June 2016.

(c) **Corporation tax repayments**

Year ended 31 March 2011 (FY2010)

- Corporation tax of £36,571 (£174,150 at 21%) will be repaid in respect of the year ended 31 March 2011, since the relevant tax rate both before and after the loss relief claim is 21%.

Year ended 31 March 2012 (FY2011)

- Taxable total profits for the year ended 31 March 2012 were originally £78,600 (£79,600 – £1,000 QCD relief)
- Taxable total profits after loss relief is £Nil
- Corporation tax of £15,720 (£78,600 at 20%) will be repaid.

Year ended 31 March 2013 (FY2012)

- Taxable total profits for the year ended 31 March 2013 were originally £50,300
- Taxable total profits after loss relief is £Nil
- Corporation tax of £10,060 (£50,300 at 20%) will be repaid.

Tutorial note

No tax is repayable in respect of the period ending 30 June 2013 or year ended 30 June 2014 as no tax will have been paid in respect of these periods. The company is not making instalments and the corporation tax return for both periods will show corporation tax payable of nil.

63 LOSER LTD (ADAPTED)

Key answer tips

A tricky question on corporation tax loss reliefs. There are two trading losses to deal with and it is important to deal with the earlier loss first. It is also important to lay out your answer using a standard pro forma.

(a) **Factors influencing the choice of loss reliefs**

- The rate of corporation tax at which relief will be obtained, with preference being given to profits charged at the marginal rate of 23.75% in FY2013, 25% in FY2012 (27.5% in FY2011) and then the main rate of 23% in FY2013, 24% in FY2012 (26% in FY2011).
- The timing of the relief obtained, with a claim against total profits in the current year and previous 12 months resulting in earlier relief than a claim to carry forward the loss against future trading profits.
- The extent to which relief for qualifying charitable donations will be lost, since these cannot be carried forward.

(b) **Loser Ltd – Taxable total profits**

	y/e 30 June 2011	*p/e 31 March 2012*	*y/e 31 March 2013*	*y/e 31 March 2014*
	£	£	£	£
Trading profit	86,600	Nil	27,300	Nil
Property profit	–	4,500	8,100	5,600
Total profits	86,600	4,500	35,400	5,600
Less: Loss relief				
– Current period		(4,500)		(5,600)
– 12 months c/b	(21,200)		(35,400)	
	65,400	Nil	Nil	Nil
Less: QCD relief	(1,400)	Wasted	wasted	wasted
Taxable total profits	64,000	Nil	Nil	Nil

Loss working		
Trading loss	25,700	78,300
Loss against total profits		
– Current period (p/e 31.3.12)	(4,500)	
– 12 month carry back (y/e 30.6.11)	(21,200)	
– Current period (y/e 31.3.14)		(5,600)
– 12 month carry back (y/e 31.3.13)		(35,400)
Loss carried forward	Nil	37,300

(c) **If Loser Ltd ceased to trade on 31 March 2014**

- The whole of the trading loss for the final twelve months of trading can be relieved against total profits for the previous 36 months under the terminal loss relief rules.
- Therefore the unrelieved losses of £37,300 could have been carried back and fully set off in the year ended 30 June 2011.

ACCA marking scheme

		Marks
(a)	Rate of corporation tax	1.0
	Timing of relief	1.0
	Qualifying charitable donations	1.0
		3.0
(b)	Trading profit	0.5
	Property business profit	0.5
	Loss relief – current and carry back 12 months	2.0
	QCD relief	1.0
	Unrelieved trading loss	1.0
		5.0
(c)	Terminal loss relief – carry back 36 months	
	Year ended 30 June 2011	2.0
		2.0
Total		10.0

64 SOFA LTD (ADAPTED)  *Online question assistance*

Key answer tips

The first part of this question involves a standard adjustment of profit computation where the company is loss making. A detailed capital allowances computation is required and care should be taken as there are many places where this computation could go wrong.

The second part is more difficult and requires detailed group relief knowledge and the calculation of the maximum surrender possible to three subsidiaries including one with a non-coterminous year end and another which only joined the group part way through the year.

The part is independent and could be answered first, before part (a), as the question tells you to assume a loss of £200,000.

(a) **Trading loss – year ended 31 March 2014**

Tutorial note

An adjustment to profits calculation is required and the fact that the company is making a loss should not change your approach in any way.

Just start with a negative figure for the loss, then make the same adjustments as you would make if it were a profit and lay out your answer in the same way.

Remember that it is important to list all the major items indicated in the question requirement, showing a zero (0) for expenditure that is allowable. This is because credit will be given for showing no adjustment where none is needed.

List the adjustments in the order they appear in the question.

If required, also add notes to show why you have not adjusted for an item, or why you have added it back. However, lengthy explanations are not required where the requirement is just to 'calculate' the adjusted profits, rather than to explain them.

Always show your workings if the figure you are adjusting for is not clear from the question.

	£	£
Loss before taxation	(88,820)	
Depreciation	150,820	
Audit and accountancy (Note 1)	0	
Legal fees – issue of share capital (Note 2)	7,800	
Legal fees – renewal of 10 year lease (Note 3)	0	
Legal fees – issue of loan note (Note 2)	0	
Construction of new wall (Note 4)	9,700	
Repairing wall (Note 4)	0	
Entertaining suppliers (Note 5)	1,360	
Entertaining employees (Note 5)	0	
Counselling employees (Note 6)	0	
Health and safety fine	420	
Profit on disposal of shares		4,300
Bank interest received		8,400
Interest payable (Note 7)	0	
Capital allowances – Plant and machinery (W1)		269,308
	81,280	282,008
	(282,008)	
Trading loss	(200,728)	

Tutorial note

1 *Audit and accountancy is allowable, as it is incurred wholly and exclusively for the purposes of the trade.*

2 *Legal fees in connection with the issue of share capital are not allowable, being capital in nature. However, the cost of obtaining loan finance is allowable as a trading expense under the loan relationship rules as the loan was used for trading purposes.*

3 *The cost of renewing a short-lease (less than 50 years) is specifically allowable as a trading expense.*

4 *The new wall is not allowable, being capital in nature. However, repairing a wall is allowable.*

5 *The only exception to the non-deductibility of entertainment expenditure is when it is in respect of employees.*

6 *The costs of counselling services for redundant employees are specifically allowable.*

7 *Interest on a loan used for trading purposes is deductible in calculating the trading loss on an accruals basis.*

Workings

(W1) **Plant and machinery – Capital allowances computation**

		Main pool	*Short life asset*	*Special rate pool*	*Allow-ances*
	£	£	£	£	£
TWDV b/f		16,700	16,400		
Additions (No AIA or FYA) (Note 1):					
Car (CO_2 > 130 g/km)				22,200	
Car (CO_2 between 96 – 130 g/km)		10,900			
Additions (with AIA):					
Fixtures (Note 2)	44,800				
Less :AIA (Max)	(44,800)				44,800
				Nil	
Equipment	211,400				
Less :AIA (Note 2)	(205,200)				205,200
		6,200			
Disposal proceeds: Short life asset			(15,800)		
Car (2)		(8,800)			
Lorry		(7,600)			
		17,400	600	22,200	
Balancing allowance			(600)		600
WDA (18%)		(3,132)			3,132
WDA (8%)				(1,776)	1,776
Additions with FYA					
Car (CO_2 < 96 g/km)	13,800				
Less: FYA (100%)	(13,800)				13,800
		Nil			
TWDV c/f		14,268		20,424	
Total allowances					269,308

Tutorial note

1 Capital allowances on car purchases are calculated based on the CO_2 emissions of the car as follows:

CO_2 emissions of < 96 g/km:
eligible for a FYA of 100%.

CO_2 emissions of between 96 – 130 g/km:
put in main pool, eligible for a WDA at 18%.

CO_2 emissions of > 130 g/km:
put in special rate pool, eligible for a WDA at 8%.

The appropriate rates are given in the tax rates and allowances.

2 Remember to include the expenditure on the fixtures and fittings in the second hand building in the special rate pool as they are integral features. The AIA should be claimed against this expenditure in priority to the main pool additions as otherwise it would only be eligible for WDAs at 8%.

(b) **Maximum group relief**

Settee Ltd

The accounting periods of Settee Ltd and Sofa Ltd are not coterminous. Therefore, Settee Ltd's taxable total profits and Sofa Ltd's trading loss must be apportioned on a time basis.

Year ended 31 March 2014 and year ended 30 June 2013

The corresponding accounting period is 1 April 2013 to 30 June 2013 (3 months)

Year ended 31 March 2014 and year ended 30 June 2014

The corresponding accounting period is 1 July 2013 to 31 March 2014 (9 months)

Settee Ltd can therefore claim the following group relief:

CAP to 30 June 2013

Sofa Ltd can surrender (3/12 × £200,000)	£50,000
Settee Ltd can accept (3/12 × £240,000)	£60,000

Therefore maximum loss claim is £50,000.

CAP to 30 June 2014

Sofa Ltd can surrender (9/12 × £200,000)	£150,000
Settee Ltd can claim (9/12 × £90,000)	£67,500

Therefore maximum loss claim is £67,500.

Couch Ltd

Couch Ltd is not a 75% subsidiary of Sofa Ltd, so no group relief claim is possible.

Futon Ltd

Futon Ltd did not commence trading until 1 January 2014, so the corresponding accounting period is the 3 months from 1 January 2014 to 31 March 2014.

Sofa Ltd can surrender (3/12 × £200,000)	£50,000
Futon Ltd can claim	£60,000

Therefore maximum loss claim is £50,000.

Examiner's report

Part (a) of this question was very well answered.

A certain amount of bad examination technique was evident as regards the adjustments in computing the trading loss.

Some candidates went into far too much detail explaining the adjustments made, thus wasting time, whilst others produced figures without any workings at all. This was fine for correct answers, but not so for incorrect ones.

Where no adjustment was necessary, such as for the interest payable, then this fact should have been clearly shown or stated.

Most candidates did not answer part (b) very well.

Many candidates wasted a lot time by performing detailed calculations showing the amount of group relief that should have been claimed rather than the amount that actually could be claimed.

ACCA marking scheme

			Marks
(a)	Loss before taxation		0.5
	Depreciation		0.5
	Professional fees		2.5
	Repairs and renewals		1.0
	Other expenses		2.5
	Profit on disposal of shares		0.5
	Bank interest received		0.5
	Interest payable		1.0
	P & M	– Purchases	1.5
		– Short life asset sold	1.5
		– Special rate motor car acquired	1.0
		– Fixtures treated as special rate pool additions	1.0
		– AIA and WDA	3.0
		– Balancing allowance	1.0
		– Pool items sold	1.0
		– Low emission car	1.0
			20.0
(b)	Settee Ltd		2.5
	Couch Ltd		1.0
	Futon Ltd		1.5
			5.0
Total			25.0

65 VOLATILE LTD (ADAPTED)  *Walk in the footsteps of a top tutor*

Key answer tips

A familiar style corporation tax losses question requiring relief to be claimed as soon as possible and a calculation of the loss left to carry forward.

Tutor's top tips

Part (a) requires a purely written answer highlighting the key factors that influence the choice of loss relief.

Only 3 marks are available, suggesting that 3 bullet points will suffice to answer this part.

This requirement is a common request in losses questions and you should learn the factors so that you can jot them down quickly in the exam.

(a) **Factors influencing the choice of loss reliefs**

- Rate of relief

  The rate of corporation tax at which relief will be obtained is an important factor. Preference should be given to profits charged at the marginal rate of 23.75% (25% for FY2012 and 27.5% for FY2011) first, then profits charged at the main rate of 23% (24% for FY2012 and 26% for FY2011) and lastly profits charged at the small profits rate of 20%.

- Cash flow

  The timing of the relief obtained is a key factor. A claim against total profits in the loss making period, then carry back will result in earlier relief than a claim against future trading profits.

- Wastage of Qualifying Charitable Donations

  The extent to which relief for qualifying charitable donations will be lost is another factor, since these cannot be carried forward.

Tutorial note

Remember that for companies, a carry back election cannot be made until the current year total profits have been relieved first.

(b) **Taxable total profits**

	y/e 31 Dec 2011	*9 m/e 30 Sept 2012*	*y/e 30 Sept 2013*
	£	£	£
Trading profit	15,200	78,700	Nil
Property business profit	6,500	–	–
Chargeable gains	–	–	9,700
Total profits	21,700	78,700	9,700
Less: Loss relief (W)			
Current year			(9,700)
Carry back – 12 months	(5,425)	(78,700)	
	16,275	Nil	Nil
Less: QCD relief	(1,200)	wasted	wasted
Taxable total profits	15,075	Nil	Nil

Loss working

	£
Trading loss	101,800
Current year relief (Note)	(9,700)
Carry back relief (previous 12 months)	
– 9 m/e 30 September 2012	(78,700)
	13,400
– y/e 31 December 2011 (£21,700 × 3/12)	(5,425)
Unrelieved loss as at 30 September 2013	7,975

Tutorial note

For the year ended 31 December 2011 loss relief is restricted to the lower of:

(i) the proportion of the profits of that period of account that falls into the 12 months carry back period preceding 1 October 2012 (i.e. 3 months)

= (£21,700 × 3/12) = £5,425

(ii) the remainder of the loss = £13,400

Examiner's report

This question was not particularly well answered.

In part (a) far too many candidates explained the loss reliefs available rather than the factors influencing the choice of claims.

In part (b) many candidates approached this on a year by year basis, rather than one computation with a column for each of the periods. This not only wasted time in having to write out several computations, but also made it very difficult to calculate the correct loss relief claims.

Other common mistakes included treating the chargeable gains separately (rather than as part of the taxable total profits), and deducting qualifying charitable donations from trading profits rather than total income after loss relief.

ACCA marking scheme

		Marks
(a)	Rate of corporation tax	1.0
	Timing of relief	1.0
	Impact on qualifying charitable donations	1.0
		3.0
(b)	Trading profits	0.5
	Property business profits	0.5
	Chargeable gains	0.5
	Loss relief – Year ended 30 September 2013	1.0
	– Period ended 30 September 2012	1.0
	– Year ended 31 December 2011	2.0
	Qualifying charitable donations	1.0
	Unrelieved trading losses	0.5
		7.0
Total		10.0

WITH GROUP ASPECTS

66 STRAIGHT PLC (ADAPTED)

Key answer tips

This question starts with a diagram of a group but most of the marks in the question can be obtained without having to think about the group aspects at all. However, be careful to answer the question set, so that in part (a) you are asked simply to calculate the trading profit.

When writing an explanation of why the companies form a gains group, it is important to give enough detail in your answer and to apply your knowledge to the facts of the question. A calculation of the effective interest of Straight plc in each of the companies is necessary to illustrate your answer.

(a) **Tax adjusted trading profit – year ended 31 March 2014**

	£	£
Operating profit	173,915	
Depreciation	21,200	
Car lease costs (15% × £8,500) (Note 1)	1,275	
Entertaining customers (Note 2)	10,000	
Entertaining staff (Note 2)	0	
Fine (Note 3)	1,250	
Capital allowances (W)		18,992
	207,640	18,992
	(18,992)	
Tax adjusted trading profit	188,648	

Tutorial note

1 *A flat rate disallowance of 15% of the leasing costs applies to cars with CO_2 emissions exceeding 130 g/km. Note that there is no disallowance for cars with CO_2 emissions of 130 g/km or less.*

2 *The only exception to the non-deductibility of entertainment expenditure is when it is in respect of employees.*

The £150 limit per head for staff entertaining is only relevant in determining whether the party represents a taxable benefit on the employees, all of the cost is an allowable deduction for the company.

3 *Fines for breach of regulations are disallowable.*

Working: Plant and machinery capital allowances

		Main pool	*Special rate pool*	*Allowances*
	£	£	£	£
TWDV b/f		35,200	18,400	
Addition (with AIA)	12,400			
Less: AIA (Note 1)	(12,400)			12,400
		Nil		
Disposal proceeds			(15,200)	
		35,200	3,200	
Less: WDA (18%)		(6,336)		6,336
Less: WDA (8%) (Note 2)			(256)	256
TWDV c/f		28,864	2,944	
Total allowances				18,992

Tutorial note

1 There is only one AIA of £250,000 for a group of companies which can be allocated to any of the group companies in whatever proportions the group requires. However, this aspect of capital allowances is not examinable, so you should assume that the maximum AIA is claimed by Straight plc.

2 A balancing allowance can only arise on the main and special rate pools on the cessation of trade. Therefore the disposal of the only asset in the special rate pool does not result in a balancing allowance.

(b) (i) **Capital gains group**

- Companies form a capital gains group if at each level in the group structure there is a 75% shareholding.
- The parent company must have an effective interest of over 50% in each group company.
- Arc Ltd, Bend Ltd and Curve Ltd are all 75% subsidiaries, and Straight plc has an effective interest of 100% in Arc Ltd, 80% in Bend Ltd and 60% (80% × 75%) in Curve Ltd. Therefore all of the companies form a capital gains group.
- If Straight plc's holding in Arc Ltd were 80%, it would have an effective interest of less than 50% in Curve Ltd (80% × 80% × 75% = 48%) and Curve Ltd would not be part of Straight plc's capital gains group.

(ii) **Corporation tax computation – year ended 31 March 2014**

	£
Trading profit (part (a))	188,648
Less: Loss relief b/f	(15,000)
	173,648
Net chargeable gains (W1)	70,000
Taxable total profits	243,648
Plus: FII (£9,000 × 100/90) (Note)	10,000
Augmented profits	253,648
Corporation tax (W2) (£243,648 at 23%)	56,039
Less: Marginal relief	
3/400 × (£375,000 – £253,648) × £243,648/£253,648	(874)
Corporation tax payable	55,165

Tutorial note

Group dividends are not included as franked investment income. Therefore only the dividend from Triangle plc is included in the calculation of augmented profits.

Workings

(W1) **Net chargeable gain**

	£
Chargeable gain	140,000
Less: Rollover relief (see below)	(60,000)
Chargeable gains after rollover relief	80,000
Less: Capital loss b/f	(10,000)
Net chargeable gain	70,000

Sale proceeds of £80,000 (£350,000 – £270,000) are not reinvested in qualifying business assets.

Therefore £80,000 of the £140,000 gain will be chargeable in the year ended 31 March 2014.

A rollover relief claim can be made to defer the balance of the gain of £60,000 (£140,000 – £80,000). The gain is rolled over against the base cost of the replacement asset.

(W2) **Corporation tax rates**

		£
Upper limit	(£1,500,000 × 1/4)	375,000
Lower limit	(£300,000 × 1/4)	75,000
Augmented profits		253,648
		Marginal relief applies

There are four associated companies in the group.

(iii) **Joint election for capital gains**

- Straight plc and Arc Ltd must make the election by 31 March 2016 (i.e. within two years of the end of the accounting period of the company making the disposal outside of the group).
- Arc Ltd's unused capital loss of £40,000 can be set against Straight plc's gain of £70,000, leaving £30,000 net chargeable gain.
- This is beneficial as relief for the capital loss is obtained at the highest marginal rate of corporation tax in FY2013 of 23.75%, and would otherwise be unused and carried forward.

67 ANIMAL LTD (ADAPTED)

Key answer tips

A familiar style of group loss relief question which requires group losses to be allocated to group members in the most beneficial manner.

The group relief calculations are quite tricky, involving companies joining and leaving the group and recognising the different rates of tax paid by the group members. The examiner has however made the question slightly easier by telling you how many associated companies to use when calculating the small profits limits.

Note also that 40% of the marks for this question do not relate to the group relief calculations – so do not get bogged down in these and make sure you pick up the marks for the written sections which were easy marks if the relevant definitions had been learnt.

There were easy marks available for explaining the definition of a group for group loss relief purposes. Note that for 3 marks you would expect to make three separate points.

Similarly there were three easy marks for explaining when companies are associated. The examiner has kindly given you additional guidance by stating how many associates there are in the Animal Ltd group. Again for three marks you would be expected to make three separate points.

(a) **Group relief group**

- One company must be a 75% subsidiary of the other, or both companies must be 75% subsidiaries of a third company.
- The holding company must have an effective interest of at least 75% of the subsidiary's ordinary share capital.
- The holding company must have the right to receive at least 75% of the subsidiary's distributable profits and net assets on a winding up.

(b) **Associated companies**

- Bat Ltd, Cat Ltd, Dog Ltd, Fox Ltd and Gnu Ltd are all under the common control (shareholding of over 50%) of Animal Ltd, and are therefore associated companies.
- Where a company such as Elk Ltd has been dormant throughout the accounting period, it does not count as an associated company.
- Companies that are only associated for part of the accounting period, such as Cat Ltd and Dog Ltd, count as associated companies for the whole of the period.

(c) **Taxable total profits – year ended 31 March 2014**

	Animal Ltd	*Bat Ltd*	*Cat Ltd*	*Dog Ltd*	*Fox Ltd*
	£	£	£	£	£
Trading profit	450,000	65,000	85,000	100,000	60,000
Property income	5,000	15,000			
	455,000	80,000	85,000	100,000	60,000
Less: Group relief (W)	(95,000)	(30,000)	(35,000)	(25,000)	(15,000)
Taxable total profits	360,000	50,000	50,000	75,000	45,000

Reasons for group relief strategy

- The primary aim for the group is to save as much tax as possible when utilising the loss.
- Gnu Ltd's trading loss is most effectively relieved so as to bring the augmented profits of as many group companies as possible down to the small profits rate limit (see working below).
- The relevant lower and upper limits for corporation tax purposes are £50,000 (£300,000 ÷ 6) and £250,000 (£1,500,000 ÷ 6) respectively.

Tutorial note

It has been assumed that neither Cat Ltd nor Dog Ltd have any further associated companies arising from the periods when they were not part of the Animal Ltd group of companies.

- Given the level of TTP and FII, Gnu Ltd should bring the augmented profits of Bat Ltd, Cat Ltd, Dog Ltd and Fox Ltd down to £50,000.

  This saves corporation tax at the highest marginal rate of 23.75%%.
- As Dog Ltd has only been part of the group for three months of the year, group relief is restricted to a maximum of £25,000, being 3/12ths of its TTP (£100,000 × 3/12).
- Cat Ltd left the group part way through the year, however loss relief given to Cat Ltd is not restricted as the maximum group relief is the lower of the available loss of Gnu Ltd of £150,000 (£200,000 × 9/12) and the available profits of Cat Ltd of £63,750 (£85,000 × 9/12). Only £35,000 loss is required to bring its augmented profits down to £50,000.
- The balance of Gnu Ltd's trading loss of £95,000 (£200,000 – £30,000 – £35,000 – £25,000 – £15,000) is surrendered to Animal Ltd.

  This saves corporation tax at the main rate of 23%.

Working: Augmented profits

	Animal Ltd	*Bat Ltd*	*Cat Ltd*	*Dog Ltd*	*Fox Ltd*
	£	£	£	£	£
TTP before group relief	455,000	80,000	85,000	100,000	60,000
Plus: FII	20,000				5,000
Augmented profits	475,000	80,000	85,000	100,000	65,000
Lower limit	50,000	50,000	50,000	50,000	50,000
Group relief required to bring to lower limit	425,000	30,000	35,000	75,000	15,000
Rate of tax saving	23%	23.75%	23.75%	23.75%	23.75%

Tutorial note

Strictly, the rate of tax saving in Fox Ltd is not exactly 23.75%, as FII received by a company paying tax at the marginal rate will slightly change the rate of tax in the margin. However, for the purposes of the F6 exam it is perfectly acceptable to assume that the marginal rate applies.

ACCA marking scheme

		Marks
(a)	75% subsidiary	1.0
	Ordinary share capital	1.0
	Distributable profits/Net assets	1.0
		3.0
(b)	Identification of companies	1.0
	Dormant companies	1.0
	Associated for part of accounting period	1.0
		3.0
(c)	Trading profits	1.0
	Property business income	0.5
	Group relief – Relevant limits	1.0
	Group relief – Tax rates	1.0
	Group relief – Animal Ltd	1.0
	Group relief – Bat Ltd	0.5
	Group relief – Cat Ltd	1.0
	Group relief – Dog Ltd	1.0
	Group relief – Fox Ltd	1.0
	FII	1.0
		9.0
Total		15.0

68 TOCK-TICK LTD (ADAPTED)

Key answer tips

A long question requiring a computation of corporation tax with some group aspects included as a separate requirement.

It is important to have a methodical way of working through the question so you do not miss any important information. Use the standard pro formas for adjustment of profit and for capital allowances.

When considering the group aspects in part (c), don't forget that a subsidiary is counted as an associate, so reducing the small profits limits for calculating corporation tax.

(a) **Tax adjusted trading profit – year ended 31 March 2014**

Key answer tips

In the adjustment to profits calculation it is important to list all the major items indicated in the question requirement, showing a zero (0) for expenditure that is allowable.

This is because credit will be given for showing no adjustment where none is needed. List the adjustments in the order they appear in the question.

If required, also add notes to show why you have not adjusted for an item, or why you have added it back. However, lengthy explanations are not required where the requirement is just to 'calculate' the adjusted profits, rather than to explain them.

Always show your workings if the figure you are adjusting for is not clear from the question.

Tutorial note

1 *Impaired debts charged in accordance with financial accounting guidelines by a company are allowable for tax purposes, as they will be specific in nature.*

2 *Gifts to customers are an allowable deduction if they cost less than £50 per recipient per year, are not of food, drink, tobacco or vouchers exchangeable for goods, and carry a conspicuous advertisement for the company making the gift.*

Therefore the gift of the pens is allowable, but the gift of hampers of food is not allowable.

3 *The long service award is deductible in calculating the trading profit.*

4 *A donation to a national charity by a company is a qualifying charitable donation and is allowable as a deduction from total profits in the company's taxable total profits computation. It is not also allowable in the adjustment of profits computation; therefore it must be added back in this computation.*

Small gifts to local charities, where the company receives some benefit (e.g. advertising) are an allowable deduction from the trading profits.

5 *Audit and accountancy fees, costs of registering a trademark and debt collection fees are all allowable as incurred wholly and exclusively for the purposes of the trade.*

6 *Legal fees in connection with the issue of share capital are not allowable, being capital in nature. However, legal fees in connection with the* ***renewal*** *of a* ***short*** *lease (i.e. life of 50 years or less) are specifically allowable.*

7 *The replacement of the roof is allowable since the whole structure is not being replaced. The office extension is not allowable, being capital in nature.*

8 *The only exception to the non-deductibility of entertainment expenditure is when it is in respect of employees.*

9 *The costs of counselling services for redundant employees and of seconding an employee to charity are allowable.*

10 *Interest on a loan used for trading purposes is deductible in calculating the trading profit* on an accruals basis.

	£	£
Profit before taxation	186,960	
Impaired debts (Note 1)	0	
Depreciation	99,890	
Gifts to customers – pens (Note 2)	0	
Gifts to customers – food hampers (Note 2)	720	
Donation to political party	6,450	
Long service awards (Note 3)	0	
Qualifying charitable donation (Note 4)	600	
Donation to local charity (Note 4)	0	
Audit and accountancy (Note 5)	0	
Legal fees – issue of share capital (Note 6)	2,900	
Costs of registering a trademark (Note 5)	0	
Legal fees – renewal of a short lease (Note 6)	0	
Legal fees – debt collection (Note 5)	0	
Legal fees – court action	900	
Replacing roof (Note 7)	0	
Office extension (Note 7)	53,300	
Entertaining suppliers (Note 8)	2,160	
Counselling services for staff (Note 9)	0	
Secondment of staff to a charity (Note 9)	0	
Disposal of office building		78,100
Loan interest received		12,330
Capital allowances (W)		13,136
Interest payable (Note 10)	0	
	353,880	103,566
	(103,566)	
Tax adjusted trading profit	250,314	

Working – Plant and machinery

		General pool	*Special rate pool*	*Short-life asset*	*Allowances*
	£	£	£	£	£
TWDV b/f		12,200	21,600	2,300	
Additions (with AIA)					
Equipment	6,700				
Less: AIA	(6,700)				6,700
		Nil			
Less: Disposal proceeds (Note 1)			(33,600)	(460)	
		12,200	(12,000)	1,840	
Balancing charge (Note 2)			12,000		(12,000)
Balancing allowance				(1,840)	1,840
Less: WDA (18%)		(2,196)			2,196
Additions (with FYA)					
Car (CO_2 < 96 g/km)	14,400				
Less: FYA (100%)	(14,400)				14,400
		Nil			
TWDV c/f		10,004	Nil	Nil	
Total allowances					13,136

Tutorial note

1 *The sale proceeds for the high emission motor car sold are restricted to original cost.*

2 *A balancing allowance can only arise on the general or special rate pools when a company ceases trading, however a balancing charge can arise on any pool at any time if the balance on the pool becomes negative.*

(b) **Taxable total profits – y/e 31 March 2014**

	£
Trading profit	250,314
Interest income – Loan interest	12,330
Chargeable gain (W)	16,211
	278,855
Less: QCD relief	(600)
Taxable total profits	278,255

Working: Chargeable gain

	£
Sale proceeds	300,000
Less: Cost	(197,900)
	102,100
Less: Indexation allowance (given)	(85,889)
Chargeable gain	16,211

(c) **Effect on taxable total profits**

(i) **Group relief**

- Tock-Tick Ltd owns more than 75% of the share capital of Clock Ltd. They therefore form a group for group relief purposes.
- The accounting periods are not coterminous, so the claim for group relief would be restricted to the lower of:
  (i) Available loss of Clock Ltd
  (1 April 2013 – 31 December 2013) = (£62,400 × 9/12) = £46,800
  (ii) Available profits of Tock-Tick Ltd
  (1 April 2013 – 31 December 2013) = (£278,255 × 9/12) = £208,691
- Tock-Tick Ltd's taxable total profits would therefore have been reduced by £46,800.

Group rollover relief

- Tock-Tick Ltd owns more than 75% of the share capital of Clock Ltd. They therefore form a gains group. In a gains group, gains realised by one group company can be rolled over into assets acquired by another group company.
- The sale proceeds from the disposal of the office building are not fully reinvested, and so £6,000 (£300,000 – £294,000) of the capital gain cannot be rolled over.
- Tock-Tick Ltd's taxable total profits would therefore have been reduced by £10,211 (£16,211 – £6,000).

(ii) **Corporation tax liability – year ended 31 March 2014**

	£
Original taxable total profits	278,255
Less: Group relief	(46,800)
Gain rolled over	(10,211)
Revised taxable total profits	221,244
Corporation tax (£221,244 at 23%) (W)	50,886
Less: Marginal relief	
3/400 × (£750,000 – £221,244)	(3,966)
Corporation tax liability	46,920

Working: Corporation tax rates

Tock-Tick Ltd has one associated company.

The small profit rate limits are therefore £750,000 (£1,500,000 × 1/2) and £150,000 (£300,000 × 1/2).

The company is therefore a marginal relief company.

69 MUSIC PLC (ADAPTED)

Key answer tips

In this question there are 9 marks for written explanations of the gains group and associated company rules. It is important to state the basic rule and then apply to the facts of the question. Be careful with the overseas company, which is included but unable to enjoy the benefits of gains group status.

When calculating property business profit, always watch out for furnished lettings which will need a calculation of wear and tear allowance. Property 3 has a lease premium received which is a tricky area but is examined fairly regularly and so you should learn the pro forma calculation.

(a) **Capital gains group**

- Companies form a capital gains group if at each level in the group structure there is a 75% shareholding, provided the parent company has an effective interest of at least 50%.
- Alto Ltd, Bass Ltd, Cello Ltd, Echo Inc and Flute Ltd are all 75% subsidiaries, and Music plc has an effective interest of 60% (80% × 75%) in Flute Ltd. All of these companies therefore form a capital gains group.
- However, Bass Ltd and Cello Ltd will only be included in respect of assets acquired or disposed of whilst they were members of the group.

- Drum Ltd and Gong Ltd are not included since Drum Ltd is not a 75% subsidiary, and Music plc's effective interest in Gong Ltd is only 48% (80% × 75% × 80%).
- Although Echo Inc is included in the definition of the capital gains group, companies that are resident overseas are not able to take advantage of the provisions applicable to a capital gains group.

(b) **Associated companies**

- Alto Ltd, Bass Ltd, Cello Ltd, Echo Inc, Flute Ltd and Gong Ltd are all under the common control of Music plc, and are therefore associated companies.
- For associated company purposes, it does not matter where a company is resident. Echo Inc is therefore included despite being resident overseas.
- Companies that are only associated for part of the accounting period, such as Bass Ltd and Cello Ltd, count as associated companies for the whole of the period.
- Drum Ltd is not included as an associated company since Music plc's effective interest in this company is only 45%.

(c) **Property business income – year ended 31 March 2014**

	£	£
Rent – Property 1 (£2,500 × 4 × 7/12)		5,833
– Property 2 (£650 × 9) + £700 (Note)		6,550
– Property 3 (£2,000 × 9/12)		1,500
– Property 4 (£500 × 9)		4,500
		18,383
Lease premium – Property 3 (W1)		36,900
		55,283
Allowable deductions:		
Irrecoverable debt – Property 2	650	
Decoration – Property 1	2,500	
Advertising/fees (£1,500 + £250)	1,750	
Council tax/water rates (£1,200 + £600)	1,800	
Repairs – Property 2	500	
Wear and tear allowance – Property 1		
(£5,833 – £1,800) × 10% (Note)	403	
		(7,603)
Property business income		47,680

Key answer tips

The company is assessed on the net profits from all properties.

It is therefore not necessary to compute profits/losses for each property separately and one combined computation is all that is needed.

Tutorial note

Property 1

The replacement dishwasher is disallowed as it is an item of capital as Music plc claims the wear and tear allowance. The wear and tear allowance is calculated on rent received less council tax and water rates paid by the landlord.

Property 2

Property business income is calculated on the accruals basis. The date that rent is received is irrelevant.

Relief is available for irrecoverable debts.

Similarly the invoice received in April for work carried out in March 2014 should be accrued for in the accounts to 31 March 2014.

Property 4

Expenditure incurred on making the property inhabitable is capital and is therefore not deductible.

Workings

(W1) **Property business income – Property 3**

	£
Premium received	45,000
Les: 2% × £45,000 × (10 – 1)	(8,100)
Assessment on premium received (Note)	36,900

Tutorial note

Alternative calculation of the assessment on the sub lease:

£45,000 × (51 – 10)/50 = £36,900

(d) **Corporation tax liability – year ended 31 March 2014**

	£
Trading profit	92,000
Interest income	12,000
Property business income (part (c))	47,680
Net chargeable gains (W1)	23,000
Taxable total profits	174,680
Plus: Franked investment income	15,000
Augmented profits	189,680
Corporation tax (£174,680 × 23%) (W2)	40,176
Less: Marginal relief	
3/400 × (£214,286 – £189,680) × £174,680/£189,680	(170)
Corporation tax liability	40,006

Tutorial note

1 *The capital gain of £120,000 is included in Music plc's taxable total profits since an appropriate election has been made with Alto Ltd. Capital losses may be set against this gain.*

2 *Group dividends are not included as franked investment income.*

Workings

(W1) **Net chargeable gain**

	£
Net chargeable gain in the year (by election)	120,000
Less: Capital losses in the year	(65,000)
	55,000
Less: Capital losses b/f	(32,000)
Net chargeable gain	23,000

(W2) **Corporation tax rates**

		£
Upper limit	(£1,500,000 × 1/7)	214,286
Lower limit	(£300,000 × 1/7)	42,857
Augmented profits		189,680
		Marginal relief applies

There are seven associated companies in the group.

(e) **Bank loan**

All costs incurred in connection with the loan will be taxed in accordance with the loan relationship rules. Therefore the tax treatment of the loan interest and the arrangement fee will be the same.

Under the loan relationship rules costs incurred in relation to loans used for the purposes of the trade are deductible as trading expenses. If the loan was therefore used to acquire plant and machinery, the interest and arrangement fee would be deducted from the company's trading profit.

Costs incurred in relation to loans used for non-trade purposes are deductible from interest income. If the loan was used to acquire a property which was to be rented out, the interest and fees would therefore be deducted not from trading income, and not from property business income (as for individuals), but from the company's interest income.

70 GASTRON LTD (ADAPTED)  *Walk in the footsteps of a top tutor*

Key answer tips

This was a classic corporation tax computational question, requiring an adjustment of profits and capital allowances computation, corporation tax computation, and some self-assessment.

All these areas are highly likely to be tested and should be well practiced.

Parts (d) and (e) involve capital gains groups, which may be seen as tricky, but most of the marks can be won by simply stating the rules, rather than needing application to the question.

Tutor's top tips

This question has clear mark allocations, which should be used to allocate the time spent on each section. You need to adopt a logical approach, using the requirements to break down the information and plan your answer.

It is possible to score very well on this sort of question, which is not technically difficult, as long as you do not panic over the quantity of information.

Part (a) gives you clear guidance on the approach that is needed, and you should follow this – starting with the profit before tax and then making the necessary adjustments.

Work through the notes in order, and ensure you have dealt with every single item, as credit is given for showing an adjustment of nil where one is not necessary, as stated in the requirement.

If you are not sure of how to deal with an item, make a sensible assumption and move on, but do not ignore it, or waste unnecessary time.

Note that as the question has asked you to 'calculate' the adjusted profits you do not need to explain each adjustment that you make, but you should show any workings.

Make sure you do a separate capital allowances working, which is clearly referenced, as there are a number of purchases and disposals in the period, and a full working is required.

(a) **Trading profit – year ended 31 March 2014**

	£	£
Profit before taxation	640,000	
Depreciation	85,660	
Amortisation of leasehold property (Note 1)	6,000	
Deduction for lease premium (W2)		4,920
Gifts of pens to customers (Note 2)	1,200	
Gifts of hampers to customers (Note 2)	1,100	
Donation (Note 3)	0	
Legal fees re renewal of lease (Note 4)	0	
Legal fees re issue of a loan note (Note 4)	0	
Entertaining suppliers (Note 5)	1,300	
Entertaining employees (Note 5)	0	
Income from investments		87,000
Profit on disposal of shares		80,700
Interest payable (Note 6)	0	
Capital allowances (W1)		45,848
	735,260	218,468
Allowable deductions	(218,468)	
Tax adjusted trading profit	516,792	

Tutorial note

1 *The amortisation of a lease is disallowable (just like depreciation), but there is relief for the 'revenue' element of the premium. See working 2 for the calculation of the allowable deduction.*

The annual allowable deduction is calculated as the assessment on the landlord spread over the length of the lease.

2 *Gifts to customers are only an allowable deduction if they cost less than £50 per recipient per year, are not of food, drink, tobacco, or vouchers exchangeable for goods, and carry a conspicuous advertisement for the company making the gift.*

The pens cost £60 and the hampers contain food, therefore neither are allowable.

3	*Small donations to a local charity are allowable where they benefit the trade (e.g. free advertising).*
4	*The cost of renewing a short-lease (less than 50 years) is specifically allowable. The legal fees in connection with the loan note which was used for trading purposes is deductible from trading profits under the loan relationship rules.*
5	*The only exception to the non-deductibility of entertainment expenditure is when it is in respect of employees.*
6	*Interest on a loan used for trading purposes is deductible in calculating the trading profit on an accruals basis.*

Workings

(W1) **Plant and machinery – year ended 31 March 2014**

		Main pool	*Special rate pool*	*Allowances*
	£	£	£	£
TWDV b/f		16,700	18,400	
Additions (no AIA or FYA):				
Car (CO_2 between 96 – 130 g/km)		9,800		
Additions (with AIA):				
Equipment	6,800			
Lorry	17,200			
	24,000			
Less: AIA (100%)	(24,000)			24,000
		Nil		
Disposal proceeds – equipment		(3,300)		
		23,200	18,400	
WDA (18%)		(4,176)		4,176
WDA (8%)			(1,472)	1,472
Addition qualifying for FYA				
Car (CO_2 < 96 g/km)	16,200			
Less: FYA (100%)	(16,200)			16,200
		Nil		
TWDV c/f		19,024	16,928	
Total allowances				45,848

Tutorial note

Capital allowances on car purchases are calculated based on the CO_2 emissions of the car as follows:

- *CO_2 emissions of < 96 g/km:*
  eligible for a FYA of 100%.
- *CO_2 emissions of between 96 – 130 g/km:*
  put in main pool, eligible for a WDA at 18%.
- *CO_2 emissions of > 130 g/km:*
  put in special rate pool, eligible for a WDA at 8%.
- *The appropriate rates are given in the tax rates and allowances.*

(W2) **Deduction for lease premium**

Tutor's top tips

Many students find dealing with lease premiums tricky; however, it is simply a case of learning the formula and applying it to the figures in the question.

There is no other way to attempt to deal with this question if you haven't learnt the formula!

The office building has been used for business purposes, and so the proportion of the lease premium assessed on the landlord can be deducted from trading profits.

The allowable deduction is the amount assessed on the landlord, spread over the life of the lease.

Assessment on landlord:

	£
Premium received	60,000
Less: 2% × £60,000 × (10 – 1)	(10,800)
Assessment on landlord (Note)	49,200
Allowable deduction (£49,200 ÷ 10)	4,920

Tutorial note

Alternative calculation of the assessment on the landlord:

£60,000 × (51 – 10)/50 = £49,200

(b) **Corporation tax computation – year ended 31 March 2014**

Tutor's top tips

Part (b) requires a corporation tax computation, which will incorporate the figure calculated in part (a).

As long as you use the adjusted trading profit figure you have calculated correctly you can score full marks here, even if you have made errors earlier in the question.

The year-end falls entirely in FY2013 and therefore the corporation tax liability can be calculated in one computation.

	£
Trading profit	516,792
Property business profit (W1)	12,800
Bank interest	12,400
Chargeable gain	74,800
Taxable total profits	616,792
Plus: FII (£36,000 × 100/90) (Note)	40,000
'Augmented profits'	656,792
Corporation tax	
FY2013: (£616,792 at 23%) (W2)	141,862
Less: Marginal relief	
3/400 × (£750,000 – £656,792) × £616,792/£656,792	(656)
Corporation tax liability	141,206

Tutorial note

Group dividends are not included as franked investment income. Therefore only the dividends received from Tasteless plc, the unconnected company will be grossed up and added to the taxable total profits to calculate augmented profits.

Workings

(W1) **Property business profit**

		£	£
Rent receivable	– First tenant (£1,800 × 9)		16,200
	– Second tenant (£1,950 × 2)		3,900
			20,100
Irrecoverable rents (£1,800 × 2) (Note)		3,600	
Decorating costs		3,700	
			(7,300)
Property business profit			12,800

Tutorial note

The rent is taxable on an accruals basis, and therefore all 9 months of rent for the first tenant are included. However, as the tenant left owing two months' rent, the irrecoverable rent is an allowable deduction.

(W2) **Corporation tax rate**

Gastron Ltd has one associated company, so the upper limit is reduced to £750,000 (£1,500,000 × ½) and the lower limit £150,000 (£300,000 × ½).

Augmented profits fall in between the limits, therefore marginal relief applies.

(c) **Corporation tax due dates and interest**

Tutor's top tips

Part (c) requires the due date for payments of corporation tax and the interest that will be charged if the tax is paid late.

It is important to actually calculate the interest here, rather than simply stating the way it will be calculated. All calculations should be to the nearest month unless the question says otherwise.

Note that the rates of late payment interest and repayment interest are given in the tax tables.

- Gastron Ltd's corporation tax liability for the year ended 31 March 2014 must be paid by 1 January 2015.
- If the company does not pay its corporation tax until 31 August 2015, then interest of £2,824 (£141,206 at 3% = £4,236 × 8/12) will be charged by HM Revenue and Customs for the period 1 January 2015 to 31 August 2015.

(d) **Definition of a capital gains group**

Tutor's top tips

This part requires only a definition of a capital gains group for 2 marks.

It is useful to learn this definition, as this is a common requirement in a question involving groups.

- Companies form a capital gains group if at each level in the group structure there is a 75% shareholding.
- However, the parent company must also have an effective interest of over 50% in each group company.

(e) **Gains group election**

Tutor's top tips

Knowledge of time limits and deadlines is very useful for obtaining easy marks.

The most common deadline for claims and elections for corporation tax is two years from the end of the accounting period, and if you don't know the deadline, this can be a good guess to make!

However, it is important to state the actual date, not just the general rule, so you must apply the rule to the dates in the question.

- Gastron Ltd and Culinary Ltd must make the election by 31 March 2016 (i.e. within two years of the end of the accounting period in which the disposal outside of the group occurred).
- Culinary Ltd's otherwise unused capital loss of £66,000 can be set against Gastron Ltd's chargeable gain of £74,800.
- It is beneficial for the balance of the chargeable gain of £8,800 (£74,800 – £66,000) to arise in Culinary Ltd as it will only be taxed at the rate of 20%, instead of at the marginal rate (23.75%) in Gastron Ltd.

Tutorial note

It is not necessary to do a further corporation tax computation in order to calculate the most beneficial way of making this election.

The question states that Culinary is paying tax at 20%, and in part (b) you have calculated that Gastron Ltd is paying tax at 23% less marginal relief. This means that profits falling into the marginal band suffer tax at an effective rate of tax of 23.75%.

It can be useful to learn the effective rate of tax in the margin, as this will help you to quickly calculate the benefit of any tax or loss relief.

Examiner's report

This question was very well answered, with only part (e) consistently causing problems.

In part (a) candidates were instructed to list all of the items referred to in the notes, and to indicate by the use of zero any items that did not require adjustment. This method should be quicker for candidates than writing separate explanatory notes, and shows that they have considered any non-taxable and non-deductible items, rather than simply forgetting about them.

Candidates are advised that this will be a standard approach in future and they should ensure they follow this instruction to be able to score full marks.

Despite the instruction some candidates did not list those items not requiring any adjustment.

Parts (a) and (b) were kept separate for a very good reason – namely to help candidates. Therefore those candidates who attempted to combine both parts into one calculation not surprisingly often had problems.

Given the new capital allowances rules, it was pleasing to see many candidates correctly calculate the correct figure for capital allowances. Although I can applaud candidate's attempts to save paper, it is not good examination technique to try and squeeze a capital allowances computation of this size into 5 or 6 lines at the end of a page.

In part (c) a disappointing number of candidates gave 31 January as the payment date.

Only a few candidates appreciated that interest would be due, and fewer still correctly calculated the actual amount payable.

In part (d) most candidates appreciated that a 75% shareholding was necessary, but were then often unsure where the 50% limit fitted in. The holding company must have an effective interest of 50%.

In part (e) many candidates simply stated that losses could be set against profits, without making any attempt to use the information given in the question.

ACCA marking scheme

		Marks
(a)	Profit before taxation	0.5
	Depreciation	0.5
	Amortisation of leasehold property	0.5
	Lease premium – assessable amount	1.5
	Lease premium – deduction	1.0
	Gifts of pens to customers	0.5
	Gifts of hampers to customers	0.5
	Donation	0.5
	Legal fees re renewal of lease	0.5
	Legal fees re issue of loan note	0.5
	Entertaining suppliers	0.5
	Entertaining employees	0.5
	Income from investments	1.0
	Disposal of shares	0.5
	Interest payable	0.5
	Plant and machinery – Main pool	2.0
	– AIA	1.5
	– Special rate pool	1.0
	– FYA	1.0
		15.0
(b)	Trading profit	0.5
	Property business profit	2.0
	Bank interest	0.5
	Chargeable gain	0.5
	Franked investment income	1.0
	Group dividends	0.5
	Corporation tax	2.0
		7.0
(c)	Due date	1.0
	Interest	2.0
		3.0
(d)	75% shareholding	1.0
	50% effective interest	1.0
		2.0
(e)	Time limit	1.0
	Set off of capital losses	1.0
	Tax rate	1.0
		3.0
Total		30.0

71 MICE LTD (ADAPTED)  *Walk in the footsteps of a top tutor*

Key answer tips

This corporation tax question is lengthy and time pressured with a lot of information to assimilate quickly and efficiently.

Part (a) starts with some detailed property income calculations and then the application of the corporation tax loss rules. With the removal of overseas aspects of corporation tax from the syllabus, this part is now simpler than when the question was originally set.

Parts (b) and (c) have a less familiar style in that they require advice and explanations (without revising previous calculations) in respect of the maximum possible surrender of losses within a group for 3 marks, and the maximum capital allowances that can be claimed.

The answers show that what the examiner expected was not difficult and only applied mainstream knowledge, however in an unfamiliar style. They also involved concentrating on specific aspects of the calculations, which may have caused some problems if unprepared.

Part (d) was also unusual in that students would not have come across this style of question before. It required advice about the increased tax cost to both the company and the individual should they increase the remuneration of a higher paid employee.

Again, the calculations are not difficult but it is necessary to be able to understand the impact of transactions on tax and "think in the margin". All that was required is the additional tax chargeable, not the total tax cost.

Tutor's top tips

This question can appear daunting on first reading; however it is possible to score very well on this sort of question as long as you do not panic over the quantity of information.

Remember to read the requirements carefully.

The requirements to this question lead you through how to tackle the question in the correct logical order, and it has clear mark allocations, which should be used to allocate the time spent on each section.

The first part requires a calculation of the property business profit before you consider the impact of the losses.

(a) (i) **Property business profit – year ended 31 March 2014**

Tutor's top tips

Where a company (or individual) has several rental properties, the profits and losses are pooled/aggregated to calculate the net profit or loss (i.e. current period losses are automatically set off against current period profits).

There is no need to do separate calculations of the profit and loss for each property, only one computation is required.

Set up your answer with sub-headings "Income" and "Allowable expenses" and leave space underneath to insert the relevant information as you go through each property in the question.

	£	£
Rent accrued – Property 1 (£3,200 × 4)		12,800
– Property 2		6,000
– Property 3		Nil
		18,800
Premium received for sub-lease (Property 2)	18,000	
Less: £18,000 × 2% × (8 – 1)	(2,520)	
		15,480
		34,280
Business rates	2,200	
Repairs	1,060	
Rent paid	7,800	
Advertising	680	
Insurance (£460 + £310 + (£480 × 3/12))	890	
Loan interest	Nil	
		(12,630)
Property business profit		21,650

Tutorial note

1 *The enlargement of the car park is capital expenditure which cannot be deducted when calculating the property business profit.*

2 *For Property 2, the rental paid by Mice Ltd for the original lease is an allowable deduction from the income received from the sub-lease.*

3 *For Property 3, rents accrued up to 31 March are assessed in the year ended 31 March 2014. As the property is not let until 1 April 2014, there is no assessable income. The rent received in advance before 1 April 2014 is not relevant to this question and will be assessed next year.*

4 *Interest paid in respect of a loan used to purchase property by a company is not an allowable deduction against property income, but is an allowable deduction against interest income under the loan relationship rules.*

(ii) **Taxable total profits**

Tutor's top tips

Note that the question asks for the taxable total profits of the current year, which is clearly loss making, and the previous years as the loss will be carried back if reliefs are to be claimed as soon as possible.

The examiner's answer did this in two sets of computations; however one set of computations including all of the years would gain equal credit and may save time.

Remember to highlight the "total profits" subtotal against which the loss is deducted (i.e. total profits before qualifying charitable donations).

	p/e 31.3.11	*y/e 31.3.12*	*y/e 31.3.13*	*y/e 31.3.14*
	£	£	£	£
Trading profit	83,200	24,700	51,200	Nil
Property business profit	2,800	7,100	12,200	
part (a)(ii)				21,650
Interest income (Note 1)				
(£6,400 + £3,200 – £1,800)				7,800
Chargeable gain				10,550
Total profits	86,000	31,800	63,400	40,000
Less: Loss relief (Note 3)				
Current year				(40,000)
Carry back 12 months			(63,400)	
	86,000	31,800	Nil	Nil
Less: QCD relief	(1,000)	(1,500)	–	–
Taxable total profits	85,000	30,300	Nil	Nil

Loss working

	£
Trading loss	180,000
Current year relief – y/e 31 March 2014	(40,000)
Carry back relief (12 months) – y/e 31 March 2013	(63,400)
Unrelieved loss as at 31 March 2014	76,600

Tutorial note

1 *Interest income includes all interest received and receivable (i.e. accrued) to 31 March 2014 and interest paid and payable in respect of the loan to purchase Property 3 is deducted.*

2 *Remember that, for companies, a carry back election for losses cannot be made unless the current year total profits have been relieved first.*

3 *There is no restriction to the amount of loss relief that can be claimed for carry back to the previous 12 months (i.e. year ended 31 March 2013).*

4 *Note that the dividend received grossed up by 100/90 is treated as franked investment income when calculating the applicable rate of corporation tax, but this is not part of the requirement of this question.*

(b) **Maximum amount of group relief – year ended 31 March 2014**

Tutor's top tips

Web-Cam Ltd has been a subsidiary throughout the whole of Mice Ltd's year ended 31 March 2014, however it has a June year end, not March.

As a result, time apportionment of the profits and losses is required to calculate the maximum group relief in each corresponding accounting period.

*It was not necessary to consider the optimum use of the loss here, as the requirement asked only for the **maximum** amount of group relief which could be claimed.*

Any time spent considering how the loss should be used would be wasted, and would not score any marks.

- For the three-month period ended 30 June 2013, the maximum group relief is:

  The lower of

  (i) Available profits of Web-Cam Ltd = £28,000

  (ii) Available loss of Mice Ltd for the corresponding period

  = (£180,000 × 3/12) = £45,000

- For the year ended 30 June 2014, the maximum group relief is calculated for the corresponding period of 9 months from 1 July 2013 to 31 March 2014 as:

  The lower of

  (i) Available profits of Web-Cam Ltd = (£224,000 × 9/12) = £168,000

  (ii) Available loss of Mice Ltd = (£180,000 × 9/12) = £135,000

- The total maximum group relief that Mice Ltd can surrender to Web-Cam Ltd in respect of its £180,000 loss in the year ended 31 March 2014 is therefore:

  (£28,000 + £135,000) = £163,000

(c) **Maximum amount of capital allowances claim**

Tutor's top tips

Two alternative purchases are to be considered here and 4 marks are available in total. Make sure an equal amount is spent on each part and try not to overrun on this part.

Remember that the requirement is to explain and not to just calculate a number.

Equipment

- The first £250,000 of expenditure will qualify for the annual investment allowance (AIA) at the rate of 100%, whilst the balance of expenditure will qualify for the writing down allowance (WDA) at the rate of 18%.
- The maximum capital allowances claim will therefore be: (£250,000 + (£100,000 at 18%)) = £268,000

Ventilation system

- The AIA will be available in the same way as for the equipment. However, the ventilation system will be integral to the factory and is therefore classified as 'special rate pool' expenditure.

  The balance of expenditure will therefore only qualify for a writing down allowance (WDA) of 8%.

- The maximum capital allowances claim will therefore be: (£250,000 + (£100,000 at 8%)) = £258,000

(d) **Additional amount of income tax and National Insurance**

Tutor's top tips

The managing director is clearly a higher rate taxpayer already and will remain so after the bonus payment. Therefore tax will be paid at the marginal rate of 40%.

Calculations can therefore be performed 'in the margin'; i.e. calculating the additional tax due at the marginal rate, rather than working the full income tax computation.

- The managing director's additional income tax liability for 2013/14 will be:
  (£40,000 at 40%) = £16,000
- The additional employee's Class 1 NIC will be:
  (£40,000 at 2%) = £800
- The additional employer's Class 1 NIC will be:
  (£40,000 at 13·8%) = £5,520

Tutorial note

As the managing director is clearly higher paid with taxable income in excess of £32,010, any additional income will be taxed to income tax at 40%.

Additional Class 1 Primary NICs payable by the managing director will be payable at 2% as the upper limit for NIC of £41,450 is also clearly exceeded.

Employers pay 13.8% Class 1 Secondary NICs on all of an employee's cash earnings in excess of £7,696, with no upper limit.

The MD has no other income in 2013/14, therefore his total taxable income will not exceed £100,000 and there will be no restriction of the personal allowance.

Examiner's report

This question was generally very well answered, especially the calculation of the property business profit in part (a) where most candidates scored virtually maximum marks.

In part (b) several candidates explained whether or not group relief would be available rather than calculating the amount of relief.

In part (c) most candidates were aware of what capital allowances were available.

Many candidates complicated part (d) by performing long calculations, making this much more time consuming than necessary for 3 marks. However, they should have appreciated that this was additional remuneration so the calculations were simply £40,000 × 40%, £40,000 × 2% and £40,000 × 13.8% for the 3 marks.

ACCA marking scheme

			Marks
(a)	(i)	Lease premium received	1.5
		Rent receivable – Property 1	1.0
		– Property 2 and 3 (0.5 marks each)	1.0
		Business rates	0.5
		Repairs	1.0
		Rent paid	0.5
		Advertising	0.5
		Insurance	1.5
		Loan interest	0.5
			8.0
	(ii)	Year ended 31 March 2014 – Property business profit	0.5
		Loan interest	1.5
		Dividend income not taxed	0.5
		Chargeable gain	0.5
		Loss relief	0.5
		Other periods – Trading profit	0.5
		Property business profit	0.5
		Loss relief	2.0
		QCD relief	0.5
			7.0
(b)		Period ended 30 June 2013	1.5
		Year ended 30 June 2014	1.5
			3.0
(c)		Equipment	2.0
		Ventilation system	2.0
			4.0
(d)		Income tax	1.0
		Employee's NIC	1.0
		Employer's NIC	1.0
			3.0
Total			25.0

72 NEUNG LTD (ADAPTED)  *Walk in the footsteps of a top tutor*

Key answer tips

This corporation tax question is fairly lengthy and may be time pressured.

Part (a)(i) involves application of the associated companies rules in a relatively simple scenario. It is only for 2 marks and time must not be wasted here, however you are asked to give reasons and therefore cannot get full marks for simply stating which companies are associated.

Part (a)(ii) covers the bulk of the marks for this part, in respect of a short adjustment of profits calculation, a fairly detailed capital allowances computation, the calculation of taxable total profits and then the calculation of the corporation tax liability. The question originally contained some overseas income and branch losses, however these aspects are no longer in the syllabus and have been replaced by a trading loss in a group company. This is a relatively straightforward group relief scenario. You must also be careful to remember the implications of the associated companies you have determined in the previous part.

Part (a)(iii) also related to overseas aspects of corporation tax and has been replaced by a further question regarding group relationships.

Part (b) was a VAT question, and although it involves the same company as part (a) it is a stand-alone question.

Part (b)(i) asks you to calculate the output VAT payable rather than the overall VAT payable, therefore there is no information regarding expenses and you do not need to deal with input VAT at all. You need to apply the tax point rules here, as well as dealing with the fuel scale charge.

Part (b)(ii) relates to the default surcharge, which is regularly tested and should not have caused any problems for a well prepared student who knows these rules.

Part (b)(iii) is a VAT administration question regarding invoicing and some common sense comments may have received marks here, but to get full marks it is important to know the rules.

Tutor's top tips

This question can appear daunting on first reading; however it is possible to score very well on this sort of question as long as you do not panic over the parts where you may be less confident.

Remember to read the requirements carefully. In particular make sure you provide the explanations required in part (a)(i) and to consider all the taxation consequences of the disposal of the shares – think about associates and the gains group as well as the group relief group. However, do not be tempted to discuss any chargeable gain on the disposal of the shares as you have specifically been told not to!

(a) (i) **Associates**

- To be associated there must be a shareholding of more than 50% therefore Second Ltd is not an associated company.
- Dormant companies are not included as associates therefore Fourth Ltd is not an associate.
- Third Ltd and Fifth Ltd are associated companies as Neung Ltd has a shareholding of more than 50% in both, and they are trading companies.

Tutorial note

You need to learn the rules to determine associates, as this is regularly tested in F6. It is also important to know what the implications of these rules are, which has an impact in the next part.

(ii) **Neung Ltd – Taxable total profits – year ended 31 March 2014**

Tutor's top tips

It is important to take a logical step by step approach here. Think through which calculations you will need to do in workings and in particular make sure that your workings for the capital allowances are clearly laid out (on a new sheet of paper) and well referenced.

Remember to consider how to deal with the group loss.

Be careful to consider the impact of the associates on the tax computation – what effect will they have on the limits? Will there be any effect on the FII?

	£
Trading profit (W1)	374,466
Interest income (£25,200 + £12,600)	37,800
	412,266
Less: Group relief	(15,700)
Taxable total profits	396,566
Plus: FII (£37,800 × 100/90)	42,000
Augmented profits	438,566

	£
Corporation tax at marginal rate (W4):	
£396,566 × 23%	91,210
Less: Marginal relief	
3/400 × (£500,000 – £438,566) × £396,566/£438,566	(417)
Corporation tax liability	90,793

Tutorial note

Fifth Ltd's trading loss is available to Neung Ltd as it is a 100% subsidiary and therefore in a group relief group. Since the only other company in the group (Fourth Ltd) is dormant, the whole loss should be surrendered to Neung Ltd.

The dividend received from Second Ltd is grossed up by 100/90 to calculate the FII but the dividend received from Third Ltd is not included as the company is an associate.

Workings

(W1) **Trading profit**

		£
Operating profit		627,300
Depreciation		11,830
Amortisation		7,000
Less:	Lease deduction (W2)	(4,340)
	Capital allowances (W3)	(267,324)
Trading profit		374,466

(W2) **Lease deduction**

	£
Premium paid	140,000
Less: £140,000 × 2% × (20 – 1)	(53,200)
Assessment on landlord	86,800
Allowable deduction per year (£86,800 ÷ 20)	4,340

Tutorial note

Since the property is used for business purposes, a deduction is allowed for the revenue element of the lease premium (which is the amount assessable on the landlord), spread over the life of the lease.

Alternative calculation of the assessment on the landlord:

£140,000 × (51 – 20)/50 = £86,800

(W3) **Capital allowances**

	£	Main pool £	Short life asset £	Special rate pool £	Allowances £
TWDV b/f		4,800	22,800	12,700	
Additions (no AIA)					
Motor car (1)				15,400	
Motor car (2)		28,600			
Additions (with AIA)					
Ventilation system	312,000				
Less: AIA	(250,000)				250,000
				62,000	
		33,400	22,800	90,100	
WDA (18%)		(6,012)			6,012
WDA 18%			(4,104)		4,104
WDA (8%)				(7,208)	7,208
TWDV c/f		27,388	18,696	82,892	
Total allowances					267,324

Tutorial notes

1 *Capital allowances on new car purchases are calculated based on the CO_2 emissions of the car as follows:*

- *CO_2 emissions of ≤ 95 g/km:*

  eligible for a FYA of 100% (none in this question)
- *CO_2 emissions of between 96 – 130 g/km:*

  put in main pool and eligible for a WDA at 18% (i.e. Motor Car (2))
- *CO_2 emissions of > 130 g/km:*

  put in special rate pool and eligible for a WDA at 8% (i.e. Motor Car (1))

2 *The short life asset is an item of machinery and is eligible for a WDA at 18%.*

3 *The ventilation system is an integral feature of the freehold office building and is therefore included in the special rate pool. The AIA should always be given against special rate pool expenditure in priority to any other expenditure as it is only eligible for allowances at 8%.*

(W4) **Corporation tax rate**

Neung Ltd has two associated companies as identified in part (a)(i), therefore there are three associated companies in total.

		£
Upper limit	(£1,500,000 ÷ 3)	500,000
Lower limit	(£300,000 ÷ 3)	100,000
Augmented profits		438,566
		Marginal relief applies

(iii) **Taxation consequences of selling 40% of the shares in Fifth Ltd**

- Neung Ltd will hold 60% of the shares in Fifth Ltd after the disposal, therefore Fifth Ltd will continue to be an associated company and there will be no change in the limits.
- Neung Ltd is currently claiming group relief for Fifth Ltd's losses, but loss relief will no longer be available from 1 April 2014 as Fifth Ltd will cease to be in the group relief group, since the shareholding will fall below 75%.
- Fifth Ltd will also no longer be in the capital gains group as the shareholding will fall below 75% and therefore all gains group advantages will cease to be available.

Tutorial note

There are only 3 marks available for this part, therefore it is not necessary to go into great detail about the group definitions. Three short bullet points is sufficient to gain all the marks.

(b) (i) **Output VAT payable – quarter ended 31 March 2014**

Tutor's top tips

Calculation of output VAT payable is effectively half of the VAT return. You are not being asked to calculate input VAT at all.

Calculating the VAT payable is a common requirement and you need to remember to look out for certain common elements:

1 *Be careful with the distinction between exempt and zero rated supplies – one is taxable and the other is not.*

2 *Are the figures inclusive or exclusive of VAT? It will always state somewhere in the question, and it is possible that some figures will be inclusive and others will be exclusive – check the wording carefully.*

3 *Be careful to check the tax point rules in relation to any transactions as it is possible that some sales will not be taxable in the period covered in the question.*

4 *Fuel scale charges are commonly tested – you need to calculate the VAT element of the scale charge given in the question.*

	£
Sales to VAT registered customers:	
(£44,600 – £35,200) × 20%	1,880
VAT invoice issued on 1 March 2014:	1,600
Sales to non-VAT registered customers:	
(£289,300 – £241,300) × 20/120	8,000
Fuel scale charge (£404 × 20/120)	67
Output VAT payable	11,547

Tutorial notes

1 *Exempt sales are not subject to VAT and must therefore be excluded from the calculations.*

2 *The basic tax point for a contract for services is when the services are completed. However, the basic tax point will be overridden by the actual tax point if payment is received prior to that date or an invoice is issued either prior to or within 14 days after the basic tax point. The actual tax point is therefore the date of invoice and the whole contract is taxable within this period.*

3 *When calculating the VAT from a VAT inclusive amount the gross figure should be multiplied by 20/120 or 1/6.*

(ii) **Default surcharge implications of late VAT return**

- The late submission of the VAT return for the quarter ended 30 September 2012 will have resulted in HM Revenue & Customs issuing a surcharge liability notice specifying a surcharge period running to 30 September 2013.
- The late submission of the VAT return for the quarter ended 30 June 2013 will have resulted in an extension to the surcharge period to 30 June 2014.
- The late submission and VAT payment for the quarter ended 31 March 2014 will therefore be the second default within the surcharge period, and will result in a surcharge of 5% of the VAT due for the period. This surcharge will not be collected if it is less than £400.
- In addition, the surcharge period will be extended to 31 March 2015.

(iii) **VAT invoices**

- Neung Ltd is required to issue a VAT invoice when it makes standard rated sales to a VAT registered business
- Neung Ltd is not required to issue a VAT invoice when it makes sales to the general public (i.e. non-VAT registered customers), unless the customer requests one.
- They are also not required to issue VAT invoices in respect of any exempt sales.
- A simplified invoice can be issued if the supply is less than £250.
- VAT invoices must be issued within 30 days of the date the taxable supply is treated as being made.

Examiner's report

This question was generally well answered, and there were many very good answers.

In **part (a)(i)**, candidates should realise that when given a list of four companies, it is good exam technique to explain for each company whether it is or is not treated as being associated.

In **part (a)(ii)**, the only aspect which consistently caused problems was the asset that was integral to a building. Although candidates correctly claimed the annual investment allowance against this expenditure, many candidates then claimed the 40% first year allowance on the balance of expenditure, rather than adding it into the special rate pool. *[Note that the 40% FYA is no longer available so this would no longer be a potential issue in this question].*

Several candidates treated the lease premium as income rather than as a deduction.

Candidates should try to use a new page for large capital allowances computations.

[The examiner's comments on part (a)(iii) related to overseas income, which is no longer examinable, and therefore these comments have been deleted.]

Part (b)(i) was well answered, although a number of candidates did not appreciate that the tax point for services supplied was when the invoice was issued, as this was before the basic tax point or the date of payment.

Some candidates showed (an incorrect) input VAT figure for the cost of fuel despite the question only requiring a calculation of the output VAT.

Part (b)(ii) was not as well answered as would have been expected, and too many candidates simply explained the default surcharge rules without applying them to the company's situation.

Part (b)(iii) was also often not well answered, with far too many candidates stating that a VAT invoice would not have to be issued if the company was not registered for VAT, when quite clearly it was registered.

ACCA marking scheme

				Marks
(a)	(i)	Second Ltd		0.5
		Fourth Ltd		0.5
		Third Ltd and Fifth Ltd		1.0
				2.0
	(ii)	Operating profit		0.5
		Depreciation		0.5
		Amortisation		0.5
		Lease premium	– Assessable amount	1.5
			– Deduction	1.0
		Capital allowances	– AIA	1.5
			– Pool	1.5
			– Short life asset	1.0
			– Special rate pool	1.5
		Loan interest		1.0
		Group relief		1.0
		Franked investment income		1.0
		Group dividend		0.5
		Corporation tax		2.0
				15.0
	(iii)	Associated company		1.0
		Group relief group		1.0
		Gains group		1.0
				3.0
(b)	(i)	Sales to VAT registered customers		1.0
		Additional contract		1.0
		Sales to non-VAT registered customers		1.0
		Fuel scale charge		1.0
				4.0
	(ii)	Previous late submissions		1.0
		Surcharge		1.0
		Extension of surcharge period		1.0
				3.0
	(ii)	Circumstances		2.0
		Period		1.0
				3.0
Total				30.0

VALUE ADDED TAX

73 CONFUSED LTD

Key answer tips

A more difficult question than usual testing less mainstream topics in VAT.

The first part requires clear explanation of the differences between standard rated, zero rated and exempt supplies. Do not worry if you missed the point that traders making wholly zero rated supplies need not register.

The last part has some tricky points on sale of a business and the difference between selling assets individually or as a complete business.

(a) **Standard rated supplies**

- Confused Ltd will be required to register for VAT as it is making taxable supplies in excess of the registration limit of £79,000.
- Output VAT of £16,000 (£80,000 × 20%) per month will be due, and input VAT of £1,667 (£10,000 × 20/120) per month will be recoverable.

Zero-rated supplies

- Confused Ltd will be required to register for VAT as it is making taxable supplies in excess of the registration limit of £79,000.
- However, as it is making zero-rated supplies, when it is required to register it can apply for an exemption from registration if it wishes.
- Output VAT will not be due, but input VAT of £1,667 per month will be recoverable if it registers for VAT.

Exempt supplies

- Confused Ltd will not be required or permitted to register for VAT as it will not be making taxable supplies.
- Output VAT will not be due and no input VAT will be recoverable.

(b) **Disclosure of errors**

- If the net errors total less than the greater of £10,000 or 1% of turnover (max £50,000), then they can be voluntarily disclosed by simply entering them on the next VAT return.
- If the net errors total more than this limit then they can be voluntarily disclosed, but disclosure must be made separately to HM Revenue & Customs (HMRC).
- Default interest will be charged if the net errors total more than the limit.

(c) **Sale of assets on a piecemeal basis**

- Perplexed Ltd will cease to make taxable supplies so its VAT registration will be cancelled on 31 December 2014 or an agreed later date.
- The company will have to notify HMRC by 30 January 2015, being 30 days after the date of cessation.
- Output VAT will be due in respect of fixed assets on which VAT has been claimed (although output VAT is not due if it totals less than £1,000).

Sale of business as a going concern

- If the purchaser is already registered for VAT then Perplexed Ltd's VAT registration will be cancelled as above.
- If the purchaser is not registered for VAT then it can take over Perplexed Ltd's VAT registration.
- A sale of a business as a going concern is not treated as a taxable supply , and therefore output VAT is not due.

74 ASTUTE LTD (ADAPTED)

Key answer tips

A straight forward question on the three special accounting schemes available to small businesses.

Make sure you illustrate your answer by referring to the numbers in the question and do not just write about the schemes in general.

(a) **Annual accounting scheme**

- Astute Ltd can apply to use the annual accounting scheme if its expected taxable turnover for the next 12 months does not exceed £1,350,000 exclusive of VAT.
- In addition the company must be up to date with its VAT returns.
- The reduced administration from only having to submit one VAT return each year should mean that default surcharges are avoided in respect of the late submission of VAT returns.
- In addition, making payments on account based on the previous year's VAT liability will improve both budgeting and possibly cash flow where a business is expanding.

(b) **Flat rate scheme**

- Bright Ltd can use the flat rate scheme if its expected taxable turnover for the next 12 months does not exceed £150,000.
- The main advantage of the scheme is the simplified VAT administration. Bright Ltd's customers are not VAT registered, so there will be no need to issue VAT invoices.

- Using the normal basis of calculating the VAT liability, Bright Ltd will have to pay annual VAT of £10,833 (£82,000 – £17,000 = £65,000 × 20/120).
- If Bright Ltd uses the flat rate scheme then it will pay VAT of £9,020 (£82,000 × 11%), which is an annual saving of £1,813 (£10,833 – £9,020).

Tutorial note

In the first 12 months of VAT registration, HMRC allow a 1% reduction in the appropriate percentage for that trade group. However, knowledge of this is not required in the exam.

Therefore, the examiner will give you the rate that should apply in the first 12 months and you do not need to deduct 1%, just use the rate given.

(c) **Cash accounting scheme**

- Clever Ltd can use the cash accounting scheme if its expected taxable turnover for the next 12 months does not exceed £1,350,000 exclusive of VAT.
- In addition, the company must be up to date with its VAT returns and VAT payments.
- Output VAT will be accounted for three months later than at present since the scheme will result in the tax point becoming the date that payment is received from customers.
- The recovery of input VAT on expenses will not be affected as these are paid in cash.
- The scheme will also provide automatic bad debt relief should a customer default on the payment of a debt.

(d) **Group VAT registration**

- Companies under common control may apply for group VAT registration.

  For these purposes control only needs to be via a 'person' which can include individuals as well as companies in traditional parent/subsidiary relationships.
- As Robert controls both Talented Limited and Gifted Limited, it is possible for these two companies to be group VAT registered.
- The effect of a group registration would be that the two companies are effectively treated as a single entity for VAT purposes.
- One of the companies will be nominated as the representative member and will submit only one VAT return for the group. This can save in administration costs.
- As the two companies trade with each other, output VAT would not be charged on intra-group supplies and therefore the purchasing company would not need to reclaim input VAT. This provides a cash flow advantage.

75 VICTOR STYLE  *Online question assistance*

Key answer tips

This is a question covering the common issues of registration and the flat rate scheme and also asks for the effect of registration on profit. This is unusual because traders usually pass on the cost of VAT to their customers, but in this case the question clearly states that it was not possible to raise prices as a consequence of becoming registered.

Provided you work carefully through the numbers, this should be a straight forward question.

(a) **Compulsory registration**

- A trader must register for VAT when taxable supplies during any 12-month period exceed £79,000.
- This will have happened on 30 November 2013 when taxable supplies amounted to £79,800 ((£5,800 × 10) + (£10,900 × 2)) for the previous 12 months.
- Victor therefore had to notify HM Revenue & Customs by 30 December 2013, being 30 days after the end of the 12-month period.
- Victor was liable to register from 1 January 2014, i.e. from the end of the month following the month in which the limit was exceeded.

(b) **VAT payable – y/e 31 December 2014**

- Output VAT will be £21,800 (£10,900 × 12 = £130,800 × 20/120) since Victor must absorb this himself rather than pass it on to his customers.
- Input VAT will be £800 (£400 × 12 = £4,800 × 20/120).
- The total VAT payable by Victor during the year ended 31 December 2014 is therefore £21,000 (£21,800 – £800).

(c) **Flat rate scheme**

- The main advantage of the flat rate scheme is the simplified VAT administration. Victor's customers are not registered for VAT, so there will be no need to issue VAT invoices.
- If Victor had used the flat rate scheme from 1 January 2014, then he would have paid VAT of £17,004 (£130,800 × 13%) during the year ended 31 December 2014.
- This is a saving of £3,996 (£21,000 – £17,004) for the year.

Tutorial note

In the first 12 months of VAT registration, HMRC allow a 1% reduction in the appropriate percentage for that trade group. However, knowledge of this is not required in the exam.

Therefore, the examiner will give you the rate that should apply in the first 12 months and you do not need to deduct 1%, just use the rate given.

(d) **Reduction in net profit**

- If Victor had not increased his prices, his net profit for the year ended 31 December 2014 based on the information given would have been £64,800 (£5,800 – £400 = £5,400 × 12).
- As a result of increasing his prices, Victor's net profit will be as follows:

	£
Sales (£130,800 – £21,000)	109,800
Less: Expenses (£4,800 – £800)	(4,000)
Net profit	105,800

- This is an increase in net profit of £41,000 (£105,800 – £64,800).
- If the flat rate scheme had been used from 1 January 2014 there would have been an increase in net profit of £44,996 (£41,000 + £3,996).

76 VECTOR LTD (ADAPTED)

Key answer tips

A typical mixed bag of VAT topics. The first part requires a calculation of VAT for a quarter including overseas transactions within and outside the EU. Remember to check carefully to see if figures are given inclusive of VAT or exclusive of VAT.

The tricky points are the scale charge for private fuel, the treatment of impaired debts and the overseas aspects.

There are some easy marks in part (b) for stating the conditions for and effects of cash accounting, and part (c) should be straightforward provided the topic has been revised!

(a) **VAT Return – Quarter ended 31 March 2014**

	£
Output VAT	
Sales in UK (£128,000 × 97.5% × 20%)	24,960
Advance payment (£4,500 × 20/120)	750
Motor car scale charge (£523 × 20/120)	87
Sales outside EU (zero rated)	Nil
Sales within EU (VAT registered companies) (zero rated)	Nil
Sales within EU (non VAT registered companies) (standard rated) (£14,250 × 20%)	2,850
	28,647
Input VAT	
Expenses (£74,800 – £4,200) × 20%	(14,120)
Impaired debt relief (£4,000 + £4,000) × 20%	(1,600)
VAT payable to HMRC	12,927

Notes

(1) The calculation of output VAT on UK sales must take into account the discount for prompt payment, even if customers do not take it. VAT is therefore calculated on 97.5% (100% – 2.5%) of the sales value.

(2) Input VAT on business entertainment is not recoverable unless it relates to overseas customers.

(3) Relief for an impaired debt is not given until six months from the time that payment is due. Therefore relief can only be claimed in respect of the invoices due for payment on 15 August and 15 September 2013.

(4) Input VAT cannot be recovered in respect of the motor car as it is not used exclusively for business purposes.

Tutorial note

Although the examiner uses a VAT fraction of 20/120 you may find it easier and equally valid to use a VAT fraction of 1/6.

Amounts due from customers are recorded inclusive of VAT. However the question clearly states that all figures are VAT exclusive unless stated otherwise. Hence the two invoices of £4,000 due from a customer and written off as impaired debts are treated as VAT exclusive.

(b) **Cash accounting scheme**

- Vector Ltd can use the cash accounting scheme if its expected taxable turnover for the next 12 months does not exceed £1,350,000.
- In addition, the company must be up to date with its VAT returns and VAT payments.
- The scheme will result in the tax point becoming the date that payment is received from customers.
- This will provide for automatic impaired debt relief should a customer not pay.
- However, the recovery of input VAT on expenses will be delayed until payment is made.

(c) **Group VAT registration**

Advantages

- VAT does not have to be accounted for on any intra-group sales as supplies by one group company to another are outside the scope of VAT.
- A representative member for the group is responsible for accounting for all output and input VAT on behalf of the group and only one VAT return is required for all members of the VAT group.
- Membership of the VAT group is optional and flexible. Vector Ltd can choose whether or not to be a member of the VAT group – it is not compulsory for all group companies to join the VAT group.

Disadvantages

- All members of a VAT group are jointly and severally liable for the VAT for the group as a whole.
- Increased administration may arise in collecting and collating the information for the one joint return.
- The input VAT recovery of Vector Ltd may be reduced if a company making wholly or mainly exempt supplies is included in the VAT group.

Tutorial note

Companies under common control can elect for group VAT registration, provided they are UK resident or are trading in the UK via a permanent establishment in the UK.

77 LITHOGRAPH LTD (ADAPTED)

Key answer tips

Monthly payments on account under the annual accounting scheme are based on the VAT payable for the previous year.

This first part of the question was only worth two marks and therefore it should be clear that detailed computations are not required and that the reason for the previous year information in the question is for the purposes of this part.

Calculations based on the current year position were not required until the next part of the question, which required a VAT return and should be an expected standard requirement.

(a) **Monthly payments on account of VAT**

- Each payment on account of VAT will be £1,020 (£10,200 × 10%), being 10% of the VAT payable for the previous year.
- Lithograph Ltd will have made nine payments on account, and these will have been paid for the months of April to December 2014, being months 4 to 12 of the annual VAT return period.

(b) (i) **VAT payable – year ended 31 December 2014**

	£	£
Output VAT		
Sales (£160,000 × 20%)		32,000
Motor car scale charge (£2,160 × 20/120)		360
Office equipment (£8,000 × 20%)		1,600
		33,960
Input VAT		
Purchases (£38,000 × 20%)	7,600	
Expenses (Note 1) (£28,000 × 20%)	5,600	
Machinery (£24,000 × 20%)	4,800	
Impaired debt (Note 3) (£4,800 × 20%)	960	
		(18,960)
VAT payable		15,000

Tutorial note

1 *Input VAT on business entertainment is not recoverable unless it relates to overseas customers.*

2 *Input VAT cannot be recovered in respect of the motor car as this is not exclusively for business purposes.*

3 *Relief for the impaired debt is available because the claim is made more than six months from the time that payment was due, and the debt has been written off in the company's books.*

4 *Amounts due from customers are recorded inclusive of VAT. However the question clearly states that all figures are VAT exclusive unless stated otherwise. Hence the impaired debt of £4,800 has been treated as VAT exclusive.*

5 *The tax is calculated as 20/120 for transactions quoted gross, however the use of 1/6 is also acceptable.*

(ii) **Annual VAT return**

- Lithograph Ltd made payments on account totalling £9,180 (£1,020 × 9), so a balancing payment of £5,820 (£15,000 – £9,180) would have been due with the annual VAT return.
- The annual VAT return, along with the balancing payment, would have been due by 28 February 2015, being two months after the end of the annual VAT period.

78 DENZIL DYER (ADAPTED)

Key answer tips

A question ranging over a number of VAT issues. Make sure you consider each part and write enough for each part.

Remember also to relate your answer to the specific circumstances of the business.

Numbered points or bullet points are the best way to make your answer 'marker friendly'.

(a) **Identification of the type of supply**

- The type of supply, whether standard rated or zero-rated, has no effect on the recovery of input VAT for Denzil.
- However, output VAT is only due in respect of standard rated supplies. Incorrectly classifying a supply as zero-rated would not remove Denzil's liability to pay the output VAT which is calculated on the actual price charged. This would then be an additional cost to the business.

(b) **Accounting for output VAT**

- Output VAT must be accounted for according to the VAT period in which the supply is treated as being made. This is determined by the tax point.
- The printing contracts are supplies of services, so the basic tax point for each contract will be the date that it is completed.
- Where payment is received before the basic tax point, then this date becomes the actual tax point. The tax point for each 10% deposit is therefore the date that it is received.
- If an invoice is issued within 14 days of the basic tax point, the invoice date will usually replace the basic tax point date and becomes the actual tax point. This will apply to the balance of the contract price since Denzil issues invoices within three to five days of completion.

(c) **VAT implications of discounts**

- Where a discount of 5% is given for an order of more than £500 then output VAT is simply calculated on the revised, discounted, selling price.
- As regards the 2.5% discount offered for prompt payment, output VAT is calculated on the selling price less the amount of discount offered.
- There is no amendment to the amount of output VAT charged if the customer does not take the discount but instead pays the full selling price.

(d) **Conditions for the recovery of input VAT**

- The supply must be made to Denzil since he is the taxable person making the claim.
- The supply must be supported by evidence, and this will normally take the form of a VAT invoice. Denzil will therefore not be able to recover any input VAT in respect of the purchases of office supplies for cash, where there is no invoice.
- Denzil must use the goods or services supplied for business purposes, although an apportionment can be made where supplies are acquired partly for business purposes and partly for private purposes.

(e) **Circumstances for issuing VAT invoices**

- Denzil must issue a VAT invoice when he makes a standard rated supply to one of his VAT registered customers.
- A VAT invoice is not required if the supply is zero-rated
- the supply is to a non-VAT registered customer (e.g. a member of the public) then an invoice need not be issued unless the customer requests
- A simplified invoice can be issued if the supply is less than £250.
- A VAT invoice should be issued within 30 days of the date that the supply of services is treated as being made.

79 ANNE ATTIRE  *Walk in the footsteps of a top tutor*

Key answer tips

Standalone VAT questions are not as common as seeing VAT as part of a longer income tax or corporation tax question, but either way VAT will be tested (a guaranteed 10%) and there are easy marks to be had if you have learnt the rules, as they are very straightforward to apply.

It is an important area of the syllabus and you should take care to ensure you have covered all areas.

The question has three independent parts, which have clear requirements and mark allocations. If you do not have the required knowledge to deal with part (b) do not allow this to put you off attempting the other parts.

Tutor's top tips

Part (a) is a standard VAT return, which does not have any particularly difficult items.

Cash and credit sales are both dealt with in the same way, except that the discount is only applicable to the credit sales.

Be careful to ensure you deal with the discounts correctly, in respect of both the credit sales and the impaired debts.

(a) **VAT return – Quarter ended 31 May 2014**

	£	£
Output VAT		
Cash sales (£28,000 × 20%)		5,600
Credit sales (Note 1) (£12,000 × 95% × 20%)		2,280
		7,880
Input VAT		
Purchases and expenses (£11,200 × 20%)	2,240	
Impairment loss (Note 2) (£800 × 95% × 20%)	152	
		(2,392)
VAT payable		5,488

The VAT return for the quarter ended 31 May 2014 should have been submitted by 7 July 2014, being one month and seven days after the end of the VAT period.

Tutorial note

1 *The calculation of output VAT on the credit sales takes into account the discount for prompt payment, even for those 10% of customers that did not take it.*

2 *Relief for an impairment loss is not given until six months from the time that payment is due. Therefore relief can only be claimed in respect of the invoice due for payment on 10 November 2013. Relief is based on the amount of output VAT that would originally have been paid taking into account the discount for prompt payment.*

3 *Amounts due from customers are recorded inclusive of VAT. However the question clearly states that all figures are VAT exclusive unless stated otherwise. Hence the impaired debt of £800 has been treated as VAT exclusive.*

(b) **Cash accounting**

Tutor's top tips

Part (b) requires students to recall a reasonable amount of knowledge regarding the cash accounting scheme, which is not difficult if learnt, but extremely difficult if neglected in revision. These are not rules that you will be able to make up in the exam, so do take the time to learn them!

When answering written elements in the exam, keep your comments short and to the point.

Bullet points or a numbered answer (one mark per well explained point), are useful both in structuring your answer and for the marker reading it. Don't take the opportunity to write everything you know about VAT. Keep your comments relevant to the question.

- Anne can use the cash accounting scheme if her expected taxable turnover for the next 12 months does not exceed £1,350,000.
- In addition, Anne must be up-to-date with her VAT returns and VAT payments.
- Output VAT on most credit sales will be accounted for up to one month later than at present since the scheme will result in the tax point becoming the date that payment is received from customers.
- However, the recovery of input VAT will be delayed by two months.
- The scheme will provide automatic relief for impaired losses should a credit sale customer default on the payment of a debt.

(c) (i) **Sale of assets on a piecemeal basis**

Tutor's top tips

Part (c) concerns the disposal of a VAT registered business.

Again, it is important to make short, clear points, matched to the number of marks available. Therefore two points are required for each part of the answer, although here the same point can be made twice!

If you do not know all the rules, you could still potentially pick up a mark or two, with some sensible comments, such as the need to deregister when you cease trading.

- Upon the cessation of trading Anne will cease to make taxable supplies, so her VAT registration will be cancelled on the date of cessation or an agreed later date.
- Output VAT will be due in respect of the value of the fixed assets at the date of deregistration on which VAT has been claimed (although output VAT is not due if it totals less than £1,000).

(ii) **Sale of business as a going concern**

- Since the purchaser is already registered for VAT, Anne's VAT registration will be cancelled as above.
- A sale of a business as a going concern is not treated as a taxable supply, and therefore output VAT will not be due.

Tutorial note

If the purchaser was not already registered for VAT, they could consider taking over Anne's VAT registration. However, that point would not be relevant to this scenario.

Always make your comments relevant to the circumstances in the question.

Examiner's report

This was the first time that VAT has been examined as a separate question, and it was therefore pleasing to see many very good answers.

In part (a) candidates often did not appreciate that output VAT on credit sales had to take account of the discount for prompt payment even if it was not taken by customers.

In part (b) the answers of many candidates lacked sufficient depth to gain full marks. For example, the turnover limit of £1,350,000 was usually known, but only a minority of candidates correctly stated that it applied for the following 12-month period.

The same comment applies to part (c). For example, candidates generally appreciated that the taxpayer's VAT registration would be cancelled, but few stated that the reason for the cancellation was the cessation of making taxable supplies.

Many candidates stated that on a sale of the business as a going concern the VAT registration could be taken over by the purchaser despite the question clearly stating that the purchaser was already registered for VAT.

ACCA marking scheme

		Marks
(a)	Output VAT – Cash sales	1.0
	– Credit sales	1.5
	Input VAT – Purchases and expenses	1.0
	– Impairment loss	1.5
	Due date	1.0
		6.0
(b)	Limit	1.0
	VAT returns and VAT payments	1.0
	Output VAT	1.0
	Input VAT	1.0
	Relief for impairment loss	1.0
		5.0
(c) (i)	**Sale of assets on a piecemeal basis**	
	Cancellation of VAT registration	1.0
	Output VAT	1.0
		2.0
(ii)	**Sale of business as a going concern**	
	Cancellation of VAT registration	1.0
	Output VAT not due	1.0
		2.0
Total		15.0

80 ASTON MARTYN (ADAPTED)  *Walk in the footsteps of a top tutor*

Key answer tips

This is a standalone VAT question with a mixture of straightforward and difficult marks to obtain.

The classic popular topics of compulsory registration, contents of a valid invoice and payment dates should not have caused any problems, provided the topics had been revised.

However, the overseas aspects of VAT rules are complicated and difficult to explain succinctly and the penalty regime needed to be applied to the scenario to gain the marks available.

Overall, not an easy question, particularly if the rules have not been learnt, you are not clear in your explanations and do not apply to the facts of the question.

(a) **Compulsory registration**

- Aston would have been liable to compulsory registration for VAT when his taxable supplies at the end of any month exceeded £79,000 for the previous 12-month period (or since the commencement of trade if less than 12 months).
- This occurs on 28 February 2014 when taxable supplies amounted to £79,200 (£2,300 + £6,400 + £25,700 (Note) + £10,700 + £16,100 + £18,000 (Note)).
- Registration is required from the end of the month following the month in which the limit is exceeded.
- Therefore, Aston should have notified HMRC within 30 days (i.e. by 30 March 2014) and registration will have been effective from 1 April 2014 or from an agreed earlier date.

Tutorial note

Taxable supplies include zero-rated supplies.

The notification date is 30 days after the end of the month in which the limit is exceeded.

(b) **Additional pieces of information on VAT invoice**

The following information is required:

(1) Aston's VAT registration number.

(2) An identifying number (invoice number).

(3) The rate of VAT for each supply.

(4) The amount of VAT payable.

Tutor's top tips:

There are only 2 marks for this part, and four things to mention. As only half a mark is available for each point you need to be efficient with time and not take too long on this part.

(c) **Supply of services received from EU VAT registered businesses**

- VAT will have to be accounted for according to the time of supply.
- This is the earlier of the date that the service is completed or the date it is paid for.
- The VAT charged at the UK VAT rate should be declared on Aston's VAT return as output VAT, but will then be reclaimed as input VAT on the same VAT return.
- This is known as the reverse charge procedure.

Tutor's top tips:

This part is tricky, however marks were given for recognising that there is both input and output VAT to account for on the supply of a service from EU VAT registered businesses.

(d) **Errors on a VAT return**

- Provided Aston has taken reasonable care and informs HMRC promptly of any errors after he has discovered them, HMRC will not charge a penalty.
- However, Aston would be expected to check the VAT classification of each of his supplies when making the supply and invoicing. Therefore, applying the incorrect rate of VAT is more likely to be treated by HMRC as careless, rather than taking reasonable care.
- The maximum amount of penalty for carelessness is 30% of the VAT underpaid.
- However, with unprompted disclosure to HMRC by Aston, the penalty could be reduced to £Nil.

Tutor's top tips:

Be careful not to answer this part in general terms. The penalty table could have been presented and would have been mark earning – but only if you then applied the rules to the specific scenario given in the question.

(e) (i) **Quarterly VAT returns**

- Aston must file his VAT returns online and pay the VAT that is due electronically.
- The deadline for submission and payment is one month and seven days after the end of each quarter.

  For example, for the quarter ended 30 June 2014 Aston will have until 7 August 2014 to file his VAT return and pay the VAT that is due.

(ii) **Annual accounting scheme**

- Aston will have to make nine payments on account of VAT commencing in month four of the annual VAT return period.

  These will be due electronically.
- Each payment on account will be 10% of the VAT payable for the previous year, although for the first year an estimated figure will be used.
- The annual VAT return, along with the balancing payment, will be due two months after the end of the annual VAT period.

  The VAT return will have to be filed online.

Tutorial note

The filing of the annual VAT return online is two months after the end of the annual VAT period, with no seven day extension, as the deadline is already longer than normal.

Examiner's report

With the exception of part (b), this question was generally answered quite poorly.

In part (a) most candidates did not appreciate that the zero-rated supplies had to be included when calculating taxable supplies for registration purposes.

Part (b) was well answered, although many candidates wasted time by stating more than four additional pieces of information.

For example, common sense should mean that the business could not possibly state the VAT registration number of the customer.

Many candidates simply ignored part (c), but marks were awarded for any sensible answer such as input VAT and output VAT would contra out.

In part (d) too many candidates simply reproduced the penalty table without relating it to the facts given. Again, marks were awarded for any sensible conclusion.

There was little knowledge of the new online filing requirement for quarterly returns in part (e), although the annual accounting scheme aspects were answered much better.

ACCA marking scheme

			Marks
(a)	Registration limit		0.5
	28 February 2014		2.0
	Date of registration		0.5
			3.0
(b)	Aston's VAT registration number		0.5
	An identifying number		0.5
	The rate of VAT for each supply		0.5
	The amount of VAT payable		0.5
			2.0
(c)	Time of supply		1.0
	Entries on VAT return		1.0
			2.0
(d)	No penalty if reasonable care		1.0
	Treated as careless		1.0
	Amount of penalty		1.0
			3.0
(e)	(i)	Online filing	0.5
		Electronic payment	0.5
		Deadline	1.0
			2.0
	(ii)	Payments on account	1.0
		Amount of each payment	1.0
		Deadline	1.0
			3.0
Total			15.0